D1674267

www.standort-deutschland.com

Wirtschaftsstandort Frankfurt am Main

Schrittmacher einer europäischen Spitzenregion

Pacemaker for an European Top Region

EUROPÄISCHER WIRTSCHAFTS VERLAG
Frankfurt am Main
2001/2002

Sehr geehrte Damen und Herren,

Weltweit konkurrieren die Städte heute um die Gunst der Investoren. Dabei wird es immer wichtiger, sich von anderen Wirtschaftsstandorten durch seine standorteigenen Vorteile positiv zu unterscheiden. Jeder Unternehmensstandort in Deutschland bietet spezielle Vorteile für die Ansiedlung von neuen Betrieben und nationalen und internationalen Investoren. In der Vielzahl von miteinander konkurrierenden Regionen liegt auch die Chance einer Stadt, durch besondere Qualifikationen die Entscheidung zur Standortwahl positiv für sich zu beeinflussen.

Frankfurt am Main ist das Zentrum einer der dynamischsten Regionen Europas, in der Mitte des Kontinents hat es mit seiner hervorragenden Verkehrsinfrastruktur zu Luft, zu Wasser und zu Lande einen schnellen Zugang zu allen wichtigen Schlüsselmärkten Europas. In Mainhattan, wie die Stadt stolz genannt wird, herrscht eine Atmosphäre von Weltoffenheit und globalem Handeln.

Bis 2004 wird Frankfurt, so sagt eine seriöse Studie, weitere 17.000 neue Arbeitsplätze haben – den Bedarf für den Ausbau des Flughafen noch nicht mitgerechnet. So wird vor allem das Business to Business-Gewerbe wachsen, wo heute bereits 70.000 Menschen beschäftigt sind. Auf

diesem Gebiet der unternehmensorientierten Dienstleistungen hat die Information, die Ware der Zukunft, inzwischen einen besonderen Platz eingenommen – Frankfurt ist heute auch das deutsche Zentrum für Informationstechnologien und für Kommunikation. Hier stehen die Server, die die deutschen User mit der Welt verbinden, hier sind die großen internationalen Network-Agenturen.

Aber Frankfurt am Main ist nicht nur ein dynamischer Wirtschaftsstandort, nicht nur das Finanzzentrum „Bankfurt" , sondern lebenswerte Weltstadt für mehr als 650.000 Menschen. Das amerikanische Consulting-Unternehmen William M. Mercer setzte die Stadt im weltweiten Ranking für Lebensqualität auf Platz 11, weit vor dem schärfsten Rivalen London, das nur auf den 35. Rang kam. Wohl auch deshalb wird Frankfurt als touristisches Ziel immer attraktiver. Mehr als zwei Millionen Gäste übernachten hier jährlich und über 30.0000 Arbeitspätze sind inzwischen vom Tourismus abhängig.

Dieses in Zusammenarbeit mit der Wirtschaftsförderung Frankfurt GmbH entstandene Werk soll neben dem informativen und unterhaltenden Stellenwert auch eine praktische Aufgabe erfüllen. Es soll Kooperationen und neue Geschäftskon-

takte mit den im Buch präsentierten Firmen und Ihnen als Leser fördern.

Das Buch ist ein wichtiger Bestandteil des Standardwerkes zu deutschen Wirtschaftsregionen und international auch im Internet unter der Adresse „www.standort-deutschland.com" präsent.

Möglicherweise ist die Stadt Frankfurt am Main ja auch Ihr „Unternehmensstandort der Zukunft"?!

Dear Reader

Worldwide cities are competing today to be favoured by investors. It is becoming increasingly important to be distinguished from other business locations through ones own location advantages positively. Each location for enterprises in Germany offers its special advantages for the settlement of new companies and national and international investors. The many regions in competition with each other, however, also provide the city with a chance to influence for itself positively, through special qualifications, the decision for a location selection.

Frankfurt on the Main is the centre of one of the most dynamic regions of Europe, where in the last 30 years the number of inhabitants has more than doubled. Frankfurt lies in the middle of Europe and has with its excellent transport infrastructure by air, water and land, a rapid access to all important key markets in Europe. In Mainhattan, as the city is proudly called, there exists an atmosphere of openness to the world and of global activities.

Up to 2004, a serious study says, Frankfurt will have further 17.000 new workplaces – not counting the demand for the extension of the airport. Thus, above all the business-to-business sector will grow, where even today 70.000 people are employed. In this field of company-oriented services, information, the merchandise of the future, has meanwhile taken a very special place – Frankfurt is today also the German centre of information technologies and of communication. Here, the servers that connect the German users with the world are located; here are the great international network agencies.

But Frankfurt on the Main is not only a dynamic business location, not only the finance centre "Bankfurt", it is a city worth living in for more than 650.000 people. The American consulting company William M. Mercer has placed the city in the worldwide ranking for quality of living on place 11, far above the strongest rival London, which only reached rank 35. Surely this is why Frankfurt is becoming more and more attractive as a goal for tourism. More than two million

guests stay overnight here every year and more than 30.000 workplaces depend on tourism meanwhile.

This work, produced in co-operation with the City of Frankfurt Magistrates, shall apart from the information and entertaining content also fulfil a practical task. It is meant to promote cooperations and new business contacts with the companies presented in the book and you as reader. The book is an important component of the standard work about German business regions and internationally also present in the Internet under the address www.standort-deutschland.com.

Maybe, the city of Frankfurt on the Main is also your "company location of the future"?!

Christian Kirk
Managing Director of
MEDIEN GRUPPE KIRK HOLDING AG

Sehr geehrte Damen und Herren,

Frankfurt – die große Metropole Hessens in der Region Rhein-Main, einem der wirtschaftlich bedeutendsten Räume Europas. Wenn der Name Frankfurt fällt, denkt man zunächst an den Finanzplatz, den internationalen Verkehrsknotenpunkt mit dem Rhein-Main-Flughafen und dem meistfrequentierten Bahnhof Europas oder auch nur an eine auf unserem Kontinent einzigartige Wolkenkratzer-Skyline, die der größten Stadt Hessens den liebenswürdigen Spitznamen „Mainhatten" eingebracht hat.

Frankfurt ist der zentrale deutsche Banken- und Börsenplatz, Sitz des Bundesaufsichtsamtes für den Wertpapierhandel und Sitz der Europäischen Zentralbank. Die Frankfurter Wertpapierbörse ist die viertgrößte Börse der Welt. In der Finanzwirtschaft sind im Raum Frankfurt gut 100.000 Menschen beschäftigt.
Wer vom Ausland aus nach Deutschland kommt, der landet zumeist in Frankfurt. Der Rhein-Main-Flughafen ist über seine Bedeutung als internationaler Verkehrsknotenpunkt hinaus also nicht nur ein wichtiger Wirtschaftsfaktor, sondern für viele Menschen das Tor nach Deutschland und Europa.
Tatsächlich sind Frankfurt und sein Umfeld aber noch vielfältiger, als es diese bekannten Schlaglichter zunächst vermuten lassen. Viele

Unternehmen haben nicht ohne Grund gerade in Frankfurt und Umgebung ihre Forschungs- und Entwicklungszentren. Hier liegen die Wurzeln für viele hochwertige Produkte im Bereich der Spitzentechnologie. An nur wenigen europäischen Standorten gibt es ein solch breites und ausgeprägtes wissenschaftliches Umfeld wie in Frankfurt. Die New Economy hat in Frankfurt früher Einzug gehalten als anderswo. So ist die Stadt Knotenpunkt für 85 Prozent aller Internet-Anwendungen in Deutschland.

Frankfurt ist eine bedeutende Messestadt. 1999 wurden in der Mainmetropole 51 Messen mit 37.129 Ausstellern und mehr als 2,2 Millionen Besuchern ausgerichtet.

Bei aller Wirtschaftskraft hat sich Frankfurt auch seine Liebenswürdigkeit bewahrt. Wer in Frankfurt-Sachsenhausen schon mal eine echte Frankfurter Äppelwoi-Gaststätte besuchte, hat erlebt, wie gemütlich es in „Mainhattan" sein kann. Auch vor den Toren der Stadt – z. B. im Taunus oder im Odenwald – kann man sich jederzeit bestens erholen. Ein Besuch an der Bergstraße oder im Rheingau lohnt sich nicht nur wegen der vorzüglichen Weine, die dort angebaut werden.
Frankfurt ist nicht zuletzt auch wegen seines reichhaltigen Kulturangebotes auf internationa-

lem Niveau bekannt. Dafür steht nicht nur Goethe, der berühmteste Sohn der Stadt. Deutsche Bibliothek, Internationale Buchmesse, Oper und Alte Oper sind nur die schillerndsten Kulturfacetten. Frankfurt, die weltweit bekannte „City of the Euro", wird sich deshalb nicht nur als Wirtschafts-, sondern ebenso auch als Lebensstandort im globalen Wettbewerb behaupten.

Dear Reader

Frankfurt: The great metropolis of Hesse in the Rhein-Main region, one of the economically most important areas in Europe. When the name of Frankfurt is mentioned, one first thinks of a finance centre, the international transport intersection with the Rhein-Main airport and the most-frequented train station of Europe or even only of a skyscraper skyline that is unique on our continent and which has given to this largest city in Hesse the nickname of "Mainhatten".

Frankfurt is the main German banking and stock exchange centre, seat of the Federal Regulatory Authority for securities trade and headquarters of the European Central Bank. The Frankfurt securities exchange is the fourth largest stock exchange in the world. Around 100.000 people work in the finance economy within the Frankfurt region.
Whoever comes from abroad to Germany mostly lands in Frankfurt. The Rhein-Main airport is beyond its importance as international transport intersection also not only an important economic factor but for many people it is the gate to Germany and Europe.

In fact, Frankfurt and its surroundings are much more versatile than this well-known highlights may reveal at first. Not without a reason, do many enterprises have precisely in Frankfurt and its surroundings their research and development centres. Here lay the roots for many high-quality products from the fields of top-technologies. Only very few European locations offer such a broad and characteristically scientific environment as Frankfurt. The New Economy settled in Frankfurt earlier than anywhere else. Thus, the city is an interconnecting node for 85 percent of all Internet applications in Germany.

Frankfurt is an important city of trade fairs. In 1999, in the cosmopolitan city on the Main 49 trade fairs with 37.129 exhibitors and more than 2,2 million visitors were organized.

With all its economic power Frankfurt has maintained its charm. Whoever has visited once a real Frankfurt apple-cider (Äppelwoi) bar in Frankfurt-Sachsenhausen, must have experienced how cosy it can be in "Mainhattan". Also in front of the city

gates – for example in the Taunus Mountains or in the Odenwald – one can find relaxation at its best. A visit to the Bergstraße or the Rheingau is not only worthwhile because of the excellent wines that are cultivated there.

Last not least, Frankfurt is also known because of its rich cultural possibilities on an international level. Not only Goethe bears witness of this, the most famous son of the city. The German Library, International Book Fair, the opera and Alte Oper (old opera) are only some of the most illustrious facets of culture. Frankfurt, the worldwide known "City of the Euro" will succeed in maintaining its hold not only as a business location but also as a location for living, in the global competition.

Dieter Posch
Hessian Minister for Commerce, Transport and Regional Development

Wirtschaftsstandort Frankfurt am Main
Business Location Frankfurt on the Main

Inhalt/Contents

7

Lebenswerte Weltstadt in einer der dynamischsten Regionen Europas

*A Cosmopolitan City worth living in,
Within one of the most dynamic Regions of Europe*

Das Rhein-Main-Gebiet zählt zu den wichtigen Verdichtungsräumen Europas. Auf dem Gebiet von rund 11.000 km², das sich über Südhessen, den östlichen Teil von Rheinland-Pfalz und den nordwestlichen Teil Bayerns erstreckt, konzentrieren sich 4,8 Mio. Einwohner, 320.000 Unternehmen und 2,2 Mio. Arbeitsplätze. In der Region wird ein Bruttoinlandsprodukt von 143 Mrd. Euro erwirtschaftet, ein Drittel davon allein in Frankfurt.

Jeder siebte Einwohner, jedes achte Unternehmen und jeder dritte Arbeitsplatz der Region befindet sich im Stadtgebiet Frankfurt, das hinsichtlich der Fläche lediglich zwei Prozent der Region ausmacht. Auch wenn die Region mit den großen Städten Wiesbaden, Mainz, Darmstadt und Offenbach eine polyzentrische Struktur aufweist, ist Frankfurt mit diesen Zahlen das herausragende Zentrum der Region.

Obwohl wirtschaftliche Aspekte das Image der Region prägen, lässt es sich hier aber auch sehr gut leben. Die Flusslandschaften von Main und Rhein, eingebettet in die Mittelgebirgszüge des Taunus, Vogelsberges, Odenwalds, Spessarts und den südlichen Teil des Hunsrücks bieten eine reizvolle Szenerie mit hohem Freizeitwert, die auch zahllose Touristen aus aller Welt anzieht. Das lockere Nebeneinander von Siedlungsflächen, ausgedehnten Waldlandschaften, Seen und weiten landwirtschaftlich genutzten Flächen bietet einen hohen Erholungswert. Zahlreiche Studien zur Identifikation der Bevölkerung mit ihrer Region belegen, dass der weitaus überwiegende Teil der Menschen sehr gern im Rhein-Main-Gebiet lebt.

Das Rhein-Main-Gebiet ist in den letzten Jahrzehnten sowohl in der Fläche – wegen der

Der Messeturm, weithin sichtbares Wahrzeichen Frankfurts.
The Fair Tower, far visible symbol of Frankfurt.

Petra Roth

Petra Roth wurde 1944 in Bremen als Tochter einer alteingesessenen Bremer Kaufmannsfamilie geboren. Sie absolvierte die Höhere Handelsschule und machte eine Ausbildung als Arzthelferin. 1972 trat Petra Roth der CDU bei, als Kandidatin für den Wahlkreis Frankfurt-Ost wurde sie seit 1987 dreimal direkt in den Hessischen Landtag gewählt. Ab 1993 war sie wieder als MdL Hessen auch Mitglied der Frankfurter Stadtverordnetenversammlung. 1993 wurde sie zur Stadtverordnetenvorsteherin gewählt; das Amt übte sie bis zum 31. Januar 1994 aus. 1995 wurde Petra Roth bei der ersten Direktwahl in Frankfurt am Main zur Oberbürgermeisterin gewählt. 1997 bis 1999 war sie Präsidentin des deutschen Städtetages, seitdem ist sie dessen Vizepräsidentin.

Petra Roth was born in 1944 in Bremen as daughter of a traditional merchants family of Bremen. She finished the Higher School of Economics and completed training as dental assistant. In 1972 Petra Roth joined the Christian Democratic Union (conservative party); as candidate of the electoral district of East-Frankfurt she was elected three times since 1987 directly into the parliament of Hesse. From 1993 on she was again a Member of the Town Council of Frankfurt being a Member of the Parliament of Hesse; she held this office until the 31st January 1994. In 1995, Petra Roth was elected Mayor of the City of Frankfurt at the first direct election to this office. From 1997 till 1999 she was President of the German Parliament of City Magistrates, and since then has been its Vice President.

Frankfurt ist eine grüne Stadt, der Siedlungsflächenanteil beträgt nur 32 %.

Frankfurt is a green city; the share of settlement areas is only 32 %.

The Rhein-Main region is amongst the most densely populated areas of Europe. On an area of approx. 11.000 sq. km. that extends across the South of Hesse, the Eastern part of Rhine-Palatine land and the North-Western part of Bavaria, there is a concentration of 4,8 million inhabitants, 320.000 enterprises and 2,2 million workplaces. The region achieves a gross domestic product of 143 billion Euro, one third of this only in Frankfurt.

Each seventh inhabitant, each eighth enterprise and each third workplace of the region is located within the urban area of Frankfurt, which in respect to its area only occupies 2 % of the total region. Even if the region with its large cities of Wiesbaden, Mainz, Darmstadt and Offenbach shows a polycentric structure, Frankfurt still remains with these figures the most distinguished centre of the region.

Although mainly economic aspects shape the image of the region, one can still live a very good life here. The landscapes near the rivers of Main and Rhine, imbedded into the Central Mountains of the Taunus, Vogelsberg, Odenwald, Spessart and the Southern part of the Hunsrück provide a picturesque scenery for high quality leisure time that also attracts countless tourists from all over the world. The loosely adjacently situated areas of set-

tlements, extensive landscapes of woods, lakes and wide areas used for agriculture have a high value for relaxation. Many surveys for identification of the population with its region prove that the large majority of people enjoy living in the Rhein-Main area very much.

The Rhein-Main region has grown tremendously in the last decades in terms of its area – because of the increased radius for action of spatial inter-connected relations – but above all, in terms of its population. Thus, the number of inhabitants of the region has more than doubled in the past 30 years.

There is a whole bunch of factors that explain the dynamic development of the region. With a view on Frankfurt, being the heart of the region, four strategically important influential factors can be mentioned:

Central location and infrastructure

When one looks for the centre of Europe, one lands directly in Frankfurt on the Main. Together with the excellent transport infrastructure (roads, rail, air and water) this guarantees a rapid access

to all-important key markets in Europe. Furthermore, the Frankfurt Airport is a gate to the world. The central location of Frankfurt within the region opens up in an excellent way regional economic powers and purchasing powers.

Diversity of the Economy

Despite the high share of the service sector in the economy (83 % of people employed) Frankfurt disposes with just below 70.000 employees of a strong industrial base with a focus on Life Science. The largest field in the economy is the business-to-business commerce, that is the company-oriented services, followed by the financial sector, which also employs 70.000 people. But also the skilled trade sector with 55.000 employees plays an important role. Of course, also the commercial sectors as well as the news and transport systems belong to the pillars of the economy of Frankfurt, a city of commerce and exhibitions. Especially the sectors of telecommunication and Internet are among the markedly dynamic fields of growth. Through an early co-operation with private network providers, even before the fall of the network monopoly of the German Telekom, the magistrate of the city created the framework con-

Die Zeil, Frankfurts berühmte Einkaufsstraße.

The Zeil, Frankfurt's famous shopping mall.

Rund 10 % der Unternehmen sind ausländischer Herkunft und die meisten der Frankfurter Unternehmen pflegen Geschäftsbeziehungen mit dem Ausland, sei es im Import/Export, sei es, dass sie dort Dependancen unterhalten. Die Frankfurter Messe weist eine starke internationale Orientierung auf. Im Schnitt kommen 60 % der Aussteller aus dem Ausland.

Die Liste der Merkmale der Internationalität Frankfurts ließe sich fortsetzen. Aber bereits jetzt wird deutlich, dass Internationalität in Frankfurt alltägliche Normalität ist. Unsere Stadt ist stolz auf ihre Weltoffenheit und ihre Toleranz gegenüber anderen Kulturen. Mit dieser Haltung sind wir stets gut gefahren.

Lebensqualität

Frankfurt ist eine grüne Stadt. Fast die Hälfte des Stadtgebietes entfällt auf Grün- und Freizeitflächen. Der Siedlungsflächenanteil beträgt gerade einmal 32 %. Das ist zum Beispiel deutlich weniger als Münchens Anteil von über 50 % Siedlungsfläche. Frankfurts Architektur ist von einem interessanten Mix von Tradition und Moderne geprägt und natürlich sind wir stolz auf unsere Skyline.

Das Kulturangebot in der Stadt zeichnet sich durch große Vielfalt aus. Die Oper, Konzerthallen, 33 deutsch- und fremdsprachige Theater, 37 Museen, Blues-Clubs und über 100 Kunstgalerien bieten jedem Interesse und Geschmack etwas.

Natürlich ist auch für das Sportliche gesorgt. 466 Sportvereine, zahllose Fitness-Studios, Tennis- und Golfplätze laden zu sportlichen Aktivitäten ein. Aber auch wer nur zusehen möchte, findet die ganze Palette vor: Fußball, Handball, Basketball, American Football, Eishockey und vieles andere mehr. Das Kultur- und Freizeitangebot Frankfurts entspricht den vielseitigen Lebesstilen der Menschen, die hier leben, und dem Anspruch, dass die Menschen dort gerne arbeiten, wo sie gute Lebensbedingungen vorfinden.

Frankfurt ist eine weltoffene und international orientierte Metropole. Ihr Rang wird von ihrer wirtschaftlichen Bedeutung und von der Rolle als Ort des Euros bestimmt. Frankfurt gehört zum Kreis der Städte, in denen die europäische Integration vorangetrieben wird. Die Perspektive heißt „Europäisches Zentrum".

Frankfurt ist von den Zahlen her eine kleine Metropole, eine Metropole der kurzen Wege, wo weltstädtische Atmosphäre im reizvollen Kontrast zu dörflichem Ambiente steht. Weltstadt und Dorf zugleich, das macht den speziellen Charme Frankfurts aus. Überzeugen Sie sich selbst. ■

gewachsenen Aktionsradien der räumlichen Verflechtungsbeziehungen –, aber vor allem auch hinsichtlich der Bevölkerung sehr stark gewachsen. So hat sich die Bevölkerungszahl der Region in den letzten 30 Jahren mehr als verdoppelt.

Es gibt ein ganzes Bündel von Faktoren, die die dynamische Entwicklung der Region erklären. Mit Blick auf Frankfurt, als dem Herzen der Region, sind vier strategisch wichtige Einflussfaktoren zu nennen:

Zentrale Lage und Infrastruktur

Auf der Suche nach der Mitte Europas landet man direkt in Frankfurt am Main. In Verbindung mit der hervorragenden Verkehrsinfrastruktur (Straße, Schiene, Luft und Wasser) garantiert das den schnellen Zugang zu allen wichtigen Schlüsselmärkten Europas. Der Frankfurter Flughafen ist darüber hinaus das Tor zur Welt. Die zentrale Lage Frankfurts in der Region erschließt in hervorragender Weise die regionale Wirtschafts- und Kaufkraft.

Vielfalt der Wirtschaft

Trotz des hohen Anteils der Dienstleistungswirtschaft (83 % der Beschäftigten) verfügt Frankfurt mit knapp 70.000 Beschäftigten über eine starke industrielle Basis mit dem Schwerpunkt Life Science.

Der größte Wirtschaftsbereich ist das Business to Business-Gewerbe, also die unternehmensorientierte Dienstleistungen, gefolgt vom Finanzsektor, der ebenfalls 70.000 Menschen beschäftigt. Aber auch das Handwerk mit seinen 55.000 Beschäftigten spielt eine bedeutende Rolle. Natürlich gehört auch der Handel sowie das Nachrichten- und Verkehrswesen in der Handels- und Messestadt zu den Säulen der Frankfurter Wirtschaft. Gerade die Bereiche Telekommunikation und Internet zählen zu den besonderen dynamischen Wachstumsbereichen. Durch frühzeitige Kooperation mit privaten Netzanbietern, noch vor dem Fall des Netzmonopols der Deutschen Telekom, hat der Magistrat der Stadt die Rahmenbedingungen dafür geschaffen, dass Frankfurt europaweit nicht nur als Mekka der Telekommunikationswirtschaft gilt, sondern auch für alle Firmen interessant ist, die bei ihren Geschäften die Vorteile einer Real-Time-Kommunikation nutzen wollen.

Internationalität

Fast 30 % der Frankfurter sprechen eine ausländische Muttersprache. Hier gibt es 80 Konsulate und mehr als 60 ausländische Handelsvertretungen. Acht internationale Schulen sorgen für die Betreuung und Ausbildung der Kinder der Expatriates. 180 ausländische Business- und Kulturclubs vermitteln ein Stück Heimat. Ein breites Angebot internationaler Geschäfte, Restaurants sowie fremdsprachige Theater und Kinos tragen den Freizeit- und Kulturbedürfnissen der ausländischen Bürgerinnen und Bürger Rechnung.

ditions for Frankfurt to be considered not only as a Mecca of the telecommunication economy, but also for being interesting to all firms that in their business transactions want to use the advantages of real-time communication.

Internationalism

Almost 30 % of people in Frankfurt speak a foreign mother tongue. There are 80 consulates and more than 60 foreign commercial representations here. Eight international schools are concerned with the care and training of children of expatriates. 180 foreign businesses and cultural clubs transmit a piece of homeland. A broad offer of international shops, restaurants as well as theatres in foreign languages and cinemas take account of the leisure time and cultural needs of the foreign male and female citizens.

Around 10 % of enterprises are of foreign origin and most of the enterprises in Frankfurt maintain business relations abroad, be it in import and export, be it that they sustain dependencies there. The Frankfurt Fair also shows a strong orientation towards internationalism. On average, 60 % of exhibitors are from abroad. One could continue listing the characteristics of internationalism of Frankfurt. But even now it becomes clear that internationalism in Frankfurt is everyday normality. Our city is proud of its openness towards the world and its tolerance against other cultures. Things have always worked out well for us with this attitude.

Quality of Life

Frankfurt is a green city. These areas cover almost half of the city zones. The share of settlement areas is only 32 %. This is markedly less, for example, than Munich's share of settlement areas of more than 50 %. Frankfurt's architecture is characterised by an interesting mix of traditional and modern styles and of course we are proud of our skyline.

The possibilities for cultural activities in the city are marked by a great variety. The opera, concert halls, 40 German and foreign language theatres, 37 museums, blues clubs and more than 100 art galleries offer something for every interest and taste.

Naturally, also sporting activities have been taken care of. 466 sport clubs, countless fitness studios, tennis and golf courses invite to be active in sports. But also only spectators can find a wide range of

possibilities: football, handball, basketball, American football, ice hockey and much more. The possibilities for cultural and leisure time activities in Frankfurt corresponds with the varied life styles of the people that live here and the claim that people like working in a place where they can find good living conditions.

Frankfurt is a metropolis open to the world and internationally oriented. Its rank is determined by its economic importance and by its role of city of the Euro. Frankfurt belongs to the circle of cities in which the European integration is enhanced. Its perspective is therefore: "European Centre". In terms of numbers Frankfurt is a small cosmopolitan city, a metropolis of short paths, where a cosmopolitan atmosphere stands in charming contrast to a village environment. Metropolis and village at the same time, this is what gives Frankfurt its special charm. Convince yourself. ■

Frankfurts Architektur ist von einem interessanten Mix aus Tradition und Moderne geprägt.
Frankfurt's architecture is characterised by an interesting mix of traditional and modern styles.

Everything starts in Frankfurt
Rhein-Main – The Gateway to Europe

Everything starts in Frankfurt
Rhein-Main – The Gateway to Europe

Vielfalt und Dynamik der Wirtschaftsregion spiegeln sich in drei strategischen Zielen wider, die die Industrie- und Handelskammer Frankfurt am Main als Selbstverwaltungsorgan der gewerblichen Wirtschaft verfolgt: Stärkung der internationalen Verflechtungen, Engagement für die Zukunft junger Menschen sowie Förderung von Wirtschaft und Beschäftigung. Das ist zugleich der Beitrag der IHK zum Ausbau der sozialen Marktwirtschaft, deren Grundprinzipien vor über 50 Jahren von Ludwig Erhard in der IHK Frankfurt formuliert wurden. Rund 70.000 Unternehmen gehören der IHK Frankfurt am Main an. Unter ihnen haben die kleinen und mittleren besonderes Gewicht. Darum verstehen wir uns als Partner vor allem auch des gewerblichen Mittelstandes.

Viele Wege führen in die Region Rhein-Main – einen Wirtschaftsraum mit vielen Gesichtern. Zwischen Aschaffenburg und Mainz, zwischen Gießen und Darmstadt arbeiten an die 300.000 Unternehmen aller Größen und Branchen für nationale und internationale Märkte. Schlüsselindustrien sind Chemie, Maschinenbau und Elektrotechnik. Mehr als ein Drittel aller Erzeugnisse der Region werden exportiert. Das Unternehmen Frankfurt Rhein-Main liegt mitten in Europa, umfasst 13.500 km² Fläche, hat 4,5 Mio. Einwohner, 1,8 Mio. Beschäftigte und eine Bruttowertschöpfung von 291 Mrd. DM. Mit anderen Worten: 6 Prozent der Bevölkerung erarbeiten auf 4 Prozent der Fläche des heutigen Deutschlands knapp 10 Prozent der gesamten Wertschöpfung. Das pro Kopf erwirtschaftete Bruttoinlandsprodukt in der Region Rhein-Main wird nur von den Räumen London, Hamburg und Brüssel übertroffen. Dem international zugeschnittenen Branchenmix des Wirtschaftsraums entspricht seine polyzentrische Struktur.

Es dominiert keine Branche und kein Zentrum. Dafür gibt es kurze Wege und engmaschige,

**Dr.
Frank
Niethammer**

Der Autor wurde 1931 in Leipzig geboren. Er studierte Rechtswissenschaften in Tübingen und Marburg und promovierte 1958 an der Universität Marburg. Seitdem nahm er erfolgreich Führungsaufgaben in verschiedenen deutschen Unternehmen wahr. Er ist Mitinhaber und Ehrenvorsitzender des Aufsichtsrates der Kübler & Niethammer Papierfabrik Kriebstein AG in Kriebethal/Sachsen. Dieses, der Familie seit 1856 gehörende und 1945 enteignete Unternehmen kaufte er zusammen mit drei Vettern noch zur Zeit der DDR zurück. Von 1991–2000 war er Präsident und ist seit 2001 Ehrenpräsident der Industrie- und Handelskammer Frankfurt am Main. Bis Februar 2001 war er einer der vier Vizepräsidenten des Deutschen Industrie- und Handelstages (DIHT).

The author was born in 1931 in Leipzig. He studied law in Tübingen and Marburg and obtained his PhD in 1958 at the University of Marburg. Since then he has carried out successfully management tasks in various German enterprises. He is co-owner and honorary chairman of the supervisory council of Kübler & Niethammer Papierfabrik Kriebstein AG in Kriebethal/Saxony. This enterprise, belonging to his family since 1856 and disowned in 1945, he bought back together with three cousins in the time of the rule of the German Democratic Republic. From 1991– 2000, he was president and since 2001 he is honorary president of the Chamber of Commerce and Industry Frankfurt on the Main. Until February 2001 he was one of the four vice presidents of the DIHT.

Kammergebäude der Industrie- und Handelskammer Frankfurt am Main.
Building of the Chamber of Commerce and Industry Frankfurt on the Main.

In der Region Rhein-Main erarbeiten 6 Prozent der Bevölkerung auf 4 Prozent der Fläche des heutigen Deutschlands knapp 10 Prozent der gesamten Wertschöpfung.

In the Rhein-Main region 6 percent of the population on 4 percent of today's German area achieve almost 10 percent of the total net product.

Diversity and dynamism of the economic region is mirrored in three strategic aims that the Chamber of Commerce and Industry Frankfurt on the Main (IHK) is pursuing, being a self-administered body of the commercial sector of the economy: Strengthening of international interconnections, engagement for the future of young people as well as promoting the economy and employment. At the same time this is the contribution of the IHK for an extension of the social market economy whose basic principles were laid down over 50 years ago by Ludwig Erhard in the IHK Frankfurt. Around 70.000 enterprises belong to the IHK Frankfurt on the Main. Special importance is given to the small and medium-sized businesses. For this reason we also see ourselves as partners of the commercial middle-class.

Many ways lead into the Rhein-Main region, a multi-faceted economic area. Between Aschaffenburg and Mainz and between Gießen and Darmstadt almost 300.000 enterprises of all sizes and branches work for national and international markets. Key industries are the chemical, mechanical construction and electro-technique. More than a third of all products of the region are being exported. The greater enterprise Frankfurt Rhein-Main lies in the middle of Europe, encompasses an area of 13.500 km², has 4,8 million inhabitants, 1,8 million employees and a gross net product of 291 billion DM. In other words, 6 percent of the population on 4 percent of today's German area achieve almost 10 percent of the total net product. The per capita gross national income of the Rhein-Main region is only surpassed by London, Hamburg and Brussels. The internationally tailor-made mix of branches of the economic region corresponds with its polycentric structure.

No single branch and no single centre is dominant. Instead there are short distances and tight, efficient networks, which are a precondition for internationalised as well as flexible economic methods of our time. The productivity of the areas lies in its diversity. To make these transparent and to make aware its main protagonists that the region is a network of multi-faceted relations and possibilities is the aim of the IHK-Forum Rhein-Main, an association of the nine Chambers of Commerce of the region.

The financial centre number 1 in Germany is without doubt Frankfurt on the Main with 370 credit institutions and more than 4.000 financial service providers. The international nature of Frankfurt as a banking centre becomes clear through the great number of foreign banks. In total, 243 foreign institutes from 48 different countries are represented in the metropolis on the Main. The decision by the EU Counsel of Ministers, to make Frankfurt the seat of the European Monetary Institute, then of the European Central Bank, has made Frankfurt – besides London – an international financial centre of Europe.

Whoever speaks of the international turning wheel of transport Rhein-Main, mainly means the Airport Frankfurt-Main. But region and airport keep each other flourishing. The economy needs fast communication. The airport attracts companies, whose mix and focus make Rhein-Main an important node in the network of worldwide economic relations. This is where Frankfurt and its region directly lie at the limits of Bombay or Buenos Aires. 45 million flight passengers a year feel that the centres of the world are barely some short time leaps away.

Its location favourable for transport in the intersection of traffic routes by land, water and air has

leistungsfähige Netze, die Voraussetzung für die internationalisierten wie flexiblen Wirtschaftsweisen unserer Zeit sind. Die Produktivität dieses Raumes liegt in der Vielfalt. Diese transparent zu machen und die Region als Netz vielgestaltiger Beziehungen und Möglichkeiten, als attraktiven Wirtschafts- und Lebensraum ins Bewusstsein der Akteure zu bringen, hat sich das IHK-Forum Rhein-Main, ein Zusammenschluss der neun Industrie- und Handelskammern der Region, zum Ziel gesetzt.

Der Finanzplatz Nummer eins in Deutschland ist zweifellos Frankfurt am Main mit 370 Kreditinstituten und über 4.000 Finanzdienstleistern. Die Internationalität des Frankfurter Bankenplatzes wird verdeutlicht durch die Vielzahl der Auslandsbanken. Insgesamt sind in der Mainmetropole 243 ausländische Institute aus 48 verschiedenen Ländern vertreten. Mit der Entscheidung, Frankfurt zum Sitz des Europäischen Währungsinstitutes, dann der Europäischen Zentralbank zu machen, hat der EU-Ministerrat Frankfurt – neben London – zu dem internationalen Finanzplatz Europas gemacht.

Wer von der internationalen Verkehrsdrehscheibe Rhein-Main spricht, meint meist den Flughafen Frankfurt/Main. Doch Region und Flughafen halten sich gegenseitig in Schwung. Die Wirtschaft braucht schnelle Kommunikation. Der Flughafen zieht Unternehmen an, deren Mix und Konzentration Rhein-Main zu einem wichtigen Knoten im Netz weltweiter Wirtschaftsbeziehungen machen. Hier grenzen Frankfurt und die Region direkt an

Bombay oder Buenos Aires. 45 Millionen Fluggäste jährlich spüren, dass die Zentren der Welt nur knappe Zeitsprünge entfernt sind.

Die verkehrsgünstige Lage im Schnittpunkt von Verkehrswegen zu Lande, zu Wasser und in der Luft hat die wirtschaftliche Entwicklung der Region Frankfurt-Rhein-Main nachhaltig beeinflusst. Das 1956 eröffnete Frankfurter Autobahnkreuz bewältigt täglich mehr als 300.000 Pkws. Ein Totalumbau wird es fit machen für die Erfordernisse des 21. Jahrhunderts. Der neue Flughafenbahnhof verbindet zusammen mit dem Frankfurter Hauptbahnhof, dem größten Personenbahnhof in Europa, das Rhein-Main-Gebiet mit dem Ruhrgebiet. Mit dem Projekt Hafen 2000 plus wird der Osthafen auf die Aufgaben der kommenden Jahrzehnte optimal vorbereitet. Infrastrukturell liegt der Osthafen im Schnittpunkt wichtiger nationaler Fernstraßen, Bahntrassen und Wasserwege (Rhein, Main, Donau) und ist damit ein hervorragender Standort der Güterverkehrslogistik für die Stadt und die Region. Er ist als größtes Ver- und Entsorgungszentrum für Güter aller Art Garant für eine optimale Versorgung der Wirtschaft und Industrie. Allein der Ausbau vorhandener Infrastruktur wird nicht ausreichen, um Wirtschaftskraft und Lebensqualität im Rhein-Main Gebiet zu gewährleisten. Verkehrs-System-Management heißt das Stichwort. Ziel ist die bessere Vernetzung von Straße, Schiene, Wasser, Luft und ihrer jeweiligen Systeme sowie die punktgenaue, verkehrsflussabhängige Information an die Verkehrsteilnehmer.

Als Marktplatz internationaler Möglichkeiten ist der Messeplatz Frankfurt, der über das drittgröß-

te Gelände der Welt verfügt, ein entscheidender Wirtschaftsfaktor. Insgesamt 55 Messen ziehen pro Jahr fast 50.000 Aussteller und rund 2,5 Millionen Besucher an. 16 der weltgrößten Branchenmessen aus dem Konsum-, Investitionsgüter- und Dienstleistungssektor haben in Frankfurt ihren Standort gefunden. Durch ihre globale Ausstrahlung unterstützen gerade diese „Leitmessen" die Stadt Frankfurt am Main und das Rhein-Main-Gebiet im europäischen Wettbewerb der Regionen. Dadurch werden jährlich nicht nur 20.000 Arbeitsplätze gesichert, sondern auch eine zusätzliche Nachfrage für die gesamte Region von über 3 Mrd. DM bewirkt.

Der Standort als Messe- und Kongressstadt erleichtert das Anbahnen von Geschäftskontakten. Der wichtigste Handelspartner Hessens sind die USA. Dies gilt sowohl für den Export als auch für den Import. Während Frankreich und das Vereinigte Königreich im Außenhandel ebenfalls von großer Bedeutung sind, haben die USA bei den ausländischen Direktinvestitionen in Hessen mit rund 30 Prozent unangefochten den ersten Platz inne. Exportiert werden entsprechend den industriellen Schwerpunkten vor allem Maschinen, Kraftfahrzeuge und chemische Erzeugnisse, wobei die beiden letztgenannten Erzeugnisse gleichzeitig auch den größten Importgüteranteil ausmachen.

Bis in die Vereinigten Staaten ist auch der Ruf der Postproduction-Unternehmen der Region gelangt. Die am stärksten expandierenden Branchen sind die Presse- und Verlagshäuser, Bild- und Informationsdienste, Netzprovider, Marktforschungsunternehmen sowie Werbe- und PR-Agenturen. Auf dem Weg ins Informationszeitalter liegt Frankfurt Rhein-Main als Zentrum der New Media Industry ganz vorne.

Im 21. Jahrhundert wird Frankfurt Rhein-Main unverändert eine internationale Wirtschaftsregion für internationale Konzernzentralen mit einem internationalen Finanzplatz Frankfurt – eben ein Gateway to Europe – sein. Neben Berlin und München wird Frankfurt als „Finanzhauptstadt Europas" eine starke Stellung behalten, wobei es sich in einigen Punkten von anderen Metropolen unterscheidet: Frankfurt hat nach wie vor etwas Bürgerliches, Intimes mit einer wunderschönen Umgebung. Innerhalb von 30 Minuten erreicht man in jede Richtung das Mittelgebirge. Neben dem vielfältigen kulturellen Angebot gibt es z. B. auch das besondere Flair Sachsenhausens mit seinen Apfelweinkneipen, die eher kleinstädtisch wirken. Frankfurt zeichnet sich sowohl durch Weltoffenheit und Internationalität einer Metropole als auch durch die überschaubaren Konturen einer Kleinstadt aus. Das ist in den Riesenstädten wie London, Paris oder Berlin schwer zu finden. ∎

Auf dem Weg ins Informationszeitalter liegt Frankfurt Rhein-Main als Zentrum der New Media Industry ganz vorne.

On its way into the information age Frankfurt Rhein-Main lies right in the front, as a centre of the New Media Industry.

14

with around 30 % of foreign direct investments in Hesse. The exports comprise, according to the industrial main focus, above all machines and engines, motor vehicles and chemical products, whereby the latter two mentioned products also make up the largest share of imported goods.

The reputation of the postproduction enterprises of the region has reached as far as the United States. The most rapidly expanding branches are the press- and editing houses, picture and information services, network providers, market research companies as well as advertising and PR-agencies. On its way into the information age Frankfurt Rhein-Main lies right in the front, as a centre of the New Media Industry.

In the 21st century Frankfurt Rhein-Main shall remain unchanged as international economic region for international headquarters of company groups with its financial centre Frankfurt – thus a Gateway to Europe. Besides Berlin and Munich, Frankfurt shall maintain a very strong position as „Financial Capital of Europe", whereby it differs from other metropolitan cities in some points: Frankfurt still keeps some of its middle-class charm, something intimate within a beautiful surrounding. Within 30 minutes into any direction one reaches the Central Mountains (Mittelgebirge). Apart from the multicultural alternatives there is the special flair of Sachsenhausen for example its cider bars that have a rather small-town character. Frankfurt distinguishes itself through its openness to the world and international character as well as through the clear contours of a small town. This is hard to find in huge cities like London, Paris or Berlin. ■

Bulle und ...

Bull and ...

influenced the economic development of the region Frankfurt-Rhein-Main in a lasting way. The Frankfurt motorway crossing opened in 1956 copes with more than 300.000 vehicles a day. A complete reconstruction will make it fit for the needs of the 21st century. The new airport train station connects together with the Frankfurt main train station, the largest passenger service train station in Europe, the Rhein-Main area with the area of the Ruhr. The current project „Port 2000" is preparing the Eastern Port for the tasks of the coming decade in an optimal way. In terms of infrastructure the Eastern Port lies in the intersection of important national long-distance roads, railway lines and waterways (Rhine, Main, Danube) and thus is an excellent location for the logistics of rail cargo transport for the city and the region. It is, being the largest supply and disposal centre for goods of all kinds, a guarantee for an optimal supply of commerce and industry. Let alone the extension of the existing infrastructure is not going to be sufficient to ensure economic prosperity and quality of life in the Rhein-Main area. The key word is: Transport-System-Management. Its aim is the better networking of roads, train tracks, water, air and their individual systems as well as meticulous information independent of the traffic flow for all participants in traffic. As a market place of international possibilities the fair and exhibition centre Frankfurt, which disposes of the third largest ground in the world, is a decisive economic factor. A total of 55 exhibitions per year attract almost 50.000 exhibitors and around 2,5 million visitors. 16 of the world's largest exhibitions for branches from the consumer-, investment goods- and service sectors have found their

location in Frankfurt. Through their global energy, especially these „trend setting fairs" support the City of Frankfurt on the Main and the Rhein-Main region in the European competition of the regions. In this way, not only 20.000 workplaces are secured yearly, but also an additional demand of more than 3 billion DM is effected for the complete region. The location as a city of exhibition and congresses facilitates the initiation of business contacts. The most important business partner of Hesse is the USA. This is valid for exports as well as for imports. While France and the United Kingdom are also of great importance in exports, the USA hold the undisputable first place

... Bär vor der Frankfurter Börse.

... Bear in front of the Frankfurt Stock Exchange.

PricewaterhouseCoopers – Kompetenz im weltweiten Netzwerk

PricewaterhouseCoopers – Competence in a Worldwide Network

Die PricewaterhouseCoopers Unternehmensberatung GmbH ist mit ca. 2.150 Mitarbeiterinnen und Mitarbeitern eines der führenden Beratungsunternehmen in Deutschland. Wir beraten Wirtschaftsunternehmen aller Branchen sowie öffentliche und private Organisationen in allen Fragen der Unternehmensstrategie und -planung, des Reengineering, Change Management, im IT- und Outsourcing-Bereich. Im Verbund PricewaterhouseCoopers sind wir in über 150 Ländern und allen wichtigen Wirtschaftszentren vertreten. Weltweit stehen rund 40.000 Beraterinnen und Berater für international ausgerichtete Projekte zur Verfügung.

Die PricewaterhouseCoopers Unternehmensberatung gehört zum Unternehmensverbund PwC Deutsche Revision. Rund 10.000 Mitarbeiterinnen und Mitarbeiter aus den Bereichen Wirtschaftsprüfung, Unternehmensberatung, Steuerberatung, Corporate Finance- und Human Resource-Beratung arbeiten im Unternehmensverbund an über 40 Standorten in Deutschland für nationale und internationale Kunden und Mandanten jeder Größe.

Mit insgesamt 150.000 Mitarbeiterinnen und Mitarbeitern eröffnet PricewaterhouseCoopers globale Präsenz an allen wichtigen Wirtschaftsstandorten der Welt. PricewaterhouseCoopers International ist eine Company limited by guarantee, registriert in England und Wales. ∎

Rund 40.000 Beraterinnen und Berater stehen in mehr als 150 Ländern zur Verfügung.
Around 40.000 male and female consultants are available in more than 150 countries.

Die kontinuierliche Ausweitung unserer Produktpalette, die hohe Spezialisierung unserer Experten, die enge Einbindung in das leistungsstarke Netzwerk von PricewaterhouseCoopers und unsere hohen Investitionen in moderne Beratungs- und Prüfungssoftware kommen unseren Kunden in kleineren Projekten ebenso zugute wie bei großen, international ausgerichteten Aufgaben.

Als Mitglied im Verbund PricewaterhouseCoopers können wir weltweit einheitliche Leistungen auf hohem Qualitätsniveau anbieten.

Intelligente Lösungen.
Intelligent solutions.

Wachstumsbranche Unternehmensberatung.
Company Consulting, the growing branch.

The PricewaterhouseCoopers Unternehmensberatung GmbH is with approx. 2,150 employees one of the leading consulting companies in Germany. We advise business enterprises from all industries as well as public and private organisations in all issues of corporate strategy and planning, re-engineering, change management, and in the fields of IT and outsourcing. PricewaterhouseCoopers is represented in more than 150 countries and in all important business centres. Worldwide around 40,000 consultants are available for internationally oriented projects.

The PricewaterhouseCoopers Unternehmensberatung belongs to the Group PwC Deutsche Revision. Around 10,000 employees from the fields of auditing, consulting, tax consulting, corporate finance and human resource consulting work within this business group at more than 40 locations in Germany for national and international clients and customers of all sizes.

The continuous expansion of our service range, the high specialisation of our experts, the close integration into the most efficient network of PricewaterhouseCoopers and our high investment into modern consulting and auditing software benefit our clients in smaller projects as well as at large internationally oriented tasks.

As a member of the PricewaterhouseCoopers international, we are able to provide standardised solutions worldwide on a high qualitative level.

Mehr als 150.000 Mitarbeiter weltweit.
More than 150,000 employees worldwide.

With a total of 150,000 employees PricewaterhouseCoopers has global presence in all important business locations of the world. PricewaterhouseCoopers International is a company limited by guarantee, registered in England and Wales. ∎

PRICEWATERHOUSECOOPERS
Unternehmensberatung GmbH

PricewaterhouseCoopers
Unternehmensberatung GmbH

Geschäftsführer (Sprecher)/
Manager (Spokesman):
Dr. Jan Philip Schleth
Peter Spix

Gründungsjahr/Year of Foundation:
1998

Standorte/Locations:
Berlin, Düsseldorf, Essen, Frankfurt am Main, Hamburg,
Leipzig, München, Saarbrücken,
Stuttgart, Walldorf

Mitarbeiter/Employees:
rund 2.150 Mitarbeiterinnen und Mitarbeiter,
davon ca. 2.000 Beraterinnen und Berater
inkl. Partner (Stand 31.12.2000)
Around 2,150 male and female employees,
of these approx. 2,000 consultants incl. Partners
(status: 31.12.2000)

Umsatz/Turnover:
rund 750 Mio. DM (Geschäftsjahr 1999/00),

Ranking:
Position 3 im Ranking der
„Leading German Consultancies" (nach Umsatz)
Position 3 in the ranking of "Leading German
Consultancies" (according to turnover)

Geschäftstätigkeit/Business Activity:
Strategieberatung/Strategy Change
• Unternehmensstrategie/Corporate Strategy
• Technologische Strategie/Technological Strategy
• Organisationsstrategie/Organisational Strategy
• Operative Strategie/Operative Strategy
• Change Management

Application Outsourcing Services

Prozessberatung/Performance Improvement
• Customer Relationship Management
• Supply Chain Management
• Finanz- und Kostenmanagement/
  Finance and Cost Management
• Personalwirtschaft/Capital Solutions
• IT-Management

Technologieberatung/Technology Solutions
• Informationstechnologie/Information Technology
• Systemintegration/System Integration
• ERP-Systeme/ERP Systems

Die Zukunftsthemen der
PricewaterhouseCoopers Unternehmensberatung:
Future fields of PricewaterhouseCoopers Consulting:
• E-Business
• Knowledge Management
• Globalisierung/Globalisation
• Innovationsmanagement/Innovation Management

Anschrift/Address:
Lurgiallee 5
D-60439 Frankfurt am Main
Telefon   +49 (69) 59 76-80
Telefax   +49 (69) 59 76-81 09
Internet   www.pwcglobal.com/de
           www.ebusinessisbusiness.com

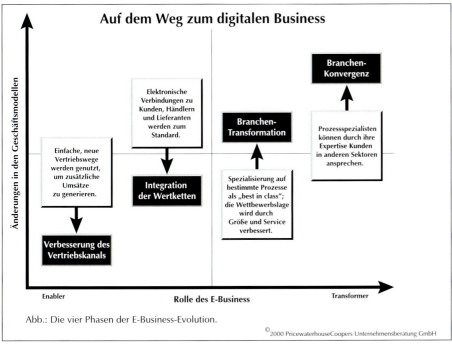

Auf dem Weg zum digitalen Business

Änderungen in den Geschäftsmodellen

Einfache, neue
Vertriebswege
werden genutzt,
um zusätzliche
Umsätze
zu generieren.

Verbesserung des
Vertriebskanals

Elektronische
Verbindungen zu
Kunden, Händlern
und Lieferanten
werden zum
Standard.

Integration
der Wertketten

Branchen-
Transformation

Spezialisierung auf
bestimmte Prozesse
als „best in class";
die Wettbewerbslage
wird durch
Größe und Service
verbessert.

Branchen-
Konvergenz

Prozessspezialisten
können durch ihre
Expertise Kunden
in anderen Sektoren
ansprechen.

Enabler   Rolle des E-Business   Transformer

Abb.: Die vier Phasen der E-Business-Evolution.

© 2000 PricewaterhouseCoopers Unternehmensberatung GmbH

E-Business: Transformation statt Revolution.
E-Business: Transformation instead of Revolution.

Frankfurt – optimal für Start ups und Neuansiedlungen

Frankfurt – an optimal Location for Start-Ups and New Settlements

Was benötigen *Start up* Firmen, um erfolgreich zu sein? Sie brauchen zunächst einmal einen ideenreichen Firmengründer. Darüber hinaus brauchen sie Kapital, Räume, Mitarbeiter, Marktzugang, Beratung und schnelle Daten- und Telekommunikationsnetze. All das brauchen sie sofort und auf möglichst hohem Niveau. Wo könnte man also diese Ingredienzien für einen erfolgreichen *Start up* besser finden als in einem der wichtigsten Wirtschaftszentren Europas? Auch etablierte Firmen haben die gleichen Anforderungen, um erfolgreich sein zu können. Anders als *Start ups* brauchen erfolgreiche, etablierte Unternehmen nicht alles zur gleichen Zeit, sondern über einen längeren Zeitraum verteilt, aber ihr Bedarf ist vorhanden. Darum finden sich die benötigten Komponenten in einem großen Wirtschaftszentrum. Was finden *Start up* Unternehmen in Frankfurt? Der innovative, einfallsreiche, entschlossene und von der Idee der Unternehmensgründung begeisterte Jungunternehmer findet in Frankfurt Kapital von den verschiedensten Venture Capital Unternehmen. Nachdem sich der Neue Markt, der Markt für Wachstums- und Technologiewerte der Deutschen Börse, hier in Frankfurt in wenigen Monaten zu einem hochinteressanten und erfolgreichen Anlagemarkt entwickelt hat, ziehen mehr und mehr Venture Capital Firmen nach Frankfurt. Da der Ausstieg aus einem Engagement über den Börsengang am Neuen Markt für die Wagniskapitalgeber nicht minder interessant ist als der Einstieg in ein Unternehmen, sind sie hier in Frankfurt präsent. Die Räume für ein *Start up* Unternehmen sind bei über 9 Mio. Quadratmeter vorhandene Bürofläche und 10 weiteren Hochhäusern, für die der Hochhausrahmenplan Planungsrecht geschaffen hat, mit Sicherheit in 1B-Lagen und ähnlichen Lagen zu finden. Allerdings fehlen in Frankfurt weitgehend die von bestimm-

Dr. Hartmut Schwesinger

Der Autor wurde 1949 in Hamburg geboren. Er studierte in Hamburg mit dem Abschluss als Diplom-Chemiker und war von 1980 bis 1993 bei Deutsche Shell AG tätig. Seit 1994 ist Dr. Hartmut Schwesinger Geschäftsführer der Wirtschaftsförderung Frankfurt GmbH.

The author was born in 1949 in Hamburg. He studied in Hamburg and graduated as a Certified Chemical Engineer and worked for the Deutsche Shell AG from 1980 until 1993. Since 1994 Dr. Hartmut Schwesinger is Managing Director of the Wirtschaftsförderung Frankfurt GmbH (Frankfurt Organization for the Promotion of Economy).

ten Firmen so geschätzten alten Schwerindustriebauten. Mitarbeiter, insbesondere junge, sind in Frankfurt ebenfalls zu finden.

Eine der wesentlichen Stärken Frankfurts ist sicherlich der Marktzugang. Mit dem Flughafen, mit dem Schnellbahnnetz und der unmittelbaren Anbindung an das Autobahnnetz sind von Frankfurt aus fast alle großen europäischen Städte sowie Städte in Nachbarländern und praktisch alle deutschen Kommunen in einer eintägigen Geschäftsreise zu erreichen. Diese zentrale Lage in einem Netz nationaler und internationaler Verkehrswege zu Luft, zu Wasser und zu Lande ist eine der herausragendsten Stärken Frankfurts. Schnelle, kurze Wege bedeuten Kostenersparnis und vor allen Dingen schnelle Reaktionsmöglichkeiten. Dieser Standortvorteil gilt für *Start ups* natürlich ebenso wie für Neuansiedlungen und alteingesessene Unternehmen.

Zahlreiche Venture Capital Firmen stehen in Frankfurt bereit, innovationsfreudigen Jungunternehmen das nötige Startkapital zu geben.

Numerous venture capital companies are prepared in Frankfurt to provide young entrepreneurs that are ready to innovate, with the initial capital they need.

What do start-up companies need to be successful? First of all they need a founder that is full of ideas. Furthermore, they need capital, space, employees, market access, consulting and fast data and communication networks. They need all this immediately and on the highest possible level. So where could one find these kind of ingredients for a successful start-up better than in one of the most important economic centres of Europe? Also already established firms have the same requirements, to be successful. Different to start-ups, successfully established companies do not need everything at the same time, but proportioned over a longer period of time, but their need exists. For this reason, the required components can be found in a large economic centre. What can start-up companies find in Frankfurt? The innovative, imaginative, determined young entrepreneur that is excited by the idea of founding a company can find in Frankfurt capital from the most varied venture capital companies. After the successful development of the New Market Economy, the market for growth and technology securities of the German Stock Exchange, here in Frankfurt after only a few months into a highly interesting and successful market for investments, more and more venture capital companies are moving to Frankfurt. Since for providers of risk capital the exit from an engagement that wants to go public in the New Market is just as interesting as getting into a company, they are present here in Frankfurt. Spaces for start-up companies can surely be found, considering more than 9 million square metres of existing office space and 10 further skyscrapers, for which the guidelines for skyscrapers have provided the necessary planning law, in 1B-locations and similar locations. However, in Frankfurt to a great extent the old heavy industrial constructions are missing, which are so highly valued by certain companies. Employees, especially young ones, can also be found in Frankfurt.

One of the decisive strengths of Frankfurt certainly is its market access. With the airport, the network of high-speed trains and the direct connection to the motorway network Frankfurt can be reached from almost all large European cities as well as cities in neighbouring countries and practically all German communities within a one-day business journey. This central location within a network of national and international traffic routes by air, water and roads is one of the most characteristic strengths of Frankfurt. Fast, short routes mean cost savings and above all a fast possibility to react. This location advantage is valid for start-ups just as much as for new settlements and traditional companies.

Thanks to international law firms, consulting companies, auditing companies and other service

Erfolgreiche Start ups – besser als in einem der wichtigsten Wirtschaftszentren Europas können die Ingredienzien für eine Unternehmensgründung nicht sein.

Successful start-ups – the ingredients for a company foundation could not be better than in one of the most important economic centres of Europe.

providers, a start-up company – just like a new settlement – finds an international, experienced consulting scenario. One special location advantage for start-ups and new settlements certainly is, the probably most unique telecommunication infrastructure worldwide. No other city has as many competing telecommunication networks as Frankfurt. With so-called Web-Hotels and Carrier-Hotels the telecommunication and Internet providers continuously extend their offers. With such infrastructures systems like a web- or carrier-hotel start-up companies as well as new settlements have the possibility to do business on the nets. The hardware, the necessary technology the

Eine der wesentlichen Stärken Frankfurts ist der Marktzugang über Straße, Schiene und Luft.
One of the essential strengths of Frankfurt is its market access via roads, rail and air.

Welt ist. Die Wettbewerbsbereitschaft, das Selbstbewusstsein zu den Siegern gehören zu können, macht einen großen Teil der Atmosphäre Frankfurts aus. Frankfurter messen sich nicht an Nachbargemeinden oder in nationalen Maßstäben. Für weite Teile der Frankfurter Business Community gilt der europäische, wenn nicht der Weltmaßstab als die eigentlich relevante Messlatte. Diese Atmosphäre von Weltoffenheit und globalem Handeln ist ein ideales Umfeld für *Start up* Unternehmen.

Frankfurt bietet daher auch Idealbedingungen für junge *Start up* Unternehmen sowie Neuansiedlungen. In Frankfurt finden Firmengründer wie Neuansiedler ein optimales Umfeld. Die Angebote an Büroraum und Gewerbeflächen decken die unterschiedlichsten Bedürfnisse. *Start up* Unternehmen finden in Frankfurt vielfältigste Unterstützung. Zahlreiche Venture Capital Firmen stehen bereit, innovationsfreudigen Jungunternehmen das nötige Startkapital zu geben. Die IVC hat mit ihrem Venture Lab darüber hinaus einen in Deutschland einmaligen Incubator für Jungunternehmen geschaffen. Die Anwaltskanzleien beraten hochprofessionell und auch spezialisiert. So finden sich in Frankfurt zahlreiche Anwälte mit internationaler Erfahrung, sei es mit Biotech *Start ups* in Kalifornien oder mit Telekommunikationsunternehmen, sei es im IT-Bereich oder auch im Bereich von Film- und Fernsehproduktionen.

Dank internationaler Anwaltskanzleien, Unternehmensberatungen, Wirtschaftsprüfern und anderen Dienstleistern für Unternehmen trifft ein *Start up* Unternehmen, genau wie eine Neuansiedlung, in Frankfurt auf eine international erfahrene Beratungskulisse. Ein besonderer Standortvorteil für *Start ups* und Neuansiedlungen ist mit Sicherheit die wohl weltweit einmalige Telekommunikationsinfrastruktur in Frankfurt. Keine andere Stadt hat so viele miteinander im Wettbewerb stehende Telekommunikationsnetze wie Frankfurt. Mit sogenannten Web-Hotels und Carrier-Hotels erweitern die Telekommunika-

tions- und Internetinfrastrukturanbieter ständig ihr Angebot. Mit solchen Infrastruktureinrichtungen wie einem Web- oder Carrier-Hotel wird *Start up* Unternehmen wie Neuansiedlungen die Möglichkeit geboten, auf den Netzen Geschäft zu machen. Die Hardware, die nötige Technologie halten die Betreiber der Hotels vor. Der deutsche Internetknotenpunkt DE-CIX, über den 85 % des Internettraffics in Deutschland geführt werden, ist ein Beleg für die Leistungsstärke der IT-Infrastruktur am Main.

Aber nicht nur Technologie- und Infrastruktureinrichtungen, wie der Flughafen, bestimmen die Qualität eines Standortes. Mindestens ebenso wichtig sind die Menschen, die diesen Standort zu ihrem Lebensmittelpunkt erkoren haben. Frankfurts Schnelligkeit, seine Wettbewerbsorientierung, seine Kompromisslosigkeit und Bereitschaft, Konflikte auszutragen, haben sicherlich dazu beigetragen, dass Frankfurt nach den Worten von Frau Prof. Sassen heute das innovativste und aggressivste Finanzzentrum der

Darüber hinaus bieten die zahlreichen Agenturen im Bereich Werbung, Öffentlichkeitsarbeit das notwendige Know-how, um Firmen ein schnelles, erfolgreiches Wachstum am Markt zu ermöglichen. Der Neue Markt schließlich, das Segment für Technologiewerte der Börse, ermöglicht den Börsengang. Damit wird den Kapitalgebern der „Exit", der Verkauf ihrer Anteile, ermöglicht. Den Unternehmen selbst erschließt der Börsengang den Kapitalmarkt. In Frankfurt sind die Banken und Investmenthäuser zu Hause, die einen „Going public" begleiten müssen. Außerdem haben die PR Agenturen und ihre Partner im Event-Bereich vielfältige Erfahrungen hinsichtlich von Börsengängen und der sie ergänzenden Maßnahmen.

Auch über die Straße ist die Stadt mit den europäischen Metropolen verbunden.
The city is also connected by road with the European cosmopolitan cities.

providers of the hotels have in stock. The German Internet interface DE-CIX, through which 85 % of Internet traffic in Germany is handled, is proof of the strength of performance of the IT-infrastructure on the Main.

But not only technology and infrastructure institutions, like the airport, determine the quality of a location. Just as important are the people that have chosen this location as the central focus of their lives. Frankfurt's fastness, its orientation towards competitiveness, its uncompromising nature and its willingness to confront conflicts have certainly contributed to the fact that Frankfurt, according to the words of Mrs. Prof. Sassen, today is the most innovative and most aggressive financial centre in the world. The willingness to be competitive, the awareness to possibly be part of the winners has a great share in Frankfurt's atmosphere. People in Frankfurt do not measure themselves against neighbouring communities or according to national standards. For large parts of the Frankfurt Business Community the European if not the world standard is the really relevant yardstick. This atmosphere of openness towards the world and of global action is an ideal environment for start-up companies.

Therefore, Frankfurt also offers ideal conditions for young start-up companies and new settlements alike. In Frankfurt, company founders and new settlers alike find an optimal environment. The offers of office space and industrial areas cover the most varied needs. Start-up companies can find in Frankfurt the most divers support. Numerous venture capital companies are ready to provide the necessary initial capital to young entrepreneurs that are ready to innovate. The IVC, with its venture lab, has furthermore created an incubator for young entrepreneurs, uniquely in Germany. Law firms consult in a highly professional and also very specialised manner. Thus, in Frankfurt can be found numerous lawyers with international experience, be it with biotech start-ups in California or with telecommunication companies, be it in the IT-field or also in the areas of film- and TV-productions.

Furthermore, the numerous agencies in the field of advertising, public relation work provide the necessary know-how, in order to enable companies a fast and successful growth in the market. Finally, the New Market, the segment for technology securities of the stock exchange, enables companies to go public. Thus, the possibility to "exit", i.e. the sale of their shares, is given to providers of capital.

Going public opens up the capital markets to the companies themselves. In Frankfurt those banks

Neun Millionen Quadratmeter Bürofläche stehen in Frankfurt zur Verfügung.
Frankfurt disposes of nine million square metres in office space.

and investment houses are at home that must accompany a "going public". Furthermore, the PR-agencies and their partners in the event sector possess varied experiences regarding introductions into the stock exchange and their complementing measures.

But not only companies, whose aim it is to conquer the global market and position themselves in the stock exchange, find in Frankfurt the appropriate environment. At the polytechnic a programme for the promotion of university gradu-

ates was developed together with the Frankfurter Sparkasse (savings bank), which enables a comprehensive consultation and training for university graduates that want to be self-employed. For others that do not want to walk this way or were not able to, the city has created – together with the department of employment and other responsible bodies – the project "Kompass". People, who want to take the step into self-employment is given the possibility to try their capacities as entrepreneurs, without having to question their subsistence. It is only natural, that chambers and institutions pro-

Symbolisch: Die Wettbewerbsbereitschaft, das Selbstbewusstsein zu den Siegern gehören zu können, macht einen großen Teil der Atmosphäre Frankfurts aus.

Symbolical: The preparedness to compete, the confidence of belonging to one of the winners, these attitudes make up a great part of Frankfurt's atmosphere.

Companies in Frankfurt umfassende, vielfältige Netzwerke zur Verfügung. Selbstverständlich gibt es in Frankfurt einen „First Tuesday", wie aber auch andere Gruppen und Kreise, die den Meinungs- und Erfahrungsaustausch sowie der Beratung von und mit jungen Unternehmern gelten. Nicht zuletzt haben Firmen aus der IT-Branche zusammen mit der Wirtschaftsförderung den Preis „Frankfurt IniTiative 21" ins Leben gerufen, der in diesem Jahr erstmals an einen jungen, erfolgreichen Unternehmer, Herrn Benken, Firmengründer der Logo Gruppe, vergeben wurde. Ein nicht zu unterschätzender Vorteil Frankfurts gerade auch für Menschen, die die ersten Schritte auf den Märkten dieser Welt tun wollen, sind die zahlreichen international hochrangigen Kongresse. Bei ihnen treffen die Teilnehmer zwanglos mögliche Geschäftspartner, können Erfahrungen austauschen und mit interessanten Gesprächspartnern diskutieren.

zu Hause, über die ersten Schritte bis hin zur Marktreife und anschließend zur industriellen Produktion sind ebenso geglättet wie der Weg vom eigentümergeführten *Start up* über Venture Capital bis hin zur am Neuen Markt notierten Aktiengesellschaft. Der „Humus Frankfurt" lässt die Saat der *Start ups* optimal erblühen und zu beständigen und wetterfesten Pflanzen heranwachsen.

Für Firmen, die neu nach Frankfurt kommen, insbesondere für ausländische, bietet die Wirtschaftsförderung ein umfassendes Beratungs- und Betreuungsangebot. Die Hilfe bei der Erlangung von Arbeits- und Aufenthaltsgenehmigungen und Unterstützung bei der Suche nach geeigneten Immobilien sind die am stärksten nachgefragten Dienstleistungen. Allgemeine wie spezielle Standortinformationen, Erläuterungen über die rechtlichen und fiskalischen Rahmenbedingungen sind weitere, immer wieder verlangte Leistungen der Frankfurter Wirtschaftsförderer. Selbstverständlich stehen den Kunden der Frankfurter Wirtschaftsförderer auch die jeweiligen, relevanten Branchennetzwerke zur Verfügung. ∎

Aber nicht nur Firmen, deren Ziel es ist, den globalen Markt zu erobern und sich an der Börse zu platzieren, finden in Frankfurt das richtige Umfeld. An der Fachhochschule wurde ein Förderungsmodell für Hochschulabsolventen entwickelt zusammen mit der Frankfurter Sparkasse, das eine umfassende Beratung und Schulung für Hochschulabsolventen ermöglicht, die sich selbstständig machen wollen. Für andere, die diesen Weg nicht gehen wollen oder nicht gehen konnten, hat die Stadt zusammen mit dem Arbeitsamt und weiteren Trägern das Projekt „Kompass" geschaffen. Menschen, die den Schritt in die Selbstständigkeit gehen wollen, wird die Möglichkeit gegeben, ihre Fähigkeiten als Unternehmer zu erproben, ohne dabei ihre Existenz in Frage stellen zu müssen. Dass die Kammern und die Wirtschaftsförderung ein umfassendes Beratungsangebot für Firmengründer bereit halten, ist selbstverständlich. Insgesamt stehen Firmengründern und *Start up*

Acht Universitäten und Hochschulen in der Region sind ein Beleg für die hohe Forschungskapazität in Frankfurt/Rhein-Main. Das Max-Planck-Institut für Biophysik mit dem Nobelpreisträger Michel unterstreicht das internationale Spitzenniveau der Forschung in Rhein/Main. Die Stadt will den Leistungen der Forschung im BioTech-Bereich an der Frankfurter Uni wie in Darmstadt und andernorts im Rhein-Main-Gebiet mit dem Bau eines Frankfurter Innovationszentrums an der Universität Rechnung tragen. Die aus dem Hoechst-Verbund hervorgegangene Firma Infra-Serv bietet jungen Unternehmen darüber hinaus die ideale Infrastruktur und Rahmenbedingungen im Industriepark Höchst, um den Schritt von der forschungsnahen Entwicklung in die industrielle Produktion erfolgreich zu bewältigen. Mit anderen Worten: In Frankfurt sind die Wege für *Start ups* geebnet. Der Weg von der Idee, sei es im Forschungslabor, sei es im stillen Kämmerchen

Frankfurt. Euro-City.

motion of the economy offer a comprehensive provision of consultation for company founders. On the whole, there are extensive and numerous networks at the disposal of company founders and start-up companies in Frankfurt. Of course there exists in Frankfurt a "First Tuesday", as also other groups and circles that are dedicated to the exchange of opinions and experiences as well as the consultation of and with young entrepreneurs. Last but not least, companies from the IT-branch have brought to life – together with the Organization for the Promotion of Economy – the award "Frankfurt Initiative 21", which was bestowed this year for the first time to a young, successful entrepreneur, Mr. Benken, company founder of the Logo Group. One advantage of Frankfurt that must not be underestimated, especially for people that want to take their first steps on the markets of the world, are the numerous international high-ranking congresses. At these, participants can meet possible business partners informally, can exchange experiences and can take part in discussions with interesting partners.

Eight universities and polytechnics in the region are proof of the high capacity for research activi-

Mit dem ICE sind vom Frankfurter Hauptbahnhof innerhalb weniger Stunden die meisten deutschen Großstädte zu erreichen.

By ICE, most of the large German cities can be reached within a few hours from the Frankfurt mainstation.

ties in Frankfurt Rhein-Main. The Max-Planck-Organization for biophysics with its Nobel Prize-winner Michel highlights the international top level of research in the Rhein-Main region. The magistrate of the city want to honour the achievements of science in the field of biotechnology at the university of Frankfurt, as well as in Darmstadt and other cities of the Rhein-Main area by building the Innovation Centre Frankfurt at the university. The company InfraServ that emerged from the Hoechst-Group offers young entrepreneurs furthermore an ideal infrastructure and framework conditions within the industrial park Höchst, in order to cope with steps from a development close to research into the industrial production successfully. In other words, the ways from the idea, be it in the research lab or in a quiet room at home, then overcoming the first steps until arriving at market maturity and finally at industrial production are just as levelled as the ways of a start-up initiated by the owners themselves or by venture capital or through a holding noted at the New Market. The "humus Frankfurt" leaves the seed of start-ups to blossom in an optimal manner and to grow into firm and weatherproof plants.

The Organization for the Promotion of Economy provides for companies that are new in Frankfurt, especially for foreign ones, a comprehensive offer of consultation and service. Support with the attainment of work and residence permits and aid in the search for suitable properties are the most commonly demanded services. General services, like special location information, explications about legal and fiscal conditions are further, repeatedly asked services of the promoters of economy in Frankfurt. Of course, the clients of the promoters of economy in Frankfurt can also dispose of the corresponding and relevant branch networks.

Frankfurt. The-Euro-City.

3i – Ihr kompetenter Partner für Venture Capital und Private Equity

*3i – Your experienced partner
for Venture Capital and Private Equity*

Mit einem derzeitigen Beteiligungsportfolio von über 300 Unternehmen, die mit über 1.247 Millionen Euro zum 31. März 2000 bewertet wurden, einem jährlichen Investitionsvolumen von rund 1 Milliarde Euro, 70 Beteiligungsmanagern und einer Erfolgsbilanz von mehr als 30 neuen Unternehmen, die in den vergangenen drei Jahren an die Börse gebracht wurden, ist 3i der führende Venture Capital-Geber in Deutschland. 3i, das vor über 50 Jahren zur Unterstützung der Umstrukturierung der britischen Industrie gegründet wurde (3i geht auf den ursprünglichen Namen „Investors in Industry" zurück), ist heute eine global orientierte Aktiengesellschaft und ein Hauptinvestor in neuen Technologien, welche die Unternehmen im 21. Jahrhundert vorantreiben werden. Das schnelle Wachstum von 3i in Deutschland hat entscheidend dazu beigetragen, dass sich das Unternehmen zur führenden Venture Capital Gesellschaft in Europa mit einem Gesamtbeteiligungsportfolio von 3.000 Unternehmen entwickelt hat, die mit rund 10 Milliarden Euro bewertet wurden.

Expertise in vielen Branchen, regionale Präsenz

Der Umfang der 3i Expertise lässt sich jedoch mit Zahlenmaterial alleine nur begrenzt veranschaulichen. Nach der Akquisition und erfolgreichen Integration der Technologieholding mit Sitz in München im Februar 2000 bietet 3i Deutschland Venture Capital für alle Entwicklungsstufen eines Unternehmens an – angefangen von der Seed-Finanzierung von viel versprechenden Ideen bis zur Early-Stage-Finanzierung, Wachstumsfinanzierung für Wachstumsunternehmen und komplexen Finanzierung von Transaktionsgeschäften für größere Management Buy-Outs von reifen Unternehmen, die sich in der Umstrukturierungsphase befinden oder bei denen ein Eigentümerwechsel stattfindet.

Die Philosophie von 3i ist eine Kombination seiner Expertise in den unterschiedlichsten Branchen mit seiner regionalen Präsenz, um den Unternehmen, an denen 3i sich beteiligt, die bestmögliche Unterstützung zu gewähren. Mit Büros in Frankfurt, München, Stuttgart, Düsseldorf, Hamburg, Berlin und Leipzig stellt das Unternehmen Teams von Investmentmanagern für jede größere Region in

Deutschland bereit, die den 3i-Portfolio-Unternehmen Beratung vor Ort sowie globale Unterstützung durch das 3i Netzwerk – bestehend aus über 30 Büros in drei Kontinenten – bieten. Ob Branchenwissen oder Expertise betreffend Management und Transaktionsgeschäften – 3i stellt Experten und Expertise zur Verfügung, um seinen Beteiligungen die bestmögliche Lösung zu bieten.

Neuer Markt eröffnet neue Dimension

3i beteiligt sich schon seit 1988 an Unternehmen in Deutschland, jedoch eröffnete die Einführung des Neuen Marktes im Jahre 1997 3i neue Möglichkeiten und verlieh dem gesamten Venture Capital Geschäft eine neue Dimension. Der Börsengang von Mobilcom im März 1997, einer der zwei ersten Zulassungen im Neuen Markt und einer

Die 3i Geschäftsleitung – Andreas Kochhäuser (Direktor Stuttgart), Ulrich Eilers (Direktor Düsseldorf), Rudolf Franz (Direktor München), Peter Cullom (Direktor Frankfurt), Stefan Friese (Direktor Berlin und Leipzig) und Andrew Richards (Geschäftsführer), v. l. n. r.

The management of 3i – Andreas Kochhäuser (Director Stuttgart), Ulrich Eilers (Director Düsseldorf), Rudolf Franz (Director Munich), Peter Cullom (Director Frankfurt), Stefan Friese (Director Berlin and Leipzig) and Andrew Richards (Managing Director), f. l. t. r.

der erfolgreichsten in diesem neuen Marktsegment, war eine 3i Beteiligung. Durch das schnelle Wachstum des deutschen Venture Capital Marktes seit 1997 wurde durch die Erweiterung des Neuen Marktes vorangetrieben, dessen Marktkapitalisierung von 25,9 Milliarden Euro Ende 1998 auf über 200 Milliarden Euro im September 2000 stieg. Von der Einführung des Neuen Markts im März 1997 bis zum Juli 2000 unterstützte 3i (zusammen mit der Technologieholding) den Börsengang von

32 Beteiligungen in Deutschland. Hiervon wurden 28 am Neuen Markt zugelassen, darunter Unternehmen wie ACG, Intershop, Brokat und Morphosys neben Mobilcom.

Ein Börsengang stellt für 3i lediglich eine von vielen potenziellen Exitkanälen dar. So machen Börsengänge weiterhin nur ca. 20 % der 3i Veräußerungen in Deutschland aus, wobei der verbleibende Anteil in erster Linie auf Trade Sale (Veräußerung von Unternehmensanteilen an industrielle Investoren), Secondary Purchase oder Rückkäufe durch Dritte oder ehemalige Eigentümer eines Unternehmens entfällt. Darüber hinaus hält 3i auch nach der Durchführung eines Börsengangs weiterhin einen Anteil an seinen Beteiligungen, um das betreffende Unternehmen weiterhin zu unterstützen und von seinem künftigen Wachstum zu profitieren.

Neue Marktpsychologie – Möglichkeiten für 3i

Der überragende Erfolg des Neuen Marktes und das wieder aufkommende Interesse an Kapitalbeteiligungen in Deutschland hat neben der Bereitstellung neuer Kapitalquellen die Marktpsychologie grundlegend verändert. Obwohl Venture Capital Beteiligungen als prozentualer Anteil am Bruttosozialprodukt weiterhin rund einem Viertel des reiferen US-amerikanischen Marktes entsprechen, wird diese Kluft geschlossen, da VC Beteiligungen parallel zum Wachstum des breiteren Kapitalmarktes schnell zunehmen.

Dies ist ein ideales Umfeld für 3i mit seinem Doppelfokus auf Unterstützung von Technologie-Start-up-Unternehmen und Umstrukturierung von Unternehmen in etablierten Sektoren. Aufgrund der zunehmenden Dynamik des Marktes, der zunehmenden Unterstützung neuer Unternehmen und Hightech, der Deregulierung von wichtigen Industrien sowie den Steuer- und sonstigen Reformen, die es größeren Unternehmen ermöglichen wird, ihr Portfolio umzustrukturieren, blickt 3i Deutschland auf eine Periode mit anhaltendem Wachstum, die seine führende Position auf dem deutschen Markt untermauern wird. ∎

With a current investment portfolio of over 300 companies valued at more than 1,247 million at 31 March 2000, an annual investment volume on the order of 1 billion, 70 investment executives, and a track record of more than 30 new companies brought to the stock market through IPO's in the last three years, 3i is the leading venture capital investor in Germany.

Founded more than 50 years ago to help restructure British industry, 3i (from the original name of "Investors in Industry") is today a globally oriented public company and a major investor in the new technologies that will drive business in the 21st century. The company's rapid growth in Germany is a key to 3i's position as the leading European venture capital company with a total investment portfolio of 3,000 enterprises valued at some ø 10 billion.

Multispecialist expertise, regional presence

Numbers alone are only a partial indication of the scope of 3i's expertise. Following the acquisition and successful integration of Munich-based Technologieholding in February of this year, 3i Deutschland provides venture capital for all stages in the life of a company. This ranges from seed money for promising ideas to start-up financing for early phase enterprises, expansion funding for growth companies and complex transactional financings of larger buy-outs for mature companies going through a restructuring or change of ownership.

3i's philosophy is to combine its multispecialist expertise with its regional presence to provide the best support to the companies in which it invests. With offices in Frankfurt, Munich, Stuttgart, Düsseldorf, Hamburg, Berlin and Leipzig, there are teams of investment professionals in every major region of Germany to provide local advice and global support through the 3i network – with its over 30 offices on three continents – to existing and potential ventures. Whether it is industry, management or transactional expertise, 3i has the professionals and the know-how to provide the best possible solutions for its entrepreneurs.

Neuer Markt opens a new dimension

3i has been investing in Germany since 1988, but it was the launch of the Neuer Markt in 1997 which opened new opportunities for 3i and gave a new dimension to the entire venture capital business. Mobilcom, whose IPO in March 1997 was one of the first two listings on the Neuer Markt and one of the most successful in the new segment, was a 3i investment. Mobilcom's outstanding performance since its listing helped to immediately establish the credibility of the Neuer Markt as a capital market for technology and growth companies. This in turn opened a channel to large pools of capital looking for higher return equity investment vehicles, with higher risk profiles. The rapid growth of the German venture capital market since 1997 has been powered by the expansion of the Neuer Markt, whose market capitalization rose from 25.9 billion at the end of 1998 to more than 200 billion in September 2000.

From the launch of the Neuer Markt in March 1997 through July 2000, 3i (together with Technologieholding) helped bring 32 investments to market in Germany in the form of IPOs. Of this total, 28 were listed on the Neuer Markt, including companies such as ACG, Intershop, Brokat, and Morphosys in addition to Mobilcom. In the first seven months of 2000 alone, 3i accompanied 13 new IPOs on the Neuer Markt, with more in the pipeline for the rest of 2000 and beyond.

An IPO is only one of several potential exit channels for 3i. Indeed, IPOs still represent only approximately 20 % of 3i's divestments in Germany, with the remainder being primarily in the form of trade sales, secondary purchases or buy-backs by other or previous owners of a company. Moreover, in many cases, 3i continues to hold a stake in its investments even beyond the IPO in order to provide ongoing support to the company and benefit from its further growth.

New market psychology spells opportunity for 3i

In addition to providing new sources of capital, the remarkable success of the Neuer Markt and the reawakened interest in equity investment in Germany have fundamentally changed market psychology. Although venture capital investment as a percentage of GNP is still at approximately one-fourth the level of the mature U.S. market, this gap is closing as VC investment rises rapidly parallel to the growth of the broader capital market.

This is an ideal environment for 3i with its dual focus on fostering technology start-ups and supporting the restructuring of companies in more established sectors. Given the increasing dynamics of the market, the growing support for new entrepreneurs and high-tech, the deregulation of key industries, and the tax and other reforms that will allow large companies to restructure their portfolios, 3i Deutschland is looking forward to a period of sustained growth that will confirm its leadership in the German market. ■

3i Deutschland Gesellschaft für Industriebeteiligungen mbH

Geschäftsführung/Management:
Andrew Richards

Mitglieder der Geschäftsleitung/
Members of Management:
Peter Cullom
Ulrich Eilers
Rudolf Franz
Stefan Friese
Andreas Kochhäuser

Gründungsjahr/Year of Foundation: 1986

Mitarbeiter/Employees:
120 (Stand/Status 10/2000)

Geschäftstätigkeit/Business Activity:
Wachstumskapital – Beteiligungskapital
• für junge, wachstumsstarke Unternehmen,
• für etablierte Unternehmen mit
  Expansionspotenzial
• für Umstrukturierungen und
  Nachfolgelösungen – MBO und MBI
• für den Börsengang
Growth Capital – Private Equity
• for young, fast growing companies
• for established companies with potential for
  expansion
• for restructuring and solutions for successions
  MBO and MBI
• for Pre- IPO financing

Anschrift/Address:
Bockenheimer Landstraße 55
D-60325 Frankfurt am Main
Telefon   +49 (69) 71 00 00-0
Telefax   +49 (69) 71 00 00-59
E-mail   Frankfurt@3i.com
Internet   www.3i.com

Accenture – führender Architekt und Wegbereiter der neuen Ökonomie

Leading Architect and Builder of the New Economy

Accenture Firmensitz in Sulzbach bei Frankfurt.

Accenture office in Sulzbach near Frankfurt.

Accenture ist eines der weltweit führenden Beratungsunternehmen für Management und Technologie. Der Anspruch des Unternehmens ist es, als Architekt und Wegbereiter der neuen Ökonomie gemeinsam mit innovativen Organisationen die Zukunft zu gestalten.

Neue Allianzen

Accenture beschäftigt derzeit weltweit über 70.000 Mitarbeiter in 46 Ländern. Das Unternehmen erzielte im vergangenen Jahr einen Umsatz von rund 10 Milliarden US-Dollar. Accenture berät und arbeitet mit über 4.500 Organisationen weltweit; dazu gehören 91 Unternehmen aus dem Fortune Global 100-Index, mehr als die Hälfte der im Fortune Global 500 aufgelisteten Organisationen sowie die wichtigsten im Internet-Index The Industry Standard vertretenen Unternehmen. Accenture ist derzeit mehr als 100 Allianzen eingegangen, sowohl mit Weltmarktführern als auch mit aufstrebenden Technologieunternehmen.

Akzente setzen

Accenture versteht sich als führender Anbieter aller Leistungen, die zur Gründung, Entwicklung, Gestaltung, Transformation und zum Betrieb eines erfolgreichen und zukunftsfähigen Unternehmens notwendig sind. Ob es sich dabei um aufstrebende Neugründungen handelt, die Expertise und Kapital suchen, oder einen börsennotierten, international agierenden Player, der seine eCommerce-Strategie auf den neuesten Stand bringen möchte: Accenture unterstützt Unternehmen, bei der Gestaltung ihrer Zukunft die richtigen Akzente zu setzen.

Business Launch Centers

Das Unternehmen betreibt momentan über 25 Business Launch Centers, die neu gegründeten eCommerce Start-ups und Spin-offs die notwendigen Ressourcen und Werkzeuge für einen schnellen und nachhaltigen Markterfolg zur Verfügung stellen. Darüber hinaus hat Accenture unter anderem mit Microsoft und British Telecom erfolgreich tätige, eigenständige Unternehmen gegründet.

Accenture Technology Ventures

Die Risikokapitaleinheit von Accenture unterstützt Unternehmer beim Aufbau profitabler Firmen, die durch ihr Innovationspotenzial ganze Branchen verändern, neue Märkte schaffen und überdurchschnittlichen Markterfolg anstreben. Accenture Technology Ventures beabsichtigt, innerhalb der nächsten fünf Jahre weltweit mehrere hundert Millionen US-Dollar zu investieren.

In Deutschland beschäftigte Accenture (vormals Andersen Consulting) 1999 über 2.400 Mitarbeiter in fünf Niederlassungen. Im Geschäftsjahr 1999 wurde in Deutschland ein Umsatz von 1,24 Milliarden DM erzielt.

Repositionierung

Seit dem 7. August 2000 ist die Unternehmensgruppe nicht mehr mit Andersen Worldwide oder Arthur Andersen verbunden und firmiert seit dem 1. Januar 2001 weltweit unter dem Namen Accenture. ∎

Mehr als 3.000 Mitarbeiter in Deutschland.
More than 3,000 people in Germany.

Accenture is one of the leading global management and technology consulting organizations. Being an architect and builder of the new economy, the company's claim is to design the future together with innovative organizations.

New Alliances

Accenture presently employs more than 70,000 people in 46 countries around the world. Last year, the company archieved revenues of $ 10 billion. Accenture works with more than 4,500 organizations worldwide, including 91 of *Fortunes's* 1999 Global 100 companies and more than half of the organizations on *Fortune's* 1999 Global 500 list. Clients also include more than half of *The Industry Standard* 100 most important companies of the Internet economy. Accenture has at present completed more than 100 alliances both with world market leaders and up-and-coming technology enterprises.

Accent on the Future

Accenture sees itself as leading provider in every skill necessary to conceive, design, transform, launch and operate a successful organization of the future. Wether it is a new company seeking expertise and capital or an internationally operating player looking to refine its eCommerce strategy: Accenture has the capabilities to help companies create their own future.

Business Launch Centers

The company presently operates more than 25 Business Launch Centers that provide to new founded eCommerce start-ups and spin-offs the necessary resources and tools for a rapid and long-lasting market success. In addition, Accenture has launched independent successful operating companies, among others with Microsoft and British Telecom.

Accenture Technology Ventures

Accenture Technology Ventures, Accenture´s global venture capital unit, works with entrepreneurs to build profitable companies that transform industries, create new markets and generate superior economic returns. Within the next five years, Accenture Technology Ventures plans to invest worldwide several hundred million US dollars .

In 46 Ländern beraten Accenture-Experten.
Accenture experts consult in 46 countries.

In Germany, Accenture (formerly known as Andersen Consulting) employed more than 2,400 people in five offices. In 1999, Accenture achieved revenues of DM 1.24 billion in Germany.

Repositioning

Since August 7, 2000 the organization is no longer associated with Andersen Worldwide or Arthur Andersen. On January 1, 2001, Andersen Consulting changed its name to Accenture. ∎

Accenture Firmensitz ab 2002 in Kronberg/Ts.
(Zeichnung: Kaspar Kraemer Architekten BDA).
Accenture office from 2002 on in Kronberg/Ts.
(Picture: Kaspar Kraemer Architekten BDA).

accenture

Accenture GmbH

Geschäftsführung/Management:

Weltweit/Worldwide:
Joe W. Forehand, Managing Partner und CEO

Deutschland/Germany
Thomas Köhler, Sprecher der Geschäftsführung/
Country Managing Partner

Gründungsjahr/Year of Foundation:
Seit 1989 eigenständiges Unternehmen
unter dem Dach der Holding-Gesellschaft
Andersen Worldwide
Since 1989 independent company within the
holding group Andersen Worldwide.

August 2000: Trennung von Arthur Andersen
und Ausscheiden aus dem Dachverband
Andersen Worldwide
August 2000: Separation from
Arthur Andersen and Andersen Worldwide

Seit 1. Januar 2001: Accenture
Since January 1, 2001: Accenture.

Mitarbeiter/Employees:
70.000 (weltweit/worldwide)
 3.000 (Deutschland/Germany)

Umsatz 1999/ 1999 Revenues:
8,9 Mrd. USD (weltweit/worldwide)
1,24 Mrd. DM (Deutschland/Germany)

Geschäftätigkeit/Business Activity:
Unternehmensberatung für Management
und Technologie, Outsourcing, Allianzen
und Risikokapital
Management and technology consulting,
outsourcing, alliances and venture capital.

Anschrift/Address:
Otto-Volger-Straße 15
D-65843 Sulzbach
Telefon +49 (6196) 57-60
Telefax +49 (6196) 57-50
Internet www.accenture.com

Frankfurt – europäische Drehscheibe im globalen Finanzgeschäft

Frankfurt – European Turning Wheel in the Global Finance Business

Die Mainmetropole ist seit Gründung der Frankfurter Börse im Jahre 1585 als bedeutendes Handels- und Finanzzentrum in Europa fest etabliert. Vor allem vier Faktoren haben Frankfurt zu dem gemacht, was es heute ist – der wichtigste Finanzplatz Kontinentaleuropas, „The City of the Euro": die günstige geografische Lage, hohe Innovationsfähigkeit und Lernbereitschaft, Liberalität im Geschäftsleben und Weltoffenheit – und nicht zuletzt der Mut zu politisch weitsichtigen Weichenstellungen.

Frankfurt im Schnittpunkt Mitteleuropas

Frankfurts verkehrstechnisch und geografisch günstige Lage begründete die Entwicklung zur

Die Europäische Zentralbank in Frankfurt am Main.
The European Central Bank in Frankfurt on the Main.

internationalen Messestadt seit dem Mittelalter. Im Gegensatz zu anderen Messeplätzen wie Köln, Leipzig oder Straßburg hat es Frankfurt aber zumeist verstanden, seine geografischen Vorteile in eine kontinuierlich bessere Infrastruktur umzumünzen – mit Hilfe technischer Neuerungen. Dazu zählen vor allem der Ausbau und die Sicherung von Verkehrswegen. Der riesige Bau des Hauptbahnhofs im vorletzten Jahrhundert und das erste Autobahnkreuz der Republik in den fünfziger Jahren des vergangenen Jahrhunderts zeugen davon. Das zentrale Thema unserer Tage ist der Ausbau des Frankfurter Flughafens, der wirtschaftlich für die gesamte Rhein-Main-Region von grundlegender Bedeutung ist.

Zunehmend wichtiger wird aber nicht nur der effiziente Transport von Gütern und Personen: Die Information, die Ware der Zukunft, verlangt immer leistungsfähigere und komplexere Kommunikationsnetze. Deshalb hatte Frankfurts Magistrat in der Mitte der 90er Jahre mehreren Privatfirmen die Möglichkeit eröffnet, modernste Glasfasernetze zu installieren und zu vermarkten.

Aber eine wettbewerbsfähige Infrastruktur alleine reicht heute nicht aus, Bewohner – eine der Voraussetzungen dafür, dass internationale Asset-Manager und Corporate-Finance-Experten auch in Frankfurt arbeiten und leben wollen. Auf der einen Seite wird die Nähe zu den deutschen Kunden eine höhere Präsenz vor Ort erfordern. Auch die Europäische Zentralbank übt eine große Anziehungskraft aus, der sich vor allem Zins- und Devisenspezialisten schwer werden entziehen kön-

Friedrich von Metzler

Der Autor wurde 1943 in Dresden geboren und trat bereits 1964 in London bei J. Henry Schroder Wagg & Co., Ltd. in das Bankgeschäft ein. Es folgten Tätigkeiten bei Smith Barney & Co., Inc. und Brown Brothers Harriman in New York, bei Hottinguer & Cie. in Paris und bei der Deutschen Bank AG in Düsseldorf. 1969 wechselte er zum Bankhaus B. Metzler seel. Sohn & Co., Frankfurt am Main, dessen Partner er 1971 wurde. Von 1989 bis 1993 war er Vorsitzender des Vorstandes der Frankfurter Wertpapierbörse, von 1989 bis 1994 Vorsitzender des Aufsichtsrats der Frankfurter Wertpapierbörse AG/Deutsche Börse AG. Friedrich von Metzler ist Mitglied von Aufsichtsräten großer Unternehmen, u. a. der Deutschen Börse AG und der DWS Investment GmbH.

The author was born in 1943 in Dresden and joined the banking trade as early as 1964 in London with J. Henry Schroder Wagg & Co., Ltd. Activities with Smith Barney & Co., Inc. and Brown Brothers Harriman in New York followed, with Hottinguer & Cie., in Paris and with Deutsche Bank AG in Düsseldorf. In 1969 he joined the banking house B. Metzler seel. Sohn & Co., Frankfurt on the Main, whose associate he became in 1971. From 1989 till 1993 he was Chairman of the Board of the Frankfurt Securities Exchange, from 1989 till 1994 Chairman of the Supervisory Counsel of the Frankfurt Securities Exchange AG/Deutsche Börse AG (German Stock Exchange). Friedrich von Metzler is member of supervisory counsels to many great enterprises, including the Deutsche Börse AG (German Stock Exchange) and the DWS Investment GmbH.

Frankfurt am Main – der wichtigste Finanzplatz Kontinentaleuropas.

Frankfurt on the Main – the most important financial centre of continental Europe.

The metropolis on the Main has been firmly established since the foundation of the Frankfurt Stock Exchange in the year 1585 as an important trade and finance centre in Europe. Four factors above all, have made of Frankfurt what it is today – the most important financial centre of continental Europe, "The City of the Euro": its favourable geographical location, high capacity of innovation and preparedness to learn, liberal attitudes in business life and openness to the world – and last but not least a courage for setting the course in long-term political matters.

Frankfurt in the Central Point of Middle Europe

The geographical and for transport favourable location of Frankfurt caused its development into an international city of fairs since the Middle Ages. Contrary to other fair centres like Cologne, Leipzig or Strasburg, Frankfurt knew how to coin its geographic advantage into a continuously better infrastructure – with the aid of technical innovations. These include above all the extension and securing of transport systems. The huge construc-

tion of the main train station in the century before the last and the first motorway cross of the republic in the fifties of last century are witnesses to this fact. The central focus in our days lays in the extension of the Frankfurt Airport, which is economically of fundamental importance for the whole Rhein-Main region.

But not only the efficient transport of goods and persons is becoming increasingly important: Information, the product of the future, is demanding ever more efficient and complex communication networks. For this reason, the Magistrate of Frank-

29

Die Stadt bietet eine hervorragende Infrastruktur.

The city has an excellent infrastructure.

handels- Geld- und Kreditgeschäfte letztlich für alle Bürger bringen würde. Sie setzten sich durch gegen den Widerstand der Handwerker, die die Stadt lieber stärker vor Auslandskonkurrenz geschützt und gegen großzügige Zuwanderung abgeschottet hätten. Auch die jüdischen Einwohner genossen die schützende Hand der Patrizier familien: Schließlich waren sie auf jüdische Großkredite angewiesen.

Diese Internationalität ist auch heute noch prägend für das Stadtbild: Im Nachkriegsdeutschland entwickelte sich Frankfurt zur deutschen Großstadt mit dem höchsten Ausländeranteil von mittlerweile rund 30 %. Frankfurt bot sich daher schon früh als Knotenpunkt im Netz der einsetzenden Globalisierung an. Die wachsende Präsenz der Auslandsbanken in Frankfurt beweist, dass der Rückstand Frankfurts im internationalen Wettbewerb der Finanzplätze verkürzt und seine Attraktivität gesteigert werden konnte.

nen. Auf der anderen Seite haftet Frankfurt immer noch der notorisch schlechte Ruf als herzloses „Bankfurt" an – unverdientermaßen, wie eine aktuelle weltweite Studie des amerikanischen Consulting-Unternehmen William. M. Mercer in puncto „Lebensqualität" belegt: Darin lässt Frankfurt mit einem beachtlichen 11. Rang seinen schärfsten Rivalen London weit hinter sich, der sich mit dem 35. Rang bescheiden muss. Für Investmentbanker mit jungen Familien bietet Frankfurt zudem durch das nahegelegene attraktive Umland eine höhere Lebensqualität als London. Und das Entwicklungspotenzial des deutschen Kapitalmarktes ist ohnehin für jeden Investmentbanker hochattraktiv.

Frankfurts Liberalität zog Spitzenkräfte aus ganz Europa an

Bereits im späten 16. und frühen 17. Jahrhundert erlebte Frankfurt seine erste Hochblüte als Finanzplatz. Im Zuge der kriegerischen Auseinandersetzungen während der Gegenreformation in Frankreich und Spanien flüchteten Tausende nach Frankfurt. Zum Teil waren es weltläufige Kaufleute aus Antwerpen – dem damals bedeutendsten Finanzzentrum jenseits der Alpen. Sie besaßen modernste Kenntnisse in Finanzgeschäften und weitreichende internationale Kontakte. An der Gründung der 1585 eingeführten regelmäßigen Kaufmannsversammlungen, der Keimzelle der Frankfurter Börse, waren sie, zusammen mit zahlreichen in Frankfurt tätigen italienischen Kaufleuten, stärker beteiligt als die alteingesessenen Frankfurter Kaufleute. Das protestantische Frankfurt zeigte damals eine größere Offenheit und Toleranz gegenüber Fremden und profitierte so vom Entwicklungsschub, den die Eingewanderten in Gang gesetzt hatten.

Die Offenheit und Toleranz hatte handfeste wirtschaftliche Hintergründe: Die den Rat der Stadt Frankfurt dominierenden Patrizierfamilien erkannten die Vorteile, die das Wachstum der Fern-

Innovationsfähigkeit und Lernbereitschaft als Motor der wirtschaftlichen Entwicklung

Der zweite große Aufschwung Frankfurts setzte im späten 18. Jahrhundert mit der Blüte des Staatsanleihegeschäftes ein. Hervorzuheben ist die Erfindung der Partialobligation im Jahre 1778, eingeführt von Frankfurter Bankhäusern wie Bethmann, Metzler und Gontard. Der fast unstillbare Kredithunger der Fürstenstaaten verlangte eine gestückelte, an der Börse handelbare Anleihe. Damit ließ sich Kapital nicht nur bei Bankiers und reichen Schichten mobilisieren, sondern auch bei vielen kleineren Anlegern. Als Vorbild dienten Erfahrungen von Amsterdamer Bankiers. Andere Bankhäuser beteiligten sich rasch an der Verbreitung dieses Finanzinstruments. Zu Beginn des 19. Jahrhunderts stieg das Haus Rothschild von Frankfurt aus in das Anleihegeschäft ein und schuf damit die Grundlage für seine europaweite Spitzenstellung.

furt conceded the possibility to several private companies in the middle of the nineties, to install the most modern glass fibre networks and to sell them.

However, a competitive infrastructure nowadays is not sufficient. Inhabitants – one of the preconditions for international asset managers and corporate finance experts to come to live and work in Frankfurt. On the one hand, the nearness to the German customer will necessitate a larger presence locally. Also the European Central Bank is extremely attractive, especially to interest and foreign currency expert. On the other hand, Frankfurt still suffers from the reputation of being notoriously heartless as "Bankfurt" – undeservingly albeit, as a current worldwide survey of the American Consulting Firm William M. Mercer proves with respect to "quality of life": In it Frankfurt leaves its sharpest rival London far behind with a considerable 11th ranking, the latter having to make do with a 35th rank. For investment bankers with young families Frankfurt furthermore offers through the nearby attractive surroundings a higher quality of life as London.
Also, the potential for development in German capital markets is highly attractive for each investment banker anyway.
Already in the late 16th and early 17th centuries Frankfurt experienced its first zenith as a financial centre. During the belligerent confrontations of the Counter Reformation in France and Spain thousands fled to Frankfurt. Partly these were widely travelled merchants from Antwerp – the most important financial centre beyond the Alps at that time. They possessed the most modern knowledge of finance transactions and far reaching international contacts. They were more involved in the establishment of the 1585 introduced regular merchants' assemblies, which were held together with the Italian merchants, than the traditional merchants of Frankfurt and thus formed the nucleus of the Frankfurt Stock Exchange. Protestant Frankfurt in those days showed more openness and tolerance towards its foreigners and thus benefited from the driving force of a development that had been initiated by the immigrants.

Openness and tolerance had their clear economic motives: The dominant Patrician families that belonged to the Counsel of the City of Frankfurt recognised the advantages that the growth of long-distance trade, money and loan businesses would bring for all citizens ultimately. They prevailed against the resistance of the craftsmen that would have rather liked to protect the city from foreign competition somewhat stronger and that would have rather closed its frontiers to a gener-

ous immigration. Also the Jewish families enjoyed the protection of the Patrician families: In the end, they depended on the big loans of the Jewish.

This international characteristic still remains prevalent in the cityscape: In post-war Germany Frankfurt evolved to become the Germany city with the highest share of foreigners of meanwhile around 30 %. Frankfurt therefore provided early the conditions of a central node in the network of the emerging globalisation. The growing presence of foreign banks in Frankfurt proves that Frank-

furt's gap in the international competition between financial centres has been closed and its attractiveness has been increased.

Capacity of Innovation and Preparedness to Learn as a Driving Force for Economic Development

The second big upsurge of Frankfurt started in the late 18th century with the golden age of the

Zeugen der Aufholjagd deutscher Banken im weltweiten Wettbewerb.
Witnesses of the catching-up race of German banks in a worldwide competition.

31

Der zentralen Finanzinnovation des 19. Jahrhunderts jedoch verschlossen sich die Frankfurter Bankiers: Sie sperrten sich mehrheitlich gegen den Handel mit Aktien überhaupt und verschliefen damit die Dynamik im Geschäftsfeld der Industriefinanzierung. Diese Geschäfte galten in Frankfurt als zu spekulativ. Eine Ausnahme in dieser Zeit machte das Bankhaus Georg Hauck & Sohn, das 1888 zusammen mit J. J. Weiller Söhne den Börsenprospekt über 12 Millionen Mark Aktien der Farbwerke Hoechst unterzeichnete. Die Kurzsichtigkeit der übrigen Bankiers, die glaubten, sich auf den Erfolgen des vergleichsweise risikoarmen Staats-anleihengeschäftes ausruhen zu können, trieb Frankfurt in eine rund 70 Jahre lang dauernde relative Bedeutungslosigkeit als Finanzzentrum.

Diese Erfahrungen zeigen, dass Frankfurt langfristige Investitionen in Innovationspotenzial braucht, das heißt, die Stadt muss in eine hochqualifizierte Ausbildung seiner Spezialisten investieren. Frankfurt kann nicht alleine auf eine Wanderung der Arbeitskräfte von der Themse an den Main bauen; vielmehr ist die Ausbildung einer eigenen neuen Generation von hochspezialisierten Bankern ein zentraler Faktor für weiteres Wachstum. Eine noch größere Herausforderung für die Banken wird sein, diese neue Generation in Frankfurt zu halten – vor allem dann, wenn die Steuernachteile gegenüber London nicht schnell beseitigt werden. Die Banken können ihren Beitrag leisten und attraktive Vergütungssysteme schaffen, um die Mitarbeiter langfristig an das Unternehmen zu binden und sie am Erfolg stärker als bisher teilhaben zu lassen.

Politische Entscheidungen stellen langfristig Weichen

Grundlage der Frankfurter Messetätigkeit waren die politischen Privilegien der deutschen Kaiser und Könige, die der Stadt den Status einer autonomen Reichsstadt verliehen. So konnte die politische Führung der Stadt auf die Bedürfnisse der Großkaufleute eingehen. Messe- sowie Geld- und Kreditgeschäfte waren eng miteinander verwoben; aus den Handelsgeschäften entwickelte sich im Laufe der Zeit der Nebenerwerbszweig des internationalen Bankgeschäfts. Dieses übertraf zum Beispiel beim Bankhaus Metzler bereits in der zweiten Hälfte des 18. Jahrhunderts das Warengeschäft an Bedeutung und wurde schließlich alleiniges Geschäftsfeld.

Als im negativen Sinne entscheidend erwies sich der Verlust des Status als Freie Reichsstadt durch die Annektierung Frankfurts durch Preußen

nach dem Sieg über Österreich 1866. Der Verlust der politischen Unabhängikeit minderte auch den Handlungsspielraum für wirtschaftspolitische Entscheidungen. Preußens weitere Dominanz schwächte zusehends die Entwicklung Frankfurts und stärkte die Bedeutung Berlins als führendes deutsches Finanzzentrum. Ihren Abschluss fand diese Entwicklung 1876 in der Umwandlung der Preußischen Bank in die Deutsche Reichsbank. Berlin übernahm eine führende Stellung als Standort für Banken und für Geld- und Kapitalmarktgeschäfte mit Deutschland im europäischen Finanzverbund. Frankfurts Bankiers konnten diese politische Entwicklung nicht beeinflussen.

Nach 1945 schwang das Pendel zugunsten Frankfurts zurück und leitete damit den dritten großen Aufschwung ein. 1948 beschlossen die Westalliierten, die Bank Deutscher Länder in Frankfurt anzusiedeln. Ausschlaggebender Grund dafür, dass deutsche Großbanken ihre Zentralen in Frankfurt wiederaufbauten. Auch die Frankfurter Börse konnte mit ihrem Handelsvolumen alle anderen Börsen in Deutschland weit hinter sich lassen. Die erfolgreiche Wirtschaftspolitik und die Stabilität der D-Mark machten Frankfurt zunehmend attraktiv für den internationalen Geld- und Kapitalverkehr. Den größten Schub erhielt Frankfurt jedoch durch weitreichende Reformen des Gesetzgebers zugunsten des Finanzdienstleistungssektors Ende der achtziger und in den neunziger Jahren und durch die Schaf-

Der Finanzplatz Frankfurt verfügt über die modernste Marktorganisation und Börsenstruktur in Europa, vielleicht sogar weltweit.

government bonds business. Of special attention is the invention of the partial obligation in the year 1778, introduced by banking houses of Frankfurt like Bethmann, Metzler and Gontard. The almost insatiable hunger for credits of the royal states demanded a subdivided, at the stock exchange tradable bond. Thus it was possible to mobilise capital not only with bankers and the rich classes, but also with many smaller investors. The experience of the bankers from Amsterdam served as an example. Other banking houses rapidly participated in the dissipation of this financial instrument. At the beginning of the 19th century the House of Rothschild entered the business of issuing bonds from its base in Frankfurt and thus created the foundation for its European-wide top position. But the bankers of Frankfurt refused their participation in the most central financial innovation of the 19th century: They opposed in the majority the trade with shares on the whole and thus missed the dynamism in the business field of industrial financing. These business transactions were regarded in Frankfurt as too speculative. One exception in those days was the banking house Georg Hauck & Son, which in 1888 together with J. J. Weiller & Sons signed the stock exchange brochure on 12 million Marks in shares of the Farbwerke Hoechst. Short-sightedness on the part of the remaining bankers, which believed that they could rest their heads on the successes of the government bond transactions, comparatively low in risk, led Frankfurt into a relative unimportance as a financial centre lasting for around 70 years.

These experiences show that Frankfurt needs long-term financial investments into innovation potentials that mean, the city has to invest into a highly qualified training of its specialists. Frankfurt cannot rely only on a shift of labour force from the Thames to the river Main; above all the training of an inherent new generation of highly specialised bankers is a central factor for further growth. A much greater challenge for the banks will be, to keep this new generation in Frankfurt, especially, if the tax disadvantages against London are not removed rapidly. The banks can contribute their share and create attractive remuneration systems, in order to ensure the loyalty of their employees to the company and to let them participate in their success even stronger than now.

Political Decisions Set the Long-Term Course

The foundations of the fair activities of Frankfurt were the political privileges of the German Emperors and Kings that conceded the city an autonomous status as Imperial City. Thus the political leaders of the city were able to attend to the needs of the big merchants. The fair activities as well as the money and loan businesses were closely connected with each other; from the trade transactions in the course of time evolved the branch industry of international banking. This surpassed in the banking house Metzler for example already in the 2nd half of the 18th century the business with merchandise and finally became the sole field of business.

As decisively in a negative sense proved to be the loss of the status as Free Imperial City through the annexation of Frankfurt by Prussia after the victory against Austria in 1866. The loss of its political independence also lessened its scope for economic and political decisions. Prussia's continuing dominance strengthened Berlin as leading German financial centre. This development ended 1876 when the Prussian Bank was transformed into the German Imperial Bank. Berlin took on a leading position as location for banking, money as well as capital market transactions with Germany within the European financial union. Frankfurt's bankers were not able to influence this development.

After 1945 the tables turned in favour of Frankfurt again and thus the third great upsurge was initiated. In 1948 the Western allies decided to locate the Bank of German Countries in Frankfurt. The main reason for this was, that the large German banks were reconstructing the headquarters in Frankfurt. Also the Frankfurt Stock Exchange was able to take the lead by far in front of all other German exchange places with its trade volume. A successful economic policy and the stability of the D-Mark made Frankfurt increasingly attrac-

Frankfurt as a financial centre disposes of the most modern market organisation and stock exchange structure in Europe, maybe in the world.

Die Deutsche Bundesbank in Frankfurt am Main.
The German Federal Bank in Frankfurt on the Main.

fung der modernsten Börsenstruktur durch die Deutsche Börse. Weiterhin stehen die Themen Steuererleichterungen und Deregulation ganz oben auf der Wunschliste der Finanzdienstleister.

Fazit und Ausblick: Frankfurt als europäische Drehscheibe im globalen Finanzgeschäft

Frankfurt hat die Chance, die europäische Drehscheibe im globalen Geschäft zu werden – nach einer gewaltigen Aufholjagd gegenüber London, Paris und Zürich in den vergangenen zehn Jahren. Die deutschen Banken haben ihre Marktposition im Investmentbanking ausgebaut und ihr Geschäft den Bedürfnissen internationaler Kunden angepasst. Amerikanische Investmentbanken haben ihre Präsenz in Frankfurt verstärkt, um das noch nicht ausgeschöpfte Potenzial des deutschen Kapitalmarktes zu erschließen. Gleichzeitig haben die politisch Verantwortlichen in Deutschland rechtliche Rahmenbedingungen geschaffen und eine Börsenaufsicht installiert, die internationalen Maßstäben standhält. Entscheidend dürfte sein, dass Frankfurt gegen harte internationale Konkurrenz den Zuschlag für den Sitz der Europäischen Zentralbank erhalten hat. Den größten Sprung hat der Finanzplatz Frankfurt jedoch bei der Qualität und Effizienz der Märkte gemacht. Er verfügt heute über die modernste Marktorganisation und Börsenstruktur in Europa, vielleicht sogar weltweit.

Die Gründung der Deutschen Börse AG 1992 war nicht nur ein Quantensprung für den Finanzplatz Frankfurt, sondern hat die gesamte europäische Börsenlandschaft nachhaltig verändert. Modernste Informationstechnologie und Neuer Markt sind nur zwei Stichworte.

Es hat sich allerdings gezeigt, dass das größte Handikap Frankfurts die hohe Einkommensbesteuerung in Deutschland ist. So war es zwingend, dass aufgrund der ungünstigen steuerlichen Auswirkungen nicht nur der juristische Sitz der neuen Börse in London sein wird, sondern auch die amerikanische Nasdaq sich entschieden hat, auf London als Sitz der Marketing- und Vertriebsgesellschaft für den Wachstumsmarkt zu drängen – auch wenn Frankfurt in diesem Bereich die natürliche erste Wahl gewesen wäre. Und nicht nur im Finanzsektor schreckt die individuelle Steuerlast ausländische Investoren ab. International tätige Unternehmen tendieren dazu, Zukunftsjobs von Deutschland ins Ausland zu verlagern oder dort gar nicht erst anzusiedeln, weil die Steuerlast für die Mitarbeiter zu hoch ist. Gerade Investmentbanker haben Übung darin, Steuervorteile genau zu kalkulieren, und verhalten sich bei ihren Standortentscheidungen ebenso mobil wie das Kapital, das sie täglich um den Globus steuern. Eine echte Steuerreform, die den Spitzensteuersatz unter 40 % drückt, und die Harmonisierung der Einkommensbesteuerung mit London könnten also wahre Mobilitätswunder bewirken.
Die grundsätzlichen Veränderungen in der privaten Altersvorsorge und in einer wertorien-

tierteren Unternehmensführung, die in nächster Zeit für den Weg des Finanzplatzes Frankfurt an die europäische Spitze eingeleitet werden müssen, sind ein Test für die Innovationsfähigkeit der deutschen Gesellschaft. Insbesondere erhöht bei den Unternehmen die zunehmende Konzentration auf Kernkompetenzen die Rentabilität und schafft neue Arbeitsplätze. Hoffnung macht, dass die Globalisierung auch hier den Anpassungsdruck weiter erhöhen wird.

Ein Finanzplatz ist keine Privatveranstaltung von Bankern. Eine Führungsstellung Frankfurts in Europa ist kein Selbstzweck. Phasen schnellen Wirtschaftswachstums und der Schaffung neuer Arbeitsplätze werden immer von einigen wenigen dynamischen Industrien getragen.

Noch mehr als in der Vergangenheit wird der Erfolg der deutschen Wirtschaft mit dem Entwicklungsstand des Finanzsektors verbunden sein. Ein europäisches Finanzzentrum Frankfurt, wo anstatt heute 60.000 morgen über 100.00 oder 150.000 Menschen an hochspezialisierten Aufgaben arbeiten, könnte das Symbol für eine erneuerte deutsche Wirtschaft werden, wenn die sich bietenden Chancen genutzt werden. Wird dieser strategische Wert des Finanzplatzes erkannt und gefördert, steht den angesprochenen Reformen nichts entgegen: Frankfurt wird dann den Weg an die Spitze Europas erfolgreich meistern. Das hat schließlich in Frankfurt Tradition. ∎

tive for international money and capital transactions. Frankfurt received its greatest push however, through the extensive reforms made in legislation in favour of the financial service sector at the end of the eighties and in the nineties and through the creation of the most modern stock exchange structure by the German Stock Exchange. Other important topics on the top of the list of requests of financial service providers are tax relief and deregulation.

Conclusion and Prospects: Frankfurt as an European Turning wheel in the Global Financial Business

Frankfurt has a chance to become the European turning wheel in global business after having attained a tremendous position in the race between London, Paris and Zurich in the past ten years. The German banks have strengthened their position in the market of investment banking and have adjusted their business to the requirements of international customers. American investment banks have increased their presence in Frankfurt, in order to open up the untapped potential of German capital markets. At the same time, the persons politically responsible in Germany have created legal frameworks and installed a supervisory commission for the stock exchange that can stand up to international standards. One decisive fact is also, that Frankfurt was awarded the contract against hard international competition to build the headquarters of the European Central Bank. The greatest leap for Frankfurt as a financial centre has been however, the quality and efficiency of the markets. Today, it disposes of the most modern market organisation and stock exchange structure in Europe, maybe even of the world. The foundation of the German Stock Exchange AG (a joint stock company) in 1992 was not only a gigantic leap for

Frankfurt as a financial centre, but has changed the whole European stock exchange landscape in a lasting way. The most modern information technology and the New Market are only two key words in this respect.

However, it has become evident that Frankfurt's greatest handicap is the high tax on income in Germany. For this reason it became mandatory, that because of unfavourable fiscal effects not only the juridical location of the new stock exchange would be in London, but also the American Nasdaq has decided to insist on London as headquarters of the sales and marketing association for this growing market – even if of course Frankfurt would have been first choice in this field. And not only in the financial sector the individual fiscal burden is deterring foreign investors. Enterprises that are internationally active tend to relocate the jobs of the future from Germany to overseas or do not settle there in the first place, because the fiscal burden for employees is too high. Especially investment bankers know how to calculate fiscal advantages exactly and behave when deciding their business location just as mobile as the capital that they control daily around the globe. A real tax reform that would push the peak tax rate below 40 % and harmonising the income tax with London could also work miracles in terms of mobility.

Basic changes in private retirement insurance and in an value-oriented management of companies – that must be initiated in the near future for Frankfurt's way to the European top as a financial centre – are a test for the capacity of innovation of the German society. Especially the increasing concentration on core competences increases profitability in enterprises and creates new jobs. A hopeful fact is, that globalisation is going to increase the pressure to adjust the situation also here even further.

A financial centre is no private show on the part of the bankers. To attain a leading position for Frankfurt in Europe is not an aim in itself. Periods of rapid economic growth and of creation of new workplaces are always carried by some few dynamic industries.

Even more than in the past, the success of the German economy will be connected with the state of the art of the financial sector. Frankfurt, as a European finance centre where instead of 60.000 today, tomorrow more than 100.000 or 150.000 people work in high-specialised jobs, could be the symbol for a renewed German economy, if the existing chances are used. If this strategic value of the financial centre is recognised and promoted, there should be nothing in the way of the mentioned reforms: Frankfurt will then be able to make its way to the top of Europe masterly. In the end, this is tradition in Frankfurt. ■

Ehrgeiziges Ziel der Deutschen Bank: weltbester Finanzdienstleister zu sein

The Ambitious Target of Deutsche Bank:
To be the Best Financial Service Provider in the World

Die Deutsche Bank ist mit fast 1.500 Niederlassungen in Deutschland sowie Filialnetzen in Italien, Spanien und Belgien die größte Bank in Euroland. Bereits 1870 wurde sie in Berlin gegründet mit dem Zweck „Betrieb von Bankgeschäften aller Art, insbesondere Förderung und Erleichterung der Handelsbeziehungen zwischen Deutschland, den übrigen Europäischen Ländern und überseeischen Märkten".

Die Deutsche Bank bietet heute als Multispezialbank eine breite Palette moderner Bankdienstleistungen an. Dazu gehören der Zahlungsverkehr, das Kreditgeschäft sowie die Geld- und Vermögensanlage. Das Online Banking ist mittlerweile zu einem festen Bestandteil geworden. Ein starkes Standbein bildet das Investmentbanking, die Begleitung von Neuemissionen und die Beratung von Unternehmen in allen Aspekten der Unternehmensfinanzierung.

Rund 96.000 Mitarbeiter betreuen weltweit in über 60 Ländern mehr als 9 Millionen Kunden. Europa ist dabei der Heimatmarkt. Zufriedene Kunden und motivierte Mitarbeiter sind die wichtigste Voraussetzung, damit die Deutsche Bank eine kontinuierliche Wertsteigerung erzielen kann.

Die Deutsche Bank hat das ehrgeizige Ziel, der beste Finanzdienstleister der Welt zu sein. Die einzigartige Breite an Erfahrung und Fähigkeiten, die finanzielle Stärke und die Leistungen eines jeden Mitarbeiters dienen einem Ziel, für die Kunden der Deutschen Bank, die Aktionäre, Mitarbeiter und die Gesellschaft insgesamt einen deutlichen Mehrwert schaffen.

Aktionäre, Kunden, Mitarbeiter und Gesellschaft setzen häufig unterschiedliche Prioritäten. Die Deutsche Bank jedoch ist auf das gesamte Quartett angewiesen und muss deshalb eine Balance der Interessen aller vier Gruppen schaffen. Die globale Vernetzung von Märkten, Wissen und Ansprüchen stellt immer höhere Anforderungen an die Bank und ihr sehr komplexes Beziehungssystem.

Die Deutsche Bank braucht Kapital von ihren Aktionären, um ihr Bankgeschäft zu betreiben und ertragsorientiert wachsen zu können. Kapital kann aber nur dann nachhaltig und gewinnbringend eingesetzt werden, wenn der Kunde mit seiner Bank zufrieden ist. Dies erfordert hervorragende Dienstleistungen, für die motivierte Mitarbeiter benötigt werden. Geschäftliche Erfolge machen zudem Arbeitsplätze wettbewerbsfähiger und damit sicherer. Das gesellschaftliche Engagement der Bank schließlich bereitet die Grundlagen dafür, als verantwortlich handelndes Unternehmen respektiert zu werden

In Frankfurt am Main hat nicht nur die Zentrale der Deutschen Bank ihren Sitz, sondern auch die für die Inlandsregion Mitte zuständige Hauptfiliale. Die 1886 gegründete Niederlassung war der dritte Geschäftssitz der Bank in Deutschland. Die Filiale Frankfurt, die sich als Teil dieser Stadt versteht, hat alle Höhen und Tiefen der Finanz- und Wirtschaftsmetropole miterlebt. Im Stadtgebiet steht die Filiale heute mit 80 Mitarbeitern in 25 Zweigstellen einem großen Kundenkreis mit einem breit gefächerten Finanzierungs-, Beratungs- und Zahlungsverkehrsservice zur Verfügung. ∎

Die Zentrale der Deutschen Bank an der Taunusanlage in Frankfurt am Main.
The Headquarters of Deutsche Bank at the Taunusanlage in Frankfurt on the Main.

Vom Handelssaal bestehen rund um die Uhr Verbindungen zu den Finanzmärkten der Welt.
From the trading hall there are connections around the clock to all the financial markets of the world.

Deutsche Bank

Deutsche Bank AG

Vorsitzender des Aufsichtsrates/
Chairman of the Supervisory Board:
Hilmar Kopper

Vorstand/The Board:
Josef Ackermann
Carl L. von Boehm-Bezing
Clemens Börsig
Rolf-E. Breuer
Thomas R. Fischer
Tessen von Heydebreck
Hermann-Josef Lamberti
Michael Philipp

Gründungsjahr/Year of Foundation:
1870

Mitarbeiter/Employees:
ca. 96.000

Jahresüberschuss/Annual Surplus:
2.571 Mio. Euro (1999)

Kreditvolumen/Volume of Credit:
284.149 Mio. Euro (1999)

Anschrift/Address:
Taunusanlage 12
D-60325 Frankfurt am Main
Telefon   +49 (69) 910-00
E-Mail   deutsche.bank@db.com
Internet www.deutsche-bank.de

With its almost 1.500 branches in Germany as well as branch networks in Italy, Spain and Belgium, Deutsche Bank is the largest bank in Euroland. As early as 1870 she was founded in Berlin with the purpose: "Operation of bank transactions of all kind, specifically promotion and facilitation of commercial relations between Germany, the remaining European countries and overseas markets".

Deutsche Bank provides today as a multi-specialist bank a broad spectrum of banking services. These include payment transactions, the credit or loan business as well as the placing of money and investments. Online banking has meanwhile become an integral part of its business. Strong business activities consist of investment banking, the accompaniment of new emissions and the consulting of enterprises in all aspects of company finance matters.

Around 96.000 employees in more than 60 countries take good care of over 9 million customers. Europe is of course the home market. Satisfied customers and motivated employees are the most important premises for the Deutsche Bank to achieve a continuous increase of its net worth.
The Deutsche Bank has the ambitious aim to be the world's best financial service provider. The unique depth in experience and capacities, the financial strength and the performances of each single employee are geared towards this aim, to create for the customers of Deutsche Bank, it share holders, employees and the company as a whole, a distinctive increment in value.

Share holders, customers, employees and the company frequently set differing priorities. The Deutsche Bank however, depends on the complete quartet and therefore has to achieve a balance between the interests of all four groups. The global networking of markets, knowledge and claims is demanding ever-increasing requirements of the bank and challenges her very complex system of relationships.

The Deutsche Bank needs capital from its share-holders in order to carry out their banking activities and to grow profit-oriented. Capital can only be utilised lastingly and profitably, if the customer is satisfied with his bank. This requires excellent banking services for which in turn motivated employees are necessary. Furthermore, business successes strengthen the competitiveness of workplaces and make them thus more secure. The social engagement of the bank finally provides the basis for the bank to be respected as an enterprise that acts socially responsible.

In Frankfurt on the Main, not only the headquarters of the Deutsche Bank are based, but also the main branch responsible for the inland region. This branch founded in 1886, was the third company location of the bank in Germany. The Frankfurt branch, that sees itself as part of the city, has passed through all highs and lows of the finance and economic metropolis. Within the city limits, the branch is today – with its 80 employees in 25 subsidiaries – at the disposal of a large clientèle providing a broad service of finance, consultancy and payment transactions. ■

Standortkosten – Frankfurt am Main ist keineswegs das „teure Pflaster"

Costs of a Business Location –
Frankfurt on the Main is by no means an "expensive place"

Die Stadt Frankfurt am Main ist ein wirtschaftlicher Mittelpunkt des Rhein-Main-Gebietes und damit Metropole der wirtschaftsstärksten Region Europas, in der rd. 4,8 Mio. Menschen wohnen, rd. 320.000 Unternehmen ansässig sind, die mit 280 Mrd. DM etwa 9 v. H. des Bruttoinlandsproduktes des Bundesrepublik schaffen.

Als verhältnismäßig kleine Stadt mit „nur" rd. 650.000 Einwohnern, in der 560.000 Menschen Arbeit finden – davon rd. 285.000 Arbeitnehmer/innen von außerhalb –, ist Frankfurt am Main gleichwohl das führende Finanzzentrum in Deutschland und in Kontinentaleuropa. Die Stadt beherbergt rd. 370 Banken, davon 230 ausländische Geld- und Kreditinstitute – daneben die Asian Development Bank und die Weltbank Gruppe und – keineswegs zuletzt – die Europäische Zentralbank als Hüterin des europäischen Währungssystems. Damit repräsentiert die Stadt finanz- und währungspolitischen Sachverstand wie keine andere Metropole in Europa.

Aber auch das in Frankfurt am Main ansässige Handwerk und die hier tätigen Industrieunternehmen tragen in erheblichem Maße zur Bedeutung der Stadt bei. Diese gewerblichen Betriebe repräsentieren einen Umsatz von insgesamt über 50 Mrd. DM (25,6 Mrd. Euro).

Als Zentrum der Kommunikation versteht sich die Stadt Frankfurt am Main auch wegen der hier ansässigen 8.200 Unternehmen der Kommunikationswirtschaft, zu denen auch 400 Verlage, 400 Werbe- und PR-Agenturen sowie 200 Filmproduktionsfirmen gehören.

Der Frankfurter Flughafen, der größte Airport Kontinentaleuropas, die Frankfurter Messe, die nach Besucher- und Ausstellerzahlen zu den größten Einrichtungen dieser Art in der Welt zählt, und die Frankfurter Börse, die mit rd. 7.000 Mrd. DM (3.579 Mrd. Euro) weltweit die 4. größte Aktienbörse ist, sind ein Zeichen einer Infrastruktur, die in Deutschland einmalig ist und weltweit wenig Vergleichbares findet.

Dass die Stadt internationalen Ansprüchen gerecht wird, belegen 78 Konsulate, Fremdenverkehrsämter aus 60 Ländern, rd. 1 Mio. ausländische Besucher jährlich und eine Verkehrsanbindung, die neben dem Flughafen mit dem Frankfurter Hauptbahnhof, dem Rhein-Main-Verkehrsverbund und dem

Albrecht Glaser

Der Autor wurde 1942 in Worms geboren. Als die Frankfurter Stadtverordnetenversammlung ihn 1995 zum Stadtrat wählte, konnte der Jurist bereits auf eine vielseitige Vita zurückblicken: persönlicher Referent des Rektors der Universität Heidelberg, Ausbildung zum Steuerjuristen, Dozent an der FH für Finanzen in Ludwigsburg, Bürgermeister von Bretten und von Waldbronn (BW), Wahlbeamter des Landeswohlfahrtsverbandes Hessen, hier als Kämmerer, Dezernent für Krankenhäuser, Jugendhilfe und andere Sozialeinrichtungen. Aufgabengebiete in Frankfurt: November 1995 bis März 1997 Wirtschaft und Gesundheit, März 1997 bis Oktober 1997 Finanzen, Wirtschaft und Gesundheit, Oktober 1997 bis März 2000 Finanzen und Gesundheit, seit März 2000 Finanzen, Personal und Organisation.

The Author was born in 1942 in Worms. When he was voted by the town council of Frankfurt into the position of chairman of the town council in 1995, the lawyer was able to look back onto a varied vita: personal Secretary to the Director of the University of Heidelberg, professional training as Legal Accountant, Lecturer at the Institute for Higher Education in Finances in Ludwigsburg, Mayor of Bretten and Waldbronn (BW), Voluntary Officer of the Public Relief Association of Hessen, here as treasurer, Head of Department in Hospitals, Youth Associations and other social institutions. Areas of work in Frankfurt were: From November 1995 to March 1997 Economy and Health, March 1997 to October 1997 Finance, Economy and Health, October 1997 to March 2000 Finance and Health, since March 2000 Finance, Personnel and Administration.

Der Römer, Frankfurts Rathaus, mit dem Gerechtigkeitsbrunnen.
The Römer, Frankfurt's Town Hall, with its Fountain of Justice.

The City of Frankfurt on the Main is an economic centre in the Rhein-Main region and therefore metropolis of the economically strongest region in Europe, which is home for around 4.8 Mio. people. Around 320.000 companies are seated here that achieve with 280 billion DM around 9 % of the gross domestic product of the Federal Republic.

As a relatively small city with "only" around 650 thousand inhabitants, in which 560 thousand people find work – of these, around 285 thousand employees come from out of town –, Frankfurt on the Main is nevertheless the leading financial centre of Germany and of continental Europe. The city houses around 370 banks, of these 230 foreign banks and financial institutes – apart from these the Asian Development Bank and the Worldbank Group and – last but not least – The Central European Bank as keeper of the European monetary system. The city represents herewith financial and monetary expertise like no other European metropolis.

But also the skilled trade seated in Frankfurt on the Main and the industrial enterprises active here contribute considerably to the importance of the city. These commercial companies generate a total turnover of more the 50 billion DM (25,6 billion Euro).

Frankfurt on the Main sees itself also as centre of communication because of 8.200 enterprises of the communication industry that are seated here, which include 400 editorials, 400 advertising and PR agencies as well as 200 film production companies.

The Frankfurt Airport, the largest of continental Europe, the Frankfurt International Fair, which is regarding visitors and exhibitors one of the largest institution of its kind in the world, and the Frankfurt Stock Market, with around 7.000 billion DM (3.579 Euro) the 4th largest stock exchange worldwide, are sign of an infrastructure that is unique in Germany and worldwide will not easily find a comparison.

Rund 370 Banken haben in Frankfurt am Main ihren Sitz.
Around 370 banks are located in Frankfurt on the Main.

Prove to the international claim of the city are 78 consulates, tourism offices of 60 countries, around 1 million foreign visitors a year and transport connection facilities that are difficult to equal, demonstrated by the airport with the Frankfurt Central Station, the Rhein-Main (regional) Transport Association and the Frankfurt motorway cross as the most important node of the German motorway network.

Further characteristics of an excellent infrastructure are the cultural and leisure time offers of the city. With 37 museums that are yearly visited by 1,4 million people, 109 art galleries, 33 theatres and 56 cinemas, as well as 2.300 restaurants, 423 ha. of city parks, a worldwide recognised botanic garden (Palmengarten) and a zoo located in the city area, more than 800 sports places, which also include the Waldstadion (football stadium in the forest), the Eissporthalle (a hall for ice sports) and the horses' race course, Frankfurt on the Main offers, apart from varied possibilities for professional and commercial engagement, also possibilities of relaxation for almost any taste.

Frankfurter Kreuz als dem wichtigsten Knotenpunkt des deutschen Autobahnnetzes seinesgleichen sucht.

Ein weiteres Merkmal hervorragender Infrastruktur sind die Kultur- und Freizeitangebote in der Stadt. Mit 37 Museen, die jährlich von 1,4 Mio. Besuchern genutzt werden, 109 Kunstgalerien, 33 Theatern und 56 Kinos neben 2.300 Restaurants, 423 ha Fläche in den städtischen Parks, einem weltweit anerkannten Palmengarten und einem im Stadtgebiet gelegenen Zoo sowie über 800 Sportstätten, zu denen auch das Waldstadion,

die Eissporthalle und die Pferderennbahn gehören, bietet Frankfurt am Main neben Möglichkeiten zu beruflichem und gewerblichem Engagement auch Entspannungsmöglichkeiten für nahezu jeden Geschmack.

Vor dem Hintergrund der vorstehend in seinen wichtigsten Bestandteilen vorgestellten Infrastruktur relativieren sich scheinbar hohe Belastungen mit Steuern und Gebühren oder die Kosten betrieblicher Investitionen. Der oft praktizierte Hinweis auf Steuern, Gebühren, Büromieten und Baulandpreise in kleinen Städten und Gemeinden

scheitert grundsätzlich an der fehlenden Vergleichbarkeit. Wer in der privaten Wirtschaft Verantwortung trägt, der weiß das – den Entscheidungsträgern ist bewusst, dass Leistung einen Preis hat und haben muss.

Unabhängig von diesen allgemeinen und sicherlich nachvollziehbaren Aussagen hat die Stadt Frankfurt am Main mit einer erheblichen Senkung der Hebesätze für die von ihr zu erhebende Gewerbe(ertrag-)Steuer und die kommunale Grundsteuer ein deutliches Signal für Standortentscheidungen gesetzt. Hinzu kommt die Entlastung des für die Stadt so wichtigen Gaststätten- und Beherbergungsgewerbes durch den Verzicht auf die Gaststättenerlaubnissteuer ab dem Jahre 1998 und die 10%ige Getränkesteuer auf alkoholische Getränke ab dem Jahre 2000.

Neben dem vom Bundesgesetzgeber bestimmten Verzicht auf die Steuer auf das Gewerbekapital – also auf das Betriebsvermögen der gewerblichen Betriebe – ab dem Jahre 1998 hat die auf die verbliebene kommunale Steuer nach dem Gewerbeertrag wirkende Senkung des Hebesatzes von 515 v. H. der Bemessungsgrundlage auf 500 v. H. im Jahre 2000 und auf 490 v. H. ab dem Jahre 2001 eine deutliche steuerliche Entlastung für die Gewinne bewirkt, die von den Frankfurter Unternehmen am Standort Deutschland erwirtschaftet werden.

Aus der Sicht des städtischen Haushaltes bedeuten die steuerlichen Erleichterungen allein bei der Gewerbesteuer einen Verzicht auf rd. 400 Mio. DM (204,5 Mio. Euro) Einnahmen aus dieser Steuer. Dieser Verzicht kommt den Unternehmen zu Gute, die in Frankfurt am Main Gewerbesteuer bezahlen müssen. Dass dies schon wegen der bei Einzelunternehmen und Personengesellschaften geltenden Freibeträge und der von der Gewerbesteuer ausgenommenen Freien Berufe (Ärzte, Rechtsanwälte, steuerberatende Berufe usw.) und Land- und Forstwirte nicht alle in Frankfurt am Main ansässigen Unternehmen sind, sei deshalb erwähnt, weil es verdeutlicht, dass die steuerliche Entlastung für die rd. 7.000 verbliebenen betroffenen Unternehmen zum Teil erheblich ist.

Bezogen auf 100 DM (51,13 Euro) jenseits des geltenden Freibetrages für Einzelunternehmen und Personengesellschaften – nicht für Kapitalgesellschaften und andere juristische Personen – und der sich anschließenden Staffelstufe zur Überleitung in die volle Steuer beläuft sich die Gewerbesteuer in Frankfurt am Main ab dem Jahre 2001 auf 19,68 v. H. der Bemessungsgrundlage. Die Stadt kann damit im Vergleich zu anderen bedeutenden Großstädten am Standort

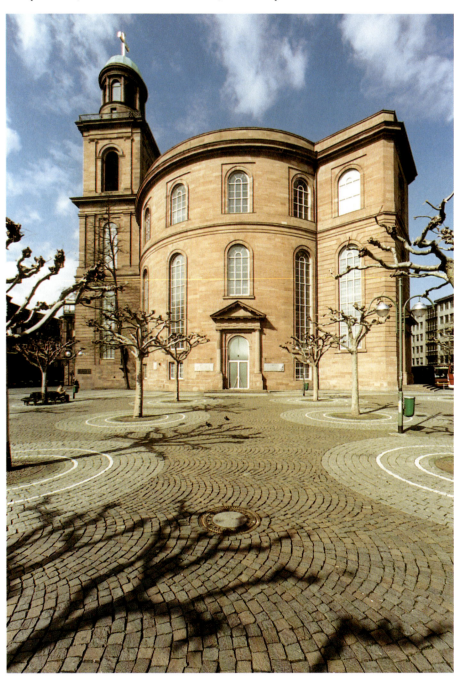

Die Frankfurter Paulskirche.

The Paulskirche (St. Paul's Cathedral) of Frankfurt.

Against the background that has been presented in the above in its most important components, seemingly high expenditures of taxes and fees or costs of commercial investments become relative aspects. The often given argument in small towns and municipalities about taxes, fees, and rents for office space and prices for real estate must principally fail because of a missing possibility for comparison. Whoever bears responsibility in the private sector economy knows this – and decision makers are conscious that a certain merit rightly has its price and should have it.

Independently of these very general and surely understandable statements, the City Administration of Frankfurt on the Main has shown a clear sign by considerably sinking the tax factor for levies to be charged for commercial earnings tax and municipal real-estate tax, for facilitating decisions on business locations. In addition should be mentioned the relief of restaurant and hotel businesses by waiving the tax for licences from the year 1998 on and the beverage tax of 10 % on alcoholic beverages from the year 2000 on.

Besides the waiver of taxes on nominal capital stipulated by federal law – as also on business assets of industrial enterprises – from 1998 onwards, the reduction of levies from 515 p.c. of the basis for assessment to 500 p.c. in the year 2000 and to 490 p.c. from 2001 on has brought considerable tax relief for earnings that are achieved by enterprises in Frankfurt from a German business location, a fact influencing the remaining municipal tax after commercial earnings.

From the point of view of the town budget, the tax relief measures mean – considering only the commercial earnings tax – renouncing around 400 Mio. DM (204,5 Mio. Euro) income from this tax alone. This waiver is in favour of the enterprises that have to pay commercial earnings tax in Frankfurt on the Main. It should be mentioned that this does not include all the enterprises located in Frankfurt on the Main, because this shows that the relief for around 7.000 affected enterprises is sometimes significant, since it precludes allowances valid for individually owned businesses and general or limited partnerships as well as freelancers and private practi-

tioners (medical doctors, lawyers, tax consulting professionals etc.) and farmers and foresters, which are exempt from commercial earnings tax.

Referring to 100 DM (51,13 Euro) above the valid allowance for individually owned businesses and general or limited partnerships – not corporate enterprises and other legal entities – as well as the following differential rates for gradation into the full tax, the commercial earnings tax in Frankfurt on the Main totals from the year 2001 19.68 p.c. of the basis of assessment. The city can thus well withstand comparison to other important large cities of the German business location that offer a somewhat equal infrastructure.

The City of Frankfurt on the Main has embarked on similar endeavours of reforms regarding the real estate or land tax. Also here, the tax factors for charges on commercially used real estate as well as the those tax factors for charges on properties used for living have been reduced considerably. For the year 2000 instead of the former tax factor of 570 p.c. of the basic assessment sum a tax factor of 510 p.c. applies and from 2001 on, a tax factor of 460 p.c. of the basis for assessment will be charged. In relation to incurred charges per square meter, including real estate or land tax, this means for the year 2000 a reduction of around 10.8 p.c. against the previous year and from 2001 on another relief of around 9.8 p.c. against the year

2000. A survey carried out as representatively as possible of mainly commercially used real estate showed that the charges for commercial earnings tax that in 1999 were between 2,20 DM (1,12 Euro) and 0,70 (= 0,35 Euro) per square metre, according to the nature and condition of the real estate, in the year 2001 will only amount from 0,57 DM (0,29 Euro) to 1,85 DM (0,94 Euro) per square meter. With real estate used for living purposes the differences in the charges are still between 0,54 DM (0,27 Euro) and 0,34 DM (0,17 Euro) in the year 1999 and between 0,44 DM (0,22 Euro) and 0,23 DM (0,11 Euro) in 2001.

With the privatisation of public services initiated by the municipality of Frankfurt on the Main itself, like the disposal of refuse mainly including shareholders from the private sector of economy – as for example the township waste disposal management – the way is prepared for private sector economic thought and action by the city council and thus competition is stimulated. Also this fact is beneficial to the investor and shall launch Frankfurt even further forward.

Independently of this, the City of Frankfurt on the Main does not take any first places regarding costs for electricity and gas supply and sewage waste management as well as waste disposal and street cleaning, according to an investigation carried out by the magazine "Capital" in the beginning of

Die Hauptwache.

The Hauptwache (historic tower).

41

Deutschland, die eine in etwa vergleichbare Infrastruktur bieten, durchaus bestehen.

Entsprechende Anstrengungen hat die Stadt Frankfurt am Main bei der kommunalen Grundsteuer unternommen. Auch hier wurden die sowohl für die Belastung des betrieblichen Grundbesitzes als auch für die Belastung des zu Wohnzwecken genutzten Grundbesitzes geltenden Hebesätze deutlich gesenkt. Für das Jahr 2000 gilt anstelle des bisherigen Hebesatzes von 570 v. H. der Bemessungsgrundlage ein Hebesatz von 510 v. H. und ab dem Jahre 2001 ein Hebesatz von 460 v. H. der Bemessungsgrundlage. Bezogen auf die pro Quadratmeter eintretende Belastung mit Grundsteuer bedeutet dies im Jahr 2000 gegenüber den Vorjahren eine Minderung um rd. 10,8 v. H. und ab dem Jahr 2001 nochmals eine Entlastung um rd. 9,8 v. H. gegenüber dem Jahr 2000. Bei möglichst repräsentativ ausgezählten gewerblich genutzten Grundstücken ergibt sich, dass die Gewerbesteuerbelastung, die im Jahre 1999 je nach Art und Beschaffenheit des Grundstückes zwischen 2,20 DM (1,12 Euro) und 0,70 DM (0,35 Euro) je Quadratmeter lag im Jahre 2001 nur noch von 0,57 DM (0,29 Euro) bis 1,85 DM (0,94 Euro) pro Quadratmeter reicht. Bei zu Wohnzwecken genutzten Grundstücken liegen die Belastungsspannen noch zwischen 0,54 DM (0,27 Euro) und 0,34 DM (0,17 Euro) im Jahre 1999 und zwischen 0,44 DM (0,22 Euro) und 0,23 DM (0,11 Euro) im Jahre 2001.

Mit der von der Stadt Frankfurt am Main selbst vorgenommenen Privatisierung städtischer Dienstleistungen wie Müllbeseitigung u. a. unter Einbeziehung privatwirtschaftlicher Anteilseigner – hier ist z. B. der Bereich der städtischen Abfallwirtschaft zu nennen – wird auch insoweit privatwirtschaftlichem Denken und Handeln von der Stadt der Weg geebnet und so der Wettbewerb gefördert. Auch dies dient dem Investor und wird Frankfurt noch weiter nach vorn bringen.

Unabhängig davon nimmt die Stadt Frankfurt am Main im Bereich der Kosten der Strom- und Gasversorgung und Abwasserentsorgung sowie der Müllabfuhr und der Straßenreinigung ausweislich einer Untersuchung, welche die Zeitschrift „Capital" Anfang 1995 für die 84 bundesrepublikanischen Großstädte mit über 100.000 Einwohnern durchgeführt hat, in keinem der genannten Bereiche einen Spitzenplatz in Form der Gebühren ein. Die Untersuchung weist vielmehr aus, dass Frankfurt am Main unter den Großstädten mit über 500.000 Einwohnern in den Bereichen Gasversorgung, Abwasser- und Müllentsorgung, was günstige Gebühren angeht, an erster bzw. zweiter Stelle steht.

Letzteres gilt für andere Kosten für Investoren. Sie sind individuell zu ermitteln und dementsprechend schwankend in ihrer Art und Höhe. Hier ist vor allem das Arbeitsfeld der Wirtschaftsförderung Frankfurt a. M. GmbH, die stets bereit ist, Investoren mit Rat und Tat zur Seite zu stehen, um nicht zuletzt die Investition in Frankfurt am Main lohnend zu machen.

Zusammenfassend gilt, dass die Stadt Frankfurt am Main im Gegensatz zu der manchmal zu hörenden Auffassung sowohl bei den Steuern als auch vielen anderen Standortkosten keineswegs ein „teures Pflaster" ist. Gemessen an dem, was die Stadt an Infrastruktur und Standortvorteilen zu bieten hat, spricht auch unter diesen Gesichtspunkten alles für den hervorragenden Standort. ∎

Hauptwache und Katharinenkirche.

1995 for 84 large cities of the Federal Republic with more than 100 thousand inhabitants, in any of the mentioned fields in form of fees. On the contrary, the investigation shows that Frankfurt on the Main is amongst the large cities with more than 500 thousand inhabitants in the fields of gas supply, sewage and waste disposal on first or second place as regards reasonable fees.

The latter is valid for other costs of the investors. These have to be calculated individually and do correspondingly fluctuate in their nature and amount. This is exactly the field of work of the Wirtschaftsförderung Frankfurt a. M. GmbH, which is always prepared to support investors in word and deed in order to make an investment in Frankfurt on the Main finally worthwhile.

In summary it can be said that the City of Frankfurt on the Main is by no means, contrary to the opinion sometimes heard, neither regarding taxes nor many other costs of location, an expensive place. Compared to the advantages that the city has to offer in terms of infrastructure and location, even under these points of view everything is in favour of this excellent location. ■

Hauptwache and the Church of St. Catherine (Katharinenkirche).

Die DG Diskontbank –
das Spezialinstitut für den Mittelstand

The DG Diskontbank –
a specialized commercial Institute for Small and Middle-Sized Businesses

Die DG Diskontbank ist eine Spezialbank, die insbesondere mittelständischen Firmen und Einkaufskooperationen ihre Finanzdienstleistungen anbietet. Alleiniger Gesellschafter ist die DG BANK Deutsche Genossenschaftsbank Aktiengesellschaft in Frankfurt am Main. Mit ihren Produkten Dynamische Absatzfinanzierung (Factoring) und Dynamische Einkaufsfinanzierung (Zentralregulierung) ergänzt die DG Diskontbank die Produktpalette des genossenschaftlichen FinanzVerbundes. In beiden Geschäftssparten ist sie mit einem Gesamtumsatz von 24.1 Mrd. DM (1999) das führende Institut am deutschen Markt. Die DG Diskontbank versteht sich als Dienstleister, der auch Geld gibt, und nicht als Geldgeber, der auch Dienstleistungen erbringt.

Dynamische Absatzfinanzierung (Factoring) Liquidität für den Mittelstand

Die DG Diskontbank wurde 1963 in Mainz unter dem Namen Inter-Factor-Bank gegründet. Sie ist somit das erfahrenste Factoringinstitut in Deutschland. Beim Factoring dient der Kunde der DG Diskontbank seine sämtlichen Forderungen aus Warenlieferungen und Dienstleistungen zum Kauf an. Die Bank kauft diese Forderungen im Rahmen vorab eingeräumter Limite an und trägt damit das Ausfallrisiko für diese Forderungen in voller Höhe. Den Kaufpreis für die Forderung erhält der Kunde sofort ausbezahlt. Hierfür zahlt er Zinsen in banküblicher Höhe. Die DG Diskontbank führt für die von ihr gekauften Forderungen die Debitorenbuchhaltung. Außerdem übernimmt sie den Einzug der Forderungen einschließlich des Mahn- und Inkassowesens. Der Kunde der DG Diskontbank erhält also mit dem Verkauf seiner Waren oder dem Erbringen seiner Dienstleistung sofort die entsprechende Liquidität und ist vor Forderungsausfällen 100%ig geschützt. Zudem wird er von administrativen Aufgaben im Forderungsmanagement entlastet. Factoring mit der DG Diskontbank ist praktisch in allen Ländern möglich, in denen ein funktionierendes Bankensystem etabliert ist.

Dynamische Einkaufsfinanzierung (Zentralregulierung) Sicherheit für Warenlieferungen

Die DG Diskontbank ist seit 1974 als Zentralregulierer und Marktführer auch der starke Partner für Einkaufskoopera-

Die Geschäftsführung:
Stefan Gerdsmeier, Katja Gollnick und
Dieter Ostheimer (v. links).

The Management:
S. Gerdsmeier, K. Gollnick and
D. Ostheimer (from left).

tionen. Unter Zentralregulierung versteht sich die zentrale Erfassung aller Lieferantenrechnungen für die Anschlusshäuser (Mitglieder) eines Verbandes und die zusammengefasste Regulierung zu festen Zahlungsterminen. Damit verbunden ist die 100%ige Delkredereübernahme im Rahmen eines Forderungskaufs für die Zahlungsverbindlichkeiten der Anschlusshäuser gegenüber den Vertragslieferanten. Die rund 3.300 Mitglieder der Einkaufskooperationen, mit denen die Bank zusammenarbeitet, sind Skontozahler. Neben der Entlastung administrativer Tätigkeiten und der Delkredereübernahme gegenüber den Vertragslieferanten übernimmt die DG Diskontbank abhängig von der gewählten Vertragsart die unterschiedlichsten Aufgaben und Dienstleistungen. ∎

Die Historie	
1963	Gründung als International Factors Deutschland AG & Co mit Firmensitz in Mainz
1969	Umwandlung in INTERFACTOR-BANK AG, Mainz
1974	Aufnahme des Zentralregulierungs-Geschäfts
1978/ 1979	schrittweiser Erwerb aller Kapitalanteile durch die DG BANK und Umfirmierung in DG Diskontbank AG, Mainz
1986	Sitzverlegung nach Frankfurt am Main
1991	Umwandlung in eine GmbH
1994	höchster Factoring-Umsatz in der Bundesrepublik, seitdem Marktführer

Hoch hinaus: die DG Diskontbank in Frankfurt am Main.
Towering high: the DG Diskontbank in Frankfurt on the Main.

The DG Diskontbank is a specialized commercial bank that offers financial services particularly to small and middle-sized enterprises as well as to purchase co-operatives. The sole shareholder is the DG BANK Deutsche Genossenschaftsbank Aktiengesellschaft in Frankfurt on the Main. With its products of dynamic factoring and dynamic purchase financing (central regulation) the DG Diskontbank extends the range of products of the co-operative financial union. In both business fields she is the leading institute in the German market with a total turnover of 24.1 billion DM (1999). The DG Diskontbank sees itself

as a service provider that also provides money, not as a moneylender that also provides services.

Dynamic Factoring – Liquidity for Small and Middle-sized Businesses

The DG Diskontbank was founded in 1963 in Mainz under the name of Inter-Factor-Bank. She is thus the most experienced factoring institute in Germany. In factoring, the client offers to the DG Diskontbank his complete accounts receivable from deliveries of goods and services for purchase.

History	
1963	Establishment as International Factors Deutschland AG & Co. with headquarters in Mainz
1969	Conversion to INTERFACTOR-BANK
1974	Start of the Central Regulation Business
1978/ 1979	step-by-step purchase of all capital shares by the DG BANK and change of company's name to DG Diskontbank AG, Mainz
1986	Relocation of headquarters to Frankfurt on the Main
1991	Conversion into a GmbH
1994	highest factoring turnover in the Federal Republic, and since market leader

The bank then purchases these trade accounts within the framework of prior granted credit facilities and thus bears the risk of default for these trade accounts receivable in full amount. The customer receives the payment for the purchase prize of the trade accounts immediately. For this he pays interest in amounts customary in banking. The DG Diskontbank keeps the books for the accounts receivable of the purchased trade accounts. Furthermore, it claims the accounts receivable while including systems of reminders and debt collection. The client of DG Diskontbank thus receives with the sale of his goods or the execution of his service immediately the corresponding liquidity and is protected from defaults of accounts receivable by 100 %. Furthermore, he is released from his administrative responsibilities of accounts receivable management. Factoring with the DG Diskontbank is practically possible in all countries, which have established a functioning banking system.

Dynamic Purchase Financing (Central Regulation) – Security for Deliveries of Goods

Being the central regulatory institution and market leader, the DG Diskontbank has been since 1974 also a strong partner for purchase co-operatives. By central regulation is meant the central data collection of all supplier invoices for the members of an association and the summarised regulation at fixed payment terms. Connected herewith is to stand 100 % delcredere within the framework of a purchase of accounts receivables for payment liabilities of the members against the appointed suppliers. The approx. 3.300 members of the purchase co-operatives that the bank works with pay cash discounts. Apart from a relief from administrative activities and standing delcredere against appointed suppliers, the DG Diskontbank takes on the most varied tasks and services, depending on the selected type of agreement. ∎

DG DISKONTBANK

DG Diskontbank GmbH

Vorsitzender des Aufsichtsrates/ Chairman of Supervisory Board: Bedo Panner

Geschäftsführung/Management: Stefan Gerdsmeier Dieter Ostheimer Katja Gollnick (Generalbevollmächtigte) (Executive Manager)

Gründungsjahr/Year of Foundation: 1963

Mitarbeiter/Employees: 209

Repräsentanzen/Representative Offices: Berlin, Düsseldorf, Hamburg, Hannover, Hong Kong, München

Geschäftstätigkeit/Business Activity: Finanzdienstleistungen für mittelständische Unternehmen Financial services for middle-sized enterprises

Anschrift/Address: Friedrich-Ebert-Anlage 2–14 D-60325 Frankfurt am Main Telefon +49 (69) 74 47-31 00 Telefax +49 (69) 74 47-32 00 E-Mail info@dg-diskontbank.de Internet www.dg-diskontbank.de

Prinzip der DG Diskontbank: Nägel mit Köpfen.
Slogan of the DG Diskontbank: Do the job properly.

Ernst & Young begleitet Unternehmen in die weltweit vernetzte Zukunft

Ernst & Young accompanies Enterprises into the Worldwide-Networked Future

Das Internet revolutioniert auch die Beziehungen der Wirtschaftsprüfer zu ihren Kunden. Jansen: „Mit einem Abonnement bei Ernst & Young Online erhalten unsere Kunden die Möglichkeit, rund um die Uhr auf unsere Wissensressourcen zuzugreifen und Fragen zu formulieren, die von unseren Experten online in einem garantierten Zeitraum beantwortet werden. Weitere Entwicklungen wie z. B. die standardisierte elektronische Auswertung von Jahresabschlüssen und die Finanzberichterstattung im Internet – das so genannte eReporting – werden folgen.

Ernst & Young wird damit seinem Ruf als „Trendsetter" in der Branche einmal mehr gerecht. Seit 80 Jahren bietet die Gesellschaft ihren Kunden eine individuelle und bedarfsgerechte Betreuung in den Bereichen Wirtschaftsprüfung, Steuerberatung, Corporate Finance und prüfungsnahe Beratung. Am Standort Frankfurt ist Ernst & Young seit 1950 präsent und pflegt dort in besonderem Maße das grenzüberschreitende Geschäft. Denn Regionalvorstand Jansen ist sicher: „Ob Konzern oder gehobener Mittelstand – die Zukunft ist international und interdisziplinär." ∎

Ernst & Young ist Trendsetter im Bereich Unternehmensberatung.
Ernst & Young is a trendsetter in the field of company consulting.

Wir sind davon überzeugt, dass künftig für kein Unternehmen der Weg am E-Business vorbeiführt", stellt Wolf Jansen, Ernst & Young-Vorstand für die Region Frankfurt sowie den Bereich Wirtschaftsprüfung und prüfungsnahe Beratung, fest.

Ernst & Young hat in den letzten Monaten mit Hochdruck an Lösungen für die neuen Herausforderungen gearbeitet: „Eigens für die Prüfung und Beratung von Unternehmen, die ins E-Business einsteigen wollen oder die sich schon jetzt dort tummeln, haben wir das Ernst & Young E-Business Center aufgebaut. Hier koordinieren wir Wirtschaftsprüfer, Steuerberater, Corporate Finance-

Experten, Rechtsanwälte und IT-Spezialisten, die allesamt auf das Thema E-Commerce spezialisiert sind. Gleichgültig, ob die kritische Durchsicht von Business Plänen, die Bewertung von Domains und Webseiten, Finanzreports im Internet, die Abbildung virtueller Geschäfte im Jahresabschluss, die steuerlich optimale Aufstellung der Server, die Sicherheit der Datenübertragung oder die Ausgestaltung von Stock Option Plänen auf der Agenda steht – hier erhalten unsere Kunden alle Dienstleistungen aus einer Hand", erläutert Jansen.

Experten bieten individuelle und bedarfsgerechte Betreuung.

Experts offer individual and tailor-made service.

We are convinced that in future no company can ignore the business in e-Commerce", thus Wolf Jansen, Member of the Board of Ernst & Young for the Frankfurt region as well as for Audit and Advisory Business Services, acknowledges.

Ernst & Young has worked with dedication in the last months towards the new challenges: "Especially for the auditing and consulting of companies that want to enter the e-commerce or that are already active in that area, we have established the Ernst & Young E-Business Center. Here, we coordinate auditors, tax consultants, corporate finance experts, lawyers and IT-specialists, who are all specialised in the field of e-Commerce. Whether it is the critical study of business plans, the evaluation of domains and web sites, financial reports in the Internet, the portrayal of virtual businesses in an annual report, the fiscal optimal positioning of servers, the security of data transfer or the arrangement of stock option plans that are on the agenda – here, our clients receive all services from one provider" Jansen explains.

The Internet is also revolutionising relations between auditors and their clients. Jansen: "With a subscription with Ernst & Young Online our clients have the possibility to access our knowledge resources around the clock and to pose questions that are answered by our experts online within a guaranteed period of time. Further developments like for example standardised electronic

evaluation of annual reports and financial reporting in the Internet – the so-called eReporting – will follow.

Ernst & Young is thus going to uphold its reputation as "trendsetter" in the branch once again. Since 80 years, the company offers its clients an individual and tailor-made service in the fields of auditing, tax consulting, corporate finance and advisory business services. At the Frankfurt location Ernst & Young has been present since 1950 and maintains here to a considerable extent its business across borders. For, board member for the region Jansen is sure: "whether corporate concern or upper middle-size business – the future is international and interdisciplinary." ∎

Ernst & Young
Deutsche Allgemeine Treuhand AG

Vorstand/Executive Board:
Dr. Dietrich Dörner
(Vorstandsvorsitzender/chairman of the board)
Dr. Herbert Müller
(stellvertretender Vorstandsvors./deputy chairman of the board)
Wolfgang Elkart
Wolf Jansen
Alfred Müller
Manfred Niehaus
Dr. Michael Schlößer
Joachim Schmidts
Antonio Schnieder
Dieter Schwankhaus
Hubertus Graf von Treuberg
Prof. Dr. Norbert Pfitzer

Gründungsjahr/Year of Foundation: 1919

Mitarbeiter/Employees:
derzeit rund/presently around 3.150,
davon rund 400 am Standort Frankfurt/
of these around 400 at the Frankfurt location

Geschäftstätigkeit/Business Activity:
Wirtschaftsprüfung/Auditing
Steuerberatung/Tax consulting
Corporate Finance/Corporate finance
Prüfungsnahe Beratung/Advisory Business Services

Anschrift/Address:
Mittlerer Pfad 15
D-70499 Stuttgart
Telefon   +49 (711) 988-50
Telefax   +49 (711) 988-53 33
E-Mail   info@ernst-young.de
Internet   www.ernst-young.de

Eschersheimer Landstr. 14
D-60322 Frankfurt am Main
Telefon   +49 (69) 152 08-01
Telefax   +49 (69) 152 08-280
E-Mail   frankfurt@ernst-young.de
Internet   www.ernst-young.de

Wolf Jansen, Mitglied des Vorstandes der Ernst & Young Deutsche Allgemeine Treuhand AG.

Wolf Jansen, Member of the Board of Ernst & Young Deutsche Allgemeine Treuhand AG.

FRA: Wirtschaftsmotor und Tor zur Welt

FRA: Driving Force of the Economy and Gate to the World

Die Flughafen Frankfurt/Main AG (FAG) blickt auf eine mehr als siebzigjährige Tradition als Luftverkehrsdienstleister zurück. Bei der Gründung im Jahre 1924 unter dem Namen „Südwestdeutsche Luftverkehrs AG" betrieb die Gesellschaft noch den alten Frankfurter Flughafen am Rebstockgelände. 1936 ging mit „Rhein-Main" der Kern des heutigen Flughafens am Autobahnschnittpunkt Frankfurter Kreuz in Betrieb. Heute umfasst das Flughafengelände mit seinen Start- und Landebahnen, allen flugtechnischen Einrichtungen, den beiden Terminals sowie der CargoCity Süd und der US-Air Base eine Fläche von 1.900 Hektar.

Der größte Flughafen des europäischen Kontinents, im internationalen Sprachgebrauch einfach „FRA", stellt für die Rhein-Main-Region, das Land Hessen und für ganz Deutschland das Tor zur Welt dar, sorgt für Mobilität und weltweiten Warenaustausch. Seit Jahren ist der Flughafen ein Ort sichtbaren Fortschritts und der Innovation auf vielen Gebieten. Baukran und Betonmischer sind und bleiben inoffizielle Airport-Wahrzeichen.

Der Flughafen ist aber auch eine imposante Job-Maschine. Ende 1999 belief sich die Zahl der bei fast 500 Firmen und Behörden am Flughafen Beschäftigten auf rund 62.000 – zur Erinnerung: 1970 waren es rund 19.000 und 1980 gerade erst knapp 32.000. Damit ist FRA die größte Arbeitsstätte Deutschlands. Und der Flughafen allein bietet die

Möglichkeit, auch weiterhin attraktive und sichere Arbeitsplätze zu schaffen: Erhöht sich die Zahl der stündlich koordinierten Flugbewegungen – der sogenannte Koordinationseckwert – von heute 78 um nur eine, so entstehen mehr als 2.000 neue Arbeitsplätze. Diese Zahl hat auch bei allen Rationalisierungsbemühungen und Produktivitätssteigerungen Bestand, denn Dienstleistungen, Servicefunktionen werden auch in Zukunft von Menschen und nicht von Maschinen geboten werden.

Ohne den Flughafen und seine Flugplan-Fülle hätte Frankfurt längst nicht den jetzigen Rang als Banken- und Dienstleistungszentrum, Messestadt und Hauptstadt des deutschen Tourismus. Um die Rolle als Wirtschafts- und Wachstumsmotor im härter werdenden Wettbewerb auch zukünftig spielen zu können, muss seine Konkurrenzfähigkeit gestärkt werden: Spätestens im Jahr 2003 sind die derzeitigen Bahn-Kapazitäten des Frankfurter Flughafens erschöpft; eine neue Landebahn ist nötig, damit nicht unnötig Verkehr und damit Prosperität ins benachbarte Ausland verlagert wird.

Denn schon heute muss in den attraktiven Spitzenzeiten ein Großteil der Nachfrage nach Lande- und Startmöglichkeiten in Frankfurt abgewiesen werden. Einem Koordinationseckwert von 78 Flugbewegungen pro Stunde stehen bereits zeitweise Anfragen von bis zu 120 Starts

Dr. Wilhelm Bender

Der Autor studierte Rechtswissenschaften und Volkswirtschaftslehre und promovierte zum Dr. jur. Von 1974 bis 1985 war er bei der Deutschen Bundesbahn, Frankfurt am Main, tätig, zuletzt Ministeralrat und Leiter des Vorstandssekretariates. Anschließend war er Geschäftsführer des Verkehrsforum Bahn in Bonn, sowie Geschäftsführer der Parlamentarischen Gruppe Bahn des Deutschen Bundestages (1985–1990). Er wechselte 1990 zur Schenker-Rhenus AG (Veba-Konzern) und war während der Zeit von 1990–1992 Vorsitzender der Geschäftsführung der Schenker & Co. GmbH, Frankfurt, Geschäftsführer der Schenker International GmbH, Frankfurt, Mitglied des Vorstandes Schenker-Rhenus AG sowie Vorsitzender des Vorstandes der Schenker Waggon- und Beteiligungs AG. Ausserdem war er während dieser Zeit Mitglied des Direktoriums der Stinnes AG. Seit Januar 1993 ist er Vorsitzender des Vorstandes der Flughafen Frankfurt/Main AG.

The author studied law and political economy to PhD level. From 1974 to 1985 he worked for the Deutsche Bundesbahn (German Railway) in Frankfurt on the Main, his last positions were Ministerial Counsellor and Head of the Management Secretariat. Afterwards he was Managing Director of the Verkehrsforum Bahn (Train Transport Forum) in Bonn and Managing Director of the Parliamentary Group for Trains of the German Parliament (1985-1990). In 1990 he joined the Schenker-Rhenus AG (Veba Group) and was from 1990 – 1992 Chairman of the Management Directors of Schenker & Co. GmbH, Frankfurt, Managing Director of Schenker International GmbH, Frankfurt, Member of the Board of Schenker-Rhenus AG as well as Chairman of the Board of Schenker Waggon and Holding AG. Furthermore he was Member of the Directorate of Stinnes AG during that time. Since January 1993 he is Chairman of the Board of the Flughafen Frankfurt/Main AG.

Rund 62.000 Personen sind auf dem Flughafen tätig.

Around 62.000 people work at the airport.

The Frankfurt Airport (Flughafen Frankfurt/Main AG, FAG) can look back on a tradition as air transport service organisation of more than seventy years. On its foundation in 1924, it still operated under the name "Südwestdeutsche Luftverkehrs AG" from the old Frankfurt Airport at the Rebstock grounds. In 1936, the core of today's airport started its operation at the motorway-node of the Frankfurter Cross with the name "Rhein-Main". Today, the terrain of the airport includes with its starting and landing runways, all aeronautical facilities, the two terminals and the Cargo-City South as well as the US-Air Base an area of 1.900 hectares.

Pro Stunde werden durchschnittlich 78 Flugzeuge abgefertigt.

Each hour an average of 78 aeroplanes are cleared.

The largest airport of the European continent, in international language use simply "FRA", presents to the Rhein-Main region, the federal state of Hesse and for the whole of Germany, the gate to the world and it provides mobility and a worldwide exchange of goods. For years the airport has been a place of visible progress and innovation in many fields. Unofficial symbols of the airport are and will remain also: the construction crane and cement mixer.

On the other hand, the airport also is a very impressive job machine. At the end of 1999, the number of employees employed with almost 500 companies and state authorities at the airport was around 62.000 – just to reiterate: in 1970 they were around 19.000 and 1980 only short of 32.000. This makes FRA the largest place of work in Germany. And the airport alone offers the possibility to keep creating further attractive and secure work places:

Because, if the number of hourly coordinated flight movements – the so-called coordination prime value – today of 78, increases by only one more than 2.000 new jobs are created. This figure is also valid when trying to account for all kinds of rationalisation measures and enhancements of productivity, for services and service functions shall be provided also in the future by humans and not by machines.

Without the airport and its dense flight plan, Frankfurt would have by no means its actual ranking as banking and service centre, city of exhibitions and fairs and capital of German tourism. In order to keep its role as driving force for the economy and growth in the ever-increasing competition in future, its competitiveness must be strengthened: in the year 2003 at the latest, the present runway capacities of the Frankfurt airport will be exhausted; a new runway is urgently needed so that traffic and thus prosperity is not transferred into the neighbouring foreign countries unnecessarily.

Even today, in the most attractive peak times a great part of the demand for landing and starting possibilities has to be rejected in Frankfurt. The coordination prime value of 78 flight movements per

Zeitweise gibt es stündlich bis zu 120 Anfragen für Starts und Landungen.

At times, there are up to 120 enquiries for starts and landings.

49

Trotz ständig steigender Passagierzahlen bleibt Zeit für freundliche Beratung.

Despite the continuous increase in the number of passengers there is time for kind consulting.

det den drohenden dauerhaften Engpass nicht ab. Selbst die weltweit Beachtung findende Philosophie der „Intermodalität", also der Verknüpfung verschiedener Verkehrsträger am Frankfurter Flughafen, verringert den Kapazitätsbedarf nicht. Zwar arbeitet die FAG insbesondere mit Lufthansa und der Deutschen Bahn an Konzepten, die das Umsteigen zwischen Zug und Flug ähnlich nahtlos und zeitsparend ermöglichen sollen, wie zwischen zwei Flugzeugen, aber der Erfolg dieses Projektes kommt vor allem der Ökologie zugute. Kurzstreckenflüge sollen möglichst durch entsprechend attraktive Zugverbindungen ersetzbar werden; hier bietet der Frankfurter Flughafen mit seinem ICE-Bahnhof, dem AIRail-Terminal unmittelbar am und einem separaten Regionalbahnhof unter dem Terminal 1 beste Voraussetzungen.

und Landungen gegenüber. Da beruhigt es die Lufthansa und die fast 180 anderen Linien- und Ferienfluggesellschaften nur wenig, dass die Deutsche Flugsicherung mit der Flughafen Frankfurt/Main AG (FAG), dem Hausherren und Betreiber des Flughafens, sowie mit Firmen und Spezialisten aus der Hochtechnologie und dem Flugzeug- und Triebwerksbau bereits Maßnahmen für eine Steigerung des Eckwertes auf stündlich 80 Flugzeugbewegungen angekündigt hat. Und auch die Tatsache, dass schon heute bei gutem Wetter gelegentlich deutlich mehr als die „offiziell" vorgesehenen Starts und Landungen ohne jegliche Einschränkung der Sicherheit möglich sind, wen-

Frankfurt und die Rhein-Main-Region sind nicht zuletzt dank des Flughafens attraktiv für hunderte in- und ausländischer Unternehmen. Die FAG tut alles, damit das so bleibt und diese einzigartige Trumpfkarte – im Interesse der Region und all der Hunderttausenden, die direkt oder indirekt vom Florieren jener Drehscheibe des Luftverkehrs abhängen – möglichst noch besser ausgespielt werden kann. ∎

Terminal in der Cargo-City Süd.

A terminal in the Cargo-City South.

hour is already being contrasted by enquiries for up to 120 starts and landings at times. The latter does not provide reassurance to Lufthansa and almost 180 other airlines and charter flight organisations, even if the German Flight Assurance including the Flughafen Frankfurt/Main (FAG), the Airport Frankfurt Company, the owner and operator of the airport, as well as firms and specialists of the high-technology sector and the aircraft and power plant construction have already announced measures for increasing the prime value to 80 flight movements an hour. Also the fact, that today already at times markedly more than the officially planned starts and landings are possible without any limitation of security, when the weather is good, does not avert the threatening lasting bottleneck situation.

Der Flughafen am Abend.

The airport at night.

Also the worldwide praised philosophy of "intermodality", that is the interconnection of various means of transport at the Frankfurt airport does not diminish the need for more capacity. On the one hand, the FAG is working on conceptual solutions, particularly with Lufthansa and the Deutsche Bahn, the German railway company, that are designed to facilitate changing between train and flight similar smoothly and time-saving as between two airplanes, but the success of this project is above all beneficial for the ecology. Short flights are to be substituted as much as possible by correspondingly attractive train connections; this is were the Frankfurt airport offers best preconditions with its ICE-train station, the AIRail-terminal directly and separately located at the regional train terminal underneath terminal 1.

Frankfurt and the Rhein-Main region are very attractive to hundreds of domestic and foreign enterprises because of the airport finally. The FAG does everything to ensure that this remains so and this unique trump card will even be better used in future – in the interest of the region and all the hundreds of thousands that depend directly or indirectly from the prosperity of this turning wheel of air transport. ■

Der ICE-Bahnhof am Frankfurter Flughafen.

The ICE-train station at the Frankfurt Airport.

**Kempinski
Hotel Gravenbruch**

FRANKFURT

Geschäftsführung/Management:
Andrea Mügge (Logisleiterin)
Heinz Imhof (Gastronomieleiter)
Jörg Fehrmann (Director Sales and Marketing)

Gründungsjahr/Year of Foundation:
1967

Gästeservice/Guest Services:
- Kostenloser Shuttle-Service zum Rhein-Main-Airport und in die Frankfurter Innenstadt
- Beheizter Innen- und Außenpool
- Große Liegewiese
- Sauna, Solarium, Massage
- 2 Tennisplätze
- Joggingpfad
- Diverse Golfplätze und Reitmöglichkeiten in unmittelbarer Nähe
- Beauty Farm
- Friseursalon „Tröndle"
- Portier
- Reinigungs- und Wäscheservice
- Boutique
- Mehrsprachige Tageszeitungen (Extrawünsche werden gerne erfüllt)
- Mietwagen über den Portier buchbar
- Business-Center
- 350 Parkplätze
- Garagen
- Busparkplätze
- Kinderbetreuung auf Anfrage
- 24 Stunden Etagenservice
- Free-of-charge shuttle-service to the Rhein-Main Airport and into the city centre of Frankfurt
- Heated indoor and outdoor pools
- Large lawn for sunbathing
- Sauna, solarium, massage
- 2 tennis courts
- Jogging path
- Diverse golf courses and riding possibilities in direct vicinity
- Beauty farm
- Hairdressing salon "Tröndle"
- Porter
- Cleaning and laundry service
- Boutique
- Multilingual Newspapers (extra wishes are complied with pleasure)
- Booking of hired cars possible at the porter
- Business centre
- 350 parking spaces
- Garages
- Bus parking spaces
- Childcare possible on request
- 24-hour service on each floor

Anschrift/Address:
An der Bundesstrasse 459
D-63263 Neu-Isenburg
Telefon   + 49 (6102) 505-0
Telefax   + 49 (6102) 505-900
Telefon-Verkauf + 49 (6102) 505-720
Fax-Verkauf   + 49 (6102) 505-915
E-Mail   reservation.fra@kempinski.com
Internet   www.kempinski-frankfurt.com

Kempinski Gravenbruch – das Business-Resort

Kempinski Gravenbruch – The Business-Resort

Vor den Toren der Mainmetropole Frankfurt, der Finanzhauptstadt Europas, empfängt Sie das Kempinski Hotel Gravenbruch in exklusivem traditionellen Landhausstil. Eingebettet in einer weitläufigen Parklandschaft genießen Sie Erholung und Entspannung mit der geschäftigen Nähe des Messezentrums.

Lage
Leicht zu erreichen sind in nur 15 Minuten das Banken- und Geschäftszentrum ebenso, wie der Frankfurter Flughafen und die Frankfurter Messe.

Zimmer und Suiten
282 geräumige und komfortable Zimmer und Suiten mit See- oder Parkblick stehen Ihnen mit den modernen Annehmlichkeiten der gehobenen Hotellerie zur Verfügung.

Restaurants
Es erwarten Sie traditionelle und regionale Spezialitäten in der rustikalen Forsthausschänke oder die Feinheit einer gehobenenen internationalen Küche im eleganten Ambiente des Forsthausrestaurants. Laue Sommerabende genießen Sie in unserem Biergarten Schoppenhof. Cocktails und Snacks mit Atmosphäre bieten Ihnen der Wintergarten und die Lobbybar.

Serviceangebote
Tagungs- und Bankettmöglichkeiten für bis zu 600 Personen und kreatives Catering, 24 Stunden Zimmerservice, beheiztes Innen- und Außenschwimmbad, Sauna und Solarium, Tennisplätze, Schönheitsfarm, Friseur und Boutique. Kostenfreier Flughafen- und Stadttransfer. ∎

Situated close to the heart of Frankfurt, the Kempinski Hotel Gravenbruch welcomes you in it's own beautiful extensive park providing an elegant retreat away from the bustle of the city. Your haven in a historical landmark travelling either on business or leisure.

Location
Just 15 minutes from the Business District as well as from Frankfurt Airport and Frankfurt Trade Fair.

Rooms and Suites
282 spacious and luxurious rooms and suites, all with park or lake view provide the amenities and the comfort of a five star hotel.

Restaurants
Enjoy a casual atmosphere for local and traditional cuisine in our Forsthausschänke or the fine dining of international flavours in the distinctive Forsthaus Restaurant. Our outside patio Schoppenhof welcomes during the summer season and for Sunday Jazz. The hotel also offers snacks in the Wintergarden and in the Lobby-bar.

Facilities
Well established conference and banquetfacilities for up to 600 guests as well as catering. 24 hours room service, heated indoor and outdoor pool, sauna and solarium, tenniscourts, a beautyparlour, hairdresser and a boutique. Free-of-charge transfers downtown and airport. ∎

52

Moving Forward into the Future

Frankfurt – der zweitgrößte Flughafen Europas.

Frankfurt – Europe´s second busiest airport.

Der Flughafen Frankfurt ist als Schaufenster zur Welt Garant für hohe Dienstleistungsqualität, qualifiziertes Know-How und jahrzehntelange Erfahrung der FAG als Flughafenbetreiber. Die Flughafen Frankfurt/Main AG (FAG) betreibt den zweitgrößten Flughafen in Europa und hält eine Vielzahl von Dienstleistungen bereit, die von vielfältigen Serviceangeboten ergänzt werden. Neben umfangreichen Serviceeinrichtungen für den Reisenden sind Konferenz-, Shopping und Unterhaltungsmöglichkeiten vorhanden.

Der Flughafen Frankfurt offeriert optimale intermodale Verkehrsanbindungen für den Passagier- und Frachtverkehr. So wird im März 2001 die Pilotstrecke Stuttgart Hbf – Flughafen Frankfurt in Betrieb genommen, die ein bequemes Umsteigen von Bahn auf Flug ermöglicht.

Frankfurt Rhein-Main wird zunehmend zur bedeutenden Logistikregion und – mit dem hochqualifiziertem Zentrum Flughafen – zum europäischen Distributionszentrum. Informations- und Transportlogistik verschmelzen hier zu einer leistungsstarken Gesamtlogistikleistung. Für internationale Unternehmen bietet die Flughafen Frankfurt/Main AG mit der CargoCity Frankfurt ausgezeichnete Ansiedlungsvoraussetzungen, wie zum Beispiel:

- Hightech Cargo Einrichtungen
- hoch qualifiziertes Fachpersonal
- Perishable Center Frankfurt.

Die Flughafen Frankfurt/Main AG ist darüber hinaus ein leistungsstarker Partner im Aviation Business bei über 50 Projekten weltweit. ∎

For Flughafen Frankfurt/Main AG – the Frankfurt Airport company – Frankfurt Airport is a showcase to the world that guarantees service quality, know-how and expertise based on many decades of airport operating experience.

The Frankfurt Airport company (FAG) operates the second busiest airport in Europe and offers a wide range of services and facilities. In addition to a multiplicity of passenger services, conference rooms, shopping facilities and entertainment areas are available at Frankfurt Airport.

Frankfurt Airport offers optimum intermodal connections for passengers and cargo. In March 2001, an intermodal pilot project will be launched on the route between Stuttgart Central Train Station and Frankfurt Airport, which will provide for fast and easy transfers between train and plane.

The Frankfurt Rhine-Main region increasingly is developing into a major logistics and European distribution center – due to the high quality airport located right at the heart of this region. Information and transportation logistics have been linked to create an efficient total logistics service. FAG's CargoCity offers optimum location conditions for international companies:

- high-tech cargo facilities
- highly qualified staff
- the Perishables Center Frankfurt.

Actively involved in 50 projects around the world, the Frankfurt Airport company also is a competent partner in the global aviation business. ∎

Fraport
Frankfurt Airport
Services Worldwide

Vorstandsvorsitzender/
Chairman of the Executive Board
Dr. Wilhelm Bender

Stellvertretender Vorstandsvorsitzender
Vorstand Verkehrsdienste und Immobilien/
Vice Chairman; Director Aviation Ground
Services and Real Estate Management
Prof. Manfred Schölch

Vorstand Verkehrs-/Terminal-Management und
Kommunikationsdienstleistungen/
Chief Financial Officer Responsible
for Traffic/Terminal Management
and Communications Services
Johannes Endler

Vorstand Arbeitsdirektor und technische Dienste/
Executive Director Labor Relations and
Technical Services
Hans Georg Michel

Vorstand Flughafenentwicklung/
Executive Director for Airport
Development and Expansion
Prof. Barbara Jakubeit

Gründungsjahr/Year of Foundation:
1924 als/as „Südwestdeutsche Luftverkehrs AG"

Mitarbeiter/Employees: 13.000

Umsatz/Turnover: DM 2,6 Mrd./DM 2.6 billion

Geschäftstätigkeit/Business Activity:
Flughafenbetreiber/Airport operator

Anschrift/Address:
Flughafen Frankfurt/Main AG (FAG)
D-60547 Frankfurt am Main
Telefon   +49 (69) 690-0
Telefax   +49 (69) 690-7 76 90

FAG im Internet
- Reise-Info/Travel homepage:
  www.flughafen-frankfurt.de
- Zum Unternehmen/Company homepage:
  www.flughafen-frankfurt.com
- Online-Flugbuchungen usw./Booking flight:
  www.airport-travelnet.de
- Informationen über die Ausbau-Optionen/
  Information about Airport expansion:
  www.ausbau.flughafen-frankfurt.com
- Informationen über die CargoCity/Cargo Information:
  www.cargocity-frankfurt.de

FAG-Videotext
- hessen 3 und SWR 3: Tafel/pages 560 – 567
- 3sat auf Tafel/page 480 ff.
- Euronews: Tafeln/pages 580–582
- TV 5: Tafeln/pages: 480–482
- n-tv: Tafeln/pages: 610–619

Modernste Transportlogistik der FAG.
State-of-the-art transport logistics.

53

In Frankfurt schlägt das Herz des deutschen Internets

Frankfurt carries the Heart of the German Internet

Nach anfänglichem Zögern beschleunigt sich die Internet-Entwicklung in Deutschland in den letzten Jahren. Hierbei hat sich im Wettstreit der Städte schon frühzeitig Frankfurt am Main als das „Herz" in der Infrastruktur des deutschen Internet herauskristallisiert. Am Interxion Internet Exchange Center (IEC) im Osten Frankfurts, im Gebiet der Hanauer Landstraße, kommen heute mehr Internet-Netze zusammen als an jedem anderen Punkt Deutschlands. Unter anderem ist im IEC der zentrale Deutsche Internet-Austauschknoten, kurz DE-CIX für „Deutscher Commercial Internet Exchange", angesiedelt.

Innerdeutscher Datenaustausch startete 1995

Die hohe Bedeutung von DE-CIX und IEC für die deutsche Internet-Landschaft wird aus der kurzen Historie der letzten Jahre deutlich. Bis zur Initiierung des DE-CIX im Jahr 1995 wurde der gesamte innerdeutsche Datenverkehr über die USA gerou-

tet, weil die deutschen Internet Service Provider keine Datenaustausch- oder Peering-Punkte, also keine direkten Verbindungen miteinander unterhielten. Da es zu diesem Zeitpunkt nur zwei Backbones zum amerikanischen Internet gab (die Vorläufer des heutigen UUNET und Xlink an den Unis in Dortmund bzw. Karlsruhe), stellten sich zwangsläufig mit der stark wachsenden Akzeptanz des Internet immer größere Kapazitätsprobleme ein. Der Zeitbedarf für den Datentransport stellte die Geduld der Anwender wiederholt auf eine harte Probe. Allerdings war und ist diese Situation keineswegs nur ein auf Deutschland beschränktes Phänomen, sondern betrifft in der einen oder anderen Weise sämtliche Betreiber von Internetzugängen.

Um dem entgegenzuwirken, riefen deshalb weltweit kommerzielle Internet Service-Anbieter zentrale Datenaustauschpunkte ins Leben, an denen der nationale oder regionale Datenverkehr von einem Provider-Netz zum andern übergeben wird. Als Betreibergesellschaften arbeiten dabei in der Regel gemeinsam betriebene, nicht gewinnorientierte Organisationen. Zu den prominentesten Vertretern solcher Datenaustauschpunkte

Gerd Simon

Der Autor ist Geschäftsführer der Interxion GmbH in Frankfurt am Main. Er hat im Frühjahr 1999 die deutschen Geschäftsaktivitäten gestartet, das erste Internet Exchange Center (IEC) in Deutschland aufgebaut und zu seiner heutigen Größe geführt. Der Dipl.-Wirtschaftsingenieur war zuvor bei der Deutschen Telekom-Tochtergesellschaft DeTe-System und bei der Beratungsgesellschaft ComConsult engagiert. Gerd Simon ist im Vorstand des Marketingclubs Frankfurt am Main und Gastdozent für Strategisches Marketing an der International MBA in Wiesbaden.

The author is Managing director of Interxion GmbH in Frankfurt on the Main. In spring of 1999 he started the German business activities, establishing the first Internet Exchange Centre (IEC) in Germany and led it to its present importance. The Certified Economic Engineer worked previously at dependency of Deutsche Telekom De Te-System and at the Consulting Group ComConsult. Gerd Simon is Member of the Board of the Marketingclub Frankfurt am Main and extramural lecturer of strategic marketing at the International MBA in Wiesbaden.

Interxion Telecom GmbH, Hauptverwaltung Deutschland, in der Hanauer Landstraße 312.
Interxion Telecom GmbH, Headquarters Germany, in Hanauer Landstrasse 312.

zählen heute MAE-East und MAE-West in den USA, der in London angesiedelte LINX, der Pariser SFINX, der Wiener VIX und der DE-CIX in Frankfurt. An allen vier europäischen Standorten sind die zentralen Austauschknoten oder die Co-location-Knoten dazu in einem Internet Exchange Center von Interxion untergebracht.

Hochmodernes Netzwerkequipment.

Highly modern network equipment.

After prior hesitation, the Internet development in Germany is gaining momentum in the recent years. In this respect, Frankfurt on the Main has crystallized in the competition of the cities already early as being the "heart" of the German Internet infrastructure. At the Interxion Internet Exchange Center (IEC) in the East of Frankfurt, in the area of the Hanauer Landstraße, today more Internet networks come together than at any other point in Germany. The IEC is home, amongst others, to the central German Internet exchange node, in short DE-CIX for "Deutscher Commercial Internet Exchange".

Domestic German data exchange began in 1995 The extreme importance of DE-CIX and IEC for the German Internet landscape can be seen from its short history of the last few years. Until the initiation of the DE-CIX in the year 1995 the complete German domestic data transfer was routed via the USA, because the German Internet service providers did not maintain any data exchange or peering points, that is no direct connections with each other. Since at that time there only existed two backbones to the American Internet (the predecessors of today's UUNET and Xlink at the universities of Dortmund and Karlsruhe), every greater problems of capacity accrued inevitably with the tremendously growing acceptance of the Internet. The duration of data transfer was repeatedly are hard test for the patience of the users. However, this situation was not whether in the past or at present, a phenomenon limited to Germany alone, but concerns in one way or another all operators of Internet access. In order to counteract this situation, commercial Internet service providers worldwide started therefore using central data exchange points at which the national or regional data traffic is handed over from one provider network to the other. The operating companies in general work together as non-profit oriented organisations. Amongst the most prominent representatives of such data exchange points today are MAE-East and MAE-West in the USA, the London-based LINX, SFINX of Paris, the VIX of Vienna and DE-CIX of Frankfurt. Interxion gathers at all four European locations for this purpose central exchange nodes or collocation nodes in one Internet exchange centre.

Central Peering optimises communication

The advantages of these central peering points are evident. They optimise on a national level the commercial communication in the Internet. Data packages between participants in Germany are not sent over the Internet exchange centres including the DE-CIX time consuming and costly via international connections around the globe, but are transferred on short routes. On the one hand, this increases speed and security for German Internet users on access of German resources (web-servers, e-mail etc.) and on the other hand, it relieves the international network connections. The principle is similar to the traditional letter mail, whose mailboxes dispose of insertion slits for inner city and for national mailings. By right, mail customers can expect in such scenarios to

Zentrales Peering optimiert die Kommunikation

Die Vorteile dieser zentralen Peering-Punkte liegen auf der Hand. Sie optimieren auf nationaler Ebene die kommerzielle Kommunikation im Internet. Datenpakete zwischen Teilnehmern in Deutschland werden über die Internet Exchange Center unter Einbezug des DE-CIX nicht mehr zeitaufwendig und kostspielig via internationaler Leitungen um den Globus geschleust, sondern auf kurzem Wege transportiert. Das erhöht zum einen die Geschwindigkeit und Sicherheit deutscher Internet-Nutzer beim Zugriff auf deutsche Ressourcen (Web-Server, E-Mail etc.) und entlastet zum anderen die internationalen Leitungsnetze. Das Prinzip ähnelt einer traditionellen Briefpost, deren Briefkästen über einen Einwurf für innerstädtische und für nationale Sendungen verfügen. Zu Recht kann der Postkunde in solchen Szenarien erwarten, im innerstädtischen Briefdienst einen Brief schneller zu erhalten als aus den großen Sortieranlagen.

Aber nicht nur die Internet-Nutzer, sondern auch die ISPs profitieren von zentralen Peering-Punkten. Denn diese machen die ansonsten not-wendigen bilateralen Verträge zwischen den Providern obsolet, die im übrigen zusätzlich durch die jeweils notwendigen Kommunikationsgerätschaften erheblich kostspieliger würden. Diese Erkenntnis hat sich auf breiter Basis durchgesetzt. Heute werden weit über 80 Prozent des

nationalen Internet-Verkehrs Deutschlands über den im IEC beheimateten DE-CIX geführt. Die Teilnahme an DE-CIX steht allen professionellen Internet-Dienstleistern offen, sofern sie den technischen und qualitativen Anschlussbedingungen gerecht werden.

DE-CIX ist vom Betreiber eco Electronic Commerce Forum e. V. (Köln) als gemanagter und neutraler Austauschpunkt konzipiert. Die Neutralität wird durch die Selbstverwaltung und einen Sprecherbeirat, der von den Teilnehmern für drei Jahre gewählt wird, sichergestellt. Zentrale und im allgemeinen Interesse der Teilnehmer liegende Angelegenheiten werden durch ein technisches Management aufgegriffen und umgesetzt.

Infrastruktur zieht Startups an

Die bundesweit einzigartige Infrastruktur in der Frankfurter Hanauer Landstraße zieht die Unternehmen der New Economy scharenweise an. Neben den DE-CIX im Internet Exchange Center hat das VentureLab entscheidend dazu beigetragen, die Rhein-Main-Metropole zur Internet-Hauptstadt Deutschlands zu erheben. Beim VentureLab, ebenfalls ansässig im Osten Frankfurts in der Hanauer Landstraße, initiiert und gestützt von Risikokapitalgesellschaften unter Federführung der IVC Venture Capital AG, handelt es sich um die größte Brutstätte für Startup-Firmen in Deutschland. Die Initiative wird unterstützt vom

Verband der deutschen Internet-Wirtschaft, vom Internet-Gründerverein Silicon City Club, vom Bundesministerium für Wirtschaft und Technologie, von der European Business School, der Wissenschaftlichen Hochschule für Unternehmensführung (WHU) und der Universität Frankfurt (Lehrstuhl E-Commerce).

Das VentureLab ist mit Gründungskapital in zweistelliger Millionenhöhe ausgestattet, die sich clevere Jungunternehmer mit guten Ideen abholen. Beinahe wichtiger als das Geld sind die fix und fertige Infrastruktur und das Kontaktnetz von VentureLab. Der angehende Unternehmer erhält praktisch alles, was er für den Erfolg braucht und was herkömmlicherweise in der Startphase besonders zeitraubend ist. Vom ersten Tag an sitzt er in einem top-eingerichteten Büro und hat ein technisch stabiles Computernetzwerk in Betrieb, das direkt an den DE-CIX im IEC angeschlossen ist (ca. 200 m Luftlinie). Den Gründern stehen im Venture-Lab Anwälte, Steuerberater und Wirtschaftsprüfer, Marketing- und Vertriebsspezialisten „auf Knopfdruck" zur Verfügung. FirstTuesday, Young Entrepreneurs Organization (YEO), Silicon City Club, das Exis- tenzgründer- und Jungunternehmerforum m-e-x und viele weitere Wirtschaftsverbände der New Economy kommen regelmäßig in die Hanauer Landstraße ins VentureLab.

Infrastruktur und Startups zusammen manifestieren die herausragende Position von Frankfurt am Main im deutschen Internet-Markt. ■

Power distribution frame.

Power distribution frame.

Die Funktionsfähigkeit des Netzes ist auch bei Stromausfällen gewährleistet.

Stand-by power units ensure a permanent operation capacity.

receive a letter within the inner-city letter service much faster than from the large sorting plants. But not only Internet users, also the ISPs benefit from central peering points. Because these make the otherwise necessary bilateral agreements between providers obsolete, which, by the way, in addition would become considerably more expensive, because of the correspondingly necessary communication equipment. This realisation has prevailed on a broad basis. Today, much more than 80 percent of national Internet traffic in Germany is routed via the DE-CIX based in the IEC. Participation in the DE-CIX is open to all professional Internet service providers, if they meet the technical and qualitative conditions for connection.

DE-CIX was designed as a managed and neutral exchange point by the operator eco Electronic Commerce Forum e. V. (Cologne). Neutrality is guaranteed through self-administration and an advisory speakers' committee, which is elected by participants for three years. Central matters and such of general interest of participants are taken up by a technical management and carried out.

Infrastructure attracts start-ups

The nationwide unique infrastructure in the Hanauer Landstraße of Frankfurt attracts enter-

prises of the New Economy in droves. Besides the DE-CIX within the Internet Exchange Center also the VentureLab has contributed decisively to elevated the metropolis in Rhein-Main to be the Internet capital of Germany. The VentureLab, also based in the East of Frankfurt in Hanauer Landstraße, initiated and supported by venture capital societies under the central coordination of IVC Venture Capital AG, is the largest breeding ground for start-up companies in Germany. The initiative is supported by the Association of German Internet Economy, by the Internet founder club Silicon City Club, by the Federal Ministry for Economy and Technology, by the European Business School, the Wissenschaftliche Hochschule für Unternehmensführung (Scientific Higher School of Management) and the University of Frankfurt (professorship of e-commerce).

The VentureLab has received a starting capital of a two-digit million amount, which are collected by clever young entrepreneurs with good ideas. Almost more important than the money are the ready-made infrastructure and the network of contacts of VentureLab. The up and coming independent businessman practically receives everything he needs for success and normally is very time-consuming in the starting phase. From day one he sits in a top-furnished office and is op-

erating a technically stable computer network that is directly connected to the DE-CIX in the IEC (approx. 200 m air-line). The founders can dispose in the VentureLab of lawyers, tax consultants and auditors, sales and marketing specialists "at the push of a button". Regularly, First Tuesday, Young Entrepreneurs Organization (YEO), Silicon City Club, Business Founders' and Forums for Young Entrepreneurs m-e-x and many other economic associations of the New Economy visit the VentureLab in Hanauer Landstraße. Infrastructure and Start-ups together manifest the excellent position of Frankfurt on the Main in the German Internet market.

Today, much more than 80 percent of the national Internet traffic in Germany is routed via the IEC-based DE-CIX.

At the Interxion Internet Exchange Center (IEC) in the East of Frankfurt, in the area of the Hanauer Landstraße, today more Internet networks come together than at any other point in Germany. Participation in the DE-CIX is open to all professional Internet service providers, if they meet the technical and qualitative conditions for connection. The VentureLab has received a starting capital of a two-digit million amount, which are collected by clever young entrepreneurs with good ideas. ∎

Die Basis für eine optimale Nutzung moderner Telekommunikation weltweit

The Basis for an optimal use of Modern Telecommunication World Wide

Weithin über Frankfurts Dächern sichtbar: das Logo der Deutschen Telekom AG.
Far visible beyond the roofs of Frankfurt: the logo of Deutsche Telekom AG.

Bundesweit sind 172.000 Mitarbeiter bei der Deutschen Telekom AG beschäftigt.

Nationally there are 172.000 employees working for Deutsche Telekom AG.

Mit ihrer hochleistungsfähigen Netz-Infrastruktur bietet die Deutsche Telekom für Wirtschaft und Privat die Basis zur optimalen Nutzung moderner Telekommunikation im Inland und rund um den Globus. Dazu wird speziell in Frankfurt die Qualität der internationalen Netzverbindungen zu 300 Carriern in 222 Ländern im neuerrichteten „International Net Management Center" rund um die Uhr zentral gesteuert und überwacht.

Mit der Errichtung von Infrastrukturen zu vollcomputerisierten Breitbandnetzen nimmt die Deutsche Telekom weltweit eine Spitzenposition unter den Telekommunikationsanbietern ein. Beispiele dafür sind das Zusammenführen von Festnetz und Mobilnetz, die Verwandlung des Anschlussnetzes mit DSL-Technologien in eine

breitbandige Auffahrtrampe zum globalen Infohighway oder die neuen Gigabit-Übertragungsverfahren auf Glasfaser. Eine Vielzahl internationaler Unternehmen sind Kooperationspartner der Frankfurter Deutschen Telekom. Ebenso wichtig sind für den Wirtschafts- und Finanzplatz Frankfurt die innovativen Anwendungen. Mit der Zielsetzung „Mehrwert durch Konvergenz" legt die Telekom die Basis für mehr Produktivität in der Frankfurter Wirtschaft, neue Problemlösungen für die Gesellschaft und mehr Lebensqualität für jeden Einzelnen.

Insgesamt sind für Kundenbetreuung, Vertrieb, Service und Netzausbau cirka 4.800 Telekom-MitarbeiterInnen in Frankfurt tätig. Elf im Stadtgebiet stationierte T-Punkte sind Anlaufstellen für Beratung und Kauf von Endgeräten, Diensten und Leistungen aus dem Angebotsspektrum

der Deutschen Telekom. Zudem vermitteln spezielle Teams den rund 30.000 Geschäfts- und 550.000 Privatkunden praxisnah die Vielfalt elektronischer Bürokommunikation mit modernen Komplettlösungen.

Frankfurt ist auch zentraler Sitz der Telekomtöchter T-Systems und DeTeMedien. ∎

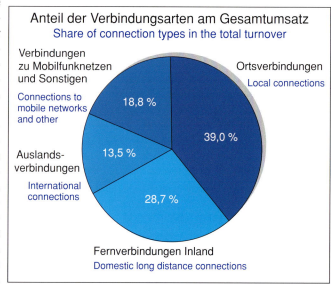

Anteil der Verbindungsarten am Gesamtumsatz
Share of connection types in the total turnover

Verbindungen zu Mobilfunknetzen und Sonstigen
Connections to mobile networks and other

Ortsverbindungen
Local connections

18,8 %

39,0 %

Auslandsverbindungen
International connections

13,5 %

28,7 %

Fernverbindungen Inland
Domestic long distance connections

Im „International Net Management Center" in Frankfurt wird die Qualität der internationalen Netzverbindungen zu 300 Carriern in 222 Ländern gesteuert und überwacht.

In the "International Net Management Center" network connections to 300 carriers in 222 countries are centrally managed and supervised.

With its high-performance network infrastructure the Deutsche Telekom offers for economy and private industry the basis for an optimal use of modern telecommunication domestically and around the globe. For this purpose, the quality of international network connections to 300 carriers in 222 countries is centrally managed and supervised in the newly-built "International Net Management Center" around the clock, especially in Frankfurt.

In der Qualität, Leistungsfähigkeit und Effizienz ihres Netzes sieht die Deutsche Telekom einen der wichtigsten Faktoren für die Informationsgesellschaft von morgen.

In the quality, performance and efficiency of its network the Deutsche Telekom sees one of its most important factors for tomorrow's information society.

With the establishment of infrastructures for fully computerised broadband networks Deutsche Telekom is holding a top position among telecommunication providers world wide.

As examples can be mentioned the merger of stationary and mobile telecommunication networks, the change of the lead network with DSL-technologies into an broadband platform for a global info highway or the new gigabyte -transfer methods via glass fibre. A number of international enterprises are co-operating partners of the Frankfurt-based Deutsche Telekom. Just as important for Frankfurt as a business and finance location are the innovative applications. Having set the objective of "added value through convergence", Telekom has laid the basis for increased productivity in the Frankfurt economy, new solutions for the problems of society and more quality of life for each individual.

In total, approx. 4.800 Telekom employees work for customer services, sales and network expansion in Frankfurt. Eleven T-Points located in the inner city are points of approach for consultation and the sale of end equipment, services and products of the spectrum of provisions of the Deutsche Telekom. Furthermore, special teams convey to around 30.000 business and 550.000 private customers the diversity of electronic office communication with modern comprehensive solutions in a way near to actual practice.

Frankfurt is also seat of the Telekom dependencies T-Systems and DeTeMedien. ∎

Deutsche Telekom

Deutsche Telekom AG

Vorstand/Board:
Dr. Ron Sommer (Vorsitzender/Chairman),
Josef Brauner, Detlev Buchal,
Dr. Karl-Gerhard Eick,
Jeffrey A. Hedberg,
Dr. Hagen Hultzsch,
Dr. Heinz Klinkhammer,
Dipl.-Ing. Gerhard Tenzer

Gründungsjahr/Year of Foundation:
1990

Mitarbeiter/Employees:
172.000 (Deutsche Telekom AG bundesweit)
172.000 (Deutsche Telekom AG Germany)

Geschäftsfelder/Fields of Business:
Netzkommunikation/Network Communication,
Carrier-Service/Carrier-Service,
Datenkommunikation/Data Communication,
Mobilkommunikation/Mobile Communication

Mehrwertdienste/Value-added Services:
Rundfunk und Breitbandkabel,
Endgeräte, Auslandsgeschäft
radio and broadband cable,
End Equipments, Foreign Business

Anschrift/Address:
Kundenniederlassung Deutsche Telekom AG
Emil-von-Behring-Str. 8–14
D-60439 Frankfurt am Main
Telefon   +49 (69) 909-30
Telefax   +49 (69) 909-332 99
Internet   www.telekom.de

Auf Kundenanliegen wird sofort reagiert.

We react immediately to requests of customers.

Breitband Business Lösungen für die Unternehmen Europas

Broadband Business Solutions for Europe´s Entrepreneurs

Priority Telecom ist einer der führenden europäischen Anbieter von Breitband Daten-, Internet- und Sprachlösungen. Mit seiner lokalen, nationalen und internationalen Netzwerk-Infrastruktur erfüllt Priority Telecom die Kommunikationsbedürfnisse von kleinen und mittelständischen Unternehmen, nationalen und internationalen Konzernen, sowie ISPs (Internet Service Providern), ASPs (Application Service Providern), Multimedia Content Anbietern und anderen Netzwerk Service Betreibern.

Priority Telecom offeriert ein umfassendes Produktportfolio, welches durch weitreichende Erfahrung im Kundenservice abgerundet wird. Unsere Breitband-Kapazitäten basieren auf einer starken Kombination von lokalen Verbindungen und globaler IP Netzwerk-Abdeckung. Mit Sitz in Amsterdam und über 20 regionalen Büros in Europa, Nord-Amerika und Asien bietet Priority Telecom Netzwerkdienstleistungen über drei Kontinente hinweg an.

Wir von Priority Telecom sind davon überzeugt, dass Breitband-Verfügbarkeit, verbunden mit der richtigen Kommunikationslösung, der Schlüssel zur Wettbewerbsfähigkeit auf dem zukünftigen globalen Marktplatz ist. Gleichzeitige Kontrolle des Backbones und der „last mile" sind die wichtigsten Elemente, um die Qualität und Zuverlässigkeit liefern zu können, die Unternehmen für ihre unternehmenskritischen Anwendungen benötigen.

• Weitreichende Glasfaser- und koaxiale lokale Netzwerke, zusammen mit einer globalen Telekommunikationsinfrastruktur, erlauben Priority Telecom die Bereitstellung von „end-to-end" Dienstleistungen über ganz Europa hinweg.
• Priority Telecoms erfahrene Account-Teams erarbeiten gemeinsam mit ihren Kunden Lösungen, die deren Geschäftsmodelle optimal unterstützen.
• Ein starkes Management Team mit umfangreicher internationaler Fachkenntnis und hervorragenden Referenzen in der Entwicklung von nationalen und internationalen Kommunikationsunternehmen gewährleistet die Auswahl der besten verfügbaren Lösungen. Chris Rooney, Vorstandsvorsitzender der Priority Telecom, hat z. B. diese Aufgabe vorher bei Cignal Global Communications und bei Global One wahrgenommen.

Internationale Reichweite

Priority Telecoms globales Netzwerk ist mit über 120 anderen IP Backbone-Carrier und Web-Hosting Unternehmen und mit über zehn großen Internet Austauschpunkten, unter anderem dem DE-CIX in Frankfurt, LINX in London, AMSIX in Amsterdam, NYIX in New York, HKIX in Hongkong verbunden. Das Netzwerk ist ferner privat und direkt mit den größten IP Backbone-Carrier der Welt – unter anderem UUnet, GTE, C&W und KpnQwest – verbunden. Diese direkten Verbindungen ermöglichen die Übermittlung von Daten an die Mehrzahl aller Internetadressen, ohne eventuell auftretende Überlastungs- und Performanceprobleme, wie sie an den öffentlichen Internet Austauschpunkten auftreten können, aufzuweisen. Das globale Netzwerk von Priority Telecom unterstützt alle Typen von Breitband Interfaces bis zu STM-4 und STM-16. Neben Frankfurt betreibt Priority Telecom lokale POPs in Düsseldorf, Hamburg und noch in diesem Jahr auch in Berlin.

In Deutschland wurde das Priority Telecom Netzwerk im September 1999 in Betrieb genommen. Frankfurt wurde als deutsche Hauptniederlassung für internationale Netzwerkdienstleistungen gewählt, da es Zentrum einer der produktivsten und dynamischsten Regionen in Europa und Hauptschnittstelle für alle wichtigen Datennetzwerke ist.

Lokaler Fokus durch Priority Telekoms Citynetze

Priority Telecoms Citynetze bieten zur Zeit Breitband-Dienstleistungen für Kunden in Österreich, den Niederlanden, Frankreich, Spanien und Norwegen an. Die Expansion in neue Märkte umfasst in diesem Jahr Deutschland, Schweden, Slowakei und Ungarn. In Deutschland liegt der Fokus im ersten Schritt auf Berlin.

Unser Netzwerk

• STM-4 und STM-16 IP/ATM Backbone mit 7 Gigabyte IP Kapazität.
• 24 Backbone POPs, welche drei Kontinente verbinden.
• Verbindungen mit über 120 IP Backbone-Carrier und Web-Hosting Unternehmen sowie Verbindungen an über 10 öffentlichen Internet Austauschpunkten.
• Exklusiver Zugang zu 12.000 km „last mile"-City Glasfaser-Netzwerken und 36.800 km Koaxialkabeln für die Bereitstellung von Breitband-Geschäftsdienstleistungen durch unsere Muttergesellschaft UPC.

Produkte und Dienstleistungen

Priority Telecom bietet eine breite Palette hochwertiger und wettbewerbsfähiger Telekommunikationsdienstleistungen für kleine, mittelständische und große Unternehmen sowie Carriers, ISPs und ASPs an.

• IP Daten Services – Breitband Internet Zugang, LAN-zu-LAN Verbindungen, Voice over IP (VoIP), Virtual Private Networks (VPNs).
• Gemanagte Datendienste – nationale und internationale Mietleitungen, ATM, maßgeschneiderte Netzwerke.
• Sprachdienstleistungen für Geschäfts- und Privatkunden – ISDN und analog (ISDN Basisanschluss, ISDN Anlagen und analoge Anschlüsse) – sowie Call Center Dienstleistungen.
• Hosting von Application Service Providern (ASPs) und E-Mail Diensten, dedizierten und gemeinsam genutzten Servern sowie Mehrwertdienstleistungen.

■

Priority Telecom is a leading European provider of broadband data, Internet and voice solutions. With its IP-powered local, national and international network infrastructure Priority Telecom meets the communication needs of small to medium enterprises, national and international corporations, ISPs, ASPs, multimedia web content and other network service operators.

Priority Telecom offers a comprehensive range of products, supported by extensive service experience. Our broadband capability is based on a powerful combination of local connectivity and global IP network coverage. Headquartered in Amsterdam and located in over 20 regional offices across Europe, North America and Asia Priority Telecom provides network services throughout three continents.

At Priority Telecom we are convinced that broadband capacity coupled with the right communications solution is the key to competitiveness in tomorrow's business market place. Control of the backbone and the local last-mile component of the network are key elements in delivering the quality and reliability that businesses require for their "mission critical" applications.

- Extensive fibre and coaxial local networks combined with global connectivity enables delivery of end-to-end quality of service across Europe.
- Experienced and focused account teams work with customers to develop solutions that support their business.
- A strong management team with broad international expertise and a proven track record in developing national and international communications companies ensures selection of the best options available. The CEO of Priority Telecom, Chris Rooney, is the former CEO of Cignal Global Communications and was previously the CEO of Global One.

International Reach

Priority Telecom's global network interconnects with over 120 other IP backbone carriers and web hosting companies, and over 10 major Internet exchange points including the DE-CIX in Frankfurt, LINX in London, AMSIX in Amsterdam, NYIX in New York, HKIX in Hong Kong. The network also interconnects privately and directly to the largest backbone carriers in the world – including UUnet, GTE, C&W and KpnQwest. These direct connections enable us to transfer traffic to a majority of Internet routes without facing the congestion and performance issues common to public Internet exchange facilities. Priority's global network is accessible from 24 POPs and supports all types of broadband interfaces up to STM-4 and STM-16.

In Germany our network was launched in September 1999. Frankfurt was chosen as the German headquarter for the international network services because it is the center of one of the most productive and dynamic regions in Europe, positioned to be an important national as well as international location in the field of telecommunications. Frankfurt is a major intersection of all important data networks and has adopted a leading role in the admission of private cable networks in Germany. It is home to branches of all leading international telephone companies.

Furthermore Priority Telecom operates POPs in Dusseldorf, Hamburg and will shortly be launching in Berlin.

City Rings/Metropolitan Area Build

Priority Telecom currently offers broadband services to metropolitan customers in Austria, the Netherlands, France, Spain and Norway and is expanding to new markets including Germany, Sweden, Slovakia and Hungary within this year. In Germany our metropolitan coverage is focused on Berlin.

Our Network

- STM-4/-16 IP/ATM backbone with 7 gigabits of IP capacity.
- 24 backbone POPs connecting three continents.
- Interconnects with 10 major Internet exchanges points and over 120 other IP backbone carriers and web hosting companies.
- Exclusive access to 12,000 kms of last mile city fibre-optic network and 36,800 kms of coaxial cable for the provision of broadband business services through our parent company UPC.

Products and Services

Priority Telecom offers a broad range of highly competitive telecommunications services for businesses of all sizes.

- IP Data Services – Broadband Internet access, LAN connectivity, VoIP, IP VPN, Internet Gateway exchange.
- Managed Data – National and international private lines, ATM, custom networks
- Voice – Business Voice – BRI and analog; Corporate Voice – PRI and call centre services.
- Hosting – Application Service Provider and email hosting, dedicated and shared server hosting, value added services. ∎

Priority Telecom Germany GmbH

Vorstandsvorsitzender/CEO:
Chris Rooney

Geschäftsführer Deutschland/
General Manager Germany:
Wilfried Röttgers

Gründungsjahr/Year of Foundation:
1998

Mitarbeiter/Employees:
600 (weltweit/world wide), 12 (Frankfurt)

Geschäftätigkeit/Business Activity:
Priority Telecom ist einer der führenden europäischen Anbieter von Breitband Daten-, Internet- und Sprachlösungen für Geschäftskunden, ISPs, ASPs, Multimedia Content Anbietern und anderen Netzwerk Service Betreibern.
Priority Telecom is a leading European provider of broadband data, Internet and voice solutions to business customers, ISPs, ASPs and other network operators.

Anschrift/Address:
Hauptsitz/Headquarter:
Amsterdam, The Netherlands

Deutsche Hauptniederlassung/German Office:
Nibelungenplatz 3
D-60318 Frankfurt am Main
Telefon   +49 (69) 95 90 95-0
Telefax   +49 (69) 95 90 95-11
E-Mail   crose@prioritytelecom.com
Internet   www.prioritytelecom.com
            www.prioritytelecom.de

Chris Rooney CEO von Priority Telecom N.V.

Chris Rooney CEO of Priority Telecom N.V.

Kommunikationszentrum Frankfurt – das Kraftzentrum am Main

Frankfurt the Communication Centre –
The Power Centre on the Main

Die Werber in Frankfurt arbeiten für die Global Player, für die „Big Spender", auch „Blue Chips" genannt, sie denken für die Start-Up's der New Economy und sie helfen caritativen Gruppen, die gar kein Geld für Werbung haben.
Viele sind in großen, internationalen Network-Agenturen angestellt und auf ihren Visitenkarten stehen Titel wie „Grouphead", „Managing Supervisor", „Creative Director", Chief Executive Officer", „Chief Creative Officer", „Vice President". Andere gehen mit ihren Talenten in inhabergeführte Agenturen, wo es übersichtlicher zugeht und wo man als Kreativer entweder Texter oder Art Director ist. Wieder andere machen ihr eigenes Ding zu zweit oder zu dritt und jedes Agenturmitglied ist auch geschäftsführender Gesellschafter.

In Frankfurt sprudelt Kommunikation und Kreativität aus allen Ecken und Enden. Allein ca. 250 Werbe- und PR-Agenturen aller Größenordnungen gibt es in der Stadt, im Rhein/Main-Umland kommt noch einmal die gleiche Anzahl dazu. Unternehmen aus aller Welt steht eine Bandbreite an Kommunikationsunternehmen zur Verfügung, die keine Wünsche offen lässt.

Natürlich dominieren in einer Stadt, in der nach dem 2. Weltkrieg vor allem amerikanische Werbeagenturen den Wachstumsmotor anwarfen, die Großen der Branche: Im Jahr 1999 hatten neun der 25 umsatzstärksten Werbeagenturen ihren Hauptsitz in Frankfurt, eine weitere ist mit einer Niederlassung vertreten. Diese 10 Agenturen erwirtschafteten 1999 ca. 36 % des Gross-Income der Top 25 in Deutschland. Die Düsseldorfer Agenturen bewegen sich in der gleichen Größenordnung, mit Abstand folgen Hamburg und München.
Und die weltgrößten Werbeholdings sind durch die deutschen Töchter ihrer größten Agenturgruppen in Frankfurt vertreten.
Erweitert man den Blickwinkel auf die 200 umsatzstärksten Werbeagenturen Deutschlands, so finden sich 23 Agenturen bzw. Agenturgruppen in Frankfurt, die im Jahr 1999 mit 4.259 Mitarbeitern ein Gross-Income von 1.031 Mrd. Mark betreuten. Rechnet man die PR- und Mediaagenturen und die Produktionsfirmen für TV, Kino, Funk und Internet dazu, liegt das Umsatzvolumen nach meiner Schätzung bei 3 bis 4 Mrd. Mark.
Düsseldorf kommt mit 24 Agenturen und einem Gross-Income von 876,77 Mio. Mark auf den zweiten Platz, Hamburg ist mit 24 Agenturen unter den Top 200 mit 681,41 Mio. Mark. Gross-Income der drittstärkste Agenturstandort in Deutschland. Fazit: Frankfurt ist der produktivste Agenturplatz Deutschlands.

Heinz Huth

Der Autor ist Gesellschafter und Geschäftsführer der 1992 in Frankfurt am Main gegründeten Werbeagentur Huth + Wenzel. Nach dem Studium der Betriebswirtschaftslehre startete er seinen beruflichen Werdegang 1976 in der internationalen Werbeagentur J. W. Thompson. 1978 wechselte er zu der damals kleinen, aber ambitionierten TBWA. Die Agentur entwickelte sich in den folgenden Jahren zu einer der besten Kreativadressen und Heinz Huth vom Kundenberater zum Geschäftsführer. 1989 erfolgte dann ein Wechsel vom Main an die Alster zu Springer & Jacoby, der erfolgreichsten inhabergeführten Agentur Deutschlands. Der Aufenthalt in Hamburg bescherte nicht nur viele Marketing- und Kreativauszeichnungen, sondern auch die Vision, mit einer eigenen Agentur in der Heimat Frankfurt eine Alternative zu den internationalen Network-Agenturen schaffen zu können.

The author is managing associate and director of the advertising agency Huth + Wenzel founded in Frankfurt on the Main in 1992. After studying economics he started out his professional career in 1976 with the international advertising agency J. W. Thompson. In 1978 he joined the hitherto small but ambitious TBWA. This agency evolved in the following years into one of the first-class addresses for creative people and Mr. Heinz Huth developed from client consultant to managing director. He then moved from the river Main to the lake Alster in 1989, where he joined Springer & Jacoby, the most successful proprietor-led agency in Germany. His stay in Hamburg did not only gain him many marketing and creative prizes, but also the vision to be able to establish an alternative against the international network agencies with his own agency in his hometown Frankfurt.

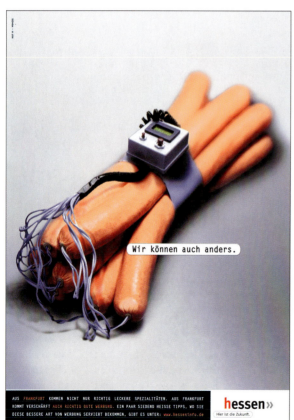

Die Siegeranzeige des Kreativwettbewerbs „Werbeagenturen in Hessen" 1999 (Agentur Huth + Wenzel).
The winning ad of the creative contest "advertising agencies in Hesse" 1999 (Agency Huth + Wenzel).

Advertisers in Frankfurt work for the global players, the 'big spenders' also called the "blue chips", they are doing the thinking for the business start-up of the new economy and they help charitable groups that have no money at all for advertising.

Many of these are employed in large international network agencies and on their business cards there are titles "Group head", "Managing Supervisor", "Creative Director", "Chief Executive Officer", "Chief Creative Officer", "Vice President". Others take their talents to proprietor-led agencies, where the work is clearly laid out and as a creative person one is either a copywriter or an art director. Others in turn, do their own thing with two or three partners and each member of the agency is a managing associate at the same time. In Frankfurt communication and creativity is bubbling all over the place. The city alone has approx. 250 advertising and PR agencies of all sizes, including the Rhein-Main suburbs this number can be doubled. Enterprises from the entire world can dispose of a broad range of communication companies that leave no wishes open.

Of course, in a city in which above all American advertising agencies were the driving force of the growth after the 2nd World war, the world leaders of this branch dominate the scene: in 1999 nine of the 25 best ranking advertising agencies had their headquarters in Frankfurt, one more is represented with a branch. These 10 agencies have achieved in 1999 approx. 36 % of the gross income of the Top 25 in Germany. The agencies of Düsseldorf are moving in the same categories, Hamburg and Munich follow with a distance.

And the German subsidiaries of their largest agency groups represent the world-largest holdings in advertising.

Extending the view on the 200 best ranking German advertising agencies, one can find 23 agencies or agency groups in Frankfurt that with 4.259 employees are in charge of 1.031 billion Marks in the year 1999. If one adds the PR and media agencies and the production companies for TV, cinema, radio and internet, the volume of turnover lies according to my estimates at 3 to 4 billion Marks. Düsseldorf holds with 24 agencies and a gross-income of 876,77 million Marks second place, Hamburg is with 24 agencies amongst the Top 200 with 681,41 million Marks gross-income the third strongest agency location in Germany. Conclusion: Frankfurt is the most productive agency location of Germany.

Also for PR-tasks is Frankfurt a first-class address and furthermore, an important centre for PR-association work and -training.

Siegeranzeige des Kreativwettbewerbs „Werbeagenturen in Hessen" 1998 (Agentur Huth + Wenzel).

The winning ad of the creative contest "advertising agencies in Hesse" 1998 (Agency Huth + Wenzel).

Frankfurt has been and is for companies that depend on communication attractive – which literally means "strongly appealing". Here, local, national and global companies have their communication made to measure, everyone find in the metropolis on the Main and in its surroundings the matching agency for his needs.

But if I speak of Frankfurt as a creative communication centre, not only the classical advertising and PR agencies are meant. A successful advertising city is unthinkable without an established, strong network of professional and creative com-

plementary and supply companies. For, also enterprises like for example the media agencies, casting, event and multimedia agencies, direct marketing and promotion agencies as well as market research companies contribute to achieve a creative end product as do also, of course, the camera people, photographers, sound studios, the speakers, the programmers and many more.

When I think of all these people I know: Frankfurt is part of a national and international network of communication. Because we do not only inspire ourselves but attract people and know-how – from

Auch für PR-Aufgaben ist Frankfurt eine erste Adresse, darüber hinaus bedeutendes Zentrum der PR-Verbandsarbeit und -Ausbildung.

Frankfurt war und ist für Unternehmen, die auf Kommunikation angewiesen sind attraktiv – was ja wörtlich übersetzt „anziehend" bedeutet. Lokale, nationale und globale Unternehmen lassen hier ihre Kommunikation maßschneidern, jeder findet in der Mainmetropole und drumherum die für seinen Bedarf passende Agentur.

Doch wenn ich vom kreativen Kommunikationszentrum Frankfurt spreche, sind nicht nur die klassischen Werbe- und PR-Agenturen gemeint. Eine erfolgreiche Werbestadt ist ohne ein etabliertes, starkes Netzwerk von professionellen und kreativen Ergänzungs- und Zulieferunternehmen nicht denkbar. Denn zum kreativen Endprodukt tragen auch Unternehmen wie z. B. die Mediaagenturen, die Casting-, Event- und Multimedia-Agenturen, die Direktmarketing- und Promotionagenturen aber auch die Marktforschungsunternehmen bei – und selbstverständlich die Film-, Video- und Internetproduktionsfirmen, die Regisseure, die Kameraleute, die Fotografen, die Tonstudios, die Sprecher , die Programmierer und viele andere.

Wenn ich an all diese Menschen denke, weiß ich: Frankfurt ist Teil eines nationalen und internationalen Netzwerks der Kommunikation. Denn wir schöpfen nicht nur aus uns selber, sondern ziehen Menschen und Know-how an – aus Hamburg, Düsseldorf, Stuttgart, Zürich, London, Paris, Mailand, New York, Rio de Janeiro und Kapstadt.

So hat es fast schon Tradition, dass immer wieder sehr gute Werber aus der Schweiz ihre etwas beschauliche Heimat verlassen und nach Frankfurt kommen, um sich an dieser aufregenden Stadt mit ihren Türmen, Ecken und Kanten zu reiben und kreativer zu werden. Unsere Partner für das kreative Produkt kommen aus der ganzen Welt in die internationalste Stadt Deutschlands: Menschen und Unternehmen, die nicht nur Zulieferer, sondern Quelle und bestimmende Faktoren für das sind, was ganz zum Schluss als Kommunikation herauskommt.

Die Rahmenbedingungen sind gut

Der Werbeberuf ist im Ansehen der jungen Generation gestiegen. Das mag daran liegen, dass die jungen Leute von heute mit permanenter Werbung aufgewachsen sind. Deshalb hat ein heller 25-jähriger heute ein umfassenderes Werbe- und Vermarktungsverständnis als mancher Fachmann vor 25 Jahren.

Die junge Generation hat Interesse an der Werbung und immer mehr bewerben sich in den Agenturen. Sie sind so flexibel wie neugierig, stellen die richtigen Fragen und sind nicht mit der erstbesten Antwort zufrieden. Und sie sind bereit, hart zu arbeiten. Aber es müssten mehr Ausbildungsplätze vorhanden sein, denn es wird jede Menge Nachwuchs gebraucht.

Die Kommunikationsbranche in Frankfurt ist eine immer schneller drehende Jobmaschine. Das wird auch noch viele Jahre so bleiben. Je ähnlicher sich die angebotenen Produkte und Dienstleistungen sind, desto mehr ist die Werbebranche gefordert, sie mit Kommunikation zu differenzieren. Auch aus diesem Grund hat sich bei den werbenden Unternehmen als gesicherte Erkenntnis durchgesetzt, dass Unernehmens- bzw. Marketingkommunikation ein wettbewerbs- und ertragsrelevanter Bestandteil des Marketing-Mix ist. Werbe-, PR- und Spezialagenturen werden zunehmend als Partner zur Erreichung von Marketing- und Werbezielen nicht nur ernstgenommen, sondern herausgefordert, weiter zu denken, nach vorne zu schauen, mutig zu sein. Das heißt: Es herrscht ein sehr förderliches Klima für Kreativität. Frankfurt und Rhein/Main ist dabei die Region, die, wegen ihrer Anzahl, Vielfalt und Qualität an Kommunikationsunternehmen hierfür das größte Potenzial besitzt.

Also: Die Macher sind da und das Klima ist positiv. Aber ist auch das Geld vorhanden? Es sieht ganz so aus. In Deutschland sind im ersten Quartal des Jahres 2000 allein die Investitionen in klassische Werbung gegenüber dem gleichen Zeitraum in 1999 um 13,6 % gestiegen. Auf 8,4 Mrd. Mark haben sich die Ausgaben für klassische Werbung erhöht, wobei der Automarkt die werbeintensivste Branche bleibt, gefolgt von den Massenmedien und der Telekommunikation als der neuen Nummer 3.

Es wird viel geworben. Die Stimmung der Agenturleiter befindet sich deshalb im grünen Bereich: Nach der Studie „Werbeklima II/2ooo" des Branchenfachblattes „werben & verkaufen" schätzen 97 % der Agenturleiter die Ertragsentwicklung als „gut" bis „sehr gut" ein. Sie erwarten für das Jahr 2000 ein Wachstum von rund 6 %, das wäre fast ein Prozentpunkt mehr als im Vorjahr (Quelle: GWA-Frühjahrsmonitor 2000)

Auch die Public Relations ist ein Wachstumsmarkt. Der Gesamtumsatz der rund 700 deutschen PR-Agenturen und -Berater wird auf rund 1 Mrd. Mark geschätzt, Tendenz weiterhin steigend. Insgesamt ist die Umsatz-Wachstumsrate der Kommunikationsbranche in Deutschland ungefähr doppelt so hoch wie die gesamtwirtschaftliche Entwicklung (Bruttoinlandsprodukt)

1994 wurde Huth + Wenzel zur Newcomer-Agentur des Jahres in Deutschland gewählt. 1998 und 99 gewann die Agentur zweimal den Kreativwettbewerb des Hessischen Wirtschaftsministeriums am Kommunikationsstandort Rhein/Main. Der Gewinn eines Marketingpreises für besonders effiziente Werbung, des Effie 1998, mit dem Kunden Miele zeigt, dass die 45 Mitarbeiter(innen) der Agentur keine selbstverliebten Kreativen sind. Zu den größeren Kunden der Agentur zählen auch Bertelsmann, Bloomberg, DaimlerChrysler, die KfW sowie Mercedes-Benz.

Ein Motiv aus der „Tageszeitungskampagne" des Jahres 1999 (Agentur Huth + Wenzel).

In 1994, Huth + Wenzel were elected "Newcomer-Agency of the Year" in Germany. In 1998 and 99, the agency won two times the competition for creatives of the Ministry of Economy for the State of Hesse at the communication location Rhein/Main. The award of a marketing prize for especially efficient advertising, the Effie 1998, with their client Miele, shows that the agency's 45 employees are creatives that are not in love with themselves. Among the major clients of the agency are also Bertelsmann, Bloomberg, DaimlerChrysler, the KfW as well as Mercedes-Benz.

One theme from the "Daily Newspaper Campaign" of the year 1999 (Agency Huth + Wenzel).

Hamburg, Düsseldorf, Stuttgart, Zurich, London, Paris, Milan, New York, Rio de Janeiro and Cape Town.

Thus, it is almost a tradition that again and again very good advertisers from Switzerland leave their somewhat quiet homeland and come to Frankfurt, to rub themselves against this exciting city with its tower peaks, bends and edges and to become more creative. Our partners for the creative product come from all over the world into the most international city of Germany: People and enterprises that are not just suppliers but a source and determining factor for the result that in the end emerges as communication.

Framework and conditions are good

The profession of advertising has risen in estimate with the young generation. This may be caused by the fact that young people today have grown up with permanent advertising. This is why today a bright 25-year-old has a more comprehensive understanding of advertising and marketing than some experts 25 years ago.

The young generation has great interest in advertising and more and more apply for jobs in agencies. They are just as flexible as curious, ask the right questions and are not satisfied with the first best answer. And they are willing to work hard. However, more training places should be available, because a lot of young blood is needed. The communication branch is an ever rapidly turning job machine. This situation is going to continue for many years. The more similar the offered products and services are, the greater is the challenge for the advertising branch to differentiate them with communication.

For this reason also, the advertising enterprises have realised with certainty that company and marketing communication is a competitive and profit related component of the marketing mix. Advertising, PR and specialist agencies are increasingly taken serious as partners for the achievement of marketing and advertising aims, and not only that, the are being challenged to think further, ahead and to be courageous. This means: There is a stimulating climate for creativity. Frankfurt and the Rhein-Main region possess because of their number, variety and quality of communication enterprises the greatest potential for this purpose.

Therefore: The makers are here and the climate is positive. But, is there also money available? It looks like it. In Germany in the first quarter of the

year 2000 alone the investments in classical advertising have risen against the same period of 1999 by 13,6 %. Expenditures for classical advertising have increased to 8,4 billion Marks, whereas the automobile branch remains the most intensively advertising, followed by the mass media and telecommunications as the new number 3.

There is a lot of advertising being done. The mood of agency heads is therefore in the green section: According to the survey "Advertising climate II/2000" of the specialist journal of the branch "werben & verkaufen" (advertising & selling) 97 % of agency heads estimate the development of profits to be "good" till "very good". They expect a growth for the year 2000 of around 6 %, which would be 1 percent point more than in the previous year (Source: GWA-Frühjahrsmonitor (spring monitor) 2000).

Also Public Relations is a growing market. The total turnover of the approx. 700 German PR-agencies and consultancies is estimated at around 1 billion Marks, having a rising tendency. In total, the turnover growth rate of the communication branch in Germany is approx. double as high as the total economic development (gross domestic product).

This shows: Communication is a higher than average factor of the economy. This is especially valid for Frankfurt on the Main as advertising city. In order to avoid a false impression: Although the mood is actually in the green section, it is not the fact that the agency heads of Frankfurt are celebrating on the opera square. They have to fight a hard battle – the challenges are:
- Cost pinch (profit on average under 2 %!)
- Eliminating competitors amongst agencies
- Competition of business locations (Berlin promotes the settlement of agencies in a most intensive way)
- State Regulations (Advertising Prohibition)
- Globalisation
- Competition with management consultancies
- Policies for small and medium sized businesses
- Lack of qualifies employees.

"Anything goes?" Yes, but ...

Times are moving faster nowadays. To a 25-year-old that does not mean anything, s/he lacks possibilities of comparison. But whoever has 20 or more years of experience feels that the pace has become speedier; that innovations happen fast, but sometimes disappear just as fast. Advertisers and agencies alike may fall into the temptation of

Ohne LASTER gibt's von allem zu wenig.

Imageanzeige des Bundesverbands Güterkraftverkehr und Logistik (Agentur Huth + Wenzel).
Image ad of the Federal Association of Cargo Transport and Logistics (Agency Huth + Wenzel).

Das zeigt: Kommunikation ist ein überdurchschnittlich starker Wirtschaftsfaktor. Für die Werbestadt Frankfurt am Main trifft das ganz besonders zu.

Damit kein falscher Eindruck entsteht: Obwohl sich die Stimmung im grünen Bereich befindet, ist es nicht so, dass die Frankfurter Agenturchefs auf dem Opernplatz feiern würden. Sie haben zu kämpfen – die Herausforderungen sind:

• Kostendruck (Rendite im Durchschnitt unter 2 %!)
• Verdrängungswettbewerb unter den Agenturen
• Standortwettbewerb (Berlin fördert die Ansiedlung von Agenturen auf intensivste Weise)
• Staatliche Reglementierung (Werbeverbote)
• Globalisierung
• Wettbewerb mit Unternehmensberatern
• Mittelstandspolitik
• Mangel an qualifizierten Mitarbeitern.

„Anything Goes?" Ja. Aber

Die Zeiten sind schnelllebiger geworden. Das sagt einem 25-Jährigen natürlich nichts, da fehlt es noch an der Vergleichsgröße. Aber wer 20 oder mehr Jahre Erfahrung hat, der spürt, dass das Tempo rasanter geworden ist; dass Neues schnell kommt, aber zum Teil auch schnell wieder verschwindet. Auf Werbungtreibende und Agenturen lauert hier die Versuchung des „kommunikativen Zappings": Eine Mischung aus Wettbewerbsdruck und Orientierungslosigkeit wird instrumentalisiert und als „Anything Goes" praktiziert. Manches Unternehmen zappt also von einer Strategie zur nächsten, von einer Werbeagentur zur anderen – alles ist irgendwie möglich, vieles wird pro-

biert. Und viele Agenturen zappen mit. Der Grund ist eine Art Gedächtnisverlust: Vor lauter Tempo und Veränderungen weiß man nicht mehr genau, wer man eigentlich ist und wo man steht. Also kann man auch nicht wissen, wohin man will.

Die Unternehmen, die ihre Marken ordentlich geführt und trotzdem frisch, auf der Höhe der Zeit sehen wollen, haben mit Frankfurter Agenturen meist Partner zur Seite, die nicht einfach kreativ an der Oberfläche surfen, sondern auch beratend an Marketingstrategien und Visionen mitarbeiten. Strategische Planung und integrierte Markenkommunikation sind in Frankfurt keine Trendthemen, sondern Arbeitsalltag.

„Anything Goes" heißt also richtig verstanden: Kundenberatern und Kreativen ist alles zu denken erlaubt, was den strategischen und kommunikativen Zielen des Kunden nützt und hilft, dessen Marke oder Dienstleistung positiv von anderen zu unterscheiden.

Es gibt viel zu tun

Die Märkte sind so agil wie nie. Wir leben und arbeiten in einer Zeit gigantischer Unternehmens-Fusionen und Start-ups von Firmen, deren Daseinszweck man sich vor fünf Jahren noch gar nicht vorstellen konnte. Alles bewegt sich, verändert sich, vieles ist neu und noch mehr wird anders. Einige Branchen sind beachtliche Newcomer in puncto Werbeausgaben: Internet- und Telekommunikationsunternehmen, aber auch Finanzdienstleister und Energieversorger. Auch die Werbewelt wird immer vielfältiger. Es geht bei der Kommunikation immer weniger darum, ob

hauptsächlich Print oder eher TV eingesetzt wird. Heute ist die ganze Bandbreite möglich – zwischen Verkaufsförderung und E-Commerce, zwischen Public Relations und Event-Marketing, zwischen Doppelseite und Homepage, zwischen Bannerwerbung und TV. Das bedeutet: Die Führungsaufgaben bei der Kommunikation werden in den Unternehmen und Agenturen immer wichtiger. In Folge dessen muss und wird es noch mehr und noch besser ausgebildete Menschen in der Kommunikationsbranche geben. Dabei hat der Standort Rhein/Main einen substanziellen Vorteil:

Frankfurt ist das Kommunikationszentrum Deutschlands

Will man sich erbsenzählerisch betätigen, könnte man sagen: Bezogen auf die Anzahl der Kommunikationsagenturen, deren Umsatz sowie deren Vielfalt und Leistungsbreite kann sich Frankfurt und Rhein/Main als Kommunikationszentrum Deutschlands bezeichnen. Hier gibt es mehr große, renommierte internationale Agenturen und mehr kleine und spezialisierte als irgendwo sonst in Deutschland. Aber es nützt nichts, wenn wir uns darauf ausruhen.

Man muss gerade dann auf ein Konto einzahlen, wenn die Zeiten gut sind. Einzahlen bedeutet: Mehr arbeiten für die Verbesserung der Standortqualität und mutiges Angehen von Visionen. Dafür können alle Beteiligten etwas tun. Zuerst die Kommunikationsunternehmen selbst – indem sie herausragende Werbung und Kommunikationsarbeit leisten, die eine Werbung für die Werbung aus Frankfurt ist.

Dann die werbetreibenden Unternehmen der Region, indem sie mehr Mut und Standortloyalität entwickeln und mit ihren regionalen oder nationalen Etats die erfahrenen und die jungen Kreativen ihrer Stadt herausfordern. Die werden sich liebend gerne darauf einlassen, weil das eine willkommene Alternative zu den häufigen Adaptionen internationaler Kampagnen ist. Und nicht zuletzt kann die Politik den Werbestandort Frankfurt stärken. Indem sie Chancen und Möglichkeiten der hiesigen Kommunikationsbranche erkennt und fördert: durch bessere Ausbildungsmöglichkeiten für junge Leute, die in eine Branche wollen, die selbst schlecht ausbildet. Die Werbebranche ist eine junge Branche, eine Branche, die von qualifizierten Einsteigern lebt und durch sie lebendig bleibt. Guter und ausreichend vorhandener Nachwuchs ist der Treibsatz für Wachstum. Und damit Basis für die Zukunft von Frankfurt als Kommunikationszentrum Deutschlands. ∎

"communicative zapping": A mixture of competitive pressure and having no sense of direction is being used as an instrument and practised as "anything goes". Some few enterprises are thus zapping from one strategy to the next, from one advertising agency to the other – everything is possible somehow and much is tried. And many agencies are joining the zapping. The reason is some kind of loss of memory: All the speed and changes make one forget who one is in reality and where one stands. Therefore one can also not know where one is heading.

Enterprises that manage their brands orderly and still fresh, that want to see them on top of time have in agencies located in Frankfurt mostly partners that not only surf creatively on the surface but that also co-operate in a consulting manner in marketing strategies and visions. Strategic planning and integrated brand communication are not trendy topics in Frankfurt but everyday work.

Therefore, "anything goes" means understood rightly: Consultants of clients and creative people are allowed to think anything that serves the strategic and communicative aims of the customer and helps him to differentiate his brand or service positively from others.

employed. Today the complete bandwidth is possible – between sales promotion and e-commerce, between public relations and event marketing, between double spread and homepage, between banner ads and TV. That means: management tasks in communication are becoming more and more important in enterprises and agencies. As a result, there will be even more and better-trained people in the communication branch in future. The business location Rhein-Main has a substantial advantage:

Frankfurt is the Communication Centre of Germany

If one wanted to be pernickety one could say: In relation to the number of communication agencies, their turnover as well as variety and service spectrum Frankfurt and the Rhein-Main region can called itself the Communication Centre of Germany. There are far more large, renowned international agencies and more small and specialised ones than anywhere in Germany. But it is of no good to us, if we sleep on this fact. One should especially pay into a good standing ac-

count when the going is good. Paying-in meaning: To work harder for the improvement of the business location quality and a courageous approach towards visions. All people involved can do something for this purpose. Firstly, the communication enterprises themselves – by providing outstanding advertising and communication work, that is an advertisement for advertising from Frankfurt. Then come, the enterprises in need of advertising in the region, by developing greater courage and loyalty to the business location and challenge the experienced as well as the young creative people of their town with their regional or national budgets. They will be glad to be part of it, because this is a welcome alternative to the frequent adaptations of international campaigns. And last but not least, the politics can strengthen the advertising location Frankfurt. In that they recognise chances and possibilities of the local communication branch and their promotion: by better training possibilities for young people that want to enter a certain branch, which does not offer good training itself. The advertising branch is a young branch, a branch, which lives from its qualified newcomers and stays vibrant through them. Good and large numbers of young people is the driving force for its growth. And thus basis for the future of Frankfurt as Communication Centre of Germany. ■

There is much to do

Markets are as agile as never. We live and work in time of gigantic corporate mergers and start-up of companies whose purpose of existence could not have been imagined even five years ago. Everything is moving, changing, so much is new and much more is becoming different. Some branches are impressive newcomers in respect of advertising expenditure: the internet and telecommunication enterprises, but also financial service providers and energy providers. Also the advertising world is becoming more and more diversified. The point of communication is becoming increasingly less, whether mainly print or rather TV is going to be

*Motiv aus der Imagekampagne der Kreditanstalt für Wiederaufbau „KfW"
(Agentur Huth + Wenzel).*

*Theme from the image campaign
the Kreditanstalt für Wiederaufbau, "KfW" (Agentur Huth + Wenzel).*

Online-Broking der neuen Generation

Online-Broking of the New Generation

**INVESTNET Deutschland
Trading-Software & Service GmbH**

Geschäftsführer Deutschland/
General Manager Germany:
Wolfgang Ebinger

Gründungsjahr in Deutschland/
Year of Foundation in Germany:
2000

Mitarbeiter insgesamt/Employees:
95

Weitere Niederlassungen/Branches:
in Italien, Spanien, Holland und Frankreich.
in Italy, Spain, The Netherlands and France.

Geschäftstätigkeit/Business Activity:
Application Service Provider für Banken,
Sparkassen und Broker im Bereich
Börseninformations- und Tradingsysteme.
Application Service Provider for banks,
savings institutes and brokers in the field of
stock exchange information and trading systems.

Anschrift/Address:
Hochstraße 49
D-60313 Frankfurt am Main
Telefon   +49 (69) 92 10 17-0
Telefax   +49 (69) 92 10 17-80
E-Mail   info.de@investbv.com
Internet   www.investnetwork.com

Alles auf einem Screen:
Kurse, Charts, News, Ordereingabe und Depot.
Everything is on one screen:
Prices, charts, news, order entry and account.

INVESTNET wurde 1998 in Italien gegründet. Nach erfolgreichem Start auf dem italienischen Markt ist INVESTNET nun mit seinem Börseninformations- und Tradingservice auf Expansionskurs in Europa. Die Märkte in Spanien, den Niederlanden, Frankreich, Belgien und Luxemburg werden derzeit erschlossen. Seit Mitte 2000 ist das paneuropäische Investoren-Netzwerk von INVESTNET auch am internationalen Bankplatz Frankfurt am Main präsent. Eine strategisch gute Wahl, da INVESTNET hier seinen potenziellen Kunden am nächsten ist: Banken, Sparkassen und Brokern.

Der Börseninformations- und Trading-Service von INVESTNET ermöglicht Privatkunden, was bisher nur professionellen Brokern vorbehalten war: den unmittelbaren Zugriff auf die elektronischen Börsenplätze in aller Welt. Der Anleger kann über seine Hausbank innerhalb von Sekunden Wertpapiere online kaufen und verkaufen. Auf einem Bildschirm sieht er automatisch aktualisierte Echtzeitkurse, Wirtschaftsnachrichten, Chartanalysen und seinen Depotauszug und kann seine Aufträge direkt in die Ordermaske eingeben. Mit Interactive Trading von INVESTNET bleiben die Anleger mobil. Handy und Laptop genügen für die Echtzeit-Verbindung zu den Weltbörsen.

Herzstück des Service ist das Rechenzentrum in Frankfurt am Main. Als Application Service Provider stellt das 18 köpfige Team um Geschäftsführer Wolfgang Ebinger seinen Partnern eine umfassende Infrastruktur inklusive aller notwendigen Serviceleistungen zur Verfügung. Banken, Sparkassen und Broker können innerhalb kürzester Zeit das Informations- und Handelssystem von INVESTNET im eigenen Haus einsetzen und ihren Kunden zur Verfügung stellen. ■

INVESTNET was established in 1998 in Italy. After a successful start on the Italian market, INVESTNET is now on a tour of expansion in Europe with its stock exchange information and trading service. The markets in Spain, The Netherlands, France, Belgium and Luxembourg are currently being explored. Since the middle of the year 2000, pan-European network of investors of INVESTNET is also present in the international banking centre of Frankfurt on the Main. A strategically excellent choice, since INVESTNET is here closest to its potential clients: banks, savings institutes and brokers.
The stock exchange information and trading service of INVESTNET provides its private clients with what was only possible hitherto to professional brokers: direct access to the electronic trading centres in the whole world. The investor can buy and sell online securities through his house bank within seconds. On one screen he sees automatically updated real-time market prices, economic news, chart analyses and his account statements and is able to enter his orders directly into the order mask. With interactive trading of INVESTNET investors stay mobile. Mobile phone and laptop are sufficient for a real-time connection to the stock exchange centres of the world.
Core piece of service is the computer centre in Frankfurt on the Main. Being an Application Service Provider, the team of 18 people around Managing Director Wolfgang Ebinger provides its partners a comprehensive infrastructure including all necessary service provisions. Banks, savings institutes and brokers can use the information and trading system of INVESTNET in their own house within the shortest possible time and provide it to their clients. ■

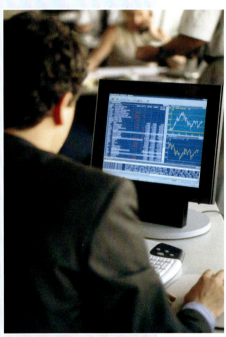

*Interactive Trading für Banken
und deren Kunden.*
*Interactive Trading for banks
and their customers.*

Interxion macht Frankfurt zur Internet-Hauptstadt

Interxion makes Frankfurt the Internet Capital

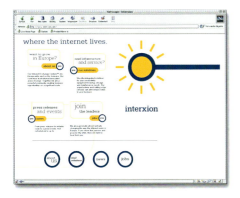

Interxion Telecom GmbH

Geschäftsführer/Managing Director:
Bart van den Dries,
Gerd Simon

Gründungsjahr/Year of Foundation: 1999

Mitarbeiter/Employees: 60

Standorte Deutschland/Locations in Germany:
• Frankfurt
• Düsseldorf
• München

Geschäftstätigkeit/Business Activity:
• Entwicklung und Betrieb
  von Internet Exchange Centers
• Integrierte Lösungen für
  Connectivity, Equipment Housing,
  Storage und Media Streaming
• Betriebsdienstleistungen u. a.
  Wartung von Netzwerkelementen
• Development and operation
  of Internet Exchange Centres
• Integrated solutions for connectivity,
  equipment housing,
  Storage and media streaming
• Operational services including
  maintenance of network elements

Zielgruppe/engl.:
• Carrier/Carrier
• ISP/ISP
• ASP/ASP
• E-Commerce-Anbieter/E-Commerce Providers
• Content Provider/Content Providers
• Mediengesellschaften/Media enterprises
• Webhostingfirmen/Web hosting companies

Anschrift/Address:
Hanauer Landstraße 312
D-60314 Frankfurt am Main
Telefon   +49 (69) 401 47-0
Telefax   +49 (69) 401 47-199
E-Mail   info@interxion.com
Internet www.interxion.com

The Interxion Telecom GmbH operates in Frankfurt on the Main one of its German Internet Exchange Centres (IEC). This forms the heart of the German Internet – around 85 percent of the complete Internet traffic in Germany flows through this Deutscher Commercial Internet Exchange (DE-CIX) located in the IEC. The IEC has made the Rhein-Main metropolis the "Internet Capital" of Germany.

Interxion, with headquarters in Amsterdam, develops and operates Internet Exchange Centres not only in Germany, but also almost all over Europe. All IEC-nodes are, as in Germany, connected with the networks of the large national and international telecommunication companies and the European Internet exchange nodes. Thus the IEC infrastructure forms a central basis for the complete European Internet. On the basis of the IEC facilities, Interxion offers integrated solutions for connectivity, equipment housing, storage and maintenance. Target groups are Internet service providers, eCommerce companies, contents providers, media enterprises and web hosting companies. Being an independent provider of highly scalable services of connection, Interxion enables its clients to connect their networks with exchange services on "neutral terrain". Interxion operates presently, apart from Frankfurt, also IEC Centres in Amsterdam, Brussels, Düsseldorf, Copenhagen, London, Madrid, Paris, Stockholm, Vienna and Zurich. In the near future, further IEC nodes will be opened in Dublin, Helsinki, Hilversum and Milan. Further information can be accessed under www.interxion.com. ∎

Die Interxion Telecom GmbH betreibt in Frankfurt am Main eines seiner deutschen Internet Exchange Center (IEC). Dieses bildet das „Herz" des deutschen Internet – rund 85 Prozent des gesamten Internetverkehrs Deutschlands fließt durch den im IEC beheimateten Deutschen Commercial Internet Exchange (DE-CIX). Das IEC macht die Rhein-Main-Metropole zur „Internet-Hauptstadt" Deutschlands.

Interxion mit Hauptquartier in Amsterdam entwickelt und betreibt die Internet Exchange Center nicht nur in Deutschland, sondern in beinahe ganz Europa. Alle IEC-Knoten sind wie in Deutschland mit den Netzen der großen nationalen und internationalen Telekommunikationsgesellschaften und den europäischen Internet-Austauschknoten verbunden. Damit bildet die IEC-Infrastruktur eine zentrale Grundlage für das gesamte europäische Internet. Auf Basis der IEC-Einrichtungen offeriert Interxion integrierte Lösungen für Connectivity, Equipment Housing, Storage und Wartung. Zielgruppe sind Internet-Diensteanbieter, E-Commerce-Firmen, Inhaltsanbieter, Mediengesellschaften und Webhostingfirmen. Als unabhängiger Anbieter von hochskalierbaren Verbindungsdiensten ermöglicht Interxion den Kunden die Verknüpfung ihrer Netze mit Austauschdiensten auf „neutralem Boden". Interxion betreibt derzeit neben Frankfurt auch IEC-Zentren in Amsterdam, Brüssel, Düsseldorf, Kopenhagen, London, Madrid, Paris, Stockholm, Wien und Zürich. In naher Zukunft werden weitere IEC-Knoten in Dublin, Helsinki, Hilversum und Mailand eröffnet. Weitere Informationen stehen unter www.interxion.com. ∎

Internet Exchange Center TM (IEC) ist ein Warenzeichen von Interxion.
Internet Exchange Center TM (IEC) is a trademark of Interxion.

Medienstadt Frankfurt – Zeitungen, Zeitschriften und Bücher für Deutschland

Frankfurt, City of the Media – Newspapers, Magazines and Books for Germany

Hans-Wolfgang Pfeifer

Vor einigen Jahren schrieb ein bekannter Unternehmer: „Wenn ich darüber nachdenke, was mir – dem in Berlin Geborenen und dem Land Bayern sehr Verbundenen – das Leben in Frankfurt anziehend und interessant erscheinen lässt, dann ist es das geistige Frankfurt, das liberal-kämpferische, das der Freiheit verpflichtete Frankfurt." Mancher mag stutzen: Gewiss, Frankfurt am Main ist eine lebhafte Handels- und Bankenstadt; es kann auf seine freiheitliche Tradition, auf Toleranz und Unvoreingenommenheit stolz sein. Aber ein „geistiges Frankfurt"?

In ihrer langen Geschichte hat die Stadt wenig getan, um mit ihren kulturellen Angeboten für die Wirtschaftsmetropole zu werben. Das ist schwer begreifbar. Denn sie sind ansehnlich und tragen Wesentliches zu dem freiheitlichen, kritischen und toleranten Geist der Bevölkerung bei, der Voraussetzung für erfolgreiches wirtschaftliches Handeln ist. Zudem braucht Wirtschaft die schöpferische Kraft und den Ideenreichtum von Menschen, die für die Kultur leben. Besonders das Verlagswesen spielt in der offiziellen Darstellung kaum eine Rolle. Auch dies ganz zu Unrecht. Denn Frankfurt am Main ist eine Stadt der Buch- und

Zeitschriftenverlage und der Zeitungsverlage. Ihre wirtschaftliche Bedeutung mag im Vergleich mit der des Flughafens, der Banken und der Börse geringer sein. Aber ihr politischer und kultureller Einfluß ist groß – weit über die Grenzen unseres Landes hinaus.

Seit dem überaus erfolgreichen Verkauf von Martin Luthers Druckschriften auf der Frankfurter Messe von 1520 entwickelte sich sehr rasch ein vielfältiges Verlagswesen mit Messrelationen, aus denen Tages- und Wochenzeitungen wurden, mit Flugschriften und Büchern und mit Druckereien. Kriege und die politischen Verhältnisse zerstörten zwar so manche Traditionslinie; aber auch heute gibt es in der Stadt Verlagsunternehmen, die eine lange Geschichte haben – die Brönner/Umschau-Gruppe oder die Frankfurter Societäts-Druckerei GmbH beispielsweise. Die Mehrzahl der rund 200 Verlagsunternehmen ist allerdings erst nach dem Zweiten Weltkrieg gegründet worden oder aus der damaligen Sowjetischen Besatzungszone hierher gekommen.

Heute werden rund 15 % der in Deutschland hergestellten Bücher in Frankfurt am Main verlegt –

Der Autor, geboren 1931 in Frankfurt am Main, war nach dem Studium der evangelischen Theologie und der Rechtswissenschaften zunächst als Rechtsanwalt tätig. Von 1968 bis 1994 war er Vorsitzender der Geschäftsführung, seitdem ist er Vorsitzender des Aufsichtsrats der Frankfurter Allgemeinen Zeitung GmbH. Er ist außerdem Vorsitzender des Aufsichtsrats der Deutschen Verlags-Anstalt und Mitglied mehrerer anderer Aufsichtsräte. Er ist Vorsitzender des Vorstands der Hessischen Kulturstiftung, Vorsitzender des Kuratoriums der Sektion Schauspiel des Frankfurter Patronatsvereins für die Städtischen Bühnen e. V. und Präsident der Frankfurter Gesellschaft für Handel, Industrie und Wissenschaft. Er wurde u. a. mit dem Großen Bundesverdienstkreuz mit Stern des Verdienstordens der Bundesrepublik Deutschland ausgezeichnet.

The author, born in 1931 in Frankfurt on the Main, worked at first as a lawyer, after studying evangelic theology and law. From 1968 till 1994 he was Chairman of the Management and since then Chairman of the Supervisory Council of the Frankfurter Allgemeine Zeitung GmbH. Furthermore, He is Chairman of the Supervisory Council of the German Publishing Institute and member of various other supervisory councils. He is Chairman of the Board of the Hessische Kulturstiftung (Cultural Foundation of Hesse), Chairman of the Board of Trustees of the Section Theatre of the Patronage Association of Frankfurt for Municipal Theatres and President of the Society of Commerce, Industry and Science. His awards include the Large Federal Cross of Merit with Star of the Order of Merit of the Federal Republic of Germany.

Projektion des FAZ-Logos auf das Hochhaus der Dresdner Bank.
Projection of the FAZ-logo onto the skyscraper of the Dresdner Bank.

70

Frankfurt / Main – Börsenplatz – Medienstandort.

Frankfurt / Main – Stock Exchange Centre – Location of the Media.

Some years ago an unknown entrepreneur wrote: „When I think about the things that make to me – born in Berlin and a lover of the region of Bavaria – life in Frankfurt seem attractive and interesting, then it is intellectual Frankfurt, the liberal fighting, the Frankfurt committed to freedom." Many may be astounded: Certainly, Frankfurt on the Main is a lively city of commerce and banks; it can be proud of its liberal tradition, its tolerance and impartiality. But an „intellectual Frankfurt"?

In its long history, the city has done little to promote itself as economic metropolis through its cultural offers. This can hardly be understood. For these are impressive and contribute considerably towards the liberal, critical and tolerant spirit of the population, a prerequisite for successful economic activities. Furthermore, economy needs the creative energy and richness in ideas from people that live for culture. Especially the publishing sec-

tor in official presentations does not play an important role. This is completely unfair. Because Frankfurt on the Main is a city of book and magazine and newspaper publishers. Its economic importance may be lesser in comparison with that of the airport, the banks and the stock exchange. But its political and cultural influence is great – and goes far beyond the limits of our country.

Since the tremendously successful sale of Martin Luther's printed publications on the Frankfurt fair of 1520, very rapidly a varied publishing system developed with connections to the fair that evolved to become daily and weekly newspapers, with pamphlets and books and with printers. Many lines in this tradition were destroyed by wars and political conditions; but even today there are publishing houses in the city that have a long history – the Brönner/Umschau Group or the Frankfurter Societäts-Printers GmbH, for example. The majority of around 200 publishing hous-

es, however, only were founded after the 2nd world war or moved here from the former Soviet occupation zone.

Today, around 15 % of books produced in Germany are published in Frankfurt on the Main – at the Aufbau-Verlag, the Büchergilde Gutenberg, Campus, Eichhorn, S. Fischer, the Frankfurter Verlagsanstalt, Insel, Fritz Knapp, Vittorio Klostermann, Suhrkamp of course, but also at the Societäts-Verlag, the book publishing section of the Frankfurter Allgemeine Zeitung (newspaper) GmbH, at Alibaba and many more. They attend to fiction and poetry, publish extraordinary reference and non-fiction books and are dedicated to books for children and for young people. Important literary developments began in the past and still do begin with books issued in Frankfurt. Almost all promote young writers and young journalists and give writers and publishers a platform for the transmission of their views and insights.

Auf der Frankfurter Buchmesse.

Visiting the Frankfurt Book Fair.

Druckmedien zählen auch einige Anzeigenblätter, die in hohen Auflagen verteilt werden, und Stadtteilzeitungen.

Mit der Verlagsgruppe Deutscher Fachverlag und mehreren Zeitschriftenverlagen nimmt Frankfurt am Main einen guten Platz auf dem Markt der Fachzeitschriften ein. Viele der insbesondere vom Deutschen Fachverlag verlegten Zeitschriften sind „Spitzentitel".

Zahlreiche weitere Verlagsunternehmen haben in der Stadt eine Niederlassung oder eine Repräsentanz – keineswegs nur der C.H. Beck Verlag, die Verlagsgruppe Handelsblatt, die Verlagsgruppe Milchstraße oder The Economist.

Die meisten der in Frankfurt ansässigen Zeitungs- und Zeitschriften-Verlage haben sich auf die Veränderungen in der sogenannten Informationsgesellschaft eingestellt. Sie bieten zur Erweiterung und Vertiefung ihrer publizistischen Angebote Informationen im Internet an und arbeiten mit dem Hessischen Rundfunk oder mit Hit Radio FFH zusammen. Auch insoweit sind sie führend.

Der Börsenverein des Deutschen Buchhandels, Journalisten- und Zeitungsverlegerverbände, Medieninstitute, die Deutsche Gesellschaft für Dokumentation, deutsche und ausländische Nachrichtenagenturen und anderen Verlagen nahestehende Organisationen haben die Stadt zum Zentrum ihrer Tätigkeit gewählt.

Die Verlage und die ihnen dienenden Unternehmen beschäftigen viele und besonders qualifizierte Menschen, die der Stadtkultur unentbehrliche Impulse geben.

Frankfurt am Main ist im Wettstreit der großen Städte auf die Medienunternehmen angewiesen, wenn die Stadt ihre Bedeutung behalten möchte. Sie sind ein wesentlicher Faktor im geistigen Leben der Stadt und das Ferment eines auch wirtschaftlich blühenden Gemeinwesens. Frankfurt am Main ist eben nicht nur die „City of the Euro". Frankfurt am Main ist auch die Medienstadt und die Stadt einer reichen Kultur. ■

beim Aufbau-Verlag, bei der Büchergilde Gutenberg, bei Campus, bei Eichborn, bei S. Fischer, bei der Frankfurter Verlagsanstalt, bei Insel, Fritz Knapp, Vittorio Klostermann, Suhrkamp natürlich, aber auch beim Societäts-Verlag, beim Buchverlag der Frankfurter Allgemeinen Zeitung GmbH, bei Alibaba und wie sie alle heißen. Sie pflegen die Belletristik, bringen bemerkenswerte Sach- und Fachbücher heraus und widmen sich dem Kinder- und Jugendbuch. Wesentliche literarische Entwicklungen begannen und beginnen mit Büchern Frankfurter Verlage. Fast alle fördern junge Schriftsteller und junge Journalisten und geben Schriftstellern und Publizisten Foren für die Vermittlung ihrer Ansichten und Einsichten. Ohne die Verlage wäre die Kultur in Frankfurt am Main ein „arm Ding".

Nicht von ungefähr ist hier alljährlich das Weltfest der Bücher, die Frankfurter Buchmesse. In der Paulskirche wird der Friedenspreis des Deutschen Buchhandels verliehen, im Römer der Wächterpreis der Tagespresse. Und die Deutsche Bibliothek hat auch deshalb hier einen Sitz, weil Frankfurt am Main eine Verlagsstadt ist. Das Literaturhaus ist zu einer Heimstatt für Literaturen geworden, die Autorinnen und Autoren anzieht, die sich ihren Frankfurter Verlagen verbunden fühlen oder ein immer

aufgeschlossenes Publikum suchen. Im Frankfurter Presse-Club versammeln sich nicht nur die für die Medien Tätigen. Er ist auch ein Forum für freimütige Diskussionen.

In kaum einer anderen Stadt der Welt erscheinen so zahlreiche selbständige und voneinander unabhängige Zeitungen wie in Frankfurt am Main. Die Frankfurter Rundschau, die Frankfurter Neue Presse, die Frankfurter Allgemeine Zeitung, die Frankfurter Allgemeine Sonntagszeitung, die Börsen-Zeitung und BILD Frankfurt verschaffen der Stadt im In- und Ausland Aufmerksamkeit und informieren in hoher journalistischer Qualität über die Stadt und das Land. Gleichzeitig geben sie Banken, Unternehmen und der mittelständischen Wirtschaft das publizistische Umfeld, das sie brauchen, um sich behaupten und entwickeln zu können.

Das vielfältige Zeitungsangebot wird durch Teilauflagen anderer Zeitungen erweitert, die hier hergestellt werden, der Financial Times, des Handelsblatts, der ZEIT, der englischen Ausgabe der F.A.Z., um nur einige zu nennen. Und unmittelbar vor den Toren der Stadt, in Zeppelinheim, werden zahlreiche ausländische Zeitungen redigiert und gedruckt. Zu den Frankfurter

Without publishers, culture in Frankfurt on the Main would be „a poor thing".

Not by chance does the yearly world feast of books, the Frankfurt Book Fair, take place here. In the St. Paul's cathedral the Peace Prize of the German Book Trade is awarded, in the Römer (town hall) the Wächterprize of the daily press. And the German Library also has its seat here, because Frankfurt on the Main is a publishing city. The House of Literature has become a home to literature that attracts male and female authors, which feel related to Frankfurt's publishing houses or always are looking for an open-minded public. In the Frankfurt Press Club, not only those people gather that are active in the media. It is also a forum for open discussions.

Hardly any other city in the world issues so many self-sufficient and from each other independent newspapers as Frankfurt on the Main. The Frankfurter Rundschau (daily), the Frankfurter Neue Presse (new press), the Frankfurter Allgemeine Zeitung (daily), the Frankfurter Allgemeine Sonntagszeitung (Sunday paper), the Börsen-Zeitung (financial paper) and BILD Frankfurt (tabloid) earn interest for the city domestically and abroad and inform in high journalistic quality about the city and the country. At the same time they provide banks, enterprises and the middle-sized businesses with the journalistic environment they need to be able to assert and to develop themselves in the market.

The various offers of newspapers are extended by partial circulations of other newspapers that are produced here, the Financial Times, the Handelsblatt (commercial paper), the ZEIT, the English edition of the F.A.Z., just to name a few. And immediately in front of the city gates in Zeppelinheim, numerous foreign newspapers are edited and printed. Amongst the printed media of Frankfurt there are also some newspaper advertisers that are distributed in high circulation numbers and district newspapers. With publishing group Deutscher Fachverlag and various newspaper publishers Frankfurt on the Main holds a good place on the market of specialist journal. Many of the published titles, especially those of the Deutscher Fachverlag, are „top titles".
Numerous other publishing companies have a branch or representation in the city – and not only the C.H. Beck Verlag, the Handelsblatt publishing group, the Milchstraße publishing group or The Economist.

Most of the newspaper and magazine publishers located in Frankfurt have adjusted to the changes in the so-called information society. They provide for extending and deepening their journalistic offers information in the Internet and work in co-operation with the Hessischer Rundfunk (radio station of Hesse) or with Hit Radio FFH. Also in this respect they are leading.
The Stock Exchange Association of the German Book Trade, Journalists and Newspaper Publishers Associations, Media Institutes, the German Society of Documentation, German and foreign news agencies and other organisations close to publishers have chose the city as the centre for their activities.

The publishers and the companies serving them employ many and especially qualified people that provide the city with indispensable impulses.

Frankfurt on the Main depends in the competition of the large cities on the media enterprises, if the city wants to maintain its importance. They are an essential factor in the intellectual life of the city and also ferment an economically flourishing society. Frankfurt on the Main is thus not only the „City of the Euro". Frankfurt on the Main is also the city of the media and city of a rich culture. ■

In der Frankfurter Messe.

In the Frankfurt fair.

Frankfurter Allgemeine Zeitung

F.A.Z.-Verlagsgebäude, Hellerhofstraße, Frankfurt.
F.A.Z. Publishing House, Hellerhofstraße, Frankfurt.

Mit der Gründung der Frankfurter Allgemeinen Zeitung, die am 1. November 1949 ihre erst Ausgabe herausbrachte, waren hohe Ansprüche verbunden. Mit der neuen Zeitung wollte man den „nachdenklichen Kreisen aus allen Berufen und Altersgruppen" eine geistige Heimat bieten. Die vorurteilsfreie Schilderung der Tatsachen und die Darstellung verschiedener Standpunkte und Meinungen bilden dafür die wesentliche Grundlage – damals wie heute. Der weltweite Ruf der F.A.Z. als meinungsbildendes Blatt zeigt, dass diese Ansprüche die Arbeit ihrer Macher bis heute erfolgreich prägen.

Gründungsgedanken

Seit ihrer Gründung legt die F.A.Z. größten Wert auf ihre Unabhängigkeit. Die Redaktion ist nur ihrem eigenen Gewissen verantwortlich. Sie verfolgt eine freiheitliche Linie und vertritt die soziale Marktwirtschaft. Dabei hält sie ihre Leser für urteilsfähig und lässt daher auch abweichende Meinungen zu Wort kommen. Dieses Prinzip der Meinungsvielfalt herrscht auch in den obersten Etagen der Zeitung: Hier legt nicht ein Chefredakteur die Position der F.A.Z. fest, sondern ein Gremium von fünf Herausgebern arbeitet nach dem Kollegialprinzip zusammen.

Wirtschaftlich autark

Um die wirtschaftliche Unabhängigkeit der F.A.Z. zu sichern, wurde 1959 die FAZIT-Stiftung gegründet. Sie hält bis heute die ausschlaggebende Mehrheit an der F.A.Z. GmbH. Die Erträge aus dieser Beteiligung kommen keinen Einzelpersonen zu, sondern müssen ausschließlich für gemeinnützige Zwecke verwendet werden. Aus ihren Mitteln fördert die FAZIT-Stiftung Forschungsvorhaben an deutschen Hochschulen oder die Ausbildung von Nachwuchskräften im Zeitungswesen.

Eine Zeitung, die jeder kennt

Die F.A.Z. ist nicht nur weltweit bekannt, sie unterhält auch Beziehungen in die ganze Welt. Ihr Korrespondentennetz ist größer als das der Times und der New York Times und liefert Eindrücke und fundierte Meldungen aus vielen Regionen der Erde. Dies ermöglicht eine Exklusivität, Aktualität und Kontinuität der Berichte und Kommentare, die kaum eine andere Zeitung weltweit für sich in Anspruch nehmen kann. Nicht umsonst genießt die F.A.Z. auch international einen hervorragenden Ruf. Aber die F.A.Z. importiert nicht nur Informationen, sie wird auch täglich in 148 Länder exportiert – sogar in so abgelegene Länder wie Kasachstan oder Papua-Neuguinea.

Logistische Höchstleistungen

Damit die F.A.Z. auch jeden Tag frisch bei ihren Lesern ankommt, muss so manches Hindernis überwunden werden. Nicht, dass es leicht wäre, sie zu schreiben, aber sie zu verteilen ist eine fast unmöglich scheinende Aufgabe: Bis zu 650.00 Exemplare müssen innerhalb weniger Stunden an Kioske und Abonnenten in aller Welt geliefert werden. Die Routen sind aufs kleinste von Logistikexperten ausgeklügelt, und der Aufwand lohnt: Die „Zeitung für Deutschland" ist wirklich überall in Deutschland zu haben. Selbst auf dem höchsten Punkt Deutschlands, der Zugspitze, gibt es die F.A.Z. druckfrisch ab 9.00 Uhr morgens.

Etwas Einmaliges aus Deutschland

Etwas ganz Besonderes in der publizistischen Landschaft Deutschlands ist die „F.A.Z. English Edition": Seit April 2000 können auch englischsprachige Leser eine der führenden überregionalen deutschen Tageszeitungen in ihrer Muttersprache lesen. Die achtseitige Ausgabe enthält ausgesuchte Texte aus der F.A.Z. und wird in Deutschland der International Herald Tribune beigelegt. Die macht nicht nur in 182 Ländern ihrem guten Ruf alle Ehre, sondern wird auch in Deutschland besonders gern von Mitarbeitern global operierender Unternehmen gelesen. ■

In der Frankfurter Societäts-Druckerei in Mörfelden-Walldorf wird die F.A.Z. gedruckt.
The F.A.Z. is printed in the Frankfurter Societäts-Druckerei in Mörfelden-Walldorf.

Demands of high standards were connected with the foundation of the Frankfurter Allgemeine Zeitung, which was published on 1st November 1949 for the first time. The new newspaper was designed to offer to "thoughtful circles from all professions and age groups" an intellectual home. Account of unprejudiced facts and the portrayal of various viewpoints and opinions are the fundamental basis for this – in those days and as it is today. The world-wide reputation of the F.A.Z. as an opinion-making paper shows that these demands still characterise successfully the work of their makers until today.

Principle Guiding Thoughts on Foundation
Since its foundation, the F.A.Z. maintains the utmost emphasis on its independence. The editors are only accountable to their own conscience. It follows a liberal line and also represents the social market economy. It regards its readers however as capable of judgement and allows diverting opinions to be heard. This principle of diversity in opinions is also prevalent in the upper floors of the newspaper: here does not stipulate only one chief editor the position of the F.A.Z., but a board of five publishers works together according to a co-operative principle.

Economically Self-sufficient
In order to ensure the economic independence of the F.A.Z. the FAZIT-Foundation was established in 1959. It holds till today the decisive majority of the F.A.Z. GmbH. Profits from this holding of equity capital do not go to any individual person, but must exclusively be used for charitable purposes. From these funds the FAZIT-Foundation supports research ventures at German universities or the training of young people in the newspaper sector.

A newspaper that everyone knows
The F.A.Z. is not only known worldwide, it also maintains contacts and relationships with the whole world. Its network of correspondents is larger than that of the Times and the New York Times and supplies impressions and well-founded reports from many regions of the world. This enables a kind of exclusiveness, relevance and continuity of reports and comments that can hardly be claimed by any other newspaper worldwide. Not for nothing does the F.A.Z. also enjoy internationally an excellent reputation. But the F.A.Z. does not only import information, it also exports daily into 148 countries – even into such remote countries like Kazakhstan or Papua-New Guinea.

Maximum Logistic Performance
For the F.A.Z. to arrive each day anew at its readers, many obstacles must be overcome. Not that it would be easy to write it, but to distribute it is an almost impossible seeming task: Up to 650.000 copies must be supplied within a few hours to kiosks and subscribers in the whole world. The routes are ingeniously mapped into the smallest detail by logistic experts and the work is worthwhile: The "Newspaper for Germany" can really be obtained everywhere in Germany. Even on the highest spot in Germany, the Zugspitze, the F.A.Z. can be bought fresh from the press from 9 a.m. onwards.

Something Unique from Germany
Something very special in the landscape of German publishing activities is the "F.A.Z. English Edition": Since April 2000, also English speaking readers can read one of the leading supraregional German daily newspapers in their mother tongue. The eight page edition contains selected texts taken from the F.A.Z. and is enclosed as supplement to the International Herald Tribune in Germany. It is not only honouring its good reputation in 182 countries, but is also especially well read amongst employees of globally operating companies in Germany. ∎

Frankfurter Allgemeine
ZEITUNG FÜR DEUTSCHLAND

Geschäftsführer/Manager:
Jochen Becker
Klaus Rudloff
Edmund Keferstein

**Vorsitzender des Aufsichtsrates/
Chairman of the Supervisory Board:**
Hans-Wolfgang Pfeifer

Gründungsjahr/Year of Foundation:
1949

Mitarbeiter/Employees:
1.315 festangestellte Mitarbeiter
  360 Redakteure
   77 Korrespondenten Inland
   47 Korrespondenten Ausland

1.315 permanent employees
  360 editors
   77 domestic correspondents
   47 correspondents abroad

Anschrift/Address:
Hellerhofstraße 2–4
D-60327 Frankfurt am Main
Internet www.FAZ.de
          www.FAZ.com
          www.FAZ.net

Mehr als fünf Tonnen Zeitungen werden werktags als Luftfracht transportiert, an den Wochenenden sind es mehr als elf Tonnen.

More than five tons of newspapers are transported as air cargo on weekdays, on weekends it is more than eleven tons.

CommerceBay

CommerceBay GmbH

Geschäftsführer/Manager:
Hassan El Manfalouty
Thoms Deininger

Gründungsjahr/Year of Foundation:
Juli 2000

Mitarbeiter/Employees:
5 Interne/4 Externe
(Stand Januar 2001)
5 internal/4 external
(status January 2001)

Geschäftstätigkeit/Business Activity:
Partner für unsere Kunden bei dem
Ausbau ihrer nationalen/internationalen
E-Commerce-Lösungen.
Partner for our customers in building
their national/international eCommerce
solutions.

Anschrift/Address:
Hamburger Allee 2–10
D-60486 Frankfurt am Main
Telefon   +49 (69) 7 92 04-0
Telefax   +49 (69) 70 04 86
E-Mail   info@commercebay.de
Internet www.commercebay.de

Warum gerade CommerceBay?

Why CommerceBay of all Others?

Heute stehen Großkonzerne wie mittelständische Unternehmen oder Kleinbetriebe gleichermaßen vor der Herausforderung, sich in der vom Internet veränderten Marktwirtschaft zu behaupten. Die Zeichen dieser Veränderungen könnten in den dramatischen Verschärfungen des Wettbewerbs, der Aufhebung der geografischen und physischen Marktgrenzen und der Abnahme der Kundenloyalität liegen. Der elektronische Handel über das Internet ist das Mittel, diesen Herausforderungen erfolgreich zu begegnen. Zwei Einsatzmöglichkeiten sind zu betrachten: Business To Consumer (B2C) und Business To Business (B2B). Wie es in dem Diagramm links unten zu sehen, sind die Geschäftsbeziehung A ein B2C und B ein B2B.

CommerceBay, ein neu gegründetes Unternehmen der Deininger Unternehmensberatung Gruppe, hat die Beratung und Unterstützung mittelständischer und kleiner Unternehmen bei dem Aufbau eine E-Commerce Lösung als Hauptziele definiert. Das Hauptgeschäftsfeld der Gesellschaft ist eBusiness Transformation Service. Dies umfasst Consulting- und Implementation-Dienstleistungen bei der Umstellung der bestehenden Geschäftsprozesse auf die Erfordernisse der New Economy.

Warum CommerceBay?
CommerceBay kann die Wirtschaftlichkeit einer eBusiness Lösung errechnen und die Ersparnisse für ein Unternehmen durch Zahlen belegen.
Das Unternehmen zeichnet sich aus durch:
• Ausgezeichnetes Branchen-Know-how durch Senior Business Consultants,
• eine eigene eSolution-Mannschaft für Umsetzung der Lösungen,
• Partnerschaft mit System-Management/ Content-Management Providers.
CommerceBay verfügt über eine eResearch Gruppe, die sich ständig mit der technologischen Entwicklung des Internets befasst. Bei der Konzeption und die Durchführung der Lösungen werden Produkte ausgewählt, die auf standardisierte Plattformen aufbauen.

Unser Ziel ist: Der richtige Partner für unsere Kunden bei dem Aufbau ihrer nationalen/internationalen E-Commerce-Lösungen. ∎

Today, large corporations as well as middle-sized enterprises or small companies have to face the same challenge of holding its stand within a market economy changed by the Internet. Signs of this change could be seen in the dramatic intensification of competition, the elimination of geographical and physical market limits and the demand of customer loyalty.

The electronic commerce via the Internet is a means to confront these challenges successfully. Two possible uses are to be considered: Business to Consumer (B2C) and Business-to-Business (B2B). As can be seen in the diagram below left, business relation A is a B2C and B a B2B.

CommerceBay, a newly founded enterprise of the Deininger Consulting Group, has defined the consultation and support of middle-sized and small enterprises in developing an e-commerce solution as main target. The main business field of the society is the eBusiness Transformation Service. This comprises Consulting and Implementation Services at transformation of existing business processes into the requirements of the New Economy.

Why CommerceBay?
CommerceBay is able to calculate the profitability of an eBusiness solution and prove the savings in figures for an enterprise. The company is distinguished because of:

• Excellent branch know-how of senior business consultants
• It's own eSolution team for implementation of the solutions
• Partnership with system-management/ content-management providers.

CommerceBay disposes of an eResearch group that is continuously engaged in following the technological developments of the Internet. At conception and when executing solutions, such products are selected that can build on standardised platforms.

Our aim is: The right partner for our customers in building their national/international eCommerce solutions. ∎

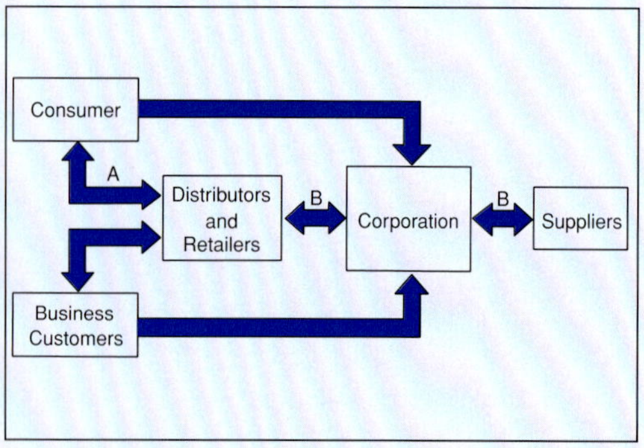

Deininger – internationale Beratungskompetenz

Deininger – International Consulting Competence

Die Deininger Unternehmensberatung GmbH, 1981 gegründet, gehört zu den fünf großen der in Deutschland ansässigen Personal- und Unternehmensberatungen. Ihr Unternehmenssitz ist Frankfurt, der Aktionsradius ist international. 1999 wurde in Berlin ein Büro eröffnet, 2000 in München. Auf Deiningers Beratungskompetenz setzen Unternehmen aus allen Sektoren der Wirtschaft. Die Stärken liegen in den Bereichen Finanzdienstleistungen, Industrie vom Mittelstand bis zum Global Player, Marketing und Handel, Telekommunikation, Medien, IT und Beratungen.

Deininger Unternehmensberatung sucht per Direktansprache Führungskräfte der ersten und zweiten Management-Ebene, Mitglieder von Aufsichts- und Beratungsgremien sowie Spezialisten in allen Hierarchien.

Das Wachstum geschah aus eigener Kraft und durch Gründung oder gezielten Erwerb von Beteiligungsunternehmen im In- und Ausland.

Das Umsatzvolumen der Deininger Gruppe stieg 1999 um 12,5 Prozent auf 71,3 Millionen DM bei einem Eigenkapital von über 5 Mio. DM. Diese Dynamik verdeutlicht den wirtschaftlichen Erfolg, ist aber vor allem Ausdruck des Vertrauens, das Deininger über die Jahre hinweg bei den Klienten aufgebaut hat. ∎

Gründliche Recherche vor jeder Beratung.
Thorough research before each consultancy.

Die Zertifizierung nach DIN EN ISO 9002.
Certification according to DIN EN ISO 9002.

The Deininger Unternehmensberatung GmbH, founded in 1981, is one of the five great personnel and management consulting companies in Germany. Its headquarters are in Frankfurt, its range of action is international. In 1999, an office was opened in Berlin and 2000 in Munich. Companies from all sectors of the economy rely on the consulting competence of Deininger. Its strength lies in the fields of financial services, industry from medium-size enterprises to the global players, marketing and trade, telecommunications, media, IT and consulting.

Deininger Unternehmensberatung searches by direct approach management personnel of the first and second hierarchical level, members of supervisory boards and consulting panels as well as specialists on all management levels.

The growth of the company is due to its own efforts and through the establishment of targeted acquisitions of direct investment companies domestically and abroad.

The turnover of the Deininger Group has risen in 1999 by 12,5 percent to 71,3 million DM, while owning capital resources of over 5 million DM. This dynamism demonstrates the economic success, but is as well a clear sign of confidence that Deininger has been able to develop over the years with its clients. ∎

DEININGER UNTERNEHMENSBERATUNG

Deininger Unternehmensberatung GmbH

Geschäftsführer/Manager:
Sabine von Anhalt
Richard Bensch
Thomas Deininger
Ernst Pálffy-Daun
Fred Dosenbach
Siegfried Lamprecht
Susanne Scherp
Dr. Markus Tschernig
Heide Winkler

Gründungsjahr/Year of Foundation:
1981

Umsatz/Turnover:
71,3 Mio. DM (1999)

Geschäftstätigkeit/Business Activity:
Personal- und Unternehmensberatung
Personnel and management consulting

Anschrift/Address:
Hamburger Alle 2–10
D-60486 Frankfurt am Main
Telefon   +49 (69) 79 20 40
Telefax   +49 (69) 70 04 86
E-mail   heide.winkler@deininger.de
Internet   www.deininger.de

Der Firmensitz in Frankfurt am Main.
Headquarters in Frankfurt on the Main.

Frankfurt –
ohne Sorgen auf dem Arbeitsmarkt?

Frankfurt – No Worries On The Labour Market?

In der FAZ vom 4. Mai 2000 erschienen zwei Artikel, die die Stimmungslage der Wirtschaft schon in der Überschrift wiedergeben. Die eine Überschrift lautete: „Um Frankfurt braucht man sich keine Sorgen zu machen, Frankfurt stockt auf". Der Autor dieses Artikels hat nicht nur beispielhaft die imponierende Zahl der Banken, die Silhouette der Hochhäuser, die vorgesehenen Neubauten der Wolkenkratzer, den Ausbau der Messe und des ICE-Bahnhofes sowie die Untertunnelung des Hauptbahnhofes und den Ausbau des Flughafens angesprochen, sondern in geradezu liebevoller Weise die Menschen beschrieben, die schroff und zugleich liebenswürdig sein können, die den Anspruch auf eine europäische Metropole erheben, aber in einem Dorf leben wollen. Diese Menschen waren und sind in ihrem Handeln an Wirtschaft, Handel und Finanzen aus-

gerichtet. Gleichzeitig waren und sind sie stolz auf ihren mit Mäzenatentum verbundenen Bürgersinn, auf ihr soziales Engagement und nicht zuletzt auf ihre Liberalität und Offenheit gegenüber den Fremden, den Menschen aus anderen Regionen und Ländern.

Die zweite Überschrift lautete: „Frankfurt soll internationales IT-Zentrum werden". Dieser Optimismus, diese Aufbruchstimmung zeigt sich auf dem Arbeitsmarkt bereits seit 1998. Nachdem ab 1992 die Arbeitslosigkeit auch in Frankfurt a.M. in die Höhe ging, ist die Zahl der Arbeitslosen von März 1998 bis März 2000 um über 20 % zurückgegangen. Es ist durchaus realistisch, bis März 2001 eine weitere Abnahme um 13 % zu prognostizieren, für 2003/2004 sogar einen Rückgang von 50 % gegenüber dem Höchststand von 1997 an-

Hans-Peter Griesheimer

Der Autor wurde 1941 in Berlin geboren. Er besuchte das Humanistische Gymnasium und studierte Rechtswissenschaften. Nach dem 2. Staatsexamen (1970) Eintritt in die Bundesanstalt für Arbeit, Personalreferent, Leiter der Abteilung Verwaltung im Landesarbeitsamt Hessen. Seit 1989 ist Hans-Peter Griesheimer Direktor des Arbeitsamtes Frankfurt am Main.

The author was born in 1941 in Berlin. He went to the Humanistic Grammar School and studied law. After the second state examination (1970) he joined the Bundesanstalt für Arbeit (State Department of Employment), Personnel Officer, Head of Department of Administration in the Regional Dept. of Employment of Hesse. Since 1989 Hans-Peter Griesheimer is Director of the Department of Employment of Frankfurt at the Main.

Auch durch zusätzliche Ausbildungsmaßnahmen ist die Arbeitslosigkeit in Frankfurt am Main zwischen März 1998 und März 2000 um mehr als 20 Prozent zurück gegangen.

Also through additional training measures unemployment has decreased in Frankfurt on the Main between March 1998 and March 2000 by more than 20 percent.

zunehmen. So haben wir in der Region Frankfurt a. M. trotz immer noch hohem Stand an Arbeitslosen, trotz hoher Investitionen in die berufliche Qualifizierung nicht erst seit heute das Problem, vorhandene Ausbildungs- wie Arbeitsplätze zu besetzen. Diese Entwicklung auf dem Arbeitsmarkt ging einher mit einer Umstrukturierung auf dem Arbeitsmarkt, sprich Abbau der industriell gewerblichen Arbeitsplätze zugunsten der oft zu pauschal umschriebenen Dienstleistungen. Gewinner dieses Prozesses sind seit Jahren die beratenden Tätigkeiten wie Rechts-, Finanz-, Unternehmensberatung und Zeitarbeitsunternehmen, aber auch Werbung sowie einfache Dienstleistungen wie Sicherheits- und Reinigungsdienste. Verbunden mit dieser Entwicklung ist ein weiterer

Das Frankfurter Arbeitsamt.

The Department of Employment in Frankfurt.

Arbeitsamtsdirektor Hans-Peter Griesheimer
in seinem Dienstzimmer.

*The Director of the Department of Employment
Mr. Hans-Peter Griesheimer in his office.*

The Frankfurter Allgemeine Zeitung (FAZ) of 4th May 2000 published two articles that convey the present mood of the economy. One heading read: "No need to worry about Frankfurt, Frankfurt is picking up". The author did not only refer excellently to the impressing number of banks, the silhouette of sky scrapers, the planned new constructions of sky scrapers, the enlargement of the fair and exhibition centre and the ICE-train station as well as the tunnelling of the main train station and the expansion of the airport, but he described in really loving terms the people of Frankfurt that can be rough and kind at the same time, that claim to be an European metropolis, but want to live in a village. These people have always tended to orient their actions towards economy, trade and finance. At the same time, they have always been proud of their middle-class way of life connected with their spirit of patronage, of their social engagement and, last not least, on their liberal nature and openness towards foreigners, the people from other regions and countries.

The second heading read: "Frankfurt shall become an international IT-centre". This optimism, this stimulating atmosphere is present on the labour market already since 1998. After unemployment began to rise from 1992 also in Frankfurt a. M., the number of unemployed persons decreased from march 1998 till March 2000 by over 20 %. It is quite realistic to presume a further reduction till March 2001 by 13 % and for 2003/2004 even a reduction of 50 % compared to the highest level of 1997. In the region of Frankfurt a. M. the problem of job placements for existing training- and work vacancies is not new, despite the continuing high rate of unemployed and the high investments into professional qualification through further education. This development on the labour market has happened in parallel with the re-structuring of the labour market that is the decrease of workplaces of industrial skills in favour of services often described in too general terms. Winners of this ongoing process have been for many years now the consulting services like law, finance and man-

Anstieg der Akademisierung, so dass Frankfurt neben München der Standort mit den höchsten Dienstleistungs- und Akademisierungsanteil in der Bundesrepublik Deutschland sein dürfte. Neben dem Dienstleistungsschwerpunkt und der Internationalität – Frankfurt beherbergt Menschen aus 160 Ländern – ist schließlich ein weiteres Spezifikum, dass der Arbeitsmarkt in Frankfurt aufgrund der Strukturen der Arbeitsplätze für Frauen Möglichkeiten wie kaum in einer anderen Stadt bietet.

Einer der Gewinner dieser rasanten Entwicklung ist die Kommunikationsbranche. Hier gebührt der Wirtschaftsförderungs GmbH hohe Anerkennung, wobei das Arbeitsamt bei der Erteilung von Arbeitserlaubnissen für IT-Fachkräfte sich nicht vorrangig als Wahrer der Ordnungspolitik, sondern als Teilchen der Pflege und der Ausweitung des Standortes Frankfurt für zukunftsorientierte Branchen verstanden hat. Neben der Diskussion um IT-Spezialisten zeichnet sich immer deutlicher ab, dass die Arbeitsplätze in der Frankfurter Region ohne einen arbeitsmarktorientierten Zuzug nicht zu besetzen sein werden. Nach einer Studie wird Frankfurt a.M. bis 2004 mehr als 17.000 zusätzliche Arbeitsplätze haben. Wenn man den Ausbau des Flughafens unterstellt, so kommen noch Tausende Arbeitsplätze hinzu. Die demographische Entwicklung ist bekannt. Schon in den letzten Jahren suchen wir junge Menschen in Thüringen und Mecklenburg, um Ausbildungsplätze zu besetzen. Ausbildungsplätze im IT-Bereich werden auch in diesem Jahr offen bleiben, weil qualifizierte junge Menschen attraktive Alternativen in Frankfurt finden. All dies zwingt zu der Schlussfolgerung, dass wir gerade für eine Region wie Frankfurt ein Einwanderungsgesetz brauchen, das die Erfordernisse des Arbeitsmarktes als Überschrift hat.

Bei aller Dynamik in der Wirtschaft und den Auswirkungen auf den Arbeitsmarkt sollen aber die Probleme, Sorgen und Ängste der Menschen, die den Anforderungen des Marktes nicht entsprechen, nicht vernachlässigt werden. Es muss Pflicht und Verantwortung der Gesellschaft bleiben, die Schwächeren, die trotz aller Hilfestellung auf dem Arbeitsmarkt nicht zu integrieren sind, nicht fallen zu lassen. Dies betrifft nicht die, die können, aber nicht wollen, sich Arbeitsangeboten verweigern. Hier müssen verstärkt leistungsrechtliche Konsequenzen gezogen werden. Für die Verlierer wie für Jüngere ohne Schulabschluss, für ältere Langzeitarbeitslose und Schwerbehinderte muss sich ein Standort wie Frankfurt mit seiner Wirtschaftskraft weiter sozial engagieren, Signale setzen, wie dies in den letzten Jahren in Zusammenarbeit zwischen Kommune, Arbeitsverwaltung, Trägern, Verbänden und Aktivitäten von sozial engagierten Menschen in der Stadt geschehen ist. Erst dann kann ich mich der Überschrift „Um Frankfurt braucht man sich keine Gedanken zu machen" anschließen, wobei es nicht schaden kann, wenn man dies immer mal wieder tut. ∎

Menschen aus 160 Ländern leben und arbeiten in Frankfurt am Main.
People from 160 countries life and work in Frankfurt.

agement consulting companies as well as temporary agencies, but also advertising and simple services such as security and cleaning services. Together with this development goes a further increase of the academic sector, so that Frankfurt possibly is, apart from Munich, the location with the highest share of service providers and academies in the Federal Republic of Germany. Besides the focus on services and international flair – Frankfurt is home to people from 160 countries – another specific characteristic of the Frankfurt labour market are the job vacancies, arising from the structure of its workplaces, offered to women as hardly another city has these great possibilities.

One of the winners of this rapid development is the communication sector. Much recognition should be given here to the Wirtschaftsförderung GmbH, whereby the issuing of work permits for IT-specialists has not been for the Department of Employment a question of keeping the legal policies, but one of contributing to the maintenance and expansion of Frankfurt as a location for future oriented branches. Besides the discussion around IT-specialists, there are increasing signs that workplaces in the Frankfurt region will not be able to be filled without labour market oriented immigration. A survey shows that Frankfurt a. M. will have more than 17.000 additional workplaces until 2004. If one presumes the expansion of the airport as well, thousands of workplaces can be added to this. The demographic development is known. Already in the last years, young people have been sought for filling training vacancies in Thuringia and Mecklenburg. Training vacancies in the IT-field will remain open also in this year, because qualified young people will find alternatives in Frankfurt. All this indisputably leads to the conclusion that we need, especially for a region like Frankfurt, an immigration law that deals with the requirements of the labour market as a main topic.

With all the dynamism in the economy and its effect on the labour market the problems, worries and fears of people that do not correspond with the requirements of the labour market shall not be disregarded. It must remain duty and responsibility of society not to let down the weak that despite all help and assistance cannot be integrated into the labour market. This does not refer to such people that can do something but do not want to, those that refuse to accept offers of work. These cases should be dealt with legal consequences in benefits. For the losers like the youth without a finished school education, for the long-term unemployed and disabled persons a location like Frankfurt has to continue to be socially engaged and set signals as it has been done in the last years in co-operation with the municipalities, employ-

ment authorities, supporting organizations, associations and the activities of socially engaged persons in the city. Only then, can I support the heading: "Do not worry about Frankfurt", whereby it would not do any harm if one did, every now and then. ∎

Frankfurt, bei Feinschmeckern auch bekannt durch die „Frankfurter Grüne Soße" und den „Äppelwoi", bietet Arbeitsplätze in wachsender Zahl auch in der Gastronomie.
Frankfurt, gourmets also know it because of the "Frankfurter Grüne Soße" and the "Äppelwoi" (apple cider) provides workplaces in growing numbers also in the hotel and restaurant business.

Amadeus AG
Personal-Dienstleister und Solution Provider
Personnel Services and Solution Provider

Leitung/Management:
Günter Spahn,
(Vorstandsvorsitzender/Chairman of the Board)
Peter Haas,
(Finanzvorstand/Member of the Board for Finance)

Gründungsjahr/Year of Foundation: 1990

Mitarbeiter/Employees: ca./appox. 750

Umsatz 1999/2000/Turnover: 67,1 Mio. DM

Geschäftstätigkeit/Business Activity:
Personal-Dienstleistung ausschließlich
mit kaufmännischen Fach- und
Führungskräften sowie Spezialisten
im Finanz- und Rechnungswesen
Personnel-Services exclusively with
specialists and management personnel
of commerce as well as specialist from
the finance and accounting sector

Niederlassungen/Branches in:
Frankfurt am Main, Düsseldorf, Hamburg, Berlin,
Köln, München, Stuttgart, Essen, Mannheim,
Hannover, Nürnberg, Bonn, Mainz, Krefeld,
Darmstadt, Amsterdam, Wien

Beteiligungen/Participations in:
FiRe AG – Zeitpersonalservice und Zeitmanagement
im Finanz- und Rechungswesen;
FIRE Outsourcing GmbH;
Amadeus IT Consulting – Komplettlösungen in SAP;
Steuer-Fachschule Endriss/
FiRe AG – Temporary Personnel Service and
Temporary Management in the Finance- and
Accounting Sector;
FIRE Outsourcing GmbH;
Amadeus IT Consulting –
Complete Solutions in SAP;
Vocational School for
Tax Consultants Endriss

Anschrift/Address:
Stresemannallee 30
D-60596 Frankfurt am Main
Telefon   +49 (69) 9 68 76-314
Telefax   +49 (69) 9 68 74-399
E-mail   Info@AmadeusAG.de
Internet   www.AmadeusAG.de

Umsatzkunden der Amadeus Gruppe
Turnover clients of the Amadeus Group

11,6 %

Xerox Gruppe
Pro Markt Holding
Coca Cola
DETE CSM
GE Compunet AG
Nokia
Ford Werke AG
DETE Immobilien
Sega Deutschland
Rockwell Automation

ca. 1.700 sonstige Kunden / 88,4 %
Approx 1,700 other clients / 88,4 %

Amadeus AG – Lieferant von Ergebnissen

Amadeus AG – Supplier of Results

Die Amadeus AG, Personal-Dienstleister und Solution Provider mit Hauptsitz in Frankfurt am Main, hat seit ihrer Gründung konsequent auf Spezialisierung gesetzt. Als erste Zeitarbeitsfirma bot sie zunächst ausschließlich Spezialisten im Finanz- und Rechungswesen an. Seit 1996 erweiterte sie die Dienstleistung um kaufmännische Fach- und Führungskräfte der Bereiche Vertrieb sowie Personal- und Beschaffungswesen.

Die Amadeus-Gruppe hat ihre Dienstleistung frühzeitig differenziert. Neben Zeitpersonalservice wurde mit der FiRe Outsourcing GmbH seit 1996 Interim- und Projekt-Management angeboten. Top Führungskräfte werden seither für anspruchsvolle Managementaufgaben bei Kunden eingesetzt: Von Aufbau eines internationalen Reportings wegen Firmenfusion, Übernahme des Controllings bei Beteiligungen, Unterstützung bei Reorganisationen oder als Personal- oder Vertriebsleiter sind Interim-Manager der Amadeus-Gruppe professionelle und effektive Dienstleister. In den Bereichen Zeitpersonalservice, Personalberatung und -vermittlung, sowie dem Qualitätssegment Interim-Management ist die Amadeus-Gruppe heute strategischer Partner führender Unternehmen der New- und der Old-Economy in fast allen Großstädten Deutschlands sowie Amsterdam und Wien.

Die Amadeus AG sieht ihre Positionierung am Markt als Lieferant von Ergebnissen im Kundeninteresse und nicht nur in der Bereitstellung von Human-Ressourcen. Die Wertschöpfungskette wird in sechs Stufen definiert: Zeitpersonalservice, Interim-/Projekt-Management, Stellenvermittlung, Unternehmensberatung, IT-Beratung, Personalberatung.

Mit dem Börsengang wurde 1999 der Grundstein gelegt, diese Wertschöpfungskette auszubauen. Seither wurden acht neue Standorte eröffnet und die Amadeus IT Consulting GmbH gegründet. Amadeus IT bietet Komplettlösungen im SAP Umfeld an und ist spezialisiert auf Implementierung, Customizing, Releasewechsel und die Entwicklung von kundenspezifischen SAP/R3® Add Ons. Über 20 hochqualifizierte IT-Spezialisten kommen bundesweit bei Kunden zum Einsatz.

Zum Januar 2001 wurde eine 60-prozentige Beteiligung an der Steuer-Fachschule Dr. H. W. Endriss vereinbart. ∎

The Amadeus AG, a human resource service company and solution provider with its headquarter in Frankfurt am Main, has consequently concentrated on specialisation since its foundation and being the first temporary staffing company offering exclusively experts in the field of finance and accounting. In 1996 services were extended in the commercial field and experts are supplied in the areas of sales support, marketing, personnel and logistics.

The Amadeus Group has diversified its services early. Besides services in temporary staffing, interim and project management services have been offered since 1996 with the opening of the FiRe Outsourcing GmbH. Since then Top Interim Managers are employed for demanding management tasks with clients: They can establish a reporting system according international standards, define a controlling system for direct investments, support a restructuring process or act as professional and effective Amadeus interim managers in areas like sales or personnel.

In the fields of temporary staffing services, personnel consulting and – recruitment as well as in the quality sector of interim management, the Amadeus Group has become a strategic partner of leading enterprises of the new and old Economy in almost all large cities of Germany as well as in Amsterdam and Vienna.

Amadeus AG is positioned in the market as a supplier of results to the client and not only as a supplier of human resources. The value chain is defined in six steps: temporary staffing services, interim-/project management, permanent placement/recruitment, management consultancy, IT-consultancy, Executive Search.

The Amadeus share was successfully placed in official trading on the Stock Exchange. The purpose of going public was to accelerate the groth and the development of the value chain. Since then, 8 new locations were opened and the Amadeus IT Consulting GmbH was established. Amadeus IT offers complete solutions in the SAP environment and is specialized in implementation, customizing and specific taylor made SAP/R3™ add-ons. Over 20 highly qualified IT-specialists are constantly on duty with clients nationally.

For January 2001, a 60 percent participation in the tax college Dr. H. W. Endriss has been agreed. ∎

Dienstleistungen in und an Gebäuden

Services in and for Buildings

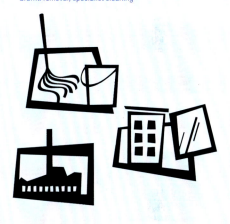

Die awell Dienstleistungs GmbH, eine eigenständige Niederlassung und awell MASTER OFFICE im Rhein-Main-Gebiet, mit Sitz in Eschborn, bietet Kunden aus Industrie, Handel, Banken, Kommunen und Behörden zuverlässige Pflege und Werterhaltung rund um deren Betriebe und Gebäude.

Der Anschluss an den bundesweiten awell Service Verbund brachte dem Unternehmen einen kräftigen Zuwachs an innovativem Know-how, Flexibilität und Effizienz aus mehr als 35 Jahren Erfahrung in der Gebäudereinigung. Qualitätssichernde Fort- und Weiterbildungsprogramme sorgen für eine gleichbleibend hohe Professionalität. Ziel von awell ist, dass sich die Mitarbeiter der Kunden in ihren Räumen wohlfühlen.

Durch die konsequente Umsetzung des Qualitätssicherungs-Systems garantiert awell, dass die vom Kunden gekaufte Sauberkeit auch in der zugesagten Qualität gründlich und pünktlich ausgeführt wird.

Wer Sauberkeit zum Wohlfühlen will und transparente Reinigungskosten wünscht, der sollte mit dem awell-Team sprechen. ∎

The awell Dienstleistungs GmbH, an independent branch of awell MASTER OFFICE in the Rhein-Main region, with headquarters in Eschborn, provides reliable care and upkeep of value to clients from industry, commerce, banks, communes and public authorities in all matters of their business enterprises and buildings.

Joining the nationwide awell Service Association brought the company a tremendous increase of innovative know-how, flexibility and efficiency from more than 35 years of experience in commercial cleaning. Quality ensuring further education programmes warrant a continuously high professionalism. It is the aim of awell that the employees of their clients feel comfortable in their work areas.

Through a consequent implementation of a quality assuring system awell guarantees that the cleanliness bought by the client is carried out thoroughly and punctually in the agreed quality.

Whoever wants cleanliness for comfort and wishes to receive transparent cleaning costs should talk to the awell-team. ∎

Handwerk – neue Anforderungen an ein traditionsreiches Gewerbe

*Skilled Trades & Crafts –
New Challenges on a Trade Rich in Traditions*

Frankfurt am Main ist mit 650.000 Einwohnern die fünftgrößte Stadt Deutschlands und eine der Wirtschaftsmetropolen Europas. In ihren Funktionen als Verkehrsdrehscheibe, als Finanzzentrum und als Messe- und Handelsplatz hat Frankfurt internationale Bedeutung. In diesem produktiven Umfeld von Unternehmen aller Größen und Branchen hat sich auch das Handwerk einen herausragenden Platz geschaffen. Von den 560.000 Menschen, die in Frankfurt arbeiten, sind 54.000 im Handwerk beschäftigt. Damit ist das Frankfurter Handwerk ein gewichtiger Beschäftigungsfaktor. Die 5.100 Frankfurter Handwerksbetriebe erwirtschaften jährlich einen Umsatz von 6,3 Milliarden DM (ohne Mehrwertsteuer). Durch seine Kunden- und Lierferverflech- tungen ist das Handwerk daher auch für andere Branchen ein entscheidender Wirtschaftsfaktor. Dazu kommt, dass vier von fünf handwerklich Beschäftigten im verarbeitenden Gewerbe tätig sind. Das Handwerk ist ein stabiler Wirtschaftsbereich, der Arbeitsplätze für Menschen mit gewerblich-technischen Qualifikationen anbietet, deren Beschäftigungschancen im Strukturwandel zur Dienstleistungsgesellschaft außerhalb des Handwerks immer ungünstiger werden. Ferner bietet das Handwerk jährlich mit etwa 3.200 Lehrstellen jungen Menschen mit gewerb-

lich-technischen Begabungen, die vom Strukturwandel immer mehr an den Rand gedrängt werden, durch eine zukunftsorientierte Ausbildung eine Chance zu beruflichem und gesellschaftlichem Aufstieg. Des weiteren ist die Rolle zu nennen, die das Handwerk für die Nahversorgung der Bevölkerung spielt. Genannt seien hier nur beispielhaft die in den einzelnen Stadtteilen ansässigen Bäckereien, Konditoreien, Fleischerbetriebe, aber auch Augenoptiker und chemischen Reinigungsbetriebe. Wer würde Heizungsanlagen installieren und den Innenausbau von Wohnhäusern vornehmen, wenn es das Handwerk nicht gäbe? Diese wenigen, in groben Strichen gezeichneten Sachverhalte belegen eindrucksvoll die wirtschaftliche und gesellschaftliche Bedeutung des Frankfurter Handwerks.

Starke Dienstleistungsorientierung der Frankfurter Wirtschaft problematisch für das Handwerk

International hat sich Frankfurt am Main vor allem als Banken- und Messestadt einen Namen gemacht. Diese Entwicklung wurde durch die Ansiedlung der Europäischen Zentralbank im Jahr 1998 bestätigt. Die Deutsche Bundesbank ist schon seit Jahrzehnten in Frankfurt zu Hause. Von den zehn größten deutschen Banken haben fünf ihren Sitz in Frankfurt. Ebenso ist Frankfurt am Main ein Zentrum der Kommunikationswirtschaft. Über alle Branchen gesehen arbeiten 80 Prozent der sozialversicherungspflichtig Beschäftigten im Dienstleistungssektor. Diese starke Dienstleistungsorientierung in der Stadt ist für das Handwerk nicht unproblematisch. Die starke Nachfrage nach Büroflächen hat die Grundstückspreise in Frankfurt am Main auf ein Niveau steigen lassen, das für Handwerksbetriebe nicht mehr rentabel ist. Gleichzeitig ist in den letzten Jahren in den Stadtteilen ein Vordringen von Bürobauten und eine verstärkte Wohnnutzung sowie die Umstrukturierung bisher gewerblich genutzter Standorte zu beobachten. Ferner reagiert die Nachbarschaft auch von alteingesessenen Handwerksbetrieben auf früher tolerierte und oft nur geringe Störungen durch Lärm und Geruch immer sensibler. Die von der Stadt verfolgte Politik der Verkehrsberuhigung trägt ebenfalls dazu bei, Handwerksbetriebe mehr und mehr aus ihren

Jürgen Heyne

Der Autor wurde 1938 in Frankfurt am Main geboren und absolvierte von 1954 bis 1957 eine Lehre im Fleischerhandwerk. 1963 legte er die Prüfung zum Fleischermeister ab und machte sich 1970 selbstständig. Seit 1984 gehört er der Vollversammlung und ab 1989 dem Vorstand der Handwerkskammer Rhein-Main an, deren Präsident er 1994 wurde. Seit 1999 ist er Präsident der Arbeitsgemeinschaft der Hessischen Handwerkskammern sowie des Hessischen Handwerkstages. 1999 wurde er zum Mitglied des Präsidiums des Zentralverbandes des Deutschen Handwerks gewählt. Außerdem ist er seit 1999 Stadtrat der Stadt Frankfurt am Main.

The author was born in 1938 in Frankfurt on the Main and completed an apprenticeship from 1954 to 1957 in the butcher crafts. In 1963 he passed his exams as a master butcher and became self-employed from 1970 on. Since 1984 he belonged to the assembly and from 1989 on to the board of the Chamber of Handicrafts Rhein-Main, whose president he became in 1994. Since 1999 he is President of the Working Group of Chambers of Handicrafts in Hesse as well as of the Parliament of Chambers of Handicrafts in Hesse. In 1999 he was elected Member of the Committee of Central Associations of German Handicrafts. Furthermore he is town counsellor of the City of Frankfurt on the Main since 1999.

angestammten Quartieren zu verdrängen, da sie von Kunden und Lieferanten nicht mehr erreicht werden können. Aufgrund dieser Entwicklung verlagern Handwerksbetriebe vermehrt ihren Sitz von Frankfurt ins Umland. Mit dem Verschwinden der Handwerksbetriebe mit ihren La-

Handwerkskammer Rhein-Main, Hauptverwaltung Frankfurt.
Chamber of Handicrafts Rhein-Main, Headquarters in Frankfurt.

With its 650.000 inhabitants, Frankfurt on the Main is the 5th largest city in Germany and one of the centres of the economy of Europe. Through its many functions as a turning wheel of transport, as financial centre and as exhibition and trading place Frankfurt has an international importance. In this productive environment of enterprises of all sizes and branches, also the skilled trades have been able to find an excellent place. Of the 560.000 people that work in Frankfurt, 54.000 are employed in the skilled trades. This makes the skilled trades of Frankfurt a weighty factor of employment. 5.100 skilled trades companies in Frankfurt account for a yearly turnover in sales of 6,3 billion DM (without VAT). Because of its customer and supply relations, the skilled trades are thus also an important economic factor for other branches. Added to this is the fact that four out of five persons employed in skilled trades work in the processing industry. The skilled trades is a very stable field of the economy that offers workplaces to persons with qualifications of manual skills and techniques whose employment possibilities are becoming increasingly unfavourable with the structural change into a service society happening outside the skilled trades. Furthermore, the skilled trades with around 3.200 apprenticeship places training young people with talents of manual skills, that are pushed more and more to the margin by the structural change, offers yearly through future-oriented training a chance for professional and social advancement. Furthermore, the role should be mentioned that the skilled trades plays for the immediate supply of the population. To mention just a few examples of trade located in the various boroughs of the city, like bakeries, confectioners, butchers as well as opticians and chemical cleaners. Who would install heating systems and carry out the interior decoration of living quarters if the skilled trades did not exist? These few facts drawn in rough outlines prove impressively the economic and social significance of skilled trades in Frankfurt.

The strong orientation towards service of the Frankfurt economy is a problem for the skilled trades

Internationally, Frankfurt on the Main has acquired fame as a banking and exhibition centre. This development has been strengthened by the establishment of the European Central Bank in the year 1998. The Federal Bank of Germany has had its main office in Frankfurt now for decades. Of the ten largest German banks, five have their headquarters in Frankfurt. There are a total of around 400 credit institutes in Frankfurt, of which approx. 240 are foreign. Frankfurt on the Main is also a centre of the communication sector. More than 250 advertising and PR agencies as well as 130 book and newspaper editorials and approx.

Zweiradmechaniker, bei jungen Männern ein besonders gefragter Ausbildungsberuf.
A two-wheel mechanic, for young men a very attractive job.

80 film production companies have settled in the city. With a view across all branches, 80 percent of the employees that are socially insured work in the service industry. This strong orientation towards the service sector in the city is not without problems for the skilled trades. The strong demand for office space has allowed the prices for real estate in Frankfurt on the Main to rise to such a level, that is not profitable for companies of the skilled trades. At the same time it can be observed in the last years that in the boroughs a penetration of office buildings and an increased used of living space is taking place as well as the re-structuring of hitherto commercially used locations. Also, the neighbourhood of even old-established skilled trades companies is reacting increasingly sensitive to noise and smells that was in earlier times tolerated and are often only small disturbances. The policy of subsiding traffic followed by the municipality also contributes to more and more displacement of skilled trades businesses from their traditional quarters, since they cannot be reached any longer by customers and suppliers. Because of this development skilled trades companies relocated increasingly from Frankfurt into the surrounding communities. The disappearance of skilled trades businesses and their shops, however, leads to a loss of attractiveness of the hitherto lively city boroughs. Nevertheless, Frankfurt on the Main is an important market for skilled trades services. This becomes especially clear, if one compares the sales and supply relations of the skilled trades of Frankfurt with the surrounding communities and also vice versa from the surrounding communities to Frankfurt.

Within the region of the Chamber of Commerce Rhein-Main one skilled trades business produces on average half of its turnover in the town or community it is based. Because of the great demand for skilled trades services that exists in Frankfurt, the companies of skilled trades that are seated in Frankfurt produce more than 70 percent of their turnover in Frankfurt itself. At the same time, Frankfurt on the Main is for the skilled trades companies located in the surrounding rural communities also an important sales market. For example, from the Main-Taunus-District, the Hoch(High)-Taunus-District and from Offenbach each third skilled trades business has clients to supply in Frankfurt and also in Darmstadt each fourth skilled trades business has clients in Frankfurt.

The role of foreign citizens working in skilled trades

Frankfurt on the Main has evolved into a city with a high rate of foreigners. For a smooth co-existence of the population the social integration of the foreign citizens is of central importance. In this respect, working life plays a decisive role. The co-operation between working colleagues in mutual tasks presents a social field in which common understanding and tolerance can be lived. This is of utmost importance to young people whose experiences in school and vocational training are formative for their further journey through life. The skilled trades sector is making, with a share of foreigners of 30,5 percent of all trainees, an important contribution to the professional and social integration of young foreign citizens. Furthermore,

dengeschäften verlieren bisher lebendige Stadtteile einen Teil ihrer Attraktivität. Dennoch ist Frankfurt am Main ein wichtiger Markt für handwerkliche Leistungen. Dies wird besonders deutlich, wenn man die Absatz- und Lieferbeziehungen der Frankfurter Handwerksbetriebe mit dem Umland und auch umgekehrt aus dem Umland nach Frankfurt hinein vergleicht.

Im Durchschnitt des Bezirks der Handwerkskammer Rhein-Main erwirtschaftet ein Handwerksbetrieb gut die Hälfte seines Umsatzes in der Stadt oder Gemeinde, in der er ansässig ist. Aufgrund der großen Nachfrage nach handwerklichen Leistungen, die in Frankfurt herrscht, erwirtschaften die in Frankfurt ansässigen Handwerksbetriebe mehr als 70 Prozent ihres Umsatzes in Frankfurt selbst. Gleichzeitig ist Frankfurt am Main auch für die in den umliegenden Landkreisen ansässigen Handwerksbetriebe ein wichtiger Absatzmarkt. So hat beispielsweise aus dem Main-Taunus-Kreis, dem Hoch-Taunus-Kreis und aus Offenbach jeder dritte Handwerksbetrieb Lieferbeziehungen nach Frankfurt und auch in Darmstadt hat jeder vierte Handwerksbetrieb Kunden in Frankfurt.

Die Rolle der ausländischen Mitbürger im Frankfurter Handwerk

Frankfurt am Main hat sich zu einer Stadt mit einem hohen Ausländeranteil entwickelt. Für ein reibungsloses Zusammenleben der Bevölkerung ist die gesellschaftliche Integration der ausländischen Mitbürger von zentraler Bedeutung. Hier spielt das Arbeitsleben eine maßgebende Rolle. Die Zusammenarbeit von Arbeitskollegen an gemeinsamen Aufgaben ist ein gesellschaftlicher Bereich, in dem gegenseitiges Verständnis und Toleranz gelebt werden können. Besonders wichtig

54.000 Menschen sind in Frankfurt im Handwerk beschäftigt.

54.000 people work in Frankfurt in skilled trades.

ist dies für junge Menschen, deren Erfahrungen in der Schul- und Berufsausbildung prägend sind für ihren weiteren Lebensweg. Mit einem Ausländeranteil von 30,5 Prozent an allen Auszubildenden leistet das Handwerk in Frankfurt einen wichtigen Beitrag zur beruflichen und gesellschaftlichen Integration von jungen ausländischen Mitbürgern. Ferner haben viele ausländische Mitbürger, die schon seit vielen Jahren in Deutschland leben, eine eigene Existenz im Handwerk gegründet und bieten ihrerseits Arbeitsplätze nicht zuletzt für ihre Landsleute an, was ebenfalls zu einer gesellschaftlichen Stabilisierung und Integration von ausländischen Mitbürgern beiträgt.

Strukturwandel im Handwerk

Nach der Handwerkszählung von 1995 hat die Zahl der im Frankfurter Handwerk Beschäftigten in den 18 Jahren seit der vorherigen Handwerkszählung im Jahr 1977 um ca. 10 Prozent zugenommen. Gleichzeitig ist aber die Zahl der Betriebe um 16 Prozent zurückgegangen, d. h. die in Frankfurt ansässigen Handwerksbetriebe sind größer geworden. Die Beschäftigtenentwicklung verlief in den einzelnen Handwerksgruppen sehr unterschiedlich. Die Beschäftigtenzahlen haben sich deutlich zugunsten der Gesundheits- und Reinigungshandwerke und der Elektro- und Metallhandwerke entwickelt. Demgegenüber ist die Zahl der Beschäftigten im Nahrungsmittelhandwerk, in der Gruppe der Bekleidungs-, Textil- und Lederhandwerke, im Bau- und Ausbauhandwerk sowie im Holzgewerbe zurückgegangen. In dieser Entwicklung spiegelt sich der Strukturwandel wider, der sich in den 18 Jahren, die zwischen den beiden Handwerkszählungen von 1977 und 1995 liegen, vollzogen hat. Der Bedeutungszuwachs der Elektro- und Metallhandwerke innerhalb des Gesamthandwerks ist auf eine veränderte Arbeitsteilung zwischen dem Handwerk und der Industrie zurückzuführen. Die Betriebe des Elektro- und Metallhandwerks sind stark im Zulieferwesen engagiert. Durch den verstärkten Wettbewerbsdruck wurde in den Unternehmen die Leistungserstellung auf allen Ebenen rationalisiert. Viele Leistungen und Vorprodukte, die bisher selbst hergestellt wurden, werden jetzt von spezialisierten Anbietern eingekauft. Für die Betriebe des Elektro- und Metallhandwerks ist damit in den letzten zwanzig Jahren der Markt für Zulieferleistungen sehr viel größer geworden. Gleichzeitig haben wichtige technologische Entwicklungen die Betriebe des Elektro- und Metallhandwerks in die Lage versetzt, Produkte und Leistungen anzubieten, die vor zwanzig Jahren noch undenkbar waren. So haben beispielsweise computergesteuerte Bearbeitungsmaschinen die Angebotspalette handwerklicher Zulieferbetriebe wesentlich erweitert.

Gleichzeitig tritt der Zulieferbetrieb, der nur ganz bestimmte Einzelteile herstellt, mehr und mehr in den Hintergrund. In den letzten Jahren haben sich verstärkt handwerkliche Zulieferbetriebe etabliert, die ganze Komponenten und Systeme entwickeln und fertigen. Ein Beispiel für die Leistungspalette des Elektrohandwerks ist der Entwurf, der Einbau und die Steuerung haustechnischer Anlagen in Banken und sonstigen Verwaltungsgebäuden. Ferner beauftragen große Industrieunternehmen bei der Neuplanung von Fertigungshallen mehr und mehr Handwerksbetriebe mit dem Entwurf und dem Einbau von Anlagen, die in früheren Jahren vom Unternehmen selbst erstellt wurden. Handwerksbetriebe profitieren auch oft von Auslandsengagements großer Firmen, zu denen sie gute Kundenbeziehungen haben. Wenn große Industrieunternehmen, Banken oder Versicherungen im Ausland neue Gebäude erstellen, werden gut eingeführte Handwerksbetriebe oft mit der Konzeption der Lieferung und der Montage von Schaltanlagen oder haustechnischen Anlagen betraut. Gleiches gilt für den Innenausbau und die Ausstattung ausländischer Filialen, um ein einheitliches Erscheinungsbild mit dem Stammhaus in Frankfurt herzustellen. Auf diese Weise ist es Betrieben der Elektro- und Metallhandwerke sowie des Bau- und Ausbaugewerbes in den letzten Jahren verstärkt gelungen, sich auch weiter entfernt liegende Absatzmärkte zu erschließen.

In den Elektro- und Metallberufen haben sich in den letzten 20 Jahren die Berufsbilder durch die beschleunigte technische Entwicklung stark verändert. Neue Werkstoffe und Verbindungstechniken, computergesteuerte Maschinen sowie elektronische Test- und Prüfverfahren haben in den Werkstätten Einzug gehalten. Die neuen Techniken erfordern nicht nur ein fundiertes Fachwissen sondern auch die Fähigkeit, sich flexibel auf neue Entwicklungen einzustellen und selbständig zu planen und zu arbeiten sowie die Bereitschaft, Verantwortung zu übernehmen. Dieser Wandel in den Anforderungen spiegelt sich in den veränderten Ausbildungsordnungen wider. Insgesamt hat der Anteil der in der Ausbildung vermittelten Kenntnisse zugenommen. So wurden in die Ausbildungsordnungen aller Metallberufe Grundkenntnisse der Elektrotechnik aufgenommen. Ferner wurden mit der Novellierung der Ausbildungsordnungen mehrerer Handwerksberufe, z. B. in der des Metallbauers, die Themen Aufbau und Organisation des Betriebes, Arbeitssicherheit, Umweltschutz und rationelle Energieverwendung, Planen und Vorbereiten des Arbeitsablaufes sowie Kontrollieren und Bewerten der Arbeitsergebnisse, Lesen, Anwenden und Erstellen von technischen Unterlagen usw. in die Ausbildung einbezogen.

a number of foreign citizens that are living in Germany for many years have established an existence for themselves in skilled trades and finally offer jobs to their country people, a fact that also contributes to the social stabilization and integration of foreign citizens.

Structural Change in Skilled Trades

After the skilled trades count of 1995, the number of persons employed in skilled trades in Frankfurt has risen by approx. 10 percent, within the 18 years since the last skilled trades count in 1977. At the same time however, the number of businesses has declined, that means, the skilled trades companies located in Frankfurt are grown in size. The development of the number of employees in each of the branches of skilled trades has been very varied. The number of persons employed has had a marked development in favour of the health-, cleaning-, electrical professions-, and metalworkers in skilled trades. In comparison to this, the number of persons that are employed in the food trade, the group of clothing, textile and leather trade, in the construction trade and interior fitting out as well as in the timber working trade, has decreased. The structural change that has taken place in the 18 years that lie between the two skilled trades counts of 1977 and 1995 is mirrored in this development. The growth of the importance of the electrical and metalworking branches in skilled trades within the whole conglomerate skilled trades can be led back to the fact of a changed division of labour between skilled trades and the industry. The companies of the electrical professions and metalworking skilled trades are very much engaged within the supply industry. Through an increased pressure in competition, the services offered by enterprises were rationalised on all levels. Many of the services that where hitherto self-produced are now acquired from specialist providers. For the companies of the electrical professions and metalworking trade the market for supply services has grown considerably in the last twenty years. At the same time have important technological developments enabled the companies of the electrical professions- and metalworking trade to offer products and services that were unthinkable even only twenty years ago. Thus have, for example, computer-aided processing machines considerably extended the product offers of skilled trades supply companies. At the same time, supply companies that only produce certain single parts move more and more into the background. In the past years skilled trades companies that develop and produce complete components and systems have established themselves increasingly. One example of products and services offered by the electrical professions of skilled trades is the planning, fitting

and control of building technology in banks and other buildings of administration. Furthermore, large industrial enterprises give orders of initial planning of production halls increasingly to skilled trades companies for the design and fitting of systems that were in earlier years carried out by the enterprises themselves. Skilled trades companies also benefit from the activities abroad of larger companies to which they maintain good customer relations. Banks or insurances or other large industrial enterprises that erect new buildings abroad, often assign very reliable skilled trades companies with the conception, supply and assembly of switch board systems and other systems of building technology. The same goes for the fitting out and the interior decoration of foreign branches, in order to create a uniform image with the headquarters in Frankfurt. In this way, the companies of the electrical professions and metal working trade as well as of the construction and fitting out trade have increasingly achieved in the past years to find also sales market located in further distances.

In the electrical professions and metalworking professions the nature of vocations has dramatically changed in the past twenty years because of the rapid technological development. New materials, communication techniques, computer-aided machines as well as electronic test and control methods have entered the workshops. The new technologies not only require a well-founded specialist knowledge but also the capacity to be flexible towards new developments and to be able to plan and work with self-motivation as well as to be prepared to take on responsibility.

This change in requirements is also mirrored in the adjusted training programmes of various skilled trades professions. On the whole, the share of imparted skills has risen in apprenticeships. Thus have been included into the training programmes of all metal professions basic skills of electro-techniques. Further, with the re-enacted apprenticeship regulations for various skilled trades professions, like the one of the metal craftsman, the topics of organization and structure of a company, security, environmental protection and

Die Handwerkskammer verfügt über eine Reihe moderner Ausbildungsstätten.

The Chamber of Handicrafts Rhein-Main disposes of a number of modern training workshops.

rational energy use, planning and preparation of the work process as well as control and evaluation of results, the reading, application and compiling of technical documents etc. have been included. But not only the electrical professions and metal processing professions have had to adjust to new requirements in these past twenty years. In the other fields of craft-based professions the development did not come to a halt either. Thus have also changed the activities of the optician and the acoustics specialist for hearing aids. Glasses and hearing aids are being produced in the last years increasingly in industrial production and have to be adjusted to the individual bearer, that is, against the production process the customer service of the optician and the acoustic craftsperson for hearing aids is becoming more and more dominant. As with the metal processing professions, also the changed outline of this profession has become visible in the re-enacted apprenticeship regulations. Whereas the apprenticeship regulations of 1976 focussed its contents on technical manufacturing skills, the apprenticeship regulations of 1997 is increasingly aiming at the consultation of customers, the sale of goods and services and on topics about the management of enterprises.

Jährlich bietet das Handwerk in Frankfurt 3.200 Lehrstellen.

The skilled trades sector offers in Frankfurt 3.200 apprenticeship places yearly.

Es haben sich jedoch nicht nur die Elektro- und Metallberufe in den letzten zwanzig Jahren den neuen Anforderungen anpassen müssen. In den anderen Bereichen des Handwerks ist die Entwicklung ebenfalls nicht stehen geblieben. So haben sich die Tätigkeiten des Augenoptikers und des Hörgeräteakustikers ebenfalls verändert. Brillen und Hörgeräte werden in den letzten Jahren verstärkt industriell gefertigt und müssen vom Optiker bzw. Hörgeräteakustiker an die Träger angepasst werden, d. h. gegenüber der Fertigung tritt im Augenoptiker- und im Hörgeräteakustikerhandwerk mehr und mehr die Beratung der Kunden in den Vordergrund. Wie bei den Metallberufen ist auch dieses veränderte Berufsbild in der novellierten Ausbildungsordnung des Augenoptikers nachvollziehbar. Während die Ausbildungsordnung des Jahres 1976 schwerpunktmäßig fertigungstechnische Inhalte aufwies, ist die Ausbildungsordnung von 1997 verstärkt auf die Beratung von Kunden, den Verkauf von Waren und Dienstleistungen und auf Themen der Unternehmensführung ausgerichtet.

Dynamik der Betriebsformen

In den letzten Jahren waren insbesondere in den handeltreibenden Handwerken die Betriebsformen einem starken Wandel zur Filialisierung unterworfen. Im Augenoptiker- und Uhrmacherhandwerk werden selbständige Betriebe immer häufiger in der Form von Franchise-Systemen geführt. In den Nahrungsmittelhandwerken vollzieht sich verstärkt eine Trennung der Produktionsstätte von der Verkaufsstelle. Während bei Bäckereien und Fleischereien die Produktionsstätte immer öfter in Gewerbegebiete am Stadtrand verlagert wurde, nahm die Zahl der Verkaufsstellen in der Innenstadt zu. Diese Entwicklung verlangt vom Handwerksmeister neben den traditionellen Kenntnissen und Fertigkeiten künftig vermehrt Managementkenntnisse.

Bei der Auftragsakquisition, beim Verkauf von Produkten und Leistungen und beim Kontakt zu Lieferfirmen ist auch im Handwerk die Nutzung des Internet stark auf dem Vormarsch. Ferner wird vom Kunden vermehrt ein „Leistungsangebot aus einer Hand" verlangt. Hier haben sich in den letzten Jahren vermehrt Handwerksbetriebe in Kooperationen zusammengeschlossen, um gemeinsam alle vom Kunden gewünschten Leistungen erbringen oder aber größere Aufträge übernehmen zu können. Die Novellierung der Handwerksordnung im Jahr 1998 trägt dem Erfordernis eines „Leistungsangebotes aus einer Hand" ebenfalls Rechnung.

Handwerk und seine Organisation in Frankfurt

Das Handwerk hat in seiner Tradition eine feste Stütze und Stärke, aus der es schöpfen kann. Andererseits hat das Handwerk auch bei der Gestaltung gesellschaftlicher Prozesse immer an vorderster Front mitgewirkt, z. B. 1848 im Handwerkerparlament in der Frankfurter Paulskirche. In einer längeren Entwicklung, die während der stürmischen Industrialisierung im letzten Jahrhundert auch manche Turbulenzen für das Handwerk und seine Organisationen mit sich brachte, kam es dann im Jahr 1900 überall in Deutschland zur Gründung von Handwerkskammern.

Die beiden ehemaligen Handwerkskammern Frankfurt und Darmstadt wurden 1979 zur Handwerkskammer Rhein-Main zusammengelegt. Die beiden Städte Frankfurt am Main und Darmstadt sind jetzt jeweils Sitz einer Hauptverwaltung der Handwerkskammer Rhein-Main. Durch diesen Schritt konnten die überregionalen Bedürfnisse des Handwerks gebündelt und wirksamer zur Sprache gebracht werden. Gleichzeitig wurde die Verwaltungsstruktur verschlankt und das Dienstleistungsangebot ausgeweitet.

Die Handwerkskammer ist eine Körperschaft des öffentlichen Rechts, der alle selbstständigen Handwerker und die Inhaber handwerksähnlicher Betriebe sowie deren Arbeitnehmer und Lehrlinge angehören. Es ist die Aufgabe der Handwerkskammer, die übergeordneten Probleme der Handwerksbetriebe zu bewältigen und die Interessen ihrer Mitglieder gegenüber Politik, Gesetzgeber und Öffentlichkeit zu vertreten. Neben der Führung der Handwerksrolle und der Regelung der beruflichen Ausbildung im Handwerk bietet die Handwerkskammer Rhein-Main ihren Mitgliedsbetrieben ein breites Beratungsangebot. Hierzu gehört sowohl die Beratung und Information in Rechtsfragen, in Fragen der Betriebsführung und Existenzgründung als auch im Bereich Technischer Umweltschutz und Standortsicherung. Informationen zum Europäischen Binnenmarkt sowie die Außenwirtschaftsberatung wurden in den letzten Jahren in der Arbeit der Handwerkskammer immer wichtiger. Zum wirtschaftlichen Erfolg der Handwerksbetriebe leisten auch die für die berufsspezifische Interessenvertretung der Betriebe zuständigen Frankfurter Handwerksinnungen einen wichtigen Beitrag.

Zur beruflichen Aus- und Weiterbildung unterhält die Handwerkskammer Rhein-Main in Frankfurt am Main ein Berufsbildungs- und Technologiezentrum, das bereits 1913 als Gewerbeförderungsanstalt gegründet wurde. Es gehört damit zu den ältesten handwerklichen Bildungseinrichtungen seiner Art in Deutschland. Verwaltung, Lehrwerkstätten und Theorieräume sind seit 1952 in der Schönstraße 21 in unmittelbarer Nähe zum Frankfurter Hauptbahnhof untergebracht. 30 Lehrwerkstätten, 17 Lehrsäle und 3 PC-Räume bieten über 1.100, dem neuesten Stand der Technik entsprechende Plätze für den praktischen und theoretischen Unterricht. Die berufliche Aus- und Weiterbildung wird auf vielen Gebieten in Absprache mit anerkannten Institutionen betrieben, wie z. B. die Schweißtechnische Lehranstalt, die Elektronik-Kursstätte, die Kunststoff-Kursstätte, die Aluminium-Kursstätte und die Bundesfachschule für das Zweiradmechanikerhandwerk.

Daneben wurde das Berufsbildungs- und Technologiezentrum der Handwerkskammer Rhein-Main in Weiterstadt 1972 als eines der ersten Ausbildungszentren für die überbetriebliche Lehrlingsunterweisung eröffnet. Es verfügt in 35 Lehrwerkstätten, 5 Lehrsälen und 2 PC-Räumen über 1.100 Ausbildungsplätze, die den neuesten Techniken entsprechend ausgestattet sind.

Das Aus- Fort- und Weiterbildungsangebot der Berufsbildungs- und Technologiezentren wird durch eine Technologie-Transfer-Stelle ergänzt. Die Technologie-Transfer-Beratung hat das Ziel, die Verbreitung neuer Technologien im Handwerk durch Einzelberatungen, Workshops und Lehrgänge und die Herstellung von Kontakten zu Fachverbänden und Wissenschaftseinrichtungen zu unterstützen. Ferner werden Handwerksbetriebe bei der Entwicklung neuer Produkte und Fertigungsmethoden und bei Wirtschaftlichkeitsberechnungen zu neuen Techniken beraten. Die Technologie-Transfer-Stelle ist den Handwerksbetrieben auch bei der Nutzung von Förderprogrammen für neue Techniken und bei der Einführung eines Qualitätsmanagement-Systems behilflich. Durch diese Unterstützungsangebote wird die Leistungs- und Innovationsfähigkeit des Handwerks im Strukturwandel auf einem dauerhaft hohen Niveau gehalten.

Auch im Frankfurter Handwerk sind Tradition und Innovation eng miteinander verbunden. Die Handwerkskammer Rhein-Main wird gemeinsam mit den Handwerksinnungen in Frankfurt alles tun, um das hohe Leistungsniveau des Frankfurter Handwerks auch zukünftig zu gewährleisten, damit das Handwerk als wichtige Stütze der Wirtschaft in dieser Stadt seinen Platz behält und weiter gestärkt wird. ∎

The Dynamism of Forms of Business Operation

In the past years, the forms of business operations, especially the trading craft-based professions, have been subjected to a strong change towards establishing multiple branches. In the craft-based professions of opticians and watch-making self-employed businesses are increasingly run in form of franchise systems. In the food sector of skilled trades there is a strong tendency to separate the producing factory from the sales shop. While bakeries and butchers have relocated their producing factories more often into the industrial areas of the city limits, the number of sales shops in the inner city have increased. These development demands of the master craftsmen apart from the traditional know-how and skills in future increased management know-how.

For the acquisition of orders, the sale of products and services as well as the contact with supply companies, also in the craft-based professions the use of the internet is gaining momentum. Also, the customer is increasingly demanding "service from one single provider". In this field, more and more skilled trades businesses have formed co-operations in the past years, in order to fulfil all the services desired by the clients or to take on larger orders. The re-enactment of the Handicrafts Code in the year 1998 takes also account of the requirement of "service from one single provider".

The Skilled Trades Sector and its Organisation in Frankfurt

In its tradition the skilled trades sector has a firm support and strength from which it can draw motivation. On the other hand, the skilled trades sector has always been active in the foremost frontline when shaping new social processes, for example in 1848 in the Parliament of Handicrafts in the St. Paul's Cathedral of Frankfurt. After a prolonged development, which also brought a few upheavals for the skilled trades and their organisation during the turbulent industrialization of the 19th Century, in the year 1900 everywhere in Germany new Chambers of Handicrafts were established. The two former Chambers of Handicrafts of Frankfurt and Darmstadt were merged in 1979 into the Chamber of Handicrafts Rhein-Main. At the same time, the structure of administration was made lean and the services were expanded.

The Chamber of Handicrafts is a public-law corporation, which is joined by all self-employed craftsmen and owners of near-craft based businesses as well as their employees and apprentices. It is the responsibility of the Chamber of Handicrafts to solve the superior problems of skilled trades businesses and to represent the interests of their members in front of politics, law and the public. Apart from the leading role of the skilled trades sector and the regulation of vocational training in handicrafts, the Chamber of Handicrafts Rhein-Main

provides to its member companies a broad service offer. This includes the consultancy and information in legal questions, questions of management and the establishment of new businesses as well as in the field of technical environmental protection and the security of a location. Information on the European domestic market as well as consultancy in exports has become increasingly important in the last years in the work of the Chamber of Handicrafts. The economic success of skilled trades businesses is also spurred on by the contribution of the trade guilds of Frankfurt, responsible for representing the specific interests of the professions. The Chamber of Handicrafts Rhein-Main runs a Vocational Training and Technology Centre in Frankfurt on the Main for professional training and further education that was founded already in 1913 as an institution for the promotion of trade. It is thus amongst the oldest educational institutions of handicrafts. Administration offices, training workshops and theoretical classrooms have been situated since 1952 in the Schönstraße 21 in direct vicinity to the main train station of Frankfurt. 30 training workshops, 17 classrooms and 3 PC-rooms provide 1.100 places furnished with the latest techniques for practical and theoretical teaching. Professional training and further education is imparted in many fields in agreement with recognised institutions, like for example, the Institute for Welding Technology, the College of Electronics, the College of Plastics, the College of Aluminium and the Federal Polytechnic of Two-wheel Mechanic Crafts.

Furthermore, the Vocational and Technology Centre of the Chamber of Handicrafts Rhein-Main was opened in Weiterstadt in 1972 being one of the first training centres of teaching for apprentices outside their companies. It has 35 training workshops, 5 classrooms and 2 PC rooms for over 1.100 teaching places furnished with the latest technology. The offers of training and further education of the Vocational Training and Technology Centres are complemented by a Technology Transfer Office. The consultancy in technology transfer aims at supporting the dissemination of new technologies in handicrafts

through individual consultancies, workshops and courses as well as at promoting the establishment of contacts to specialist associations and scientific institutions. Also, skilled trades businesses are consulted in the development of new products and production methods as well as in calculations of profitability. The Technology Transfer Office also assists the skilled trades businesses in the use of aid programmes for new techniques and with the introduction of a quality management system. Through these offers of support the performance and innovation ability of the handicrafts professions are kept on a lastingly high level within the structural change. The Chamber of Handicrafts Rhein-Main offers together with the Academy of Handicrafts that is sponsored by it, supra-specialist further education courses in which, above all, management know-how is imparted. Here, masters of handicrafts, their wives and management personnel can qualify themselves further by completing a course, for example, that leads to the qualification "Economist in Handicrafts".

Also within the skilled trades sector of Frankfurt tradition and innovation are closely connected with each other. The Chamber of Handicrafts Rhein-Main will do, together with the trade guilds in Frankfurt, its utmost to guarantee also in future the high standard of service of the skilled trades sector in Frankfurt, so that the craft-based professions maintains its position as an important pillar of the economy and is strengthened even further. ∎

80 Prozent aller Beschäftigten in Frankfurt sind im Dienstleistungsbereich tätig.

80 percent of all employees in Frankfurt work within the service sector.

Erstklassige Lösungen für Vorsorge, Risikoabsicherung und Vermögensaufbau

Firstclass Solutions for Provisions, Cover against Market Risks and Wealth Formation

Der Tradition verpflichtet und aufgeschlossen für die Moderne – unter diesem Motto ist die Zürich Gruppe in das 21. Jahrhundert gestartet. Sechs Versicherer und die Kapitalanlagegesellschaft Zürich Invest arbeiten unter dem gemeinsamen Dach der Zürich Beteiligungs-AG (Deutschland), die mit mehr als 4.000 Mitarbeitern, einem Gesamtumsatz von 7,1 Milliarden DM und Kapitalanlagen von über 30 Milliarden DM (jeweils Geschäftsjahr 2000) einer der führenden Finanzdienstleister in Deutschland ist. Der Unternehmensverbund bietet innovative und erstklassige Lösungen zur Risikoabsicherung, zur Vorsorge und zum Vermögensaufbau aus einer Hand. Individuelle Kundenorientierung und hohe Beratungsqualität stehen dabei an erster Stelle.

In ihrer heutigen Konstruktion besteht die Gruppe seit Anfang 1996, als die wirtschaftliche Zusammenführung der Zürich Versicherungen in Frankfurt mit den Kölner Agrippina Gesellschaften eingeleitet wurde; seit dem vergangenen Jahr ist dieser Prozess auch rechtlich abgeschlossen. In ihrer Struktur wird auch die pluralistische Vertriebspolitik deutlich. Ihre Fähigkeit, den Herausforderungen des Wettbewerbs flexibel zu begegnen, beweist die Zürich mit ihrer Ausrichtung nach Kundensegmenten: Privat-, Firmen- und Industriekunden. Die adäquate Marktstrategie drückt sich zudem in der Bereitschaft zu außergewöhnlichen, manchmal sogar spektakulären Innovationen aus. So hat die damalige Agrippina bereits 1901, also in den Frühzeiten der Motorisierung, als erster deutscher Versicherer das Auto-Kaskogeschäft aufgenommen. Schon mit ihrem Start in Deutschland 1922 brachte die seinerzeitige Vita, heute aufgegangen in der Zürich Agrippina Leben, die Invaliditäts-Zusatzversicherung, besser bekannt als Berufsunfähigkeits-Zusatzversicherung, auf den Markt, bald nach dem Zweiten Weltkrieg auch die sogenannte Restschuldversicherung, die das Risiko von Finanzierungen abdeckt und inzwischen Kreditlebensversicherung heißt.

Städtebauliche Dominante im Frankfurt des ausgehenden 20. Jahrhunderts – das Zürich-Haus am Opernplatz, das in Kürze durch einen Neubau ersetzt wird.
Dominant urban construction in Frankfurt at the closing 20th century – the Zürich House at the Opera Square, which will be replaced shortly by a new building.

1977 führte die Zürich als erste Gesellschaft in Deutschland in der Allgemeinen Unfallversicherung die 350prozentige Progression ein, nach der bei Vollinvalidität das Dreieinhalbfache der ursprünglich vereinbarten Versicherungssumme geleistet wird. Außerdem bot sie, und zwar gegen den Widerstand des Marktes, ebenfalls als erste in Deutschland die unbegrenzte Deckung in der Kfz-Haftpflichtversicherung an. 1981 war die Vita der erste Lebensversicherer in Deutschland, der einen sofort mit der Antragstellung, also noch vor der Risikoprüfung und vor der tatsächlichen Antragsannahme, einsetzenden Versicherungsschutz einräumte. Dank ihrer weltweiten Präsenz ist die Zürich seit jeher ein gefragter Partner der grenzüberschreitenden Industrie. Ihr Risk Engineering hält Leistungsprogramme bereit, welche die speziellen Eigenheiten und Erfordernisse sowohl des zu versichernden Unternehmens als auch der einzelnen Länder berücksichtigen. Damit wird für alle in- und ausländischen Aktivitäten ein einheitliches Sicherheitspaket auf der Grundlage von Risiko- und Bedarfsanalysen möglich. Dieser Service für die exportierende Wirtschaft und Industrie schließt Ingenieurtechnik mit vielfältigen Methoden zum Risikoschutz und zur Schadenverhütung ein. Die Kunden werden bei der Lösung auch ungewöhnlicher technischer Probleme beraten. Zudem müssen sie sich nicht mit den teilweise komplizierten ausländischen Gesetzen und sonstigen Usancen auseinandersetzen.

Mit besonderer Aufmerksamkeit widmet sich die Gruppe dem Internet, in dem sich die DA Deutsche Allgemeine dank ihres frühzeitigen professionellen Einstiegs einen Spitzenplatz innerhalb der Branche gesichert hat. Auf der Basis der dabei gewonnenen Erfahrungen haben weitere E-Business-Projekte Marktreife erlangt, und zwar zunächst für die Zürich Invest, die Kreditversicherung, den Medienservice und die Makleranbindungen. Dabei steht, neben der Installation eines schnellen und komfortablen Informationskanals, die Einrichtung dialogorientierter Plattformen im Vordergrund, die den Kunden „online" z. B. das Abfragen von Depotwerten, den An- und Verkauf von Fondsanteilen, die Kreditprüfung oder auch den Abschluss anderer standardisierter Geschäfte ermöglichen. Gemeinsam mit der Muttergesellschaft in Zürich wird zudem an internationalen Lösungen gearbeitet. ∎

Das Call-Center der DA Deutschen Allgemeinen, die ihre Produkte ausschließlich im Direktvertrieb absetzt.
The call centre of the DA Deutsche Allgemeine that sells its products exclusively through direct marketing.

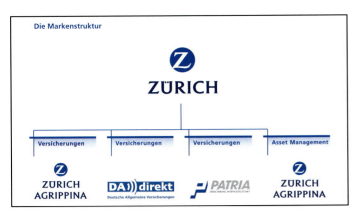

Die Markenstruktur

ZÜRICH

| Versicherungen | Versicherungen | Versicherungen | Asset Management |

ZÜRICH AGRIPPINA

DA)) direkt
Deutsche Allgemeine Versicherungen

PATRIA
VERSICHERUNG AKTIENGESELLSCHAFT

ZÜRICH AGRIPPINA

Diese vier Marken bilden mit ihren Produkten und Dienstleistungen die Zürich Gruppe.

These four brands form with their products and services the Zürich Gruppe.

C ommitted to tradition and open for modern times – this is the slogan, which the group for Zürich has chosen to start into the 21st century. Six insurance companies and the capital investment company Zürich Invest work under the mutual roof of the Zürich Beteiligungs-AG (Germany), which is with more than 4.000 employees, a total turnover of 7,1 billion DM and capital investments of more than 30 billion DM (each of financial year 2000) one of the leading financial service providers in Germany. This association of companies offers innovative and firstclass solutions of cover against market risks, for provisions and for wealth formation from one provider. Individual client orientation and a high consulting quality are of first priority in this.

The group exists in its actual structure since the beginning of 1996, when the commercial merger of Zürich Insurance in Frankfurt was initiated with the Agrippina Societies of Cologne; since last year, this process has been completed also in legal terms. Its structure also shows the pluralistic sales policy of the group. Its capacity to confront the challenges of competition with flexibility is proven by the Zürich with its orientation towards client segments: private, business and industrial clients. Furthermore, the appropriate market strategy can be observed in the readiness to opt for extraordinary sometimes even spectacular innovations. Thus, the former Agrippina was as early as 1901, that is in the early times of motorisation, the first German insurance company to start the business of insurance cover for damage to one's own car (Kasko). Also, at its establishment in Germany in 1922, the former Vita - today part of the Zürich Agrippina Leben – launched the additional invalidity insurance on the market, which is better know as additional insurance for vocational disability. Soon after the second worldwar also the so-called residual debt insurance that covers the risk of financing and is meanwhile called credit life insurance.

In 1977, the Zürich was the first company in Germany to introduce in its General Accident Insurance a 350 percent progression, which provides on full disability three-and-a-half times the originally agreed insurance sum. Furthermore she was also the first company in Germany to offer – and she did so against the resistance of the market – unlimited cover for automobile personal liability. In 1981, the Vita was the first life insurer in Germany to grant immediate insurance protection starting right with the application even before risk investigation and before the actual acceptance of the application.

Thanks to its worldwide presence, the Zürich has always been a popular partner across all branches of industry. Its risk engineering disposes of services programmes that take consideration of the special peculiarities and requirements of both the companies to be insured and also of each individual country. Thus, a standardised assurance packages on the basis of risk and requirement analyses becomes possible for all activities domestic and abroad. This service for the exporting sectors of commerce and industry includes the techniques of engineering with its diverse methods of risk insurance and for damage prevention. Clients are also consulted in the finding of solutions for unusual technical problems. Furthermore, they do not have to cope with often complex foreign laws and other usages.

The group dedicates special attention to the Internet in that the DA Deutsche Allgemeine has secured for itself a top position within the branch thanks to its early professional start-up. On the basis of the experiences gained meanwhile, further e-Business projects have attained market status, firstly for the Zürich Invest, credit insurances, media services and estate agent connections. In this, apart from the installation of a rapid and comfortable information channel also the establishment of a dialog-oriented platform is of priority that enables the client to carry out "online" for example inquiries about account values, sale and purchase of fund units, credit investigation or also the conclusion of other standardised business. Together with its parent company in Zürich also international solutions are being sought. ∎

ZÜRICH

Zürich Gruppe

Verbund von/Association of:
Zürich Agrippina Versicherung AG
Zürich Agrippina Lebensversicherung AG
Zürich Agrippina Krankenversicherung AG
mit klassischem Außendienst-Service
für alle Zielgruppen

DA Deutsche Allgemeine Versicherung AG
DA Deutsche Allgemeine Lebensversicherung AG
als Direktanbieter für den gesamten
Privatkundenbedarf

Patria Versicherung AG
als Spezialpartner für
Makler und Mehrfachagenten

Zürich Investmentgesellschaft mbH
auf dem stürmisch expandierenden
Markt der Vermögensverwaltung

Vorstandsvoritzender/Chairman of the Board:
Dr. Heinrich Focke

Gründungsjahr/Year of Foundation:
1844

Mitarbeiter/Employees:
4.000

Gesamtumsatz im Geschäftsjahr 2000/
Total turnover in the financial year 2000:
7,1 Mrd DM

Geschäftstätigkeit/Business Activity:
Versicherungen und
weitere Finanzdienstleistungen.
Insurances and other financial services.

Anschrift/Address:
Solmsstraße 27–37
D-60486 Frankfurt am Main
Telefon   +49 (69) 71 15-0
Telefax   +49 (69) 71 15-33 58
E-Mail   service@zuerich.de
Internet www.zuerich.de

Die Startseite der Kapitalanlagegesellschaft Zürich Invest im Internet.

The Homepage of the capital investment company Zürich Invest in the Internet.

Siemens Axiva – vom Konzept bis zur schlüsselfertigen Anlage

Siemens Axiva – Service from Conception to the completed Turnkey Plant

Laborentwicklung	Pilotanlage	Prozessentwicklung	Basic Engineering	Detail Engineering	Bau und Montage	Start-up
Laboratory Development	Pilot Plant	Materials Processing Development	Basic Engineering	Detail Engineering	Construction and Assembly	Start-up

Die Siemens Axiva GmbH & Co. KG, Frankfurt am Main, ist mit 570 Mitarbeitern und einem Jahresumsatz von rund 77 Millionen Euro (1999) ein führender Anbieter verfahrens- und ingenieurtechnischer Leistungen für die Prozessindustrie. Die Palette reicht von Technologieentwicklung und -realisierung über Projektbearbeitung und Prozessberatung bis hin zur Einrichtung individueller Produktionsprozesse, insbesondere im chemischen und pharmazeutischen Sektor. Siemens Axiva ist hervorgegangen aus der früheren Hoechst AG und seit Oktober 2000 eine Tochtergesellschaft des Siemens-Bereichs Automatisierungs- und Antriebstechnik (Automation & Drives, A&D), des weltweit führenden Herstellers auf diesem Gebiet. Damit verfügt Siemens Axiva neben dem verfahrenstechnischen Know-how nun auch über Kompetenzen in der Automatisierungstechnik – zum Vorteil der Kunden. Denn sowohl die Beratung als auch die Dienstleistungspalette ist jetzt umfassender. Die Bündelung dieser beiden Kernkompetenzen ermöglicht dem Kunden zudem, die Anzahl von Partnern bei der Durchführung von Projekten zu reduzieren – vom Konzept bis zur Realisierung: alles aus einer Hand.

Erfahren und kompetent

Siemens Axiva hat in der Hoechst Gruppe mehr als 75 Jahre Erfahrung in der Entwicklung neuer und der Optimierung bestehender Verfahren und Produkte gesammelt. Das Unternehmen plant, konzipiert und baut die dazugehörigen chemischen und pharmazeutischen Produktionsanlagen für unterschiedliche Zweige der Prozessindustrie. Darüber hinaus stellt Siemens Axiva Erst- und Mustermengen bereit.

Interdisziplinäre Arbeitsweise

Das Unternehmen ist so organisiert, dass es den spezifischen Anforderungen seiner Kunden und Märkte gerecht wird. In den drei Business Units Chemie, Pharma und Polymere werden komplexe Aufgaben in interdisziplinärer Zusammenarbeit gelöst. Schwerpunktmäßig wird diese fachübergreifende Arbeitsweise, je nach Projekt, mit dem Know-how aus den Kernkompetenzen gebündelt und im Team bearbeitet. Dort vernetzen Experten aus unterschiedlichen Disziplinen ihr Fachwissen. Das jeweilige Team begleitet den Kunden während des gesamten Projekts.

Modulare Dienstleistungen

Siemens Axiva setzt auf Flexibiltät, Kundenfokus und Schnelligkeit. Alle ingenieur- und verfahrenstechnischen Dienstleistungen lassen sich modular – nach den spezifischen Anforderungen des Kunden – zusammenstellen. Ob standardisierte oder maßgeschneiderte Komponenten in der Anlagentechnik, Beratung in Fragen der Logistik, ob Mustermengenbereitstellung für ein neues Produkt oder die Optimierung eines bestehenden Verfahrens – die umfangreiche Angebotspalette ist in einzelnen Modulen oder als Ganzes verfügbar.

Kernkompetenzen:
Verfahrensentwicklung und -optimierung

In eigenen Labors oder Pilotanlagen werden einzelne Bausteine eines Verfahrens optimiert und in den Gesamtprozess integriert. So entwickelt beispielsweise das Unternehmen in enger Zusammenarbeit mit der Deutschen Gesellschaft für Kunststoff-Recycling und der TU Berlin Kernprozesse eines neuen Polymer-Recycling-Verfahrens.

Anlagenbau

Von der Pilotanlage bis zum schlüsselfertigen Großprojekt – Siemens Axiva baut Anlagen nach Maß. Weltweit sind so seit 1980 mehr als 80 großtechnische Anlagen entstanden, wie beispielsweise in Frankfurt am Main. Dort hat das Unternehmen innerhalb von nur zwölf Monaten die weltweit größte Anlage zur Verteilung von Purified Water errichtet. Mit dieser Anlage, die 17 Pharmabetriebe mit Reinstwasser versorgt, haben die Siemens Axiva Ingenieure ein grundlegendes logistisches Problem gelöst: die Qulitätserhaltung von Wasser hoher Reinheitsgüte auf dem Transportweg. Bei Projekten in anderen Erdteilen verfährt das Unternehmen arbeitsteilig: Siemens Axiva übernimmt dann die Planung und das gesamte Projektmanagement, während lokale Partnerunternehmen vor Ort für die Werksinfrastruktur zuständig sind.

Consulting

Die Qualität der Beratung basiert auf der langjährigen Praxiserfahrung und der ganzheitlichen Betrachtungsweise des Produktionsprozesses. Die Leistung umfasst Prozessanalytik, Stoffdatenbeschaffung, Leit- und Sicherheitstechnik, Auditierung und Validierung sowie Prozessführung.

Produktbereitstellung

Die Business Unit Pilot Plants von Siemens Axiva ist spezialisiert auf die schnelle Bereitstellung von Erst- und Mustermengen und hilft so, die Phase bis zum Markteintritt erheblich zu verkürzen. Aufgrund der ausgezeichneten Infrastruktur und Apparateausstattung kann Pilot Plants auch die erste Produktion, beispielsweise für Markttests, übernehmen.

Innovative Technologien

Siemens Axiva erkennt frühzeitig erfolgversprechende Trends und entwickelt – im Kundenauftrag – neue Produktionstechnologien bzw. verfügt über das Know-how, um vorhandene innovative Technologien optimal zu nutzen. So setzt Siemens Axiva beispielsweise Mikrokomponenten ein und erzielt damit eine deutliche Kapazitätssteigerung von Produktionsverfahren. ∎

The Siemens Axiva GmbH & Co. KG, Frankfurt on the Main, is with 750 employees and a turnover of around 77 million EURO (1999) a leading provider of services of materials processing and engineering techniques for the processing industry. The range extends from technology development and their realisation across project work and processing consulting upto the implementation of individual production processes, particularly within the chemical and pharmaceutical sectors. Siemens Axiva emerged from the former Hoechst AG and is since October 2000 a subsidiary company of the Siemens-department Automation and Drives, A&D, the worldwide leading manufacturers in this field. Thus, Siemens Axiva disposes – apart from the know-how in matierlas processing techniques – also of competences in the techniques of automation, to the advantage of the clients. Thus, both consulting as well as the range of services are now more comprehensive. The grouping of these two core competences enables the client also to reduce the number of partners when executing projects – from concept to implementation: all services from one provider.

Experienced and Competent
Siemens Axiva has gained within the Hoechst Group more than 75 years of experience in the development of new and the optimisation of existing processes and products. The company plans, conceptualizes and builds the chemical and pharmaceutical production plants belonging to the various branches of the processing industry. Furthermore, Siemens provides first and samples amounts.

Interdisciplinary Working Methods
The company is organised in such a way, that it can comply with the specific demands of its clients and markets. In the three business units chemistry, pharma and polymere complex tasks are solved in interdisciplinary co-operation. Mainly, these working methods across specialisations are coupled with the know-how of the core competences and dealt with in a team, always according to each project. There, experts of differing disciplines network their expert knowledge. Each corresponding team attends its client during the complete project.

Modular Services
Siemens Axiva relies on flexibility, customer focus and rapidity. All services of engineering and processing techniques can be composed in a modular way – according to the specific requirements of the client. Whether standardised or tailor-made components of terotechnology, consulting in questions of logistics, whether the provision of sample amounts for a new product or the optimisation of an existing process – the extensive range of services are available as single modules or as a complete entity.

Core Competences
Development and Optimisation of Materials Processing
In the self-owned laboratories or pilot plants the single steps of a process are optimised and integrated into the complete process. Thus, the company develops in close co-operation with the German Society for Plastic-Recycling and the Technical University of Berlin for example, core processes of a new polymer recycling processing method.

Terotechnology
From the pilot plant to the large turnkey project – Siemens Axiva builds plants made to measure. Thus, worldwide more than 80 large technical plants have been established, as for example in Frankfurt on the Main. There, the company has build within only twelve months the worldwide largest plant for the distribution of purified water. With this plant, which supplies 17 pharmaceutical companies with purified water, Siemens Axiva engineers have solved a fundamental logistic problem: the maintenance of the quality of high quality purified water during transportation. In projects in other parts of the world, the company employs a division of labour: Siemens Axiva carries out the planning and the complete project management, while local partner companies are responsible for the infrastructure at their domestic location.

Consulting
The quality of consulting is based on long-year's practical experience and the integral approach towards production processes. The service comprises processing analysis, materials data collection, process control and security technology, auditing and validation as well as litigation.

Product Provision
The business unit pilot plants of Siemens Axiva is specialised in the rapid provision of primary and sample amounts and thus helps to shorten the period until introduction into the market considerably. Because of the excellent infrastructure and equipment with appliances, the pilot plants are also able to take on primary productions, for example for market tests.

Innovative Technologies
Siemens Axiva recognises early trends that promise to be successful and develops – on order of its clients – new production technologies and disposes of the know-how for an optimal use of existing innovative technologies respectively. In this way, Siemens Axiva employs for example micro components and thus achieves a significant increase in the capacity of production processing methods. ■

SIEMENS

Siemens Axiva GmbH & Co. KG

Geschäftsführer/Manager:
Michael Kirf
Dr. Norbert Schadler

Gesellschafter/Corporate member:
Siemens Axiva Verwaltungs GmbH

Mitarbeiter/Employees:
570

Umsatz/Turnover:
77 Millionen Euro (1999)

Geschäftstätigkeit/Business Activity:
- Verfahrensentwicklung & -optimierung
  Development and optimisation
  of materials processing
- Anlagenbau/Terotechnology
- Consulting/Consulting
- Produktbereitstellung/Product provision
- Innovative Technologien/Innovative Technologies

Anschrift/Address:
Industriepark Höchst, K 801
D-65926 Frankfurt am Main
Telefon   +49 (69) 305-305 69
Telefax   +49 (69) 305-305 68
E-mail   info@axiva.com
Internet www.axiva.com

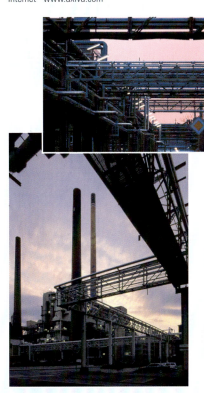

Seit 1980 hat das Unternehmen mehr als 80 großtechnische Anlagen realisiert, davon mehr als 60 im Ausland.

Since 1980 the company has realised more than 80 large technical plants; of these, more than 60 abroad.

Programmatisches zum Dialog von Wissenschaft und Wirtschaft

Programmatic Issues in the Dialogue between Science and the Economy

Frankfurt ist mehr als Drehscheibe des internationalen Bankbusiness, eines der bedeutendsten Dienstleistungszentren Europas und herausragender Standort für Life-science – Frankfurt ist Wissenschaftsstadt von besonderem Rang: Überregionale Forschungseinrichtungen, dazu zählen drei Max-Planck-Institute, Forschungs- und Entwicklungsabteilungen der chemischen und pharmazeutischen Industrie und selbstverständlich die vier Hochschulen schaffen ein forschungsfreundliches Klima mit vielfältigen Kooperationsmöglichkeiten. Die Goethe-Universität – 1914 in privater Initiative von Frankfurter Bürgern als Stiftungsuniversität gegründet, inzwischen unter den zehn größten Universitäten der Bundesrepublik platziert – spielt dabei eine entscheidende Rolle sowohl im Transfer von Grundlagenwissen in angewandte Forschung als auch im Ausbildungssektor. Die Trennung von Grundlagenforschung und angewandter Forschung verliert angesichts der sich entwickelnden Netzwerke zwischen anwendungsoffener Grundlagenforschung der Goethe-Universität und den wissensbasierten Aktivitäten der Wirtschaft an Gewicht. Wir werden den erfolgreich beschrittenen Weg, den Wissens- und Technologietransfer zu intensivieren, zu Beginn des neuen Jahrtausends spürbar verstärken.

In den kommenden Jahren, die geprägt sein werden von erheblichen Veränderungen in der Forschungs- und Bildungslandschaft und von einer zunehmenden Dynamik der „Wissensgesellschaft", wird unsere Universität ihre Profile in Forschung und Lehre zielgerichtet fortentwickeln, dabei können wir uns auf einen breiten Fundus an Aktivitäten aus unser langer Tradition stützen. An diesen Forschungsprofilen, die die Standortfaktoren der Region berücksichtigen, können sich auch unsere Partner in der Wirtschaft orientieren. Gleichzeitig wird die Goethe-Universität ihr Profil als Dienstleister im Bildungsbereich schärfen, was das Erststudium ebenso wie gezielte Angebote in der Weiterbildung umfasst.

**Prof. Dr.
Rudolf
Steinberg**

Der Autor wurde 1943 in Cochem an der Mosel geboren, studierte in Freiburg, Köln und Ann Arbor (Michigan) Jura, erstes juristisches Staatsexamen 1967, zweites juristisches Staatsexamen 1973. Stationen seiner wissenschaftlichen Laufbahn: 1970 Promotion in Freiburg als Assistent von Prof. Konrad Hesse über Staatslehre und Interessenverbände, 1978 Habilitation ebenfalls in Freiburg über Politik und Verwaltungsorganisation; 1977–1980 Professor an der Universität Hannover; seit 1977 Professur für Öffentliches Recht, Umweltrecht und Verwaltungswissenschaften am Fachbereich Rechtswissenschaft der Goethe-Universität. Von 1995 bis August 2000 war er Richter des Thüringer Verfassungsgerichtshofs. Im Juni 2000 übernahm er das Amt des Präsidenten der Johann Wolfgang Goethe-Universität in Frankfurt, die Amtszeit beträgt sechs Jahre.

The author was born in 1943 in Cochem an der Mosel, studied law in Freiburg, Cologne and Ann Arbor (Michigan), first degree legal state examination in 1967, second degree legal state examination in 1973. Stations of his scientific career: 1970 PhD in Freiburg as Assistant to Prof. Konrad Hesse in political science and syndicates, 1978 qualification as a university lecturer in Freiburg on politics and administration; 1977-1980 professor at the University of Hanover; since 1977 professorship for public law, environmental law and administrative sciences in the Faculty of Law, Goethe University. From 1995 until August 2000 he was a judge at the Supreme Constitutional Court of Thuringia. As an officially appointed expert, Prof. Steinberg works for the federal parliament, regional parliaments, regional governments and territorial corporate entities, and he has worked as counsel of proceedings and attorney in numerous court cases heard by the federal constitutional court and other courts. Prof. Steinberg took on the appointment of President of the Johann Wolfgang Goethe University in Frankfurt in June 2000; the term of office is six years.

Freundlich und einladend: Modell des Architekturbüros Nickl & Partner für den Um- und Neubau des Universitätsklinikums in Niederrad, der bis 2009 abgeschlossen sein soll. Ziel des Gesamtprojekts ist die Zusammenlegung verschiedener medizinischer Einheiten, die bislang in unterschiedlichen Gebäuden untergebracht waren. Gleichzeitig wird der Empfangsbereich neugestaltet: eine weitläufige Eingangshalle und Grünflächen bis zum Mainufer statt Parkplätzen (Modell: Architekturbüro Nickl & Partner, München).

Friendly and inviting: a model by the architects Nickl & Partner of the renovation and new building of the university clinic in Niederrad, which is to be completed by 2009. The aim of the total project is to bring together medical units that have until now been housed in different buildings. At the same time, the reception area is being redesigned: an extensive entrance hall and green areas reaching as far as the banks of the river Main will replace parking spaces (Model: Architect's Office Nickl & Partner, Munich).

Ein Meisterwerk der Architektur: die von dem Berliner Architekten Hans Poelzig entworfene, zwischen 1928 und 1931 errichtete Hauptverwaltung der I.G. Farbenindustrie AG. Ab April 2000 werden hier auf dem Campus Westend 8000 junge Menschen Gesellschafts- und Kulturwissenschaften studieren.

A masterpiece of architecture: the Main Building or the I.G. Farbenindustrie AG, designed by the Berlin architect Hans Poelzig and built between 1928 and 1931. Here on the Westend campus from April 2000 onwards, 8,000 young people will study social and cultural sciences.

Frankfurt is more than an international banking centre, one of the most important European centres in the service sector, and an excellent location for life science. The city is also a place where science enjoys a special prestige: it contains supraregional research institutes, including three Max Planck institutes, research and development departments of the chemical and pharmaceutical industry, and, of course, the four institutions of higher education. This creates a research-friendly climate with numerous possibilities for co-operation. The Goethe University – founded as a private initiative in 1914 by Frankfurt citizens as an endowed university and now among the ten largest universities in the Federal Republic – plays a decisive role both in the use of basic research in areas of applied research and in teaching. The distinction between pure research and applied research is becoming less important in the face of emerging networks linking pure research open to application at the Goethe University with the knowledge-based activities of the economic sector. At the beginning of the new millennium we shall strengthen considerably the policy that has already been successful, intensifying the transfer of knowledge and technology.

The coming years will be characterised by considerable changes in the research and education landscape and by the increasing dynamism of the "knowledge society". Our university will continue to develop its targeted profiles in research and teaching. In doing this, we are able to draw on a rich fund of experience from our long tradition. Our partners in the economy will also be able to find orientation in these research profiles, which

take account of the location of the region. At the same time, the Goethe University will sharpen its profile as a provider of services in the education sector, which encompasses undergraduate degrees as well as targeted offers in further education.

Teaching: Studying in Modules and with Credit Points

Our university, being the region's central university, is traditionally the first choice of higher education institutions for sixth-form graduates in the

densely populated Rhein-Main region; it has therefore been one of the ten largest universities in the republic for many years. Demand in the region will also remain high in future. We are striving to improve the supraregional and international attractiveness of the Goethe University; for this purpose, a range of reform measures are necessary.

University teaching must be able to react with more flexibility to new research findings and must equip its graduates for the future; for this reason all faculties are being asked to design more varied curricula. A modular structure is intended to make courses more transparent, to make available well-structured selection options, and to lay down binding requirements for teaching staff and students. Modules can be combined into new courses, and degree course be reformed rapidly through the exchange of modules. In the context of modularisation the credit point system, which has the effect of shortening study times, is being introduced. This is the only way to ensure the introduction of internationally recognised and accredited BA/MA degrees.

A number of subjects have already started their corresponding reform projects, led by the Faculty of Economics with BA courses in political economy and business studies.

With the introduction of these BA/MA courses the Goethe University is also contributing to an internationalisation of teaching: exchange programmes can be intensified and standards within the European area can be better compared. Foreign language classes and teaching programmes in foreign languages will increase.

„Klassisch modern und mit schönstem Blick auf Frankfurt", so beschreibt der Wiener Architekt Wilhelm Holzbauer das Biozentrum am Niederurseler Hang, das er zusammen mit Ernst Mayer entworfen hat. Im Herbst 1993 wurde das Biozentrum bezogen, das mit den bereits seit 1973 dort ansässigen Chemischen Instituten verbunden ist. Langfristig sollen alle Naturwissenschaften nach Niederursel verlagert werden.

"Classically modern and with the most beautiful view of Frankfurt"; this is the Viennese architect Wilhelm Holzbauer's description of the Biocentre at the Niederurseler Hang, which he designed in co-operation with Ernst Mayer. The Biocentre was opened in the autumn of 1993; it is connected with the chemical institutes located there since 1973. In the long term, all the natural sciences are to be transferred to Niederursel.

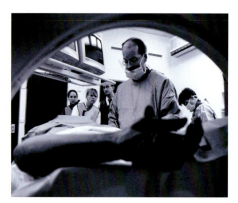

Durch die Röhre: Untersuchung mit modernsten Methoden der Computertomographie gehören zum Standard der Diagnostik im Universitätsklinikum.

Through the tube: Investigation with the most modern methods of computertomography is one of the standard methods of diagnostics in the university clinic.

Lehre: Studieren in Modulen und mit Credit Points

Unsere Universität ist als Zentraluniversität des dicht besiedelten Rhein-Main-Gebiets für dessen Abiturienten traditionell die erste Hochschuladresse; daher rangiert sie beständig unter den zehn größten Universitäten der Republik. Auch in Zukunft wird die Nachfrage aus der Region hoch bleiben. Verbessern möchten wir die überregionale und internationale Attraktivität der Goethe-Universität; dazu sind erhebliche Maßnahmen zur Studienreform erforderlich.

Die universitäre Lehre muss flexibler auf neue Forschungsergebnisse reagieren können und ihre Absolventen zukunftsfähig machen; deshalb sind alle Fachbereiche aufgefordert, die Curricula variabler zu gestalten. Durch modularen Aufbau sollen Studiengänge transparenter werden, wohlstrukturierte Wahlmöglichkeiten eröffnet und die Anforderungen an die Lehrenden wie die Lernenden verbindlich geregelt werden. Module können zu neuen Studiengängen kombiniert, Studiengänge durch Austausch von Modulen schnell reformiert werden. Im Kontext der Modularisierung wird das Credit-Point-System mit seiner studienzeitverkürzenden Wirkung eingeführt. Nur so ist auch die Einführung international anerkannter und akkreditierter BA/MA-Abschlüsse gewährleistet. Eine Reihe von Fächern haben mit entsprechenden Reform- projekten bereits begonnen, Vorreiter waren die Wirtschaftswissenschaften mit BA-Studiengänge in VWL und BWL.

Mit der Einführung der BA/MA-Studiengänge leistet die Goethe-Universität zugleich einen Beitrag zur Internationalisierung der Lehre: Austauschprogramme können intensiviert werden, Studienleistungen im europäischen Raum werden vergleichbarer, Fremdsprachenunterricht und Lehrprogramme in fremden Sprachen werden zunehmen.

Lernen im Netz: Die Online-Universität

Sowohl für Vollzeitstudierende wie auch für einen gerade in Frankfurt erheblichen Anteil von Teilzeitstudierenden sollen die Präsenzphasen des Studiums ergänzt werden durch die Arbeit mit Studienmaterialien, die über die neuen Medien vermittelt werden. Von Pilotprojekten wollen wir zu einer flächendeckenden, systematischen Nutzung der neuen Medien kommen. Ziel ist es, das Präsenzstudium durch ein konsequent ausgebautes Online-Studium zu ergänzen, das zusammen mit Kooperationspartnern erweitert werden soll.

Das Vier-Campus-Modell

Als unsere Universität 1914 eröffnet wurde, begann sie – begründet durch die in Frankfurt schon vorhandenen wissenschaftlichen Einrichtungen und im Sinne unserer Stifter und Mäzene – mit einer sozial- und wirtschaftswissenschaftlichen, einer naturwissenschaftlichen, einer geisteswissenschaftlichen und einer medizinischen Fakultät. Heute knüpfen wir an diese Tradition an und konzentrieren unsere Reformbemühungen wiederum auf der Grundlage von eigenen Stärken und spezifischen Standortvorteilen von Stadt und Region auf vier Kernbereiche: Rechts- und Wirtschaftswissenschaften, Gesellschafts- und Kulturwissenschaften, Natur- und Biowissenschaften und Medizin.

Durch den im März 1999 zwischen der Stadt Frankfurt und dem Land Hessen geschlossenen „Kulturvertrag" eröffnen sich neue Perspektiven für die Entwicklung der Goethe-Universität an vier Standorten: der rechts- und wirtschaftswissenschaftliche Campus Bockenheim soll arrondiert werden, auf dem Campus Westend können die Gesellschafts- und Kulturwissenschaften Raum finden, alle Naturwissenschaften werden auf dem Campus Niederursel vereinigt und der Medizin-Campus Niederrad wird ausgebaut. Dieses Standortkonzept soll in Zukunft interdisziplinäre Initiativen der an einem Standort vereinigten Fächer fördern und eine Folie zur Identifikation standortübergreifender Aktivitäten – einschließlich der Kooperationen mit anderen Universitäten, außeruniversitären Forschungseinrichtungen, mit Wirtschaft und Industrie und anderen Partnern – darstellen.

In welche Richtung werden sich diese vier Kernstandorte entwickeln? Über Details wird innerhalb der Fachbereiche intensiv beraten und abschließend entschieden werden müssen. Gewisse Trendlinien lassen sich bereits erkennen:

Stichwort „Finance": Innovationen in Rechts- und Wirtschaftswissenschaften

Die Rechts- und Wirtschaftswissenschaften orientieren ihre Profilbildung in Forschung und Lehre an den besonderen Standortbedingungen der Fi-

nanz- und Dienstleistungsregion Rhein-Main mit ihren Banken, Versicherungen, Unternehmensberatungen, IT- und Logistik-Unternehmen sowie Werbeagenturen: Das Center for Financial Studies wurde zu einem anerkannten internationalen Meetingpoint für Wissenschaftler und Praktiker; das von neun Professoren betreute Graduiertenkolleg „Finanzwirtschaft und Monetäre Ökonomie" versteht sich als Schnittstelle zwischen fundierter theoretischer Analyse und intensivem Praxisbezug am Finanzplatz Frankfurt; in den innovativen Feldern Investment und E-Commerce wurden zwei neue Professuren geschaffen. Es ist beabsichtigt, das traditionsreiche Institut für Ausländisches und Internationales Wirtschaftsrecht zu einem Center for Financial Law umzugestalten, das mit einer Stiftungsprofessur verbunden werden soll. In diesem Umfeld gibt es auch ein Aufbaustudium für im Ausland graduierte Juristinnen und Juristen (LLM, Magister Legum). Außerdem wird eine Weiterqualifizierung als Master of Business Administration (MBA) mit dem Schwerpunkt „finance" eingerichtet. Zudem bereitet die Mathematik zusammen mit dem Fachbereich Wirtschaftswissenschaften eine Kooperation mit Frankfurter Banken im Bereich der „mathematical finance" vor.

Internationalität: Mehr fremdsprachliche Studienangebote

In den Gesellschafts- und Kulturwissenschaften werden insbesondere interdisziplinäre Schwerpunktbildungen angestrebt: So ist an die Gründung eines Zentrums für China-/Ostasienstudien gedacht, an dem sich Wissenschaftler und Wissenschaftlerinnen der Sinologie, der Gesellschaftswissenschaften sowie der Rechts- und Wirtschaftswissenschaften beteiligen könnten. Im Fachbereich Neuere Philologien sollen die Vertreter verschiedener Sprachwissenschaften im Institut für Komparatistik fächerübergreifend kooperieren. Zum Thema „Satzarten: Variation und Interpretation" haben Vertreter der Linguistik aus unterschiedlichen Disziplinen eine Zusammenarbeit begonnen, die in einem – mittlerweile bewilligten – Graduiertenkolleg mündete. Geplant ist der Ausbau der kunsttheoretisch, kunstpsychologisch und medienwissenschaftlich ausgerichteten Frankfurter Kunstgeschichte; gleichzeitig wird im alten Gebäude der Deutschen Bibliothek in unmittelbarer Nähe zur Stadt- und Universitätsbibliothek eine umfassende Kunstbibliothek entstehen, die auch einem größeren Publikum zugänglich gemacht wird.

In der Afrika-Forschung, die beginnend mit Leo Frobenius zu den Forschungsschwerpunkten unserer Universität gehört, denken wir an eine Weiterentwicklung zu einem inner- und außeruniversitär attraktiven Afrika-Kompetenzzentrum, in dem neben den rein wissenschaftlichen Aufgaben auch afrikabezogene Beratungs- und Begutachtungsauf-

Learning on the Net:
The Online University

Both for full-time students and for Frankfurt's large number of part-time students, the periods of presence during their studies will be complemented by work with study materials transmitted via the new media. After the completion of pilot projects, we want to achieve a complete area coverage and systematic use of the new media. The aim is to complement periods in which the students have to be present at the university with consistently structured online studies that are to be extended together with co-operation partners.

The Four Campus Model

Our university was founded in 1914, on the basis of scientific institutions that already existed in Frankfurt and, in accordance with the wishes of our founders and patrons, with faculties of social science and economics, natural science, human science, and medicine. Today we are continuing this tradition and are concentrating our reform efforts, again on the basis of our existing strengths and the specific location advantages of the city and region, in four main fields: law and economics, social and cultural sciences, natural and biological sciences, and medicine.

With the "Cultural Agreement" concluded in March 1999 between the City of Frankfurt and the State of Hesse, new perspectives have been opened up for the development of the Goethe University in four locations. The Bockenheim campus will remain the home of law and economics, the social and cultural sciences will move to the Westend campus, all natural sciences will be brought together on the Niederursel campus, and the medical campus in Niederrad will be expanded. This location concept is intended to provide a basis for future interdisciplinary initiatives and for the identification of activities across locations – including co-operation with other universities, with scientific institutions outside the university, with the economic and industrial sectors, and with other partners.

In which direction will these four central locations evolve? An intensive discussion of the details is already under way within the faculties. Certain trends however, are already visible today.

Finance: Innovations
in Law and Economics

Law and economics have orientated the creation of their research and teaching profile according to the special location conditions of the Rhein-Main finance and service region with its banks, insurance companies, consultancy firms, IT and logistics companies, and advertising agencies. The Centre for Financial Studies has become a recognised international meeting point for scientists

and practitioners; the Graduate College "The Finance Economy and Monetary Economics", in which nine professors participate, sees itself as an interface between well-founded theoretical analysis and an intensive relationship to practical work in the Frankfurt finance centre; in the innovative fields of investment and e-commerce two new professorial chairs have been created. It is intended to remodel the Institute for Foreign and International Economic Law, rich in traditions, into a Centre for Financial Law, which will be connected with a foundation professorship. Within this environment there is also a course for lawyers (LLM, Magister Legum) who have already graduated abroad. Furthermore, a further qualification as Master of Business Administration (MBA) with a main focus on finance will be established. In addition, the Faculty of Mathematics is preparing, together with the Faculty of Economics, a programme of co-operation with banks from Frankfurt in the field of mathematical finance.

Internationality:
More foreign language courses on offer

The social and cultural sciences are devoting special efforts to the establishment of interdisciplinary programmes. We are intending to set up a Centre for Chinese and East Asia Studies in which sinologists, social scientists, lawyers and economists will be able to participate. In the Faculty of Modern Languages, representatives of various linguistic sciences are to co-operate in an interdisciplinary manner within the Institute for Compara-

tive Linguistics. Under the heading "Types of Sentences: Variations and Interpretations", representatives from different branches of linguistics have started to co-operate, and this has resulted in the foundation of a Graduate College which has now been approved. It is planned to extend the Institute for the History of Art, which is oriented towards the theory and psychology of art and the media sciences; at the same time a comprehensive art library is being established in the old building of the German Library close to the city and university library, which will also be accessible to a larger public.

We are planning to expand our research on Africa, which has since the beginning with Leo Frobenius been one of the main research foci of the university, into an Africa Competence Centre that will be attractive both inside and outside the university by providing, in addition to its purely scientific tasks, Africa-related consultation and expert advice. Of special interest could be the systematic further development of a new archaeology, which traditionally combines the human sciences with experimental natural scientific methods (Analytical Archaeology).

In view of the importance of comparative linguistics, renaissance studies, and urban and regional research oriented towards Europe, it would be a good idea to extend provision for foreign language study and to consider foreign language competence as a precondition for admission to certain courses. Regulations governing undergraduate and doctoral degrees are being revised to permit

Besuch eines ehemaligen Physik-Studenten der Goethe-Universität: Physik-Nobelpreisträger 1998 Prof. Dr. Horst Störmer (links) wird bei seinem Gastvortrag herzlich empfangen.

A visit from a former Goethe University physics student: The winner of the 1998 Nobel Prize for Physics, Prof. Dr. Horst Störmer (left) is cordially received on giving his guest lecture.

gaben wahrgenommen werden sollen. Von besonderem Interesse könnte die systematische Weiterentwicklung einer neuen Archäologie sein, die traditionell geisteswissenschaftliche und experimentell-naturwissenschaftliche Verfahren miteinander verbindet (Archäologische Analytik).

Insbesondere Komparatistik, Renaissance-Studien und die europäische orientierte Stadt- und Regionalforschung legen es nahe, fremdsprachliche Studienangebote zu erweitern als auch Fremdsprachen als Zugangsvoraussetzungen für bestimmte Studiengänge zu erwägen. Prüfungs- und Promotionsordnungen werden geöffnet für fremdsprachliche Arbeiten und die Beteiligung ausländischer Gutachter, Fremdsprachenkenntnisse werden zu einem Berufungskriterium.

Highlights in
Naturwissenschaften und Medizin

Drei konkrete Bauvorhaben werden den Campus Niederursel und seinen interdisziplinären Forschungsansatz deutlich stärken: das bereits im Bau befindliche Max-Planck-Institut für Biophysik und von Seiten der Universität das Zentrum für Strukturbiologie und der Neubau der physikalischen Institute. Der Realisierung des Zentrums bis Oktober 2001 ist eine wichtige Voraussetzung für den Ausbau der Strukturbiologie mit Röntgenanalytik, NMR, EPR, Massenspektroskopie, Infrarotspektroskopie und Elektronenmikroskopie. Ziel ist es, ein Zentrum für Strukturbiologie als ein international führendes Exzellenzzentrum der Strukturaufklärung zu etablieren.

Bereits im Oktober 1998 wurde eine langfristige Forschungskooperation im Bereich der Kernmagnetresonanz-Spektroskopie (NMR) zwischen der Goethe-Universität und Aventis vereinbart. Aventis unterstützt dieses Projekt über vier Jahre mit 11 Millionen Mark. So kann die NMR-gestützte Wirkstoff-Forschung und damit die weltweit führende Stellung als NMR-Forschungsstandort weiter ausgebaut werden.

Ein weiteres großes Kooperationsprojekt startete im November 2000: Die Goethe-Universität und die Henkel AG in Düsseldorf gründeten eine gemeinsame biotechnologische Forschungsgesellschaft. „Phenion" – so der Name des gemeinsamen Unternehmens – hat seinen Sitz am Biozentrum auf dem Campus Niederursel. Ziel ist es, das Unternehmen als wirtschaftlich unabhängiges Kompetenzzentrum für biologische und biotechnologische Forschung erfolgreich am Markt zu etablieren. Ein Umzug in das Frankfurter Innovationszentrum (FIZ) ist nach dessen Fertigstellung in etwa zwei Jahren vorgesehen. Auch dieses Projekt wird den zunehmenden Erwartungen nach einer engeren Zusammenarbeit zwischen Universität und Wirtschaft Rechnung trage: Die Resultate unserer Forschung werden auf diese Weise rascher umgesetzt, während wir von Management und Marketing eines internationalen Konzerns profitieren können. Diese Kooperation bedeutet für beide Partner eine „win-win-Situation".

Als flankierende notwendige Maßnahme ist die Bioinformatik in Frankfurt etabliert worden, zum Wintersemester 2000/2001 wurden die ersten 36 Studierenden im Bioinformatik-Studiengang aufgenommen. Die Forschung zu „molekularen Magneten", die von den Festkörperphysikern und – chemikern konzipiert wurde, soll in den nächsten

Jahren ausgebaut und durch Nanotechnologie verstärkt werden. Ein umfangreiches Forschungsprogramm theoretischer und experimenteller Schwerionenphysik wird in Kooperation mit der Darmstädter Großforschungseinrichtung Gesellschaft für Schwerionenforschung entwickelt.

Der Schwerpunkt IT soll in der Informatik gefördert werden. Gleichzeitig soll die informatikorientierten Mathematik verstärkt und vielfältige innovative Informatikanwendungen in den anderen Disziplinen erreicht werden.

In der Medizin existieren drei Forschungsschwerpunkte: Vaskuläre Biologie, Analyse neuronaler Systeme (Moleküle, Zellen und Schaltkreise) sowie Molekulare Diagnostik und Therapiestrategien maligner Erkrankungen. Diese Forschungsschwerpunkte sollen in Zukunft weiter vertieft und stärker mit den Niederurseler Biowissenschaften verknüpft werden.

Unterstützung und Verpflichtung:
Stiftungsprofessuren und Hochschulrat

Viele dieser Entwicklungsperspektiven lassen sich nur auf der soliden und Jahrzehnte lang gewachsenen Kooperationsbasis von Wissenschaft und Wirtschaft realisieren. Als ehemalige Stiftungsuniversität sind wir nicht nur den Bürgern Frankfurts, sondern auch der Wirtschaft der Region immer besonders verbunden. Ausdruck dieser Verbundenheit sind elf Stiftungs(gast)professuren und -dozenturen, eingerichtet von Unternehmen, Institutionen und Verbänden, um die wissenschaftlichen Fachgebiete der Universität zu erweitern. Besonders populär ist die vom S. Fischer Verlag errichtete, vom Suhrkamp Verlag übernommene Gastdozentur für Poetik, in deren Rahmen Schriftsteller und Schriftstellerinnen wie Ingeborg Bachmann, Heinrich Böll, Martin Walser, Günter Grass und Ernst Jandl Vorlesungen hielten. Im naturwissenschaftlichen Bereich gründete zum Beispiel die Hoechst AG die Rolf-Sammet-Stiftungsgastprofessur, seit 1985 hielten so namhafte auswärtige Naturwissenschaftler Vorträge an der Goethe-Universität. Der Gedankenaustausch zwischen Wissenschaft und Gesellschaft sowie die Wechselbeziehungen unterschiedlicher Wissenschaftsbereiche, insbesondere der Natur- und Geisteswissenschaften, soll durch die 1986 von der Deutschen Bank eingerichtete Stiftungsgastprofessur angeregt werden. In bester Frankfurter Mäzentradition stiftete Generalkonsul Bruno H. Schubert eine Professur für Umweltforschung.

Die Kontakte zwischen unserer Universität und ihrem Umfeld werden in den nächsten Jahren noch enger werden: Im neuen Hessischen Hochschulgesetz wurde der Hochschulrat als neues Beratungsgremium geschaffen – für uns eine Chance, externe Kenntnisse für die strategische Entwicklung der Universität zu nutzen. Dieser Hochschulrat hat nicht die Aufgabe der gesellschaftlichen Kontrolle

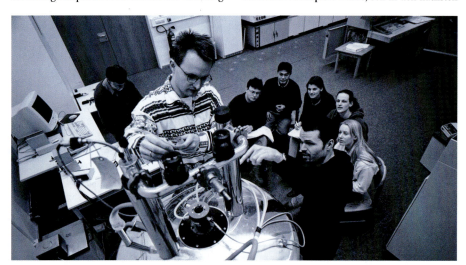

Grundlagenforschung und Wirkstoff-Forschung am NMR-Spektroskop: In der NMR-Forschung ist Frankfurt weltweit führend. Die Goethe-Universität hat mit Aventis eine langfristige Forschungskooperation auf diesem Gebiet begonnen, dabei unterstützt Aventis dieses Projekt über vier Jahre mit 11 Millionen Mark.

Pure and active substance research at the NMR spectroscope: Frankfurt is a worldwide leader in NMR research. The Goethe University has started a programme of long-term research co-operation with Aventis in this field; Aventis is supporting this project for four years with 11 million marks.

submissions in foreign languages and the participation of foreign examiners, and foreign language
competence is becoming a criterion in professorial appointments.

Highlights in Natural Sciences and Medicine
Three concrete construction plans will do much to
strengthen the Niederurusel campus and its interdisciplinary research approach: the Max Planck
Institute for Biophysics, which is already under
construction, and on the part of the university the
Centre for Structural Biology and the new building of the Institute for Physics. The completion of
the centre by October 2001 is an important precondition of the further development of structural
biology with x-ray analysis, NMR, EPR, mass spectroscopy, infrared spectroscopy, and electron mi-
croscopy. The aim is to establish a centre for structural biology as a leading international centre of
excellence for research into structures.
In October 1998 a long-term programme of research co-operation was agreed between the
Goethe University and Aventis in the field of nu-
clear magnetic resonance spectroscopy (NMR).
Aventis is supporting this project for four years
with 11 million marks. In this way NMR-assisted
research on additives and Frankfurt's worldwide
leading position as an NMR research location can
be extended further.

Another large co-operation project is starting in
November 2000: the Goethe University and
Henkel AG in Düsseldorf are founding a mutual
biotechnological research society. This joint venture, called Phenion, will have its headquarters in
the Biocentre on the Niederursel campus. The aim
is to position the enterprise as an economically independent competence centre for biological and
biotechnological research successfully in the market; it is planned to move into the Frankfurt Innovation Centre (FIZ) after its completion in
around two years. This project too will take account of the increasing expectation of close co-operation between the university and the economic
sector: The results of our research will thus be implemented faster, and we will be able to profit
from the management and marketing of an international corporation. This co-operation means
that both partners will be in a win-win-situation.
As a necessary supporting measure, a bioinformatics programme has been founded in Frankfurt. The first 36 bioinformatics students began
their studies in the winter semester 2000/2001.
Research on molecular magnets which has been
designed by solid state physicists and chemists is
due to be expanded in the next few years and
reinforced by nanotechnology. An extensive research programme of theoretical and experimental heavy ion physics is being developed in co-op-

*Arbeiten im Genlabor: In ihren Praktika lernen die Studierenden neue
biotechnologische Methoden.*

*Working in the gene laboratory:
In their practical periods the students learn new biotechnological methods.*

eration with the large research institution in
Darmstadt, the Centre for Heavy Ion Research.
A focus on IT will be promoted within information studies, and at the same time mathematics
oriented towards information studies is to be
strengthened and numerous innovative information applications in other disciplines will be
developed.
In medicine, there are three main research foci:
vascular biology, analysis of neuronal systems
(molecules, cells and switch circuits), and molecular diagnostics and therapy strategies for the treatment of malign diseases. These foci will be extended and combined more intensely with the
biosciences based in Niederursel.

Support and Obligation:
Foundation Professorships and
the board of governors
Many of these development perspectives can only be realised on the basis of decades of solid co-
operation between science and the economic sector. As a former endowed university, we are especially close not only to the citizens of Frankfurt but
also to the economic sector of this region. Expres-
sions of this closeness are eleven foundation
(guest) professorships and lectureships established by enterprises, institutions, and associations in order to expand the range of scientific
fields covered by the university. The guest lectureships for poetry founded by the publishers S.
Fischer Verlag and later taken over by the
Suhrkamp Verlag are particularly popular. Writers
like Ingeborg Bachmann, Heinrich Böll, Martin

Walser, Günter Grass, and Ernst Jandl have been
among the guest lecturers. In the field of natural
science the Hoechst AG established the Rolf Sam-
met Foundation Guest Lectureship, and since
1985 renowned foreign natural scientist have giv-
en lectures at the Goethe University. The exchange
of ideas between science and society as well as in-
teractions between the different scientific fields,
especially the natural and human sciences, have
been enhanced by the foundation professorship
established by the Deutsche Bank in 1986. In the
best Frankfurt tradition of patronage, the General
Consul Bruno H. Schubert has donated a chair for
environmental research.
The contacts between our university and its surrounding environment will become even closer in
the next few years. In accordance with the terms
of the new University Law of Hesse, the University Council has been created as a forum for consultation. This gives us an opportunity to benefit
from external expertise for the strategic development of the university. The board of governors
does not have the task of social control of the university; its function is rather to establish a bridge
between the main fields of teaching and research
in the university and its social surroundings in
the economic sector and science. The members
of the board of governors are appointed by the
Ministry of Science at the suggestion of the managing board together with the new Senate. We
have been successful in persuading seven outstanding personalities from the field of economy
and science to participate in the work of the board
of governors.

Johann Wolfgang von Goethe Universität
Frankfurt am Main

Das Jügelhaus (hier im Jahre 1906) ist heute noch das zentrale Gebäude auf dem Campus Bockenheim und war einst die Keimzelle der Goethe-Universität. Die Carl Christian Jügel-Stiftung regte 1902 die Gründung einer „akademischen Lehranstalt für die Gebiete der Geschichte, Philosophie, sowie der deutschen Sprache und Literatur" an.

The Jügel House (seen here in a photograph from 1906) remains the central building on the Bockenheim campus and was once the nucleus of the Goethe University. In 1902, the Carl Christian Jügel Foundation was instrumental in establishing an "academic teaching institute for the fields of history, philosophy as well as German language and literature".

der Universität, er soll vielmehr eine Brücke zwischen den Schwerpunktbereichen in der Universität in Lehre und Forschung und dem gesellschaftlichen Umfeld in Wirtschaft und Wissenschaft herstellen. Die Mitglieder des Hochschulrats werden durch das Wissenschaftsministerium auf Vorschlag des Präsidiums im Benehmen mit dem neuen Senat berufen. Es ist gelungen, sieben herausragende Persönlichkeiten aus dem Bereich von Wirtschaft und Wissenschaft für die Mitarbeit zu gewinnen.

Ebenso lange wie die Frankfurter Universität existiert auch die Vereinigung von Freunden und Förderern, in der sich schon seit der Gründung der Frankfurter Alma Mater Bürger und Unternehmen aus Frankfurt und dem Umland zusammenschlossen, um die Entwicklung der Hochschule finanziell und ideell zu unterstützen. Heute zählt die Vereinigung über 1.200 Einzelmitglieder, unter ihnen auch zahlreiche Alumni der Goethe-Universität, und fast 120 Unternehmen aus dem Rhein-Main-Gebiet. Viele dieser Firmen haben bereits die Entstehung der Universität aktiv vorangetrieben.

Input von außen immer wichtiger:
Die Drittmittelförderung

Ohne einen Zugewinn an Drittmitteln – sei es durch EU- oder staatliche Fördermittel, wie beispielsweise die Deutsche Forschungsgemeinschaft, sei es aber auch durch Kooperationen mit der Industrie – wird unsere Universität in Zukunft nicht lebensfähig sein. Drittmittel sind in wachsendem Ausmaß eine Finanzierungsquelle universitärer Forschung und Indikator ihrer Forschungsqualität; die Goethe-Universität strebt daher eine Erhöhung des Drittmittelvolumens an. Die Frankfurter Geschichtswissenschaften, die bei DFG-Bewilligun-

gen in ihrem Fachgebiet die bundesdeutsche Spitzenstellung einnehmen, haben unter Beweis gestellt, dass eine hohe Drittmitteleinwerbung auch in den klassischen geisteswissenschaftlichen Fächern möglich ist. Die Bedeutung dokumentiert sich in dem hohen Volumen an Drittmittelgeldern und Einnahmen aus der Auftrags- und Verbundforschung – 1999 insgesamt mehr als 92 Millionen Mark.

Kooperationsformen:
Technolgietransfer und
Gründerzentrum

Seit 1986 fördert die Abteilung Wissenstransfer schwerpunktmäßig die Kooperation zwischen der Universität und der Wirtschaft; dieses Feld soll zügig in der Region ausgebaut werden. Die im Mai 2000 gegründete Firma INNOVANTIS als Verwertungsgesellschaft universitären Wissens markiert einen weiteren Meilenstein in der Strategie anwendungsoffene Grundlagenforschung und wissensbasierte Aktivitäten der Wirtschaft zu vernetzen. Die Firma INNOVANTIS ermöglicht Unternehmen der Wirtschaft einen professionellen Zugang zu technologischem Know-how und exzellenter apparativer Ausstattung der Universität. INNOVANTIS vermittelt Forschungs- und Entwicklungs- sowie Technologiedienstleistungen der Universität für Unternehmen der Wirtschaft. Diese Firma engagiert sich außerdem bei der Vermarktung von universitärem Know-how und bietet Spin-off-Unternehmen aus der Universität verbesserte Startmöglichkeiten.

Desweiteren bemüht sich unsere Universität darum, dass in unmittelbarer Nähe des Campus Niederursel ein Gründerzentrums entsteht; dort könnten auch geplante Firmengründungen aus universitären Forschungszusammenhängen hervorragend eingebunden werden. Mit der Ansiedlung von forschungsnahen Firmen und Existenzgründungen von Hochschulabsolventen werden in den kommenden Jahren hoch qualifizierte Arbeitsplätze in Frankfurt geschaffen.

Weltweite Netzwerke
wissenschaftlicher Kooperation

Auch unsere internationalen Beziehungen werden kontinuierlich ausgebaut, wir pflegen Partnerschaften zu Universitäten in West- und Osteuropa, in den USA und Israel. Neben den gesamtuniversitären

Kontakten kooperieren unsere Wissenschaftler in EU-Projekten mit ausländischen Universitäten. Die Fachbereiche stehen im regelmäßigen Austausch mit Fachkollegen im Ausland. Darüber hinaus beteiligt sich die Goethe-Universität Frankfurt an speziellen, durch die EU geförderten Studien- und Austauschprogrammen. Im Rahmen des Erasmus- bzw. Sokrates-Programms und besonders des Lehrprogramms „Minerva" (Mobilität europäischer akademischer Institutionen) findet ein regelmäßiger Austausch von Lehrenden zwischen den Universitäten Lyon 2/Lumière, Universidad Barcelona und der Goethe-Universität Frankfurt statt. Auch zahlreiche Studierende nehmen die Möglichkeit wahr, über EU- oder DAAD-Programme an unsere Universität zu kommen oder von hier aus ins Ausland zu gehen. Jedes Jahr besuchen etwa 160 Gastwissenschaftler die Goethe-Universität, darunter eine beträchtliche Zahl international angesehener Alexander von Humboldt-Stipendiaten.

Die Goethe-Universität als wichtiger
Arbeitgeber im Rhein-Main-Gebiet

Nicht zu vernachlässigen ist zudem die Rolle der Goethe-Universität als wichtiger Arbeitgeber und Wirtschaftsfaktor in der Rhein-Main-Region: 8.000 Menschen sind in den wissenschaftlichen und nicht-wissenschaftlichen Bereichen beschäftigt. Mit rund 400 Ausbildungsplätzen ist die Goethe-Universität größter Ausbildungsbetrieb nach der Industrie in der Region. Die jährliche Ausgaben von Studierenden und Bediensteten von zirka 900 Millionen Mark sichern etwa 4.400 Arbeitsplätze in Frankfurt und Umgebung. ∎

Die Goethe-Universitäts: Facts

Studierende: 36900 (Stand Wintersemester 2000/2001)
davon:
- 9.670 in Rechts- und Wirtschaftswissenschaften
- 15.830 in Gesellschafts- und Kulturwissenschaften
- 8.750 in Naturwissenschaften
- 2.650 in Medizin
davon:
- 19.620 Frauen
- 6.250 Ausländerinnen und Ausländer
    aus 93 Nationen

Professorinnen und Professoren:	600
Wissenschaftliche Mitarbeiter:	1.500

Etat in 2000: 469 Mio. DM für Forschung und Lehre
(einschliesslich Fachbereich Humanmedizin)

Sonderforschungsbereiche: 8
davon:
- 1 in Rechts- und Wirtschaftswissenschaften
- 2 in Gesellschafts- und Kulturwissenschaften
- 4 in Naturwissenschaften
- 1 in der Medizin

Graduiertenkollegs: 12
- 2 in Rechts- und Wirtschaftswissenschaften
- 5 in Gesellschafts- und Kulturwissenschaften
- 5 in Naturwissenschaften

The Association of Friends and Supporters of the university has been in existence as long as the university itself. Ever since the foundation of the Frankfurt Alma Mater, citizens and businessmen from the city and the surrounding area have come together to support the development of the university both financially and with ideas. Today the association has more than 1,200 individual members, among them many alumni of the Goethe University, and almost 120 enterprises from the Rhein-Main area. Many of these companies were actively involved in the establishment of the university.

The growing importance of external input and funding

Without an increase in external funding, whether it comes from the EU or state grants, for example from the Deutsche Forschungsgemeinschaft (German Research Society), or through co-operation with the industrial sector, our university will not be able to survive in future. Exernal funding is a growing source of finance for university research and indicates the quality of the research; for this reason the Goethe University is endeavouring to increase the volume of its external funding. Frankfurt's historians, who receive more funding from the DFG than historians at any other university in Germany, have proved that high levels of external funding can also be attained in the classical human sciences. Its importance is documented by the high level of external funding and income from contract and cooperative research – a total of more than 92 million marks in 1999.

Digitale Bibliotheken: Literatur- und Textrecherche am Computer.
Digital libraries: Literature and text searches using computers.

The Goethe University: Facts

Students: 36.900 (status winter semester 2000/2001)
of these:
- 9.670 in law and economics
- 15.830 in social and cultural sciences
- 8.750 in natural sciences
- 2.650 in medicine
of these:
- 19.620 women
- 6.250 male and female students from abroad from 93 nations

Male and female professors: 600
Scientific employees: 1.500

Budget in 2000: 469 Mio. DM for research and teaching (including the faculty of human medicine)

Collaborative Research Centres: 8
of these:
- 1 in law and economics
- 2 in social and cultural sciences
- 4 in natural sciences
- 1 in medicine

Graduate Colleges: 12
- 2 in law and economics
- 5 in social and cultural sciences
- 5 in natural sciences

Forms of co-operation:
Technology Transfer and the Founder Centre

Since 1986, the Department of Knowledge Transfer has been promoting co-operation between the university and the economic sector as a main focus; this field is to be rapidly extended within the region. The company INNOVANTIS, founded in May 2000 for the exploitation of university knowledge, marks a further milestone in the strategy of networking between applications of basic research and the knowledge-based activities of the economic sector. INNOVANTIS gives economic enterprises professional access to technological know-how and an extremely well-equipped university. INNOVANTIS acts as an agency, making research and development as well as the technological services of the university available to enterprises from the economic sector. The company is also engaged in the marketing of university-based know-how and offers improved start-up possibilities to spin-off companies of the university.

Furthermore, our university is engaged in the establishment of a Founder Centre close to the Niederursel campus. Further company foundations resulting from university-based research are planned and could be integrated very well here. With the settlement of companies close to research and the setting up of companies by university graduates, highly qualified workplaces will be created in Frankfurt in the coming years.

Worldwide Networks of Scientific Co-operation

Our international relations are also expanding continuously. We have partnerships with univer-sities in Western and Eastern Europe, the USA, and Israel. Apart from general university contacts, our scholars co-operate in EU projects with foreign universities. The faculties maintain regular contacts with specialist colleagues abroad. Furthermore, the Goethe University participates in special study and exchange programmes supported by the EU. Within the Erasmus and Socrates programmes and especially the teaching programme Minerva, there is a regular exchange of teaching staff between the universities of Lyon 2/Lumière, Universidad Barcelona and Goethe University Frankfurt. Numerous students make use of the opportunity to study in Frankfurt through an EU or DAAD programme or to go abroad from here. Each year, around 160 guest scholars visit the Goethe University, among them a considerable number of internationally renowned holders of Alexander von Humboldt scholarships.

The Goethe University, an important employer in the Rhein-Main area

We should not forget the role the Goethe University plays as an important employer and economic factor in the Rhein-Main region: 8,000 people are employed in the scientific and non-scientific fields. With around 400 apprenticeships the Goethe University is the largest training institution in the region after the industrial sector. The yearly expenditure by students and service personnel amounts to approximately 900 million marks and supports around 4,400 jobs in Frankfurt and the surrounding area. ∎

MKI – managt die Welt der Kommunikation

MKI – Managing the World of Communications

MKI ist ein führendes Projekt Management Unternehmen für den Ausbau von Kommunikationsinfrastrukturen mit einem belegbaren Ruf für Zielerreichung, Kundenzufriedenheit, Qualität und Sicherheit. Wir beschäftigen zurzeit weit über 800 Mitarbeiter in über 30 Büros innerhalb von Europa und Asien. MKI hat seine Projekt Management-Erfahrung in einer breiten Palette von Telekommunikationsinfrastrukturen angewandt und somit ein Fachwissen entwickelt, das einzigartig für die Branche ist. MKI ist sich bewusst über den Wettbewerb in der Branche und stellt das Kundenvertrauen an erster Stelle, so dass höchste Ansprüche erfüllt werden. Alle Mitarbeiter sind sich vollends bewusst über die Bedeutung der Kundenerfordernisse, von der Projektinitiierung an bis zur Übergabe und Instandhaltung jedes einzelnen Projekts.

Service und Dienstleistungen

Projekt Management bei Kommunikationsinfrastruktur roll-out Programmen – Mobilfunknetze, Glasfaser Netzwerke, Vermittlungszentralen, Telekom- und Co-location-Plätze. Die angebotene Servicepalette beinhaltet unter anderem die Machbarkeitsstudien eines Projekts, Standortfindung und Akquisition, Planung, Entwurf, Bau, Installation & Kommissionierung sowie die Instandhaltung für diese Märkte. Weitere typische durchgeführte Aufgaben von MKIs Projekt Management sind unter anderem: Projektsteuerung, Materialbeschaffung, Zeitplanung, Programmierung, Bewertung/Projektkontrolle und Kostenplanung. Insbesondere ein Aspekt des Projektmanagements, mit dem kein anderes Telekommunikationsunternehmen konkurrieren kann, ist der Erfolg von MKI im Umgang mit den Ungewissheiten von Erstbenutzerrechten – einschließlich der Identifikation, Selektion und Akquisition der benötigten Anlagen. Diese Dienstleistungen

werden auf weltweiter Basis angeboten und von jedem MKI Standort aus unterstützt.

Bereiche, in denen MKI stark ist
- Flexibilität
- Skalierbarkeit
- Kosteneffizienz
- Alles aus einer Hand
- Qualität & Sicherheit
- Belegbarer Leistungsnachweis
- Zuverlässigkeit unserer Sub-Unternehmer und Lieferanten

Fiberglas und Switch Netzwerke

MKI hat in ganz Europa und Asien zahlreiche auf dem neuesten Stand befindliche SDH Ring-Topologie Netzwerke entworfen, installiert und aktiviert. Diese Aufträge wurden gemäß sehr hoher Anforderungen innerhalb von sehr begrenzten Zeitrahmen ausgeführt.

Nationale Netzwerke

MKI hat den Entwurf, die Fertigung und Aktivierung nationaler Glasfaser Netzwerke erfolgreich abgeschlossen, welche Sprach-, Daten- und Video-Transfer in Frankreich, Deutschland, der Schweiz, Italien, Spanien, Belgien, Holland, Irland und Großbritannien ermöglichen. Diese Netzwerke verbinden die wichtigsten Städte in den entsprechenden Ländern miteinander und bieten eine geschützte nationale Abdeckung für den Betreiber.

Technische Einrichtungen

Bis heute hat MKI über 500.000 m² technische Fläche in mehr als 20 Ländern ausgebaut. Diese Erfahrung bedeutet, dass wir auf ein großes Wissensspektrum zurückgreifen können. MKI ist in der Lage, technische Einrichtungen gemäß höchster Qualität und Spezifikation innerhalb äußerst enger Zeitrahmen fertigzustellen, um unseren Kunden die schnellstmögliche Nutzung zu ermöglichen. Unsere fundierten Beziehungen zu

bewährten Lieferanten erlauben es uns, die besten Preise und Lieferzeiten für unsere Kunden zu sichern. MKI ist Experte in Entwurf, Spezifikation und Installation von AC, DC, UPS und mit Notstrom betriebenen Systemen, um die Sicherheit der Einrichtungen zu gewährleisten und Kundenservice zu garantieren. Alle von MKI installierten technischen Einrichtungen werden einem strengen Prüfungs- und Kommissionierungsverfahren unterzogen und werden komplett dokumentiert in detailliert angefertigten Bestandsplänen und anderen Berichten.

Mobilfunk Netzwerke

Seit 1993 hat MKI Standorte akquiriert und mehr als 2.800 Mobilfunkstationen in ganz Großbritannien entworfen und errichtet. Die internationalen Verträge waren unter anderem für WLL-, GSM-, UMTS-Kunden und internationale Anlagenhersteller ausgeführt worden. In den meisten Fällen bedeutet dies die effektive Abwicklung mehrerer gleichzeitig laufender Baustellen. Bauarbeiten beinhalten unter anderem Elemente aus den Bereichen Hoch- und Tiefbau, Bautechnik, Maschinenbau und Elektrotechnik, Stahlbauarbeiten, Einrichtung von Türmen und Verstärkerstationen und, wenn nötig, Liaison mit regionalen Elektrizitätsgesellschaften. Verschiedene nennenswerte Verträge sind in West-, Zentral- und Nord-Europa abgeschlossen worden. Dazu gehören unter anderem: Belgien, Deutschland, Holland, Spanien, Portugal, Italien, Polen, die Tschechei, Ungarn und die Schweiz. ∎

MKI is a leading project manager of communications infrastructure build-out programmes, with a proven reputation for quality control, target completion, customer satisfaction and health and safety. We currently employ in excess of 800 staff with over 30 offices throughout Europe and the Asia-Pacific region. MKI has applied its project management skills to a wide range of telecommunications infrastructure, thus developing an expertise unique to the industry. MKI are very conscious of the competitive nature of the industry and prioritise client confidentiality, ensuring the fullest expectations are met. All staff are fully aware of the importance of Client reqirements, from initial project start-up to handover and maintenance of each project.

Services Provided

Project Management of Communications Infrastructure roll-out programmes – Wireless Networks; Fibre Optic Networks; and Switch, Telecoms and Co-location Space. The range of services on offer includes Feasibility Studies, Site Finding and Acquisition, Planning, Design, Construction, Installation & Commissioning, as well as Maintenance for these markets. Other typical functions carried out by MKI's project management teams include project engineering, material procurement, scheduling, programming, value engineering and cost budgeting. Specifically, one aspect of project management with which no other telecommunications company can compete, is the unprecedented success of MKI managing the uncertainties of rights of way – including the identification, selection and acquisition of the required facilities. These services are provided on a world-wide basis, supported from any MKI location.

Where MKI Adds Value

- Flexibility
- Scalability
- Cost Efficiency
- One Stop Shop
- Quality & Safety
- Proven Track Record
- Reliability of our contractors and suppliers

Fibre Optic and Switch Networks

Throughout Europe and Asia, MKI has designed, installed and activated numerous state-of-the-art SDH ring topology networks. These contracts are built to high specifications within a very restricted time frame.

National Networks

MKI has successfully completed the design, construction and activation of national fibre optic networks carrying voice, data and video traffic in France, Germany, Switzerland, Italy, Spain, Belgium, Holland, Ireland and the UK. These networks link up the major cities in the respective

countries and provide proprietary nation-wide coverage for the operator.

Technical Facilities

To date MKI has completed more than 500,000 m² of technical space in over 20 countries. This experience means that we have a huge knowledge base to draw upon. MKI are able to complete technical facilities to the highest quality and specification within extremely demanding time frames to give our clients the quickest time to market possible. Our established relationships with major suppliers allow us to secure the best prices and delivery times available for our clients. MKI are experts in the design, specification and installation of AC, DC, UPS and emergency power generation systems to ensure the security of the facility to guarantee customer service. All of the technical facilities installed by MKI are subject to rigorous testing and commissioning procedures, and are fully documented by detailed As Built drawings and other records.

Wireless Networks

Since 1993, MKI has acquired sites locations, designed and constructed in excess of 2,800 wireless base stations throughout the UK. Internationally, contracts have included WLL, GSM, UMTS clients and international equipment manufacturers. In most cases this involves the fast-track construction of a significant number of concurrent sites. Construction work has included elements of civil, structural, electrical and mechanical engeneering, steelwork manufacturing, installation of towers and cabins, rigging and where necessary liaison with regional electricity companies. Several notable contracts have been secured in Western, Central and Northern Europe. Involvement includes; Belgium, Germany, Holland, Spain, Portugal, Italy, Poland, Czech Republic, Hungary and Switzerland. ■

Managing the World of Communications

MKI GmbH

Geschäftsführer/Manager:
Nicholas Leslie Hart
Martin Thomas

Kontakt in Deutschland/Contact in Germany:
Charles Reed (International TeleCenters)
John English (Fibre Optic Networks)
Dariusz Binczyk (Wireless)

Gründungsjahr/Year of Foundation:
1991, in Deutschland/in Germany since seit 1995

Mitarbeiter/Employees:
ca. 100 Mitarbeiter in Deutschland, ca. 800 weltweit
app. 100 people within Germany, app. 800 worldwide

Geschäftstätigkeit/Business Activity:
ITC/Switch/Nodes/
ITC/Switch sites have been completed in Frankfurt (app. 1.000 m², 3.000 m², 10.000 m² and 25.000 m²), Munich (800 m²), Stuttgart (750 m²), and Düsseldorf (630 m², 4.200 m²), Hannover (970 m²), Hamburg (3,400 m² and 780 m²) and Berlin (250 m²).

Mobilfunk/Wireless:
MKI machen Projekt Management für Akquisition, Entwurf und Bau von Mobilfunkplätzen in Deutschland
MKI are project managing the acquisition, design and construction of wireless sites in Central Germany.

Netzwerke/Networks:
Eines der ambitioniertesten Projekte, die MKI bislang unternommen hat ist der Aufbau eines nationalen Netzwerks in Deutschland, welches sich über 3.000 km (3 loops) erstrecken wird und die wichtigsten Städte Deutschlands miteinander verbinden wird. MKI hat bereits 1995 mit dem Bau eines 144 Fiberglas-Netzwerks für die Metropole Frankfurt begonnen. MKI hat auch City-Netzwerke in Hamburg und Düsseldorf errichtet und baut diese City Netzwerke kontinuierlich aus.
One of the most ambitious projects undertaken by MKI is the construction of a national network in Germany, which will stretch over 3.000 km (3 loops) and link up the major cities in Germany. MKI started constructing a 144 fibre optic metropolitan area network in Frankfurt back in 1995. MKI has also constructed city networks in Hamburg and Düsseldorf and is continuously expanding the these city networks.

Standorte in Deutschland/Locations in Germany:
Frankfurt, Hamburg, Düsseldorf, Stuttgart, München

Kunden/Clients:
WorldCom, Global Crossing, GasLine, IAXIS, Nortel, Cabel & Wireless, Exodus, DigiPlex, ECRC, Lucent Technology, Mannesmann, Nokia, E-plus

Anschrift/Address:
Taunusstraße 52–60
D-60329 Frankfurt am Main
Telefon   +49 (69) 242 942-0
Telefax   +49 (69) 242 942-99
Internet   www.mki.net

Hauptsitz/Head Office:
MK International Ltd.
76-78 Chertsey Road
Woking, Surrey; GU21 5BJ
United Kingdom
Telefon   +44 (0) 148 37 48-100
Telefax   +44 (0) 148 37 15-076

Wissenstransfer von renommierten Instituten zu innovativen Unternehmen

Knowledge-Transfer from renowned Institutes to Innovative Enterprises

Wer in New York über die Rhein-Main Metropole Frankfurt spricht – dies geschieht immer öfter – denkt an Flughafen, an die europäische Zentralbank und ganz allgemein an Finanzdienstleister. Wenn man schon Forschung und Innovation à la Frankfurt bewertet, so bezieht man sich nicht auf staatliche Institutionen, sondern eher auf Unternehmen wie Hoechst und Degussa. Mancher erinnert sich auch an die führende Rolle der Sozialwissenschaftler mit Marcuse und Horkheimer, die Frankfurter Schule.

Erinnerungen trügen, besonders weil Frankfurt nie eine verträumte Universitätsstadt wie Marburg oder Tübingen war, sondern Mediziner, Naturwissenschaftler und Ingenieure sich die Anerkennung der Nachwelt mit Kultur, Finanzwelt und Politik teilen mussten. Unter vielen berühmten Namen aus der Frankfurter Wissenschaftlerszene soll beispielhaft nur an Paul Ehrlich, Nobelpreisträger und Entdecker des Salvarsans erinnert werden. Paul Ehrlich arbeitete als Forscher und Arzt am Georg-Speyer-Haus, einer privaten Stiftung für die medizinische Forschung. Mit seinem japanischen Kollegen Sachachuro Hata entwickelte er die Komponente 606 – die 605 Vorläufer zeigen keine Wirkung – das erste wirksame Medikament gegen die Plage jener Zeit, die Syphilis.

Vertrauensvolle Kooperationen zwischen Grundlagenforschung und zeitgleicher industrieller Anwendung haben in Frankfurt Tradition. Justus Liebig, der Gießener Chemiepapst, vermittelte seinen Assistenten August Wilhelm von Hoffmann als ersten Direktor an das neu gegründete Royal College of Chemistry in London. Sein Schüler Perkin sollte zwar aus dem Teerprodukt Anilin das fiebersenkende Chinin herstellen, fand dabei aber den ersten synthetischen Farbstoff Mauve, genannt nach der hellvioletten Farbe der Malven. Aufgrund der großen Nachfrage der Textilindustrie nach synthetischen Farbstoffen, entstand in Frankfurt die Anilinfabrik Lucius und Meister, die „Rothwerker", welche sich später zu dem Chemieweltkonzern Hoechst entwickelte.

Wissenschaft in Frankfurt war immer international. Man hat die besten Wissenschaftler geholt,

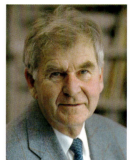

Prof. Dr. Hans Günter Gassen

Der Autor ist Geschäftsführender Direktor des Instituts für Biochemie an der TU Darmstadt. Er studierte Chemie in Marburg, Dissertation im Bereich Proteinchemie. Nach Forschungsaufenthalt am Oak Ridge Laboratorium, USA, ab 1971 Mitarbeit am Max-Planck-Institut für Experimentelle Medizin in Göttingen. Habilitation an der Universität Münster. 1973 Leiter des Fachgebietes Biochemie an der TU Darmstadt. Sechs Jahre Leiter des Forschungsverbundes „Angewandte Gentechnik" und von 1992 bis 1998 Vorsitzender der Fachgruppe Biochemie der GDCh. Gründer und Gesellschafter der B.R.A.I.N. GmbH, GENIUS GmbH und N-Zyme BioTec GmbH. Seit 1998 Beauftragter für Biotechnologie der Hessischen Technologiestiftung. Mitglied der DFG-Senatskommission „Lebensmittel" und Gutachter für Forschungsfördernde Institutionen.

The author is Managing Director of the Institut for Bio-Chemistry at the Technical University of Darmstadt. He studied chemistry in Marburg, dissertation in the field of protein chemistry. After a stay for research purposes at the Oak Ridge Laboratory, USA, from 1971 on collaboration at the Max-Planck-Institute for Experimental Medicine in Göttingen. Phd at the University of Münster. 1973 Head of Faculty of Bio-Chemistry at the TU Darmstadt. Six years Head of Research Association for "Applied Gene Technology" and from 1992 till 1998 Chairman for the Special Group Biochemistry of the GDCh. Founder and Associate of the B.R.A.I.N. GmbH, GENIUS GmbH and N-Zyme BioTech GmbH. Since 1998 Delegate for Biotechnology of the Hessian Technology Foundation. Member of the DFG-Senate Commission "Food Stuff", Expert Advisor for Institutions of Research Promotion.

Das Georg-Speyer-Haus, seit 100 Jahren ein Zentrum für die molekulargenetische Forschung. Während die Fassade fast unverändert blieb, beherbergt das Innere modernst ausgestattete Laboratorien.

The Georg-Speyer-House, since 100 years a centre of molecular-genetic research. While the façade has remained unchanged, the interior houses the most modern furnished laboratories.

Die Urkunde der Verleihung des Nobelpreises an Paul Ehrlich aus dem Jahre 1908.

The Document of the Award of the Nobel Prize to Paul Ehrlich in the year 1908.

Paul Ehrlich in der um die Jahrhundertwende üblichen Laborkleidung in seinem mikrobiologischen Laboratorium.

Paul Ehrlich, wearing the laboratory clothing used around the turn of the century, in his microbiological laboratory.

that social scientists like Marcuse and Horkheimer of the Frankfurter School played.

But memories can deceive, especially because Frankfurt has never been a dreamy university town like Marburg or Tübingen, but medical and natural scientists as well as engineers had to share the recognition of the post-world with personalities from culture, finance and politics. Amongst the many famous names of the Frankfurt scientist scene as example should be mentioned the one of Paul Ehrlich, Nobel Prize winner and discoverer of the Salvaran. Paul Ehrlich worked as scientist and medical doctor at the Georg-Speyer-House, a private foundation for medical science. With his Japanese colleague Sachachuro Hata he developed the component 606 – the prior 605 did not show any effect – the first effective medicine against the plague of the time, syphilis.

Trustworthy co-operations between basic research work and parallel industrial application are traditional in Frankfurt. Justus Liebig, pope of chemistry of Gießen, arranged for his assistant, August Wilhelm von Hoffmann, the position of the first director at the newly founded Royal College of Chemistry in London. His student Perking was supposed to produce from the tar product aniline the fever-reducing quinine, but found instead the first synthetic colouring Mauve, called after the light-violet colour of the mallow. Because of the great demand of the textile industry for synthetic colourings in Frankfurt the aniline factory Lucius and Meister, the "Rothwerker" emerged, which later became the world chemistry group Hoechst.

Science has always been international in Frankfurt. The best scientists have been brought here, but also very successful ones have been sent into the world. In the landscape of science Frankfurt as well as the area from Gießen till Darmstadt stand out through creative diversity and not through monolithic dominance. The first place in the science hierarchy belongs to the university with its excellent clinical research de-

partment, the bio-scientists with its structural research and the great thinkers of the social sciences. This core unit of research and instruction is complemented in specialist polytechnics, the Max-Planck-Institute and federal and regional research institutes. Because of their excellent international reputation the following are to be pointed out: the Max-Planck-Institutes (MPIs) for biophysics and neurological research, the Paul-Ehrlich-Institute in Langen and the Georg-Speyer-House.

Another characteristic of Frankfurt are also the associations of the chemical and pharmaceutical industry that provide a bridge between the institutions and enterprises under public law like for example the association of the chemical industry and the Dechema.

Apart from the information technology the biotechnology will become the key industry of the new century. The most important fields of application of biotechnology lie in the area of pharmaceuticals as well as in diagnostics and in therapy.

Genetically produced medicines like Insulin, Interferon and Erythropoetin achieve billions in turnover on the world market. The DNA diagnostic enables the recognition of illnesses that early, that only the therapy of a small surgery is needed. The imminent deciphering of the human genome shall make the therapy of many hitherto incurable illnesses possible through bio-informatics. Of similar importance biotechnology has become for

W hoever speaks in New York about the Rhein-Main metropolis Frankfurt – and this does happen more and more – thinks about the airport, the European Central Bank and about financial service providers in general. If one has to evaluate science and innovation à la Frankfurt at all, one does not refer to state institutions, but rather to enterprises like Hoechst and Degussa. Some few people will also be reminded of the leading role

Luftaufnahme des Paul-Ehrlich-Instituts in Langen. Das Bundesforschungsinstitut ist zuständig für die Zulassung von Blutprodukten und Diagnostika. Die Grundlagenforschung erstreckt sich über alle Gebiete der in-vitro-Medizin.

Aerial photograph of the Paul-Ehrlich-Institute in Langen. The federal research institute is responsible for the admission of blood products and diagnostica. The basic research work extends over all fields of in-vitro medicine.

aber auch die Erfolgreichen in alle Welt geschickt. In der Wissenschaftslandschaft besticht Frankfurt wie das Umfeld von Gießen bis Darmstadt durch kreative Vielfalt und nicht durch monolithische Dominanz. Der erste Platz in der Wissenschaftshierarchie gehört der Universität mit einer hervorragenden klinischen Forschung, den Biowissenschaften mit der Strukturforschung und den Vordenkern aus den Sozialwissenschaften. Dieser Kern als Einheit von Forschung und Lehre wird ergänzt durch Fachhochschulen, Max-Planck-Institute und Forschungsanstalten des Bundes und der Länder. Aufgrund ihrer exzellenten internationalen Reputationen sind hervorzuheben die MPIs für Biophysik und für Hirnforschung, das Paul-Ehrlich-Institut in Langen sowie das Georg-Speyer-Haus.

Eine Frankfurter Besonderheit sind auch die Verbände der chemisch-pharmazeutischen Industrie, die eine Brücke zwischen öffentlich-rechtlichen Institutionen und Unternehmen darstellen, so etwa der Verband der Chemischen Industrie und die Dechema.

Neben den Informationstechniken wird die Biotechnologie zur Schlüsselindustrie des begonnenen Jahrhunderts werden. Die wichtigsten Anwendungsgebiete der Biotechnologie liegen im Pharmabereich sowohl in der Diagnostik wie in der Therapie. Gentechnisch hergestellte Medikamente wie Insulin, Interferon und Erythropoetin erzielen Milliardenumsätze auf den Weltmärkten. Die DNA-Diagnostik erlaubt es, Krankheiten so rechtzeitig zu erkennen, dass mit einem geringfügigen chirurgischen Eingriff therapiert werden kann. Die bevorstehende Entschlüsselung des Human Genoms wird über die Bioinformatik die Therapie vieler bisher unheilbarer Krankheiten ermöglichen.

Eine ähnliche Bedeutung hat die Biotechnologie in der Landwirtschaft und in der Lebensmittelverarbeitung. In den USA werden bereits auf ca. 35 Millionen Hektar transgene Pflanzen angebaut. Zwar leidet die „Grüne Biotechnologie" noch unter Akzeptanzproblemen, aber da ihre Anwendung mehr Lebensqualität bedeutet, wird sie sich durchsetzen. Dass Frankfurt das deutsche Zentrum der Pharmaindustrie ist, ist allgemein bekannt, und somit existiert der Markt für medizinisch orientierte Start ups. Hessen ist aber auch ein Schwerpunkt der Lebensmittelwirtschaft mit Nestlè und Milupa. Ernährung als Motor der Gesundheit wird mit Hilfe der Biotechnologie zu der Erfolgsstory der nächsten Jahre werden.

Weltweit sind in der Biotechnologie die Amerikaner führend, während auf dem Kontinent die

Engländer von den Deutschen abgelöst wurden. Bayern hat als erstes Bundesland die Zeichen der Zeit erkannt und die Biotechnologie wie das zugehörige wissenschaftliche Umfeld kontinuierlich und mit Augenmaß gefördert. In den Wettbewerb um die Spitzenpositionen in Deutschland reihen sich dann NRW, Baden-Württemberg und Berlin-Brandenburg ein. Frankfurt hat aufgrund seiner Tradition, der Verkehrslage und der Dichte an wissenschaftlichen wie industriellen Betrieben mit Abstand die beste Ausgangslage mit Bezug auf die Biotechnologie. Was allerdings fehlt, ist die Anschubfinanzierung für Biotech-Start ups als unverzichtbare Konnektoren zwischen Wissenschaft und Industrie. Anders als IT-Firmen haben sie einen hohen anfänglichen Finanzbedarf für Investitionen. Gewinne werden aber erst nach drei bis fünf Jahren erzielt. Somit wird nicht die wissenschaftliche Idee oder die Expertise des Gründerteams zum begrenzenden Faktor der Ausgründung sondern die überlegte Finanzierung für die ersten vier bis sechs Jahre.

Unabdingbar für die Nr. 1-Position „Frankfurt Biotech" ist die Kooperation zwischen Finanzdienstleistern, der finanziellen Förderung durch Staat und Landesregierung sowie eine international renommierte Wissenschaft. Kreativität und Innovation braucht die Harmonie im Verständnis von Mensch zu Mensch und soziale Verlässlichkeit. Deshalb ist die räumliche Nähe von Grundlagenforschung, Biotech-Startups und vermarktender Industrie ein „conditio sine qua non" für den wirtschaftlichen Erfolg.

Kreative Köpfe, gleichgültig ob in Instituten oder Unternehmen, brauchen im Umfeld ein attraktive Umgebung, ob bei Kultur, Erziehung, Sport oder Entertainment. Wo könnte also Biotechnologie als Wissenstransfer von renommierten Instituten zu innovativen Unternehmen besser gedeihen als in Frankfurt? ∎

Scientific Institutions in Hesse

Kassel p

Marburg p □

p ○ Gießen

Fulda ○

□ ○ Friedberg

Frankfurt p
○ □

Mainz p □

p ○ **Darmstadt**

p **Würzburg**

Heidelberg p

p University
○ Technical College
□ other research institutes

Eine regionale Übersicht über die wichtigsten wissenschaftlichen Institute in Hessen.

A regional overview of the most important scientific institutes in Hesse.

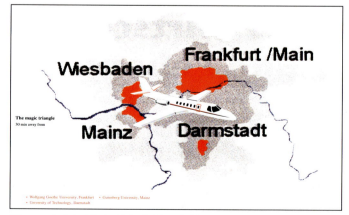

Wissenschaft im Rhein-Main Gebiet wird begünstigt durch die optimalen Verkehrsanbindungen, besonders durch den internationalen Flughafen.

Science in the Rhein-Main region profits from the optimal transport connections, especially the international airport.

agriculture and the processing of foodstuff. The USA is already cultivating around 35 million hectares of land with transgenetic plants. In fact the "green bio-technology" is still overcoming the problem of being accepted, and since its application signifies an increase in the quality of life it will be successful in the end. It is generally known that Frankfurt is the German centre of the pharmaceutical industry and therefore there exists a market for medically oriented business start-ups. Hesse is however, also a main focus of the foodstuff industry with Nestlè and Milupa. Nutrition as the driving force for health will become with the help of biotechnology the great success story of the coming years.

The Americans are world leaders in biotechnology, whereas on the continent the Germans have replaced the English. Bavaria has been the first federal state to recognise the signs of the time and has developed continuously and with sharp far sight the corresponding scientific environment. Then, in the competition for the lead positions in Germany are Nord-Rhein Westfalen (NRW), Baden-Württemberg and Berlin-Brandenburg. Frankfurt possesses because of its traditions, the transport conditions and the densely settled scientific and industrial landscape by far the best position regarding biotechnology. The only

thing missing is the initial capital for biotech-start ups since they are indispensable connectors between science and industry. Different to IT-companies, they have a high initial need of finance for investments. Profits however, are only made after three to five years. Thus, the limiting factor for forming separate enterprises is not the scientific idea or the expertise of the founder team, but the thorough financial planning for the first four to six years.

Indisputably necessary for the no. 1 position of "Frankfurt Biotech" is the co-operation between financial service providers, the financial promotion by the federal government and regional government as well as an internationally renowned science. Creativity and innovation needs harmony in comprehension of human-to-human and social responsibility. For this reason, the spatial nearness of basic research work, biotech-start ups and the selling industry is a "conditio sine qua non" for economic success.

Creative heads, regardless whether in institutes or enterprises do need an attractive environment, be it in culture, education, sports or entertainment. Where could therefore grow biotechnology as knowledge transfer from renowned institutes to innovative enterprises better than in Frankfurt? ■

Der Nobelpreisträger von 1989, Hartmut Michel, in seinem Labor am Max-Planck-Institut für Biophysik in Frankfurt.

The Nobel Prize winner of 1989 Hatmut Michel in his laboratory at the Max-Planck-Institute for biophysics in Frankfurt.

Die räumliche Nähe von Grundlagenforschung, Biotech-Start ups und vermarktender Industrie schafft in Frankfurt gute Voraussetzungen für den wirtschaftlichen Erfolg.

The spatial nearness of basic research, biotech-start ups and the selling industry creates excellent conditions in Frankfurt for an economic success.

Ice Field Dry Ice Engineering GmbH

Geschäftsführer/Manager:
Thomas Hennig

Gründungsjahr/Year of Foundation:
1998

Mitarbeiter/Employees:
15

Geschäftstätigkeit/Business Activity:
Umweltfreundliche, schnelle und schonende
Lösung komplexer Spezialaufgaben industrieller
Reinigung und Instandhaltung
Environmentally benign, rapid and conserving
solutions of complex specialist tasks for
industrial cleaning and maintenance.

Anschrift/Address:
Industriepark Höchst C343 & C346
D-65926 Frankfurt am Main
Telefon   +49 (69) 308 52-403
Telefax   +49 (69) 308 52-404
E-Mail   info@icefield.de
Internet www.icefield.de

Ice Field – Quantensprung in der industriellen Reinigungstechnik

Ice Field – Quantum Leap in Industrial Cleaning Techniques

Die Icefield (IF) löst Spezialaufgaben industrieller Reinigung und Instandhaltung. Mit dem von IF perfektionierten Hochdruck-Trockenstrahlverfahren werden selbst die komplexesten Reinigungsaufgaben schnell, umweltfreundlich und extrem oberflächenschonend bewältigt. Anlagenstillstandszeiten können drastisch verkürzt werden; eine Abtragsvermischung mit Strahlgut entfällt und ist für Dekont-Applikationen einzigartig. Das Verfahren ist weit effektiver als die meisten traditionellen Reinigungsmethoden – und dies praktisch ohne Abrieb. IF's Kunden sind Topadressen aus der Chemie-, Automobil- und Druckindustrie, die ebenfalls auf IF's individuelle Engineering-Lösungen zwecks Integration, Optimierung und Automatisierung von Reinigungsprozessen zurückgreifen. Seit kurzem wird ein kostengünstiges Verfahren zur Reinigung von kontaminierten Oberflächen, auch radioaktiv, angeboten. IF arbeitet absolut kundenorientiert und hat den Anspruch, der beste Reinigungsdienstleister zu sein. Aktuell entstehen eine Reihe technischer Entwicklungen, die die Vorteile des Hochdruck-Trockeneisstrahlens im Kundensinne weiter verstärken. ∎

Icefield (IF) solves special tasks of industrial cleaning and maintenance. The high-pressure dry ice blasting perfected by IF allows management of the most complex cleaning tasks in a rapid, non-polluting and extremely surface conserving manner. Times of equipment standstill can be shortened drastically; a mixture of removed with blasted materials does not occur and is unique for Dekont applications. The method is far more effective than most traditional cleaning methods and this practically without abrasion. IF's clients are top companies from the chemical, automobile and printing industry that also take recourse to IF's individual engineering solutions for the purpose of integration, optimisation and automation of cleaning processes. Not long ago, an inexpensive method for cleaning contaminated surfaces, also radioactive, was introduced. IF works absolutely client-oriented and claims to be the best cleaning service available. At present, a number of technical developments are being created that will enhance the advantages of high-pressure dry ice blasting for the client even further. ∎

Mit dem Hochdruck-Trockeneisstrahlverfahren werden optimale Reinigungsergebnisse erzielt.
With the high pressure-dry ice blasting method optimal cleaning results are achieved.

Strategisches Einkaufs- und Beschaffungsmanagement

Strategic Purchasing and Procurement Management

Die Büros der hpi im Industriepark Höchst.

The offices of hpi in the Industrial Park Höchst.

hpi GmbH

Geschäftsführer/Manager:
Michael Freienstein

Gründungsjahr/Year of Foundation:
1998

Mitarbeiter/Employees:
130

Umsatz/Turnover:
ca. 90 Mio. DM

Geschäftstätigkeit/Business Activity:
Dienstleistungen mit Schwerpunkt
im strategischen Einkaufs- und
Beschaffungsmanagement
Services with main focus
on strategic purchasing and
procurement management.

Anschrift/Address:
Industriepark Höchst
D-65926 Frankfurt am Main
Telefon   +49 (69) 30 58 47 80
Telefax   +49 (69) 30 58 01 85
Internet   www.hpigmbh.de

*Michael Freienstein,
Geschäftsführer der
hpi GmbH.*

*Michael Freienstein,
General Manager of
hpi GmbH.*

hpi bietet ein breites Spektrum von Dienstleistungen im Bereich Strategischer Einkauf und Beschaffungsmanagement. Global Sourcing, Marktanalysen, Preis- und Vertragsverhandlungen sind ebenso Bestandteil der Leistungspalette wie die Beratung und Unterstützung bei der strategischen Neuausrichtung und Optimierung aller materialwirtschaftlichen Aufgabenstellungen und Prozesse. Dies umfasst u. a. auch selbst entwickelte und in der Praxis erprobte Programme zur Auswahl strategischer Lieferanten und zur Leistungsmessung im Einkauf sowie die Bereitstellung von Data Warehouse-Anwendungen oder die Entwicklung individueller eProcurement-Lösungen (BtB, Kataloglösungen u. a.).

Durch das Wissen und die Erfahrung qualifizierter Einkaufsspezialisten sichert das Unternehmen seinen Kunden attraktive Beschaffungskonditionen.

Die Vorteile für hpi-Kunden:
- niedriger Einstandspreis durch unternehmensübergreifende Bündelung des Bedarfs
- Zugang zu den internationalen Beschaffungsmärkten
- Entlastung des eigenen Einkaufs
- Kooperationsmöglichkeit im Einkauf ohne Abhängigkeit und bei voller Wahrung der Vertraulichkeit. ∎

hpi offers a broad range of service in the field of strategic purchasing and procurement management. Global sourcing, market analyses, prize and contract negotiations are as much part of the service range as is the consulting and support with strategic restructuring and optimization of all material management tasks and processes. This includes for example also self-developed programmes that have been tested in practice for the selection of strategic suppliers and for procurement performance measurement as well as the provision of data warehouse applications or the development of individual eProcurement solutions (B-t-B, catalogue solutions etc.).

Through the know-how and experience of qualified purchase specialists the company ensures its clients attractive procurement conditions.

The advantages for hpi-clients are:
- low cost price through cross-company bundling of demand
- access to international supply
- relief of one's own purchasing
- possibilities of co-operation in purchasing without being dependent, while maintaining complete confidentiality. ∎

HADEN

Haden Drysys GmbH

Geschäftsführer/Manager:
Claus Andresen, John Culliford

Gründungsjahr/Year of Foundation:
1986 in Stuttgart, seit 1995 in Frankfurt
1986 in Stuttgart, since 1995 in Frankfurt

Mitarbeiter/Employees:
50

Geschäftstätigkeit/Business Activity:
Planung, Konstruktion und Erstellung von Turnkey Lackieranlagen für die Automobilindustrie.
Planning, construction and erection of turnkey paint systems for the automotive industry.

Anschrift/Address:
Berner Straße 76
D-60437 Frankfurt am Main
Telefon   +49 (69) 50 91 94-0
Telefax   +49 (69) 50 91 94-99
Internet   www.haden.com

Lackieranlage von Haden GmbH/ Frankfurt für General Motors Azambuja, Portugal.

Paint Booth System by Haden GmbH/Frankfurt for General Motors Azambuja, Portugal.

Hauptsitz in Frankfurt am Main.

Headquarter in Frankfurt at the Main.

Individuelle Oberflächen- technik für Automobile

Individual Surface Technique for Automobiles

Haden Drysys GmbH ist ein weltweit tätiger Systempartner der Automobilindustrie – unsere Lackieranlagen bestimmen das Erscheinungsbild und die Qualität der Korrosionsschutzgebung von Automobilkarossen wesentlich mit. Lackieranlagen für DaimlerChrysler und VW sowie schlüsselfertige Lackierwerke für BMW in Südafrika und für OPEL in Azambuja, Portugal, gehören zu unseren Referenzen. Designo-Farben und Effektfarben werden ebenso in den Anlagen verarbeitet, wie alle anderen Nass- und Pulverlacke. Wesentliche Fortschritte wurden in den letzten Jahren bei dem Einsatz von umweltfreundlichen Lacksystemen und Kostenreduzierungen durch Prozessänderungen erzielt.

Die vielfältigen Aufgabenstellungen werden von der Haden International Group mit Sitz in der Automobilhauptstadt der USA, Detroit, unterstützt. Von hier aus werden die amerikanischen Automobilhersteller in Nord- und Südamerika betreut und die weltweiten Haden-Aktivitäten koordiniert. In eigenen Labor- und Versuchseinrichtungen werden die Lackierlösungen für die Zukunft entwickelt. In den Forschungs- und Entwicklungsprogrammen werden die Markttrends und -anforderungen der Kunden in Amerika, Europa und Asien gleichermaßen berücksichtigt. Haden Drysys GmbH plant, konstruiert und erstellt komplette Autolackieranlagen mit Gebäude, Gebäudetechnik und dem dazugehörigen Service.

Unser Lieferprogramm umfasst:
- Vorbehandlungsanlagen,
- Elektrophoretische Beschichtungsanlagen,
- Spritzkabinen mit Zu- und Abluftanlagen und Wärmerückgewinnungsanlagen,
- Lackpartikel-Auswaschsysteme mit Lackschlammaufbereitung, -trocknung, und Abwassertechnik,
- Pulverlackieranlagen,
- Applikationssysteme für Nasslacke, Pulver und Dickstoffe,
- Farb- und Materialversorgungssysteme,
- Lacktrocknung mit AirRadiant ® oder konventionelle Trocknung,
- Fördertechnik,

Optimale Standortvoraussetzungen, ein zukunftsorientierter technischer Background und investitionsfreudige Kunden lassen uns optimistisch in die Zukunft schauen. Wir verstehen uns als globales Team und anerkannter Partner und sorgen unter Beachtung der Umwelt und Ressourcen für einen bestmöglichen Kosten/Nutzen Effekt.   ∎

Haden Drysys GmbH is worldwide active as system partner to the automotive industry. Our paint booth systems characteristically determine the appearance and quality of corrosion prevention given to the automotive car body. Our references include paint booth systems for DaimlerChrysler and VW as well as turnkey enamelling lines for BMW in South Africa and for OPEL in Azambuja, Portugal. Modern design colours and colours of intensive effect are also processed by these systems as well as all other wet and powder coatings. Considerable progress has been achieved in the last years in the use of ecological coating systems as well as in costs reduction through changes in processing. Haden International Group located in the capital of the US automotive industry, Detroit, supports the various operational tasks. From this city most of the American automotive manufacturers in North and South America are supported and furthermore, the worldwide activities of Haden are co-ordinated. In self-owned laboratories and test facilities the paint solutions of the future are being developed. Our research and development programmes evaluate the market trends and requirements of clients in America, Europe and Asia equally and thus enable the Haden Associations all over the world to produce adjusted, optimised and tailor-made concept solutions for each client. Haden Drysys GmbH designs, constructs and erects complete automotive paint booth systems with building complex, advanced building technology and the corresponding service.

Our programme of supplies includes:
- Pre-treatment systems,
- electrophoretic coating,
- spray booths with air filtration and heat processing systems
- paint sludge removal-, processing- and drying systems as well as wastewater treatment systems
- powder coating systems
- application systems for wet paint, powder and thick matter
- paint- and material supply systems
- paint drying with AirRadiant ®, or conventional drying,
- material-handling technology.

We are looking optimistically into a bright future, because of a location with optimal conditions, a future-oriented technical background and clients that are prepared to invest. We regard ourselves as a global team and recognised partner taking care that, while considering the environment and its ressources, the best possible cost/benefit effect is achieved.   ∎

ESA: Kompetenz durch Erfahrung

ESA: Competence through Experience

ESA Elektronik
Stark- und Schwachstromanlagen GmbH
Ein Unternehmen von
Thyssen Facility Management

Geschäftsführer/Manager:
Dr. Heinz-Werner Grebe,
Dipl oec. Peter Jelich
Dr. Frank Voßloh

Gründungsjahr/Year of Foundation:
1949

Mitarbeiter/Employees:
rund 300

Umsatz/Turnover:
50 Millionen Euro

Geschäftstätigkeit/Business Activity:
TGA

Anschrift/Address:
Berner Straße 35
D-60437 Frankfurt am Main
Telefon   +49 (69) 3 90 01-0
Telefax   +49 (69) 3 90 01-233
E-Mail   c.becker@esa-thyssenkrupp.de
Internet   www.esa-thyssenkrupp.de

Hessische Landesbank (li) und Maintower (re).
Hessische Landesbank (l) and Main Tower (r).

Seit rund 50 Jahren profitieren Kunden im Rhein-Main-Gebiet von ESA-Kompetenz auf den Gebieten Stark- und Schwachstrom und der Datentechnik. Etwa 300 Mitarbeiter und Auszubildende engagieren sich täglich vor Ort auf den Baustellen, bei der Planung und Abwicklung, der Objektbetreuung für die Gebäude und Anlagen der Kunden. Fachgerechte Beratung, vorausschauende Planung, effiziente Unterstützung der an den Projekten beteiligten Fachleute bis hin zur Übernahme der Gesamtverantwortung für die Abläufe gehören zum Dienstleistungsangebot des zukunftsorientierten Unternehmens. Modernstes Equipment, hervorragend ausgebildete Mitarbeiter und ein schnelles Team garantieren, dass auch auf Veränderungen beim Objekt permanent und sachgerecht reagiert wird. Das spart Zeit und Kosten.

ESA-Serviceprodukte sorgen auch dafür, dass der Strom in den Gebäuden pulsiert wie das Blut in den Adern. Ein Beratungsgespräch zeigt, welche Potentiale die Kunden nutzen können und was das für die Realisierung der einzelnen Objektes bedeutet.

ESA bietet alle Leistungen aus einer Hand, übernimmt die gesamte Verantwortung von der Beratung und Planung über die Leitung bis zur Funktions- und Betriebssicherheit der erstellten Anlagen. Dies gilt auch für die dauerhafte Betreuung dieser Anlagen, deren Modernisierung oder Erweiterung. ∎

Since around 50 years clients around the Rhein-Main area are benefitting from ESA's competence in the fields of high-voltage and weak current and of data technique. Approximately 300 employees and apprentices are daily engaged locally on construction sites in planning and transaction, technical support of buildings and facilities of the clients. Expert consulting, foresighted planning, efficient support of experts participating in the project up to the taking on of the complete responsibility for the course of events are part of the service provision of the future-oriented company. The most modern equipments, excellently trained employees and a fast team guarantee that even on unprecedented changes in the object, permanent and contextual reactions occur. This saves times and costs.

ESA service products also take care that the current pulsates in the buildings like bood in the veins. A consulting discussion shows, which potentials the clients can use and what this signifies for the realisation of each single object.

ESA offers all services from one provider, takes on the complete responsibility from consulting and planning across management up to the functional and operational security of the erected facilities. This is also valid for the permanent technical support of these facilities, their modernisation and expansion. ∎

DG Bank.

DG Bank.

Forum Frankfurt, Kastor und Pollux.
Forum Frankfurt, Kastor und Pollux.

Im Grünen wohnen, in der Stadt arbeiten: zuverlässige Leistungen im RMV

Living in a Green Surrounding, working in the City:
Reliable Services in the RMV

Die erweiterte Region Rhein-Main, die sich bis zu den Räumen Marburg, Fulda, Aschaffenburg, Erbach, Heppenheim, Bad Kreuznach, Rüdesheim und Limburg erstreckt, hat auf Grund ihrer Wirtschaftsstruktur und ihrer hohen Lagegunst hervorragende Entwicklungschancen. Der in dieser Region liegende Ballungsraum um Frankfurt RheinMain wird durch die Städte Friedberg, Hanau, Darmstadt, Groß-Gerau, Mainz, Wiesbaden, Hofheim, Oberursel und Bad Homburg definiert. In ihm funktioniert das Zusammenspiel von Natur- und Siedlungsräumen mit großem Freizeitangebot, einer modernen, leistungsfähigen Wirtschaftsstruktur und dem vorhandenen Potenzial an qualifizierten Arbeitskräften. Die hohe Lagegunst der Region im europäischen Verkehrswegenetz kennzeichnet sich durch die zentrale Schnittstellenfunktion aller Verkehrswege Schiene, Straße, Wasser und Luft. Die guten Entwicklungschancen lassen sich durch eine entsprechende Standortpolitik mit einer günstigen Beeinflussung der Standortfaktoren und einem aktiven Standortmarketing nutzen.

Im Wettbewerb der Europäischen Regionen werden die Regionen ihre Standortqualitäten erhalten und weiterentwickeln können, die unter Wahrung der Aspekte Lebensqualität und Wirtschaftskraft die erforderliche Mobilität sozial- und umweltverträglich und in vertretbaren Reisezeiten gewährleisten können. Dabei ist nicht so sehr die Reiseentfernung, sondern vielmehr die erforderliche Reisezeit das entscheidende Kriterium.

Die Stärkung des Wirtschaftsraumes und die Erhöhung der Wohn- und Freizeitqualität sind bedeutende Entwicklungsfaktoren des Standortes Hessen. Ein wichtiger Beitrag zur Sicherung der Standortqualität liegt in der Aufrechterhaltung und nachhaltigen Verbesserung der Mobilität.

Die Leistungsfähigkeit des Gesamtverkehrssystems kann durch ein regionales Verkehrsmanagement im Sinne einer integrierten dynamischen Information und einer intermodalen Verkehrslenkung auf der Basis angepasster Strategien erhöht werden. Ziel ist die Sicherung einer möglichst zeit- und ressourcenschonenden Mobilität. Das Leitbild für die Region heißt nicht nur im Grünen wohnen, in der Stadt arbeiten. Es heißt

Volker Sparmann

Nach dem Studium des Bauingenieurwesens wurde der Autor Prokurist in der Freien Planungsgruppe Berlin GmbH, anschließend übernahm er Leitungsfunktionen im nationalen und internationalen Verkehrs-Consulting. Seit dem 1. März 1994 ist Volker Sparmann Alleingeschäftsführer der Rhein-Main-Verkehrsverbund GmbH.

After studying for the civil engineer profession, the author became a fully authorized officer of the Freie Planungsgruppe Berlin GmbH; afterwards he took on management functions in national and international transport consulting. Since 1st March 1994 Volker Sparmann is Sole Managing director of the Rhein-Main Transport Union GmbH.

Jörg Lunkenheimer

Der Coautor studierte Volkswirtschaftslehre und ist seit 1995 bei der Rhein-Main-Verkehrsverbund GmbH als Leiter einer Stabsstelle verantwortlich für die Bereiche Gesellschafter, Politik und Strategie.

The co-author studied political economy and is within the Rhein-Main Transport Union GmbH as head of panel, responsible for the fields associates, policies and strategies, since 1995.

Ein modernes Verkehrssystem als Standortfaktor der Region Frankfurt-Rhein-Main.
A modern transport system as location factor or the Frankfurt Rhein-Main region.

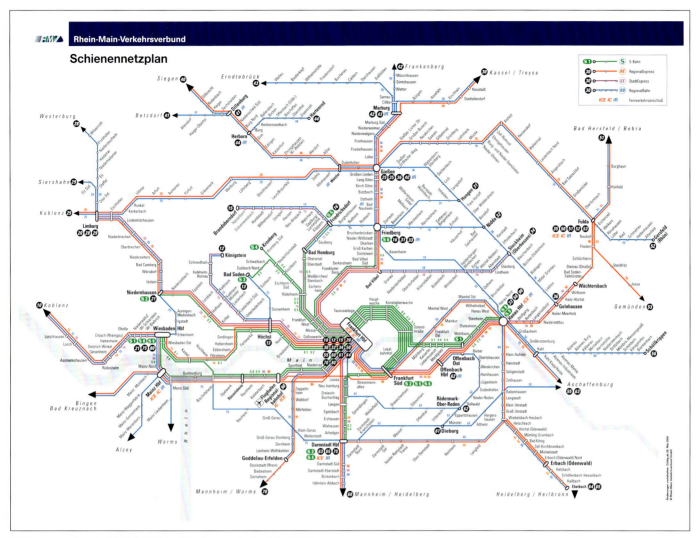

Schienennetzplan des RMV: 1.500 km Streckennetz bedient der RMV
auf einer Fläche von 14.000 km².

Map of the railway network of the RMV:
1.500 km network of tracks is served by the RMV in an area of 14.000 sq. km.

The greater Rhein-Main region that extends into the areas of Marburg, Fulda, Aschaffenburg, Erbach, Heppenheim, Bad Kreuznach, Rüdesheim and Limburg, has because of its economic structure and its highly favourable location excellent chances for development.

The congested urban area situated in this region around Frankfurt Rhein-Main is defined by the cities of Friedberg, Hanau, Darmstadt, Groß-Gerau, Mainz, Wiesbaden, Hofheim, Oberursel and Bad Homburg. Within this space the interaction between natural and settled areas with an extensive leisure time possibilities, a modern and efficient economic structure and an available potential of a qualified labour force. The highly favourable location of the region within the European network of transport is characterised by the central interconnection of all means of transport railway tracks, roads, water and air. It is therefore easily possible to use these good possibilities of development by mixing corresponding politics for the business location with beneficial influences on location factors and active location marketing. In the competition between the European regions, those regions will be able to keep and further develop their location quality that can guarantee the necessary mobility – by maintaining their aspects of the quality of life – in socially and environmentally manner and in reasonable travel times. In this respect not so much the travelling distance, but rather the necessary travel time is the determining criterion.

The strengthening of the economic region and the increase of living and leisure time quality are important factors of development for Hesse as a location. An important contribution in ensuring the location quality lies in the upkeep and lasting improvement of mobility. The efficiency of the complete transport system can be increased through a regional transport management in the sense of integrated dynamic information and intermodality of steering arrangements of transport on the basis adjusted strategies. The aim is to secure as much as possible a time and resources-saving mobility. The ideal situation for the region is not only to live in green surroundings and to work in the city. It also means, to live in a city with quality of life – also with greens – and to work in the office quarters, in the industrial areas or in the surrounding communities. A lively region is mobile and lives in constant exchange. This is the nature of the polycentric region Rhein-Main.

The requirements to revitalise our cities towards the protection of natural and living spaces and towards an energy saving and ecologically harmless transport system force a re-consideration of transport policies and a change of attitude in the trans-

Die Verkehrs-Insel Frankfurt am Main – Kundenbetreuung in der Mobilitätszentrale.
The transport island Frankfurt on the Main – Customer service in the mobility centre.

auch, in einer Stadt mit Lebensqualität – auch mit Grün – wohnen und in der Bürostadt, in den Gewerbegebieten oder im Umland zu arbeiten. Eine lebendige Region ist mobil und lebt in einem regen Austausch. Dies macht den polyzentrischen Raum Rhein-Main aus.

Die Anforderungen an die Revitalisierung unserer Städte, an den Schutz der Natur- und Lebensräume und an ein energie- und umweltfreundliches Verkehrssystem zwingen zum Umdenken in der Verkehrspolitik und im Verkehrsverhalten der Bevölkerung. Ein wirkungsvoller Ansatz ist in der Entlastung der Straßenverkehrsinfrastruktur zugunsten der Nutzung der Schienenverkehrsinfrastruktur zu sehen. Dabei geht es neben der Einbindung in das europäische Hochgeschwindigkeitsnetz der Bahnen auch um die Nutzung und den Ausbau des regionalen Schienenverkehrswegenetzes. Es wird darauf ankommen, wieweit die Regional- und Stadtplanung die Chance der integrierten Verkehrsplanung aufgreift und realisiert. Die Interessen der Gesamtregion sind sowohl auf lokaler als auch auf regionaler Ebene zu berücksichtigen. Es geht um die Entwicklung eines regionalen Bewusstseins bei Wahrung der historisch gewachsenen lokalen Identitäten. Der Rhein-Main-Verkehrsverbund (RMV) zeigt, dass dies funktionieren kann. Der RMV wird als regionale Institution von 15 Landkreisen und 11 Städten auf breiter Basis und geschlossen getragen.

Aus Sicht des optimierten Verkehrssystems ist eine Siedlungsentwicklung dann gut, wenn sie Konzentrationen schafft und Verkehrsströme bildet. Gleichzeitig ruft eine solche Entwicklung den geringsten Ressourcenverbrauch und die geringste Zeitverschwendung hervor. Aus dieser Entwicklung resultieren Einspareffekte bei Fahrzeugkilometern, insgesamt ein moderates Verkehrswachstum sowie eine gute Auslastung der Angebote im öffentlichen Verkehr, bei einer insgesamt geringeren Flächeninanspruchnahme. Im Ergebnis können mehr Mittel zur Attraktivitätssteigerung des Gesamtverkehrsangebotes eingesetzt werden.

Der Rhein-Main-Verkehrsverbund (RMV) – Mobilität für fünf Millionen Menschen
Der Rhein-Main-Verkehrsverbund (RMV) ist als Projekt lokaler und regionaler Zusammenarbeit von 15 Landkreisen, 11 Städten und dem Land Hessen gegründet worden. Er plant und organisiert in Mittel- und Südhessen den regionalen Öffentlichen Personennahverkehr (ÖPNV). Für nahezu fünf Millionen Menschen gelten einheitliche Spielregeln bei der Nutzung des regionalen und lokalen Nahverkehrs. Mit einem Fahrplan, einer Fahrkarte und einem Tarif im RMV ist die Integration des regionalen und lokalen ÖPNV erfolgreich gelungen. Dazu ist seit Verbundstart gemeinsam mit den Aufgabenträgern, den Lokalen Nahverkehrsgesellschaften (LNG) und den Ver-

bundverkehrsunternehmen (VVU) das lokale und regionale Leistungsangebot im RMV in quantitativer und qualitativer Hinsicht weiterentwickelt worden.

Die Städte und Gemeinden in der Region werden im Personenverkehr durch eine abgestufte Verkehrsbedienung miteinander verbunden (Busverkehr im ländlichen Raum, Regionalzüge bei Ober- und Mittelzentren, S-Bahn-Verkehr bei den Zentren des Ballungsraumes zu ihrem jeweiligen Umland, Stadtbahnen und Stadtbusse in den Zentren selbst). Dabei ist die Erreichbarkeit der Zentren aus dem Umland und der Zentren untereinander innerhalb von 60 Minuten sicher zu stellen.

Am 28. Mai 2000 feierte der RMV fünf Jahre Service für die Region. In dieser Zeit wurde mit einem integrierten Marketing-Konzept die Attraktivität des ÖPNV erhöht und damit die Leistungsfähigkeit des Gesamtverkehrssystems gestärkt.

Einen Schwerpunkt bildete die Weiterentwicklung des Leistungsangebotes. Mit der Einführung des Integralen Taktfahrplanes (ITF) zum RMV-Verbundstart konnte den stetig wachsenden re-gionalen Verkehrsverflechtungen im polyzentrisch strukturierten Verbundraum ein entsprechend attraktives Fahrplanangebot gegenübergestellt werden. Insgesamt wurde das Angebot auf der Schiene zwischen den Fahrplanjahren 1993/94 und 2000/2001 um rund 17 % ausgebaut. Im S-Bahn-Bereich konnte das Leistungsangebot auch aufgrund der neuen S-Bahn S9 zwischen Wiesbaden und Hanau und der Verlängerung der S3/S4 nach Darmstadt und Langen überdurchschnittlich um gut 30 % ausgeweitet werden.
Ein weiterer Ausbau und die Modernisierung von Strecken und Bahnhöfen schafft die nötigen infrastrukturellen Voraussetzungen. Diese Maßnahmen werden durch das Fahrzeugprogramm der beiden Verkehrsverbünde und des Landes Hessen begleitet. Das Land Hessen stellte umfangreiche Mittel zur Investition in komfortable Doppelstock-Reisezugwagen, in moderne Dieselleichttriebfahrzeuge und in Fahrzeuge mit Neigetechnik zur Verfügung. Damit werden vor allem die Qualitätsmerkmale Reisezeit und Komfort im Schienen-Personennahverkehr (SPNV) kundenfreundlich gestaltet.

Die Einführung eines verbundeinheitlichen Tarif- und Vertriebssystems bildete die Basis für mittlerweile über 100.000 Job-Tickets und 170.000 Semestertickets sowie für zahlreiche Kombi-Ticket-Angebote, bei denen die Eintrittskarte für das Fußball-Spiel oder das Konzert gleichzeitig die RMV-Fahrkarte ist. Durch

port behaviour of the population. One effective approach can be seen in the relief of the road transport infrastructure in favour of the used of the railway transport infrastructure. Apart from the integration into the European high-speed network of the railways the issue is also about the use and extension of the regional railway transport network. It will be decisive, how much attention the regional and city planning will give to the chance of an integrated transport planning and how far they carry it out. The interests of the whole region must be considered on local as well as on regional levels. It is important to maintain the historically grown local identity while developing a regional consciousness. The Rhein-Main Transport Association called RMV shows that this can work. The RMV as a regional institution is an organization in which 15 counties and 11 townships work on a broad basis and equally share responsibilities.

From the point of view of an optimised transport system a settlement development is of advantage if it creates concentrations and forms transport streams. At the same time, such a development does induce the least use of resources and the least waste of time. This development results in effects of savings in vehicle kilometres, on the whole a moderate growth of transport and a good utilization of the offers in public transport, while in total less surface area is being used. As a conclusion, more means can be employed to increase the attractiveness of the total transport provision.

The Rhein-Main Transport Association (RMV) – Mobility for Five Million People

The Rhein-Main Transport Association (RMV) was founded as a project of local and regional co-operation between 15 counties, 11 townships and the federal state of Hesse. It plans and organises in Middle and South Hesse the regional and public passenger service in near distance (ÖPNV). For almost five million people uniform rules are valid when using the regional and local near distance transport. With a one single timetable, one ticket and one tariff within the RMV the integration of regional and local public passenger service in near distance has been successfully achieved. For this purpose, the local and regional service provision within the RMV has been continuously

developed quantitatively and qualitatively by all the responsible bodies, the local near distance transport associations (LNG) and the companies linked in the transport union (VVU) from the beginning of its foundation.

Cities and communities in the region are systematically connected with each other in the passenger service through a graduated transport service (bus transport in rural areas, regional trains in upper and medium centres, subway trains transport in the centres of dense areas to the directions of their immediate surroundings, city trains and city busses in the centres themselves). The aim is, to ensure that the centres can be reached from their surroundings and the centres among each other within the time of 60 minutes.

On 28th May 2000 the RMV celebrated its fifth year of service for the region. In this period, by use of an integrated marketing concept the attractiveness of the ÖPNV was increased and thus the efficiency of the total transport system was strengthened.

One focus consists of the continuous development of the service provision. With the introduction of the integral rhythmic timetable (ITF) a correspondingly attractive timetable offer could be proposed at the start of the RMV association, which

was able to stand the ever-increasing demands of regional transport interrelations in a polycentric structured union.

In total, the rail provision was extended between the years of timetables 1993/94 and 2000/2001 by around 17 %. In the field of subway trains, it was possible to extend the service provision by a good 30 % above average, because of the new subways S9 between Wiesbaden and Hanau and the extension of S3/S4 to Darmstadt and Langen.

A further extension and the modernisation of tracks and train stations create the necessary preconditions of infrastructure. These measures are being accompanied by the vehicle programme of both transport unions and of the federal state of Hesse. The state of Hesse provided ample means for the investment in comfortable double-decker travel train wagons, in modern light diesel engine vehicles and in vehicles within inclining techniques. In this way, above all characteristics of quality like travel time and comfort within the passenger near distance transport on railways (SPNV) can be planned beneficially to the customer.

The introduction of a unitary tariff and sales system within the union formed the basis for meanwhile over 100.000 job tickets and 170.000 student tickets as well as for a number of combination offers for tickets, which consist of football game or

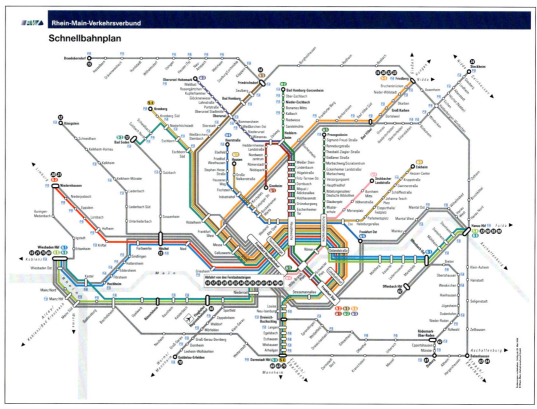

Schnellbahnplan des RMV.

Fast train map of the RMV.

ein zielgruppenspezifisches Marketing werden die Ziele Kundengewinnung und Kundenbindung unterstützt.

In der Leistungsqualität sieht der RMV ein weiteres Angebotsmerkmal und damit einen weiteren Erfolgsfaktor, den es günstig zu beeinflussen gilt. Neben den genannten Infrastrukturmaßnahmen, werden auch die Merkmale Sicherheit, Sauberkeit und Service durch entsprechende Programme kundengerecht gestaltet. Beispielsweise fährt ab 21.00 Uhr in jeder S-Bahn ein zusätzlicher Mitarbeiter zur Sicherheit der Fahrgäste mit.

Das Leistungsangebot im RMV ist für den Berufspendler, den Geschäftsreisenden und den Freizeittouristen gleichermaßen attraktiv. Wenn mehr als 35 % der Wege durch Beruf und Ausbildung initiiert werden, so ist dies für den ÖPNV ein entscheidender Teil des insgesamt wachsenden Verkehrsmarktes. Zunehmend mehr Wege werden in der Freizeit und am Wochenende angetreten. Durch ein entsprechendes Angebot an Verkehrsleistungen im Freizeitbereich, wie dem Vogelsberger Vulkan-Express-Bus werden neue Segmente bedient und neue Potentiale erschlossen.
Die Informationen über das Leistungsspektrum des RMV werden über vielfältige Medien den Menschen nähergebracht, damit Informationslücken – gleichermaßen Zugangshemmnisse zum ÖPNV – geschlossen werden können. Der RMV setzt hier unter anderem auf seine Medien wie die Internetseite des RMV (www.rmv.de) oder die Mobilitätszentralen im RMV, wie die Verkehrsinsel in Frankfurt am Main. Hier sind alle Informationen rund um die Mobilität, einschließlich des Individualverkehrs (Verkehrsmeldungen, Parkhauskapazitäten u. a.), Reise- und Freizeittipps, Hotel- und Restaurantadressen abrufbar.

Der RMV konnte seine Leistung zwischen 1995 und 1999 von 520 Millionen auf 575 Millionen Fahrten erhöhen. Im gleichen Zuge ist der Preisdeckungsgrad, als Maß der Kostendeckung von 52 % auf 57 % gewachsen. Damit konnte mehr ÖPNV für das gleiche Geld geleistet werden.

Die „Neue Mobilität"
Die Welt des Verkehrs ist vielfältiger und bunter geworden. In den letzten Jahren hat sich eine „Neue Mobilität" gebildet, die von Menschen getragen wird, die verschiedene Verkehrsmittel nutzen und dabei die Wegeketten optimal kombinieren. Dies wird realisiert über ein Mobilitätsmanagement mit einer intelligenten Mobilitätsstrategie sowie elektronischen Medien mit umfassenden Informations-, Buchungs- und Zahlungs- systemen über sämtliche Verkehrsdienst-

leistungen hinweg. Eine Möglichkeit ist das Serviceangebot des Elektronischen Fahrgeldmanagements (Electronic Ticketing) unter Verwendung einer Chipkarte. Diese Karte kann neben den Funktionen eines bargeldlosen Zahlens und einer elektronischen Fahrkarte im ÖPNV zusätzliche Anwendungen, beispielsweise als multifunktionale Eintrittskarte für Sportveranstaltungen oder Museen enthalten. Im Mittelpunkt dieser „Neuen Mobilität" wird ein Service angeboten, der umfassende Mobilitätspakete basierend auf der Kooperation der verschiedenen Verkehrsmittel organisiert. Vor diesem Hintergrund und in Kenntnis der Entwicklung anderer Märkte z. B. des Kommunikationsmarktes wird deutlich, dass ein Verkehrsangebot, das nur auf einen Verkehrsträger ausgerichtet ist, dauerhaft nicht im Verkehrsmarkt bestehen kann. Hier sind intelligente ganzheitliche Verkehrssysteme gefordert, wobei deren Vernetzung und der Koordination an den Schnittstellen eine herausragende Bedeutung zukommt. Spezifische Anforderungen und veränderte Lebensstile der Menschen ermöglichen die Bereitschaft zur Veränderung ihres Verkehrsmittelwahlverhaltens.

Zur neuen Mobilität bedarf es auch des Angebotes entsprechender Möglichkeiten – über sämtliche Systeme hinweg. Die ICE-Neubaustrecke Köln-Rhein-Main wird die Städte Frankfurt und Köln künftig in einer Stunde Fahrzeit verbinden. Innerhalb von 25 Minuten erreicht man von Limburg den Flughafen Frankfurt. Dies bedeutet auch einen Entwicklungsschub für die Region. Mit der entsprechenden Ausgestaltung der Schnittstellen zu anderen Verkehrssystemen, besonders mit einer reibungsfreien Verknüpfung des Fernverkehrs mit dem Regional- und Lokalverkehr, kann man diesen Entwicklungsschub weiter stärken.

Lange Zeit wurden ÖPNV und Auto ausschließlich als Wettbewerbsgegner im Kampf um Marktanteile des Gesamtverkehrs angesehen. Diese Betrachtung ist mittlerweile überholt, da die Wahl des Verkehrsmittels wesentlich vom Wegezweck und von strukturellen Rahmenbedingungen, wie ÖPNV-Angebot, Parkraum und ähnlichem abhängt. Mit intermodalen Verkehrskonzepten kann man überzeugen, in dem systemimmanente Schwächen eines einzelnen Verkehrsträgers durch Stärken eines anderen kompensiert werden und eine entsprechende Arbeitsteilung angeboten wird. Der Rhein-Main-Verkehrsverbund hat eine Kooperation mit CarSharing-Organisationen, Car Pool-Gesellschaften und Autovermietungen entwickelt, um sein Serviceangebot in diesem Sinne speziell für seine Jahreskarten-Kunden auszuweiten.

Zusammenfassung
Durch die Vernetzung des regionalen Verkehrs in den Europäischen Regionen können die Verkehrsprobleme wirkungsvoll gemeistert und die Chancen zu einer ökologisch und ökonomisch sinnvollen Entwicklung des Verkehrssystems eines Wirtschafts- und Lebensraumes genutzt werden. Das integrierte Gesamtverkehrssystem dient der optimalen Nutzung der vorhandenen Verkehrsinfrastruktur sowie der wirkungsvollen Umsetzung der Ziele einer modernen Verkehrspolitik. Die Realisierung eines solchen innovativen Konzeptes setzt eine intensive Öffentlichkeitsarbeit und Bürgerbeteiligung voraus. Die Maßnahmenkonzepte müssen vor allem eine ausreichende Breitenwirkung haben, um nachvollziehbare Wirkungen zur Entlastung der Region und der Umwelt erzielen zu können. In diesem Prozess des Wertewandels ist der Bürger als Partner einzubeziehen. Der Rhein-Main-Verkehrsverbund hat in den fünf Jahren seines Bestehens die Leistungen im ÖPNV qualitativ und quantitativ weiterentwickelt. Dabei wurde neben der Beförderungsdienstleistung der Servicebereich ins Zentrum gerückt. Mit neuen Wegen der Fahrgastinformation sowie einer deutlichen Verbesserung der Qualitätsmerkmale Sicherheit und Sauberkeit konnte der genannte Fahrgastzuwachs erreicht werden. Der ÖPNV kann seine Rolle als Leistungsträger im Gesamtverkehrssystem spielen und somit diesen Standortfaktor maßgeblich positiv beeinflussen. ∎

Moderne Doppelstockzüge verbinden Frankfurt mit der Region.

concert ticket and RMV-ticket at the same time. Through a target group specific marketing the aims of client acquisition and client loyalty are supported.

The quality of service provision is for the RMV another characteristic of its provision and thus another factor of success, which must be influenced favourably. Apart from the mentioned measures of infrastructure, also the characteristics of security, cleanliness and services are organised through corresponding programmes in a customer-oriented way.
For example, an additional employee for the security of the passengers accompanies each subway train from 21.00 hours on.

The service spectrum in the RMV is equally attractive for the commuter, the business traveller and the leisure time tourist. If more than 35 % of journeys are initiated by professional or training reasons, this is for the ÖPNV a decisive part of the growing transport market on the whole. Increasingly more journeys are made during leisure times and weekends. Through a corresponding provision of transport services in the field of leisure time, like the Vogelsberger VulkanExpress-Bus new segments are being serviced and new potentials tapped.

Information about the service spectrum of the RMV is brought to the people through varied media, so that gaps of information – as well as hin-

Modern double-decker trains connect Frankfurt and the region.

drances of access to the ÖPNV – can be closed. The RMV counts in this respect on its media, including for example the Internet page of the RMV (www.rmv.de) or the mobility centre s of the RMV, like the transport island in Frankfurt on the Main. Here, all information concerning mobility, including individual transport (traffic news, available parking spaces etc.), travel and leisure time tips, hotel and restaurant addresses, can be obtained.

The RMV was able to increase its efficiency between 1995 and 1999 from 520 million to 575 million journeys. At the same time, the break-even quantity, as a measure of covering expenses, has risen from 52 % to 57 %. Thus more services could be provided by the ÖPNV for the same amount of money.

The "New Mobility"
The world of transport has become more varied and more colourful. In the last years, a "new mobility" has emerged that is carried by people that use different means of transport and thus combines the chains of transport in an optimal way. This is realised through a mobility management with an intelligent mobility strategy as well as electronic media with a comprehensive information-, booking- and payment system across all transport service provisions. One possibility is the service offer of electronic transport charges management (electronic ticketing) by using a chip card. This card can contain additional possibilities of use in the ÖPNV, apart from the functions of payment without cash and an electronic ticket, like for example the multifunctional ticket for sports events or museums.

In the centre of this "new mobility" a service is offered that organises comprehensive mobility packages based on the co-operation of various means of transport. Against this background and in the knowledge of the development of other markets, for example that of communication, it becomes clear that a transport service provision that is only oriented towards one system of transport cannot be of lasting duration in the transport sector. Here, intelligent, comprehensive transport systems are needed, whereby their networking and coordination at various points of linkage becomes an important issue. Specific demands and changed life styles of the people enable the preparedness for a change in their behaviour to choose means of transport.

The new mobility necessitates also the provision of corresponding alternatives – across all systems. The newly built ICE railway stretch Cologne-Rhein-Main will connect the cities of Frankfurt

and Cologne in one hour in the future. Within 25 minutes one can reach the Frankfurt Airport from Limburg. This also means a considerably thrust in development for the region. By correspondingly fitting out the interfaces to other transport systems, especially with a smooth connection of long-distance transport with regional and local transport, one can further strengthen this thrust in development.

For a long time, the ÖPNV and automobiles were exclusively viewed as competitors in the fight for market shares of the total transport. This point of view is meanwhile outdated, since the choice of the means of transport is decisively determined by the purpose of the journey and by the structural framework conditions, like the ÖPNV-offer, parking space and other. With an intermodality of transport concepts one can convince, through compensating weaknesses inherent to the system of a single transport provider by the strengths of another and thus offering a corresponding division of labour. The Rhein-Main Transport Union has developed a co-operation with car sharing organisations, car pool associations and car rentals, in order to extend its service provision in this sense especially for its yearly ticket customers.

Summary
Through the interconnection of regional transport in the European regions the problems of transport can be overcome effectively and the chances utilised for an ecologically and economically valuable development of the transport system within a space for economy and living.
The integrated total transport system serves for an optimal use of the given transport infrastructure as well as the effective realisation of the aims of a modern transport policy. The practical realisation of such an innovative concept presumes an intensive participation of the public and public relations work. The catalogue of measures must above all have a sufficiently broad effect, in order to achieve comprehensible effects for a relief of the region
and the environment. Into his process of change in values the citizen must be included as a partner. The Rhein-Main Transport Union has in the five years of its existence continuously developed its services in the ÖPNV qualitatively and quantitatively. In this respect, apart from the transport service, the field of customer service has been focussed. With new ways of passenger information as well as a marked improvement of quality characteristics like security and cleanliness the mentioned increase in passengers was achieved. The ÖPNV can without doubt play its role within the total transport system and thus influence this location factor decisively positive. ■

Das von Oertzen Plus-Zeichen signalisiert,
wie sich verschiedene Techniken und Dienstleistungen zu
kommunikativen Lösungen verbinden lassen.
Der von Oertzen Doppel-Punkt bedeutet: Das Entstehen von
neuen Kommunikations- und Gestaltungslösungen,
die in einem Gesamtkonzept geplant und durchgeführt werden.
The von Oertzen plus-sign indicates how the differing techniques
and services can be combined to become communicative solutions.
The von Ortzen colon signifies: The emergence of new
communication and design solutions that are planned and
carried out in one comprehensive concept.

von Oertzen GmbH & Co. KG

Geschäftsführer/Manager:
Hans-Henning von Oertzen
Kleo Freese-Holzmann

Mitarbeiter/Employees:
90

Umsatz/Turnover:
7,5 Mio Euro

Geschäftstätigkeit/Business Activity:
Digitale Mediengestaltung und -produktion in
den drei Dienstleistungsbereichen
Digital media design and production in
three fields of service

• IT/Neue Medien/IT/New Media
• Mac Operations/Mac Operations
• Digitaldruck/Digital Printing

für die beiden Geschäftsbereiche/for two business fields:

• Financial Communications/Financial Communications
• Corporate Communications/Corporate communications

Es werden mehr als 100 Kunden betreut, unter anderen:
More than 100 clients receive our attention, for example:

Deutsche Bank
Geschäftsberichte, E-commerce, Werbemittelsteuerung
Business Reports, E-Commerce, control of PR-material

Dresdner Bank
Geschäftsberichte, CD-Applikationen, Internetprojekte
Business reports, CD-applications, Internet projects

Aventis
Vorstandspräsentationen, Verpackungsdesign –
datenbankgestützt
Presentations for the Board, packaging design –
database assisted

Fresenius
Geschäftsberichte, Internetschulungen
Business reports, Internet training

DG Bank
Wertpapierhandbuch – datenbankgestützt
Handbook on securities – database assisted

BHF Bank
Werbe- und Analysenmaterial/PR and analytical material

GFD
Börseneinführungsprojekte/
Projects of introduction to the stock exchange

Despa
Objektdatenbank/Object database

Kontakt/Contact::
Kleo Freese-Holzmann
Mainzer Landstrasse 250-252
D-60326 Frankfurt am Main
Telefon   +49 (69) 7 59 04-0
Telefax   +49 (69) 7 59 04-249
E-Mail   Info@von-oertzen.de
Internet   www.von-oertzen.de

VON OERTZEN
Konzeption ✚ Realisation ꞉ Digital

Das Unternehmen wurde bereits 1950 als Text- und Bildbearbeitungsunternehmen gegründet und ist heute in den Bereichen IT/Neue Medien, Mac Operations und Digitaldruck tätig.

Im Geschäftsfeld **IT/Neue Medien** werden internetbasierte Mediendatenbanken, digitale graphische Workflowprojekte, Webprogrammierungen sowie Print- und Webintegrierende Anwendungen konzipiert und realisiert. Dazu gehört auch, den Kunden beim alltäglichen Umgang mit graphischen digitalen Daten zu unterstützen.

Unter **Mac Operations** sind alle Dienstleistungen zusammengefasst, die heute am Mac realisiert werden können. Hierzu zählen sowohl Multimediadarstellungen, Internetauftritte, Intranetpflege, komplexe Bannererstellungen, Power Point Presentations, als auch Corporate Design Applikationen für Broschüren und Verpackungen sowie typographische Überarbeitungen und komplexe Satz- und Bilderstellungen bis zum fertigen Druck.

Im **Digitaldruck** ist von Oertzen mit vier Maschinen der größte Anbieter in Frankfurt. Hier werden in kürzester Zeit direkt aus dem Datenbestand vollfarbige oder s/w Druckobjekte – oft auch mit variablem Inhalt pro Exemplar – erstellt.

Unter dem Stichwort Konzeption und Realisation werden die Leistungen der einzelnen Bereiche zu Gesamtprojekten vernetzt. Das Unternehmen konzentriert sich auf die beiden Geschäftsbereiche **Financial Communications** und **Corporate Communications**.

Zu Financial Communications zählen beispielsweise Börseneinführungen, Geschäftsberichte, Analystenberichte inclusive aller multimedialer Präsentationen, Digitaldruck und Internetdarstellungen. Zu Corporate Communications gehören unter anderem die Archivierung, Adaption und Steuerung der Werbemittel von Großkonzernen durch eine internetbasierende e-Commerce Anwendung, die Entwicklung und Realisierung von 1:1 Medienlösungen und Corporate Design Datenbanken.

Diese breite Fachkompetenz und die langjährige Erfahrung unterscheidet von Oertzen damit wesentlich von anderen Dienstleistern aus den digitalen Medien. ∎

The company was established as early as 1950 as typesetting and repro company and is today active in the fields of IT/New Media, Mac operations and digital printing. In the business field of **IT/New Media** internet-based media databases, digital graphic workflow projects, web-programming as well as print and web-integrating applications are conceptualised and implemented. This includes also the support of the client in his daily use of graphic digital data.

Mac operations combine all services that can be realised nowadays at the Mac. These include both multimedia presentations, Internet presentations, Intranet maintenance, complex banner creation, power point presentations, as well as corporate design applications for brochures and packaging and typographic redesign and complex layout and picture productions up to the finished print product. In **digital printing** von Oertzen is the largest provider in Frankfurt with four machines. In the shortest possible time fully coloured or b/w printing objects are created directly from the database – often also with variable content in each copy.

Under the heading concept and realisation the services of the individual fields are networked into comprehensive projects. The company is specialized on the two business fields **financial communications** and **corporate communications**.

Financial communications include for example initial public offering, annual reports including research reports of all multimedia presentations, digital printing and Internet presentations. Corporate communications include the filing in archives, adaptation and control of promotional material for large corporations by an internet-based e-Commerce application, the development and realisation of 1:1 media solutions and corporate design databases.

This broad expert competence and its long-year's experience distinguishes von Oertzen thus considerably from other providers of the world of digital media. ∎

Direkt vom Main Tower: Hessens Wirtschaftsradio

Directly from the Main Tower: The Business Radio of Hesse

Ein hochmodernes Hörfunkstudio. Ein Blick über die Skyline Frankfurts. Ein Spitzenplatz. Seit Januar 2000 sendet das Wirtschaftsradio des Hessischen Rundfunks, hr-skyline, von 6 Uhr bis 20 Uhr aus dem 54. Stock des Main Towers mit Informationen, Analysen, Daten aus der Welt des Business. hr-skyline berichtet so schnell, wie der Puls in den Finanzzentren schlägt, so spannend, wie Wirtschaft ist, so fundiert, wie man es von einem öffentlich-rechtlichen Radio erwartet.

Der hr war 1998 die erste ARD-Anstalt, die das hohe Interesse an Wirtschaftsinformationen erkannte und eine auf Wirtschaftsthemen spezialisierte Hörfunkwelle aus der Taufe hob. „Ein Studio hoch oben im neu gebauten Main Tower, mitten in der Skyline von Frankfurt, ist für eine Wirtschaftswelle mit dem Namen „hr-skyline" natürlich besonders attraktiv, auch im Hinblick auf die Gesprächspartner aus Banken und anderen Wirtschaftsunternehmen, die wir dort live am Mikrofon haben", betont Bernd-Peter Arnold, Wellenchef von hr-skyline und hr4.

Aktuelle Börsennachrichten aus Frankfurt, New York und Fernost mit entsprechender Hintergrundberichterstattung gehören ebenso dazu wie Analystengespräche und Reportagen aus Handel, Banken, Industrie und regional ansässigen mittelständischen Unternehmen. Die Hörerschaft von hr-skyline definiert sich nicht über das Alter, sondern über Lebenseinstellung, Interessen und berufliche Orientierung.

Das hr-skyline-Team kann auf das Korrespondentennetz der gesamten ARD zurückgreifen. Die hr-Fachredaktionen sind wichtige Lieferanten von Beiträgen. Ausgewiesene externe Experten zu Wort kommen zu lassen, ist Teil des Konzepts. Eine Kooperation mit dem größten nichtkommerziellen Radiosender der USA, National Public Radio (NPR) in Washington, ermöglicht via Satellit die zeitgleiche Übernahme von Wirtschaftsnachrichtenblöcken in englischer Sprache. ∎

A highly modern audio broadcasting studio. A view across the skyline of Frankfurt. A top location. Since January 2000 the business radio of the Hessischer Rundfunk, hr-skyline, is broadcasting from 6 a.m. to 12 p.m. from the 54th floor of the Main Tower information, analyses, data from the world of business. hr-skyline reports as fast, as beat of the pulse in the finance centres, just as thrilling as the economy is in reality, as founded as one can expect from a radio station under public law.

The hr was in 1998 the first ARD-institution (Arbeitsgemeinschaft der Rundfunkanstalten Deutschlands) to recognise the high interest in business information and launched an audio broadcasting frequency that specialised in business topics. "A studio located high up in the newly built Main Tower, in the middle of Frankfurt's skyline, is of course especially attractive for a business frequency named 'hr-skyline', also in view of the invited talk-guests from banking and other business enterprises that we have live at the microphone" emphasises Bernd-Peter Arnold, chief of the frequencies hr-skyline and hr4.

Up-to-date stock exchange news from Frankfurt, New York and the Far East with corresponding background information are just as part of the service as talks of analysts and reports from commerce, banking, industry and regionally located middle-size enterprises. The listeners of hr-skyline are not defined by its age, but by its attitude to life, interests and professional orientation.

The team of hr-skyline can take recourse to the network of correspondents of the whole ARD. The hr-specialist editorial production departments are important suppliers of report contributions. To let proven external experts have the word is part of the concept. A co-operation with the largest non-commercial radio station of the USA, National Public Radio (NPR) in Washington, enables via satellite the take-over of business news blocks in English language at the same time. ∎

Hessischer Rundfunk
Anstalt des öffentlichen Rechts

Intendant/engl
Prof. Dr. Klaus Berg

Wellenchef von hr-skyline und hr 4/
Chief of the frequencies hr-skyline and hr4:
Bernd-Peter Arnold

Empfangsmöglichkeiten/
Possibilities of Reception
Terrestrisch zu empfangen ist hr-skyline über folgende Frequenzen im Großraum Rhein-Main:
Terrestrial reception of hr-skyline on following frequencies in the Larger Rhein-Main area:
Frankfurt 103,9 MHz
Wiesbaden 97,2 MHz
Darmstadt 107,0 MHz
Seeheim 88,2 MHz
Limburg 99,2 MHz.

Die Telekom bietet unter der Telefon-Nummer 0800/3300555 einen kostenlosen Auskunftsdienst zu den Kabelfrequenzen an.
In digitaler Qualität wird hr-skyline im Rahmen des hessischen DAB-Pilotprojekts (L-Band/ 1 ,5 Ghz, Block LA, LC, LG) ausgestrahlt.
Seit Januar 2000 kann hr-skyline auch über Astra Digital Radio (ADR) empfangen werden und ist somit europaweit zu hören.
The Telecom offers under their telephone number 0800/3300555 a free-of-charge information service about the cable frequencies.
Hr-skyline is broadcast in digital quality within the framework of the DAB-pilot project (Digital Audio Broadcasting) of Hesse (L-band/1,5 Ghz, block LA, LC, LG).
Since January 2000 hr-skyline can be received also via Astra Digital Radio (ADR) and can thus be heard all over Europe.

Anschrift/Address:
Bertramstraße 8
D-60222 Frankfurt am Main
Telefon   +49 (69) 15 51
Telefax   +49 (69) 155 29 00
Telex   411127
E-Mail   skyline@hr-online.de
Internet www.hr-skyline.de

The World's Complete Polyester Resource

KoSa GmbH & Co. KG

Geschäftsführer/Managing Director:
George Gregory
Knut Hartmann

Gründungsjahr/Year of Foundation:
Dezember 1998
als joint venture zwischen/as a joint venture of
Koch Industries Inc., Wichita/Kansas, und
IMASAB S.A. de C.V., Mexico City

Mitarbeiter/Employees:
10.000 weltweit
1.800 Europa

Produktionsstandorte weltweit/
Manufacturing Sites worldwide:
16

Produktionsstandorte in Europa/
Manufacturing Sites Europe:
Bad Hersfeld, Bobingen, Gersthofen, Guben,
Offenbach und Vlissingen /NL

Anschrift/Address:
Lyoner Straße 38a
D-60528 Frankfurt am Main
Telefon   +49 (69) 305-35 55
Telefax   +49 (69) 305-819 21
E-Mail   Communications.Europe@KoSa.com
Internet   www.kosa.com

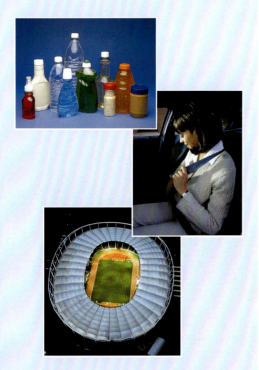

KoSa: Polyester-Lösungen für Kunden weltweit!

KoSa: Polyester Solutions to Customers Worldwide!

KoSa ist einer der weltweit führenden Polyester-Hersteller. Das Unternehmen wurde im Dezember 1998 als Gemeinschaftsunternehmen von Koch Industries Inc., Wichita, Kansas/USA und IMASAB S.A. de C.V., Mexico.City gegründet, als die beiden Partner Teile der Faseraktivitäten des ehemaligen Hoechst-Konzernes erwarben. KoSa produziert Polyester-Standard- und Polyester-Spezialprodukte in den Geschäftsbereichen Intermediates & Polymer, Verpackungsrohstoffe, Technische Filamente, Textile Fasern und Reifencord. In Europa produziert das Unternehmen Polyestervorprodukte und Fasern für technische Anwendungen:

• Zwischenprodukte und Polymere von KoSa werden für die Herstellung von Fasern, Folien und Verpackungsrohstoffen eingesetzt.
• Polyclear®, der Verpackungsrohstoff von KoSa, wird zu PET-Flaschen, Spezialbehältern oder Folien weiterverarbeitet. Einsatzgebiet: Verpackung für Getränke und Lebensmittel, Haushalts- und Reinigungsmittel.
• Polyestergarne aus KoSa Hochfest haben vielfältige Anwendungsmöglichkeiten. Zu beschichteten oder laminierten Geweben/Gewirken verarbeitet, finden sie Einsatz in LKW-Planen, Markisen, Zelten, Bedachungen. Aber auch in Industriegurten und -schläuchen, Förderbändern, Keilriemen, flexiblen Behältern, Nähfäden, im textilen Bauen und im Reifencord werden diese eingesetzt.

Der europäische Firmensitz in der Bürostadt Ffm.-Niederrad beherbergt neben der Geschäftsleitung die Unternehmenskommunikation, Marketing und Customer Service der europäischen Geschäftsbereiche, Finanzwesen, Rechtsabteilung und Information Services. ■

KoSa is one of the world's largest polyester producers, created in December 1998 when Koch Industries Inc., Wichita, Kansas/USA and IMASAB S.A. de C.V., Mexico City completed the purchase of the polyester business of Hoechst. KoSa manufactures commodity and specialty polyester products in five global businesses: Intermediates & Polymer, Packaging Resins, Technical Filament, Textile Fibers and Tirecord.

In the European region, the company produces polyester intermediates, polymers, PET Packaging Resins and fibers for industrial/technical applications:

• Intermediates and polymers from KoSa are used for the manufacture of fibers, films and packaging resins.
• Polyclear®, the KoSa packaging resin, is processed into bottles, custom containers and films for use in packaging products such as beverages, food, household chemicals and cleaning agents.
• Engineered polyester yarns made from KoSa High Tenacity filaments have a wide range of applications. They are used as reinforcing substrates in coated or laminated broadwovens and knits for truck tarpaulins, awnings, tents and roofing. They are also used in industrial belts and hoses, conveyor belts, V-belts, flexible containers, sewing threads, textile architecture and tirecord.

KoSa's European headquarters in the office district of Frankfurt-Niederrad house not only the company management team but also Corporate Communication, Marketing and Customer Services for the European businesses, Finance, Corporate Law and Information Services. ■

GESAT: Automation – Satellitecommunication – EDP-Informationtechnology

GESAT mbH
Gesellschaft für Software, Automatisierung und Technik mbH

Geschäftsführer/Manager:
Hans Pitschko
Klaus Wohlfart
Hubert Einetter
Harald Obersteiner

Gründungsjahr/Year of Foundation: 1989

Mitarbeiter/Employees: 51

Niederlassungen/Branches:
Frankfurt (Zentrale), Eschborn, Berlin, Shanghai (Representative Office)

Unternehmensbereiche/Business fields:
- Automatisierungs- und Prozesstechnik
- Elektro-, Mess-, Steuer- & Regelungstechnik
- EDV (Hard- und Softwarevertrieb)
- Satellitenkommunikation (Inmarsat und VSAT-Komplettlösungen)
- Informationstechnologie (Serverkonzepte, Internetpräsenzen, Programmierung)
- Automation and processing technique
- Electro, measuring, control and regulating technique
- EDP (sale of hard- and software)
- Satellitecommunication (Inmarsat and VSAT-Complete Solutions)
- Information technology (server concepts, Internet presence, programming)

Anschrift/Address:
Hanauer Landstr. 121a
D-60316 Frankfurt am Main
Telefon +49 (69) 96 21 80-10
Telefax +49 (69) 96 21 80-99
E-Mail main@gesat.com
Internet www.gesat.com

Wir sind eine unabhängige Ingenieurgesellschaft. GESAT umfasst verschiedene Unternehmensbereiche mit allen dazugehörigen Produkten und Dienstleistungen. Unsere Ingenieure verfügen über langjährige praktische Erfahrungen in unseren Geschäftsbereichen.

We are an independent engineering company. GESAT includes various fields of businesses with all its comprising products and services. Our engineers dispose of long-year's practical experience in our business fields.

Automatisierung
GESAT bietet Partnerschaften im Bereich technisch-kommerzieller Automatisierung an.
Wir sind Partner für Produktionsbetriebe, Ingenieur- & Planungsbüros, Maschinenbauer, Anlagenbauer etc.
Als unabhängiges Systemhaus mit langjährigen Erfahrungen sind wir dabei in der Lage, mit jedem Kunden bereits in der Planungsphase ein herstellerneutrales Anforderungsprofil auszuarbeiten. Die Umsetzung dieses Anforderungsprofils mit den jeweiligen Automatisierungs-, Steuerungs-, Bedien- und Informationssystemen ist einer unserer Tätigkeitsschwerpunkte.

Automation
GESAT offers partnerships in the field of technical-commercial automation. We are partners for production companies, engineering and planning offices, mechanical engineers, terotechnology engineers etc.
Being an independent system house with long-years experience we are in a position to work out with each client a producer-neutral profile of requirements, even in the planning phase. Implementing this profile of requirements with its corresponding automation, control, operating and information systems is one of the main points of activities.

Satellitenkommunikation
Ihr weltweit verfügbarer Telefon-, Fax- und Datenanschluss via Satellit

Sie wollen die Wüste durchqueren, in Kasachstan Öl fördern oder vom Mount Everest eine Videokonferenz abhalten und brauchen eine Telefon oder ISDN – Verbindung ?
Telefonieren, faxen, Datentransfer, Bildübertragungen, Videokonferenzen oder Fernsteuerungen von Industrieanlagen an JEDEM PUNKT DER WELT sind mit unseren Anlagen kein Problem mehr.
Unsere Stärke liegt in der Lösung der kompletten Aufgabenstellung und ist somit nicht auf die Lieferung der Satellitenanlage beschränkt.

Satellitecommunication
Your world wide available telephone, fax and data connection via satellite.

You want to cross the dessert, want to extract oil in Kasachstan or hold a video conference on Mount Everest and need a telephone or ISDN connection?
To telephone, fax, transfer data or pictures, hold video conferences or control industrial plants from a distance, all this is no problem any longer with our equipments from ANY POINT IN THE WORLD!
Our strength lies in solving the complete task required and is thus not limited to delivering a satellite equipment.

EDV
Vertrieb von Hard- und Software für gehobene Ansprüche mit individueller Vorinstallation. Hohe Qualität und guter Service ist dabei selbstverständlich.

EDP
Sale of hard- and software for sophisticated demands with individual preinstallation. High quality and good service go without saying.

Informationstechnologie
Wir entwickeln für Sie nach individuellen Vorgaben kundenspezifische Software bzw. Serverkonzepte. Eine unserer Stärken ist die Kooperation mit all unseren Geschäftsbereichen.

Information technology
We develop for you according to individual instruction customer-specific software or server concepts. One of our strengths is the co-operation with all our business fields.

Where do you want to phone today?

Olympiabotschafter Horst Scha

Satellitenkommunikation und Automatisierung.
Satellitecommunication and automation.

121

Architektur – von der Karolingerzeit bis zum ökologisch orientierten Hochhaus

Architecture – From the Time of the Carolingians to Ecologically Oriented Skyscrapers

Kurz vor der 1200-Jahrfeier der Stadt Frankfurt, wurde tief unter dem Dom das Grab eines Mädchens mit kostbaren merowingischen Beigaben aus der Zeit vor 700 freigelegt.

Die erste urkundliche Erwähnung Frankfurts war etwa 100 Jahre später, 794, als Karl der Große in Franconofurd, loco celebri, an einem damals schon bekannten Ort, ein bedeutendes Konzil abhielt. Die zwischen Dom und Römer ausgegrabenen Fundamente eines karolingischen Palatiums über den Resten einer römischen Villa zeigen, dass die Anfänge Frankfurts zwischen Braubach(straße) und Main auf einer hochwassersicheren Landzunge gefunden wurden und dort, wo jetzt der Dom steht, sich die karolingische Pfalzkapelle befand.

Das älteste erhaltene mittelalterliche Bauwerk steht jedoch auf dem hohen Ufer des Mains in Frankfurt-Höchst: die St. Justinuskirche, die wohl älteste Säulenbasilika nördlich der Alpen aus der Zeit um 830.

Die zentrale Lage von Frankfurt im Reich prädestinierte es zur Abhaltung von Reichstagen, auch weil es mit dem Schiff erreichbar war. Im Jahr 959, als Frankfurt Hauptsitz des Ostfränkischen Reiches war, empfing Kaiser Otto der Große hier in seinem Palatium supremium regale in Frankfurt viele ausländische Gäste, u. a. den Gesandten des Kalifen von Cordoba.

Im ehemaligen Saalhof stehen Reste der staufischen Pfalz mit Wehrturm und Kapelle von 1160, integriert in das Historische Museum. In staufischer Zeit wurden zu den Reichstagen in Frankfurt auch Messen abgehalten, erstmals 1150 und damit wurde der Grund gelegt für die weitere wirtschaftliche Entwicklung der Stadt. Kaiser Friedrich Barbarossa gewährte der Stadt die Erweiterung des Stadtgebiets mit einer hohen Mauer, von der östlich der Töngesgasse noch einige Bögen erhalten geblieben sind. Mit der erstmalig 1222 erwähnten Brücke in Frankfurt über den Main, wurde die Überquerung des Flusses zu jeder Jahreszeit möglich. Die Bedeutung der Stadt als Verkehrsmittelpunkt, besonders für die Messen, stieg dadurch schnell an.

Die in karolingische Zeit als Pfalzkapelle dem Salvator geweihte Kirche wurde ab etwa 1235 vergrößert und zu einer kreuzförmigen gotischen Hallenkirche umgebaut.

Als Zentralbau und eine der frühen Hallenkirchen in Deutschland, wurde die anspruchsvolle Funkti-

Prof. Rudolf von Staden

Der Autor wurde 1934 geboren. Nach Ausbildung als Steinmetz Studium der Architektur und Kunstgeschichte in München. Wissenschaftlicher Mitarbeiter von Professor Wortmann-Hannover bei städtebaulichen Projekten. Freier Mitarbeiter von Professor Guther in Darmstadt und Bonn. Oberbaurat der Stadt Heidelberg, 1976 Berufung an die Fachhochschule Frankfurt am Main als Professor für Baugeschichte und Denkmalpflege. Denkmalpflegerische Tätigkeit in Hessen, Bayern und Baden-Württemberg.

The author was born in 1934. After an apprenticeship as stonemason he studied architecture and history of art in Munich. He was a scientific employee of Professor Wortmann in Hanover in urban construction projects. The then worked freelance for Professor Gunther in Darmstadt and Bonn. Construction Council with the City of Heidelberg, 1976 appointment to the Polytechnic of Frankfurt on the Main as professor for the history of construction and preservation of historical monuments. Activities of a curator of historical monuments in Hesse, Bavaria and Baden-Württemberg.

on der Kirche für das Reich deutlich, den Titel Dom erhält die Kirche jedoch erst später.

Durch die Goldene Bulle wurde Frankfurt als Stadt für die Königswahlen bestimmt und dem Dom die Wahlkapelle angefügt. Um 1415 begann der Bau des Domturmes, entworfen von Madern Gerthener, Frankfurts bedeutendstem Baumeister im Mittelalter. Der Turmbau bedingte, dass das damals dort stehende Rathaus abgerissen und ein

Haus Wertheim am Fahrtor, erbaut um 1600.

House Wertheim at the Drive Gate, built around 1600.

Shortly before the 1200-year-celebration of the City of Frankfurt, deep underneath the Cathedral, was uncovered the grave of a girl with valuable Merovingian burial gifts from the time before 700. The first documented mentioning of Frankfurt was around 100 years later in 794, when Karl the Great in Franconofurd, loco celebri, in a then already known place, held a very important council. Foundations of a Carolingian palace exposed between Cathedral and the Römer (town hall) above the remains of a roman villa show that the beginnings of Frankfurt were found between Braubach(street) and the river Main, built on a promontory secured against flooding and on the place were now the Cathedral stands, the Carolingian Palatine chapel was situated.

The eldest preserved construction of the Middle Ages stands however on the high shore of the river Main in Frankfurt-Höchst: the St. Justinus church, the probably oldest column basilica north of the Alps from the time around 830.

Frankfurt's central location within the empire predestined it for the holding of senates or councils, because it could also be reached by ship. In the year 959, when Frankfurt was the capital of the East-Franconian Empire, Emperor Otto the Great received here in his Palatium supremium regale (Supreme Royal Palace) in Frankfurt many foreign guests, like for example the Envoy of the Caliph of Cordoba.

In the former Saalhof can be found remains of the stauffish palace with defence tower and chapel of 1160, integrated into the Historic Museum. In the times of the Stauffer, there were also held fairs in Frankfurt when the parliament held council. In 1150 for the first time, and thus was also laid the foundation for the further economic development of the city. Emperor Friedrich Barbarossa bestowed to the city his permission for extending its territory by building a high wall, of which have remained preserved some few arches east of the alley "Töngesgasse". The bridge in Frankfurt across the Main, mentioned for the first time in 1222, made it possible to cross the river in any season of the year. The importance of the city as a central node for transport, especially for the fairs, increased herewith rapidly.

The Palatine chapel, in Carolingian times consecrated as church to the Salvator, was enlarged from around 1235 on and reconstructed into a cross form gothic church hall.

As a central construction and one of the early church halls in Germany, the demanding functions of the church for the empire became appar-

ent; the church received its title as Cathedral much later, however.

Through the Golden Bull Frankfurt was determined as city for royal elections and the Cathedral had the election chapel annexed. Around 1415, the construction of the tower of the Cathedral started that had been designed by Madern Gerthener, Frankfurt's most renowned architect in the Middle Ages. The tower constructions necessitated that the town hall, which stood in that place then, was torn down and another building – the Römer – was designated as town hall.

From 1562 till 1792 the coronations of the emperors took place in the Cathedral: Goethe describes the regal pomp of a coronation, the joyous festivities and the gaiety of the Frankfurter people. In 1944, bombs destroyed the inner city and the Cathedral. The Cathedral was rebuilt – a holy and dignified place of historic status was colourfully reconstructed.

Holzhausen Schlösschen, erbaut 1727.
The small Holzhausen Castle, built 1727.

Madern Gerthener also created the tower of the Eschenheimer Gate, the highest of the former approx. 60 towers of the city wall of 1333. His head looks down cheerfully from the arch of the gate.

The purchase of the Römer by the municipality gave the Römerhill its political importance lasting until today. At first, two gabled houses formed the town hall, and then the adjoining buildings were taken over by the municipality, the last one being the Laderam House. A comparison with historic photographs from around 1870 shows, how simple the façade of the Römer was designed originally and with how much decoration the group of houses was "enriched" around 1898. The picture of the Römer as we know it today, is enormously influenced by the neo-gothic additions that also have become worthy to be classified as a historical monument after 100 years.

Also Madern Gerthener built in 1399 the Canvas House as a fair and exhibition house for the cloth

manufacturers, being one of the first fair constructions in Germany. The patrician houses and the ground floor halls of the Römer provided other spaces for the activities of the fair. Similarly to the Canvas House, in 1464 the Stone House was built, with a pewtered balustrade and small corner towers; a type of house that may have been built after the example of the residential tower of the "Grimmvogel" (Grimmbird) situated on the Liebfrauenberg, that was acquired by Sigfried zum Paradies in 1351 and that housed such illustrious guests as Karl IV, King Wenzel and later Emperor Friedrich III.

The Jewish co-citizens had their quarter in the Eastern part of the city. Their cemetery behind the former Jewish Alley has lasted over all these centuries. The eldest tombstone dates from 1284. A notable place; in its vicinity a grove was planted in memory of all Jewish citizens that were victims of the Holocaust. At the Börneplatz foundations of Jewish houses and the entrance to a Mikwe can be visited. From the time of the Renaissance there have only remained very few buildings in Frank-

anderes Gebäude – der Römer – zum Rathaus bestimmt wurde.

Von 1562 bis 1792 fanden im Dom die Krönungen der Kaiser statt: Goethe beschreibt die festliche Pracht einer Krönung, das fröhliche Teiben und die Freude der Frankfurter. 1944 zerstörten Bomben die Innenstadt und den Dom. Der Dom wurde wieder aufgebaut – eine heilige und würdige Stätte von historischem Rang, farbenprächtig wieder hergestellt.

Madern Gerthener hat auch den Turm des Eschenheimer Tores gestaltet, den höchsten der ehedem etwa 60 Türme der Stadtmauer von 1333. Sein Kopf schaut munter vom Torbogen herab.

Mit dem Erwerb des Römer durch die Stadt, erhielt der Römerberg die politische Bedeutung bis heute. Zunächst bildeten zwei Giebelhäuser das Rathaus, dann wurden die angrenzenden Gebäude von der Stadt übernommen, zuletzt das Haus Laderam. Ein Vergleich mit historischen Fotos von etwa 1870 zeigt, wie schlicht die Römerfassade ursprünglich gestaltet war, mit wieviel Zierrat die Häusergruppe um 1898 „bereichert" wurde. Das Bild vom Römer, das sich uns heute bietet, wird stark durch die neogotischen Zutaten geprägt, die nach 100 Jahren nun ebenfalls denkmalwürdig geworden sind.

Von Madern Gerthener wurde 1399 auch das Leinwandhaus als Messehaus für die Tuchhändler errichtet, als einer der ersten Messebauten in Deutschland. Andere Räumlichkeiten für den Messebetrieb boten die Patrizierhäuser und die Erdgeschosshalle im Römer. Dem Leinwandhaus ähnlich wurde 1464 das Steinerne Haus gebaut, mit gezinnter Balustrade und Ecktürmchen; ein Haustyp, dessen Vorbild vielleicht der Wohnturm zum Grimmvogel am Liebfrauenberg war, den Sigfried zum Paradies 1351 erwarb, in dem illustre Gäste Quartier nahmen, so Karl IV, König Wenzel und später Kaiser Friedrich III.

Die jüdischen Mitbürger hatten im Osten der Stadt ihr Viertel. Ihr Friedhof hinter der früheren Judengasse hat alle Jahrhunderte überdauert. Der älteste Grabstein stammt aus dem Jahr 1284. Eine denkwürdige Stätte; in ihrer Nachbarschaft ist ein Hain zur Erinnerung an alle jüdischen Mitbürger gepflanzt worden, die Opfer des Holocausts wurden. Am Börneplatz sind die Fundamente jüdischer Häuser und der Zugang zu einer Mikwe zu besichtigen.

Aus der Renaissance-Zeit sind in Frankfurt nur wenige Bauten erhalten geblieben. Dazu zählt das Haus Laderam am Römerberg, das 1595 umgebaut wurde und der liebenswürdige Treppenstein im Römerhöfchen von 1627. Die an den Römer an-

Portal des Israelitischen Friedhofs, erbaut 1828.

Gate of the Israelite Cemetery, built 1828.

grenzenden Häuser Frauenstein und das Salzhaus waren Kostbarkeiten patrizischer Renaissancekultur. Das Haus Wertheim neben dem Fahrtor, dem früheren Hauptzugang vom Fluss her in die Stadt, entstanden um 1600 mit schmückfreudigem Fachwerk, ist das einzige Fachwerkhaus der Altstadt, das den letzten Krieg überstanden hat.

Im Stadtteil Sachsenhausen, wo früher Fischer, Gemüsebauern und Handwerker lebten, steht noch eines der ältesten Fachwerkhäuser von Deutschland, das kleine Haus Schellgasse 8 aus dem Jahr 1291. Es überdauerte den 2. Weltkrieg und konnte vor dem geplanten Abriss gerettet werden. Von den Befestigungstürmen in Sachsenhausen ist nur der Kuhhirtenturm von ca. 1490 erhalten geblieben. Von 1925–1927 bewohnte Paul Hindemith den Turm und komponierte dort die Oper Cardillac.

Auf dem angrenzenden Gelände ist die gotische Deutschordenskirche mit barocker Fassade erhalten geblieben, daneben die Komturei, gestiftet 1193, eine der ältesten Niederlassungen des Deutschen Ordens, der hier ein Siechenhaus führte und berühmten Gästen Herberge bot.

Die alte Silhouette der Freien Reichsstadt Frankfurt ist aus der Vogelschau von Matthaeus Merian aus dem Jahre 1628 ablesbar: die Mainbrücke mit hohen Brückentoren, die Stadtmauern mit mehr als 60 Türmen und Toren, die Kirchen St. Nikolai, St. Leonhard, die Liebfrauenkirche, Klosterkirchen mit Reitern auf den Dächern, turmartige Patrizierhäuser mit Nebentürmchen, und alle überragend der hohe Dom mit seinem kuppelartig abschließenden Turm. Das war eines der

großen eindrucksvollen Städtebilder in Mitteleuropa, wehrhaft und offen zugleich, eng bebaut und trotzdem wohnlich – eine Bürgerstadt, würdig, Wahl- und Krönungsstadt der Kaiser des Heiligen Römischen Reiches zu sein.

Im 18. Jahrhundert wurden in Frankfurt viele Gebäude barockisiert. Es entstand eine barocke Stadt indem man u. a. Fachwerk verputzte und Kirchen, dem neuen Lebens- und Glaubensgefühl folgend, neu einrichtete. Der früheste Barockbau in Frankfurt war das schon erwähnte Deutschordenshaus von 1709. Es folgte bald der Innenumbau des Römers mit der einstmals berühmten Kaiserstiege. Die Holzhausen-Oede, ursprünglich eine kleine Wasserburg, entstand als barocker Sommersitz der Herren von Holzhausen 1727. Mit Allee und Park ein Juwel Frankfurter Wohnkultur, gestaltet von Louis Rémy de la Fosse, mit Manserddach und auf dem Dach mit einem bei den Frankfurtern so beliebten Belvedeerchen. Das Schlösschen wurde von der Frankfurter Bürgerstiftung für Kammerkonzerte und Lesungen umgebaut und damit eine Stätte zur Pflege alter und neuer Kunst. Die Hauptwache, 1730 ein Wachgebäude auf dem gleichnamigen Platz, wurde nach dem Krieg wieder aufgebaut und ist nun ein Café.

Die Frankfurter waren reichstreu und dennoch Republikaner. So gewährten sie dem kranken Kaiser Karl VII, bis er in seine Residenz nach München zurückkehren konnte, Asyl. Dass der Reichspostmeister Fürst Thurn u. Taxis sich in Frankfurt in der Gr. Eschenheimerstraße aber ein Palais bauen wollte, fand gar kein Verständnis. Nur heimlich konnte er die Grundstücke erwerben, nachbarliche Einsprüche verzögerten den von

furt. One of these is the Laderam House at the Römerhill, rebuilt in 1595 and the lovely stone stairs inside the yard of the Römer of 1627. The houses adjoining the Römer called Frauenstein and Salzhaus were valuable pieces of patrician renaissance culture. The Wertheim House next to the drive gate, the former main entrance into the city from the riverside, was built around 1600 with gaily decorated half-timbering. It is the only half-timbered house of the old part of the city centre that has survived the last war.

In the borough of Sachsenhausen, were in the past fishermen, vegetable farmers and craftsmen used to live, there still exists one of the oldest half-timbered houses of Germany, the little house of Schellgasse 8 dating from the year 1291. It outlasted the 2nd World war and could be saved from demolition. Of the fortified towers in Sachsenhausen only the Kuhhirtenturm (cow-herdsmen tower) of around 1490 has been preserved. From 1925 till 1927 Paul Hindemith lived in this tower and wrote the opera Cardillac here.

On the adjoining land, the gothic Deutschorden Church with its baroque façade has remained intact, next to it the "Komturei" (seat of the commander of the order), donated in 1193, one of the eldest branches of the German Order that kept an infirmary here and offered lodging to guests.

The old silhouette of the Free Imperial City of Frankfurt can be read from the bird's eye view by Matthaeus Merian dating from 1628: The bridge across the river Main with high bridge gates, the city walls with more than 60 towers and gates, the churches of St. Nikolai, St. Leonhard, the Liebfrauen Church, churches of monasteries with riders on their roofs, tower-like patrician houses with small adjoining towers, and rising above all these, the high Cathedral with its closing dome-shaped tower. This was one of the great impressing urban features of Middle Europe, well-fortified and open at the same time, a densely built-up area but still comfortable to live in – a residence for citizens, worthy to be the city of election and coronation of the Emperors of the Holy Roman Empire.

In the 18th Century, in Frankfurt many buildings were renovated in baroque-fashion. The result was a baroque city by for instance plastering the half-timbering and decorating the churches newly in accordance with a new faith and life-style. The earliest baroque building in Frankfurt was the previously mentioned House of the German Order of 1709. Then followed the interior reconstruction of the Römer with the formerly renowned Kaiserstiege (emperor's staircase).
The Holzhausen-Oede, originally a small castle built in water, was designed as a baroque summer residence for the von Holzhausen noblemen in 1727. With its park and avenue a jewel of living culture in Frankfurt, created by Louis Rémy de la Fosse, with an attic and a "Belvedeerchen" on the roof that is so very popular with Frankfurters. The Frankfurt Citizens Association refurbished the small castle for chamber concerts and readings and has thus become a place for the maintenance of old and new art and culture. The Hauptwache,

a guardhouse of 1730, on the place of the same name, was reconstructed after the war and is now a café.

Frankfurters were loyal to the Kaiser while being republicans at the same time. So they granted the ill Kaiser Karl VII asylum, until he was able to return to his residence in Munich. That the postmaster of the empire, Count Thurn u. Taxis, wanted to built a palace for himself in the Gr. Eschenheimerstraße of Frankfurt did not find much approval. He was only able to purchase the land in secret, protests of neighbours delayed the constructions planned by Robert de Cotte, which was finally completed, but the count did not stay in Frankfurt for very long. The two still remaining gate constructions are the last witnesses to this episode.

Johann Kaspar Goethe, father of the poet, needed appropriate housing and intended to join two houses in Hirschgraben into one, mainly by leaving the jutting out floors, which was not allowed any longer. As a lawyer he won the right to build, by applying for a reconstruction and thus cleverly evading the prohibition. This happened around 250 years ago!

Goethe's family house was reconstructed in baroque-fashion. In poetry and in truth Goethe describes details about this house worth reading, which can be found there when visiting.

The last great work before the French Revolution was the late-baroque House to Paradise and Grimmvogel (Grimm-bird) on the Liebfrauenberg, a new construction of 1775 built on the foundations of the patrician houses of the Middle Ages and reconstructed in 1995 according to the ideas of students of architecture of the Polytechnic of Frankfurt on the Main.

In 1789, when the Parisians conquered the Bastille and in Berlin the King had the Brandenburg Gate built, the citizens of Frankfurt began to build the Church of St. Paul. A centre building on an elliptic ground plan with balcony and high pitched roof – the first classicist work of architecture in Frankfurt. 1848 the church was place of the first German National Assembly. The monument of German democracy was destroyed in 1944, but soon after rebuilt, in expectation of the functions of a capital. The designation of Frankfurt as a capital failed however, mainly because of the protest of the High Allied Commissioners, because the city seemed to be endangered from the East through its position right of the Rhine. Nowadays, the church serves for receiving high guests, the presentation of awards and exhibitions.

Städelsches Kunstinstitut und Holbeinsteg.

The Städel Institute of Art and the Holbein Bridge.

Robert de Cotte geplanten Bau, der schließlich fertiggestellt wurde, aber der Fürst blieb nicht lange in Frankfurt. Die beiden noch stehenden Torbauten sind die letzten Zeugen dieser Episode.

Johann Kaspar Goethe, der Vater des Dichters, brauchte angemessene Behausung und beabsichtigte aus zwei Häusern am Hirschgraben eines zu machen u. a. durch Beibehaltung überhängender Geschosse, die nicht mehr erlaubt waren. Er obsiegte als Jurist, indem er einen Umbau beantragte und so das Verbot geschickt umging. Geschehen vor etwa 250 Jahren!

Goethes Elternhaus wurde barock umgebaut. In Dichtung und Wahrheit schildert Goethe sehr lesenswerte Details aus diesem Hause, die man als Besucher dort wiederfindet.

Das letzte große Bauwerk vor der französischen Revolution war das spätbarocke Haus zum Paradies und Grimmvogel auf dem Liebfrauenberg, ein Neubau von 1775 erbaut auf den Fundamenten der mittelalterlichen Patrizierhäuser, wiederhergestellt 1995 nach Ideen von Architekturstudenten der Fachhochschule Frankfurt am Main.

1789, als die Pariser die Bastille erstürmten, in Berlin der König das Brandenburger Tor erbauen ließ, begannen die Frankfurter Bürger den Bau der Paulskirche. Ein Zentralbau auf elliptischem Grundriss mit Empore und Zeltdach – das erste klassizistische Bauwerk in Frankfurt. 1848 wurde die Kirche Tagungsstätte der ersten deutschen Nationalversammlung. Das Monument deutscher Demokratie wurde 1944 zerstört, aber bald danach in Erwartung hauptstädtischer Funktionen wieder aufgebaut. Die Berufung Frankfurts zur Bundeshauptstadt scheiterte aber u. a. am Widerspruch der Hohen Alliierten Kommissare, weil die Stadt, rechtsrheinisch gelegen, von Osten her gefährdet schien! Jetzt dient die Kirche dem Empfang hoher Gäste, Preisverleihungen und Ausstellungen.

In der von Napoleon bestimmten Zeit musste die Stadt auf ihre Befestigungsanlagen verzichten. Nur wenig wurde in dieser Zeit gebaut, u. a. die Torgebäude am Affentorplatz und das Bethmann'sche Ariadneum für Danneckers „Ariadne auf dem Panther". Es war das erste als Museum erbaute Haus in Frankfurt, eine von Fremden bewunderte Attraktion. Später wurde daraus ein Konzertsaal, Odeon genannt, jetzt wartet es als Café auf Gäste.

1810 erbaute sich der dänische Verleger Nebbien der Bokenheimer Anlage das liebenswürdige Gartenhaus, das jetzt künstlerischen Veranstaltungen dient.

Haus zum Paradies und Grimmvogel, erbaut 1775.
House to Paradise and Grimmvogel (Grimm-bird), built 1775.

Im 19. Jahrhundert entstand das Westend als gutes Wohnviertel, im Anschluss an das Rothschild'sche Palais, mit klassizistischen Villen und qualitätsvollen Mehrfamilienhäusern, Alleen und dem exotischen Palmengarten.

Mit dem Verlust der staatlichen Hoheit, 1866, der von den republikanischen Frankfurtern tief betrauert wurde, kamen jedoch durch geöffnete Zollschranken und den Eisenbahnbau, nachhaltige wirtschaftliche Impulse. In der Gründerzeit nach 1871 entstanden in Frankfurt große Fabrikanlagen in den Vororten, ausgedehnte Wohnquartiere und mehrere prachtvolle öffentliche Bauten.

Das Opernhaus als Nachfolgebau für das in der Goethezeit bedeutende Comoedienhaus entstand 1873–1880 als Ergebnis eines Wettbewerbs unter Gottfried Semper. Architekt Lucae entwarf ein an der Grand Opera von Paris funktional orientiertes Haus, gestaltet in Formen der italienischen Renaissance. Bei der Einweihung in Gegenwart des Kaisers äußerte dieser, ein solches Haus könne er sich in Berlin nicht erlauben. 1944 ging diese Pracht unter. Nach 30 Jahren wurde die „Alte Oper" als Konzert- und Gesellschaftshaus wieder aufgebaut, mit Spenden Frankfurter Bürger. Ein Haus mit Platz für 2.400 Besucher. Im Innern konnten nur das Vestibül und das Foyer in historischer Gestalt wieder hergestellt werden. Der Opernplatz, frei vom Verkehr, erhielt, wie 100 Jahre zuvor, seinen Brunnen zurück und wurde wieder ein beliebter Treffpunkt. Der Frankfurter Hof, als Grandhotel ab 1875 erbaut, in Neo-Renaissanceformen, wurde ein Haus mit dem Flair des fin de siécle, und ist heute noch trotz

vieler Konkurrenz architektonisch und in seiner Art unübertroffen.

Der Frankfurter Hauptbahnhof entstand ab 1883 anstelle von drei Bahnhöfen, die schon bald nach der ersten Eisenbahn in Deutschland erbaut worden waren. Der Kopfbahnhof, dreischiffig für 18 Gleispaare, mit großer Empfangshalle und Flügelbauten wurde danach der größte Bahnhof des Kontinents. Die Perronhallen in Stahlbogen- und Fachwerkkonstruktion sind auch heute noch eindrucksvolle Ingenieurbaukunst. Es ist wie ein Wunder, dass bei der Schnelllebigkeit aller Technik dieser Bahnhof seine Architektur bewahrt hat, aber – wie lange noch?

Nach dem Ersten Weltkrieg und der Inflation wurde Frankfurt vorbildhaft für viele Städte durch seine großen gemeinnützigen Wohnungsbauprojekte. Unter Ernst May als Stadtbaurat entstanden für Minderbemittelte und kinderreiche Familien Stadtrandsiedlungen mit unverwechselbarer Wohnkultur, u. a. am Bornheimer Hang, in Praunheim, der Hellerhof und die Römerstadt. Gestalterisch dem Bauhaus und dem Stijl verpflichtet: lange zweigeschossige Hauszeilen, parallel zueinander, gekrümmt, mit minimalen Hausbreiten. Im Wohnungsbau hatte Frankfurt damals europäischen Rang, noch heute sind diese Wohnanlagen beliebt und gefragt.

Im Zweiten Weltkrieg wurden durch Luftangriffe 11.000 Gebäude völlig zerstört und über 40.000 schwer beschädigt. Fast 6.000 Frankfurter fanden dabei den Tod. Auch die meisten Arbeitsstätten waren zerstört worden. Nach der Währungsreform musste vor allem der enorme Bedarf an Wohnungen befriedigt werden, aber auch Geschäfte, Fabriken, Krankenhäuser, Schulen, die Universität waren wie-

In the times of Napoleon's rule, the city had to do without their fortifications. Not much was constructed in this time, like for example, the gate constructions of the Affentorplatz and the Ariadneum of Bethmann for Dannecker's "Ariadne on the Panther". It was the first house built as a museum in Frankfurt, an attraction marvelled at by foreigners. Later on, it became a concert hall, called Odeon; today it waits as a café for guests.

In 1810, the Danish editor Nebbien built in the Bockenheimer Anlage (green) a lovely garden house for himself, which now serves for cultural events. In the 19th Century, the Westend emerged as a good residential area, subsequent to the Palace of the Rothschild's, with classicist villas and high-quality multifamily residences, avenues and the exotic botanic garden, the "Palmengarten".

With the loss of its sovereignty in 1866, which was deeply regretted by republican Frankfurters, lasting economic impulses developed however through opened customs barriers and the railway construction. In the years of the rapid industrial expansion, after 1871, in Frankfurt were built large factory plants in the suburbs, extensive living quarters and various magnificent public buildings.

The opera house, being the subsequent construction for the Comoedienhaus famous during the Goethe's time, was built from 1873 – 1880 as a result of a competition under Gottfried Semper. The architect Lucae designed a house that was functionally oriented at the Grand Opera of Paris and created in the shapes of the Italian renaissance. At its inauguration in the presence of the Kaiser he exclaimed that he could not afford such a house in Berlin. In 1944 this splendour died. After 30 years, the "Alte Oper" (old opera house) was rebuilt as concert and society building with donations from Frankfurt's citizens. A house with spaces for 2.400 visitors. In the interior only the vestibule and the foyer could be reconstructed in its historic form. The opera square, free from traffic, received like 100 years ago, its fountain back and has become again a popular meeting point. The Frankfurter Hof, built as grand hotel from 1875 on, in neoforms of renaissance, became a house with the flair des fin de siécle and is still today, despite much competition, architectonically and in its kind unsurpassable.

The Frankfurt main train station was built from 1883 on, instead of three train stations, which were built soon after the first railway in Germany. The main head station, of three naves for 18 pairs of tracks, with a large entrance hall and aisle constructions became afterwards the largest train station of the continent. The Perron halls in steel arches and half-timber construction are up to today an impressive piece of architecture. It seems like a wonder that with the fast development of all modern technology this train station has maintained its architecture, but – for how long?

After the First World War and inflation, Frankfurt became an example for many cities because of its large social housing projects. Under Ernst May as councillor for construction, suburban housing estates were built for lesser fortunate and large families with an unmistakable living culture, including the ones at the Bornheimer Hang, in Praunheim, the Hellerhof and the Römerstadt.

Das Nebbiensche Gartenhaus in der Bockenheimer Anlage, erbaut um 1810.

The Garden house of Nebbien in the Bockenheimer Green, built around 1810.

der herzustellen oder mussten neu gebaut werden. Der Wiederaufbau des Römers, des Goethehauses und der alten Kirchen wurde bereits erwähnt. Erst 1960 war diese Phase abgeschlossen.

Über Jahre zog sich die Entscheidung zur Bebauung zwischen Dom und Römer hin, zwei Wettbewerbe fanden statt, bis schließlich 1978 der Wiederaufbau der Ostzeile gegenüber vom Römer als Rekonstruktion der alten Fachwerkhäuser begonnen wurde. Proteste der Architektenschaft füllten die Fachpresse. Inzwischen sind über 20 Jahre vergangen. Die Ostzeile des Römerbergs ist mit dem Römer unbestrittener Rahmen für Festlichkeiten, Empfänge und Märkte. Die nebenan in der Saalgasse zu gleicher Zeit entstandenen modernen, schmalen, hohen Giebelhäuser von jungen und namhaften Architekten wecken weit weniger Interesse, trotz ihrer Qualität. Wie relativ sind doch zuweilen unsere Wertmaßstäbe!

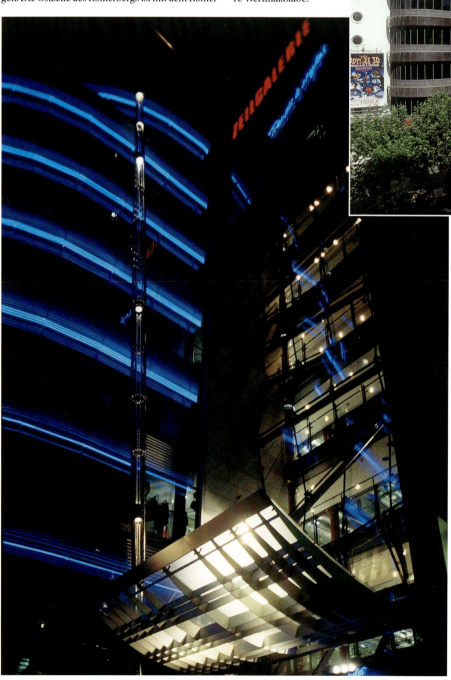

Die Zeilgalerie.

The Zeil Gallery.

Die Zeil war einst ein breiter Anger, hier standen vornehme Hotels, wo Mozart und Goethe und die Fürstlichkeiten abstiegen. Daraus wurde eine beliebte Einkaufsstraße, nach dem letzten Krieg eine Straße mit vielen Kaufhäusern und Autoverkehr, aber architektonisch nicht beeindruckend. Die Zeil wurde nach U- und S-Bahnbau, mit über hundert Platanen, mit Cafés, eine Fußgängerzone, die zu den umsatzstärksten in Deutschland zu zählen ist. Mit dem Bau der Zeilgalerie (Zeil 112–114) und ihrer zur Straße geöffneten Fassade ist eine geradezu sensationelle „Shopping Mall" entstanden. Auf einer 700 m langen, spiralförmigen Einkaufsstraße mit vielen offenen Ständen, Bistros und Geschäften, mit einer Aussichtsplattform auf 35 m Höhe, tags und nachts geöffnet, ist sie Publikumsmagnet (dessen sich der Bauherr allerdings nicht lange erfreuen konnte).

Seit dem Bau der berühmten Städelschen Kunstgalerie am Schaumainkai vor 125 Jahren sind insgesamt 14 Museen und Galerien beidseits des Mains eingerichtet worden, z. T. spektakuläre Museumsneubauten, besonders in den letzten Jahrzehnten - inspiriert von Hilmar Hoffmann. Das Museum für Kunsthandwerk, eines der führenden Museen seiner Art, wurde 1985 von Richard Meier, New York, erbaut. Die klassizistische Villa Metzler und alter Baumbestand wurden behutsam in die lockere Baumasse integriert. Eine beschwingte architektonische Lösung mit Museumspark, die zum Verweilen einlädt. Das Deutsche Architekturmuse-

Dedicated in design to the Bauhaus and the Stijl: long two-storey rows of houses, opposite in parallel, bent, with minimal house width. In housing construction Frankfurt enjoyed European ranking in those times, and even today these housing estates are very popular and sought after.

In the Second World War, 11.000 buildings were completely destroyed by air raids and over 40.000 were heavily damaged. Almost 6.000 people died in Frankfurt then. Also most of the workplaces had been destroyed. After the monetary reform, above all, the enormous demand for housing had to be satisfied, but also all businesses, factories, hospitals, schools and the university had to be reconstructed or newly built. The reconstruction of the Römer, the house of Goethe and of the old churches has already been mentioned. Only in 1960 this phase was completed.

It took many years to decide to build-up the area between the Cathedral and the Römer, two competitions took place, until finally in 1978, the reconstruction of the Eastern row opposite the Römer was started as reconstruction of the old half-timbered houses. Protests of the architectural world filled the expert press. Meanwhile 20 years have passed. The Eastern row of the Römerhill is without doubt the undisputed setting for festivities, receptions and markets. The adjoining and at the same time modern built, narrow and high gabled houses of the Saalgasse designed by young and famous architects do not receive as much interest despite their high quality. Alas, how relative sometimes our value judgements can be! The Zeil used to be once a broad meadow, elegant hotels stood here, where Mozart and Goethe and the noblesse used to take lodging. It then became a popular shopping mall after the last war, a street with many department stores and auto car traffic, but architectonically not very impressive. After the U- and S- subway constructions, the Zeil became with more than hundred plane trees, with cafés, one of the most selling pedestrian zones in Germany. With the construction of the Zeil Gallery (Zeil 112–114) and its façade opened towards the street side an almost sensational shopping mall has been created. On a shopping street that winds 700 m upwards, spiral-shaped, with many open stands, bistros and shops, with an sightseeing platform at 35 m height, open day and night, she is a magnet for the public (a fact that could not be enjoyed by the builder for very long).

Since the construction of the famous Städel Art Gallery on the Schaumainkai 125 years ago, a total of 14 museums and galleries have been established on both sides of the Main, partly spectacular new buildings of museums, especially in the last decades – inspired by Hilmar Hoffmann. Richard Meier, New York built the Museum for Craftsmanship, one of the leading of its kind, in 1985. The classicist Villa Metzler and the old trees were integrated carefully into the loose solidium. The result was a gay architectonic solution with a museum park that invites one to stay. The German Museum of Architecture by architect O.M. Ungers 1984 was built as a house in a house in a Palladian-shaped villa that had to be decentralised for this purpose. Well-received exhibitions, encounters and lecture cycles on architecture continue to attract friends of architecture also from abroad. The students of architecture attending the Städel-School and the Polytechnic of Frankfurt on the Main do find here a mutual forum. The museum of Modern Art, by Hans Hollein, near the Cathedral on a long triangular piece of land, built from 1987 to 1991, is an expressive work of construction with unusual rooms and possibilities of presenting new art forms.

The reconstruction of Frankfurt into one of the great finance, stock exchange and exhibition centres of the world does find in architectural terms its far visible expression through the many office towers. Preconditions for this development were the central transport location of the region and the favourable conditions for business locations, which in turn promoted the demand for office space tremendously. This trend still prevails.

One of the earliest office skyscrapers in Frankfurt is the Zürichhaus at the opera square dating from 1961, 68 m high, with 20 storeys. Today, it is regarded as technically outdated, like many houses of the reconstruction era that have meanwhile been torn down; it is however classified as a historical monument! During the course of the following years, office towers were built at very characteristic points of the inner city, standing more and more close together at the Bockenheimer Landstraße, at the Mainzer Landstraße and next to the river Main. Finally, the construction of skyscrapers was concentrated in the Westend, in the banker's quarter on both sides of the Taunus-/

Blick von der Fachhochschule auf die City.

View from the Polytechnic onto the City.

um von Architekt O. M. Ungers 1984 wurde in einer palladianisch gestalteten Villa als ein Haus im Haus gebaut, das dazu entkernt werden musste. Viel beachtete Ausstellungen, Begegnungen und Vortragszyklen über Architektur ziehen immer wieder Architekturfreunde auch aus dem Ausland an. Die Architekturstudenten der Städelschule und der Fachhochschule Frankfurt am Main finden hier ein gemeinsames Forum. Das Museum für Moderne Kunst, von Hans Hollein, nahe dem Dom auf einem langgestreckten dreieckigen Grundstück 1987–1991 erbaut, ist ein expressiver Baukörper mit ungewöhnlichen Räumen und Möglichkeiten zur Präsentation neuer Kunst.

Der Umbau von Frankfurt zu einem der großen Finanz, Börsen – und Messezentren der Welt, findet architektonisch seinen weithin sichtbaren Ausdruck durch die vielen Bürotürme. Voraussetzung für diese Entwicklung waren die zentrale Verkehrslage der Region und günstige Standortbedingungen, die die Nachfrage nach Büroflächen rasant steigen ließen. Dieser Trend hält immer noch an.

Zu den frühesten Bürohochhäusern in Frankfurt gehört das Zürichhaus am Opernplatz aus dem Jahr 1961, 68 m hoch, 20 Geschosse. Heute gilt es als technisch verbraucht, wie viele Häuser des Wiederaufbaus, die inzwischen schon abgerissen wurden, es steht aber unter Denkmalschutz! Im Laufe der folgenden Jahre entstanden Bürotürme an sehr markanten Punkten des Stadtgebietes, in immer dichterer Folge an der Bockenheimer Landstraße, an der Mainzer Landstraße und am Main. Schließlich konzentrierte sich der Hochhausbau im Westend, im Bankenviertel beiderseits der Taunus-/Gallus-Anlage, in Niederrad und am Flughafen. Das City-Haus

von 1975, am Platz der Republik, übersprang mit 143 m erstmals deutlich die Hundertmeter-Höhe. Die Nachfrage für Bürofläche führte auch zu stärkerem Druck auf den Magistrat, höhere Grundflächenzahlen und immer größere Bauhöhen zu genehmigen. Der Euro-Tower, jetzt der Sitz der Europäischen Zentralbank, 148 m, am westlichen Zugang zur Altstadt und an der Gallus-Anlage, wurde zum Signal einer neuen Entwicklung in der Altstadt, die auch gestattete höher als der Domturm ist (94 m) zu bauen. Hiermit begann auch die Gruppierung von Hochhäusern beidseits der Taunus-/Gallus- Anlage, die mit ihrem breiten Grün und den Kolonnaden einen wohltuenden Ruheraum bietet. Jetzt sind diese Anlagen fast vollständig umgeben von Hochhäusern. Ein beeindruckender großer Architektur-Raum, sowohl von der Alten Oper aus wie von Süden her zu erleben. Die Zwillingstürme der Deutschen Bank, Höhe 155 m, 1984, haben in diesem städtebaulichen Konzept eine hervorragende raumbildende Wirkung. Die sich spiegelnden, schräg zueinander hoch aufragenden Glasflächen auf prismatischem Fuß prägen das Stadtbild von Frankfurt entscheidend mit.
Die Besucher der Messen in Frankfurt können schon von fern her den Messeturm mit seinen 256 m Höhe, Architekten Murphy und Jahn, in seiner teleskopartigen Form und mit der Pyramide als oberer Abschluss wie ein Messezeichen wahrnehmen. Das gilt auch für das im westlichen Teil des Messegeländes aufragende Torhaus mit 117 m Höhe von O. M. Ungers, das meisterhaft die schwierige Situation in einem Gleisdreieck mit einer Toröffnung überbrückt.

Ein Büroturm, der alle in Europa überragen sollte, dessen Bau aber am Nein einer Nachbarin

scheiterte, war der südlich des Hauptbahnhofs mit 265 m Höhe geplante sog. Campanile. Eine Milliardeninvestition scheiterte am nachbarschützenden Baurecht und an der Unbeugsamkeit eines Menschen! Auch das ist Frankfurt.
Inzwischen ist am Kaiserplatz die Commerzbank-Zentrale als höchster Büroturm Europas entstanden, mit 259 m plus Antenne 300 m Höhe. Ein gigantisches und zugleich beschwingt wirkendes Bauwerk für 2.400 Arbeitsplätze und beispielhaft für die neue Hochhausgeneration.

Sir Norman Foster hat mit der Commerzbank nicht nur einen wichtigen städtebaulichen Akzent und die Spitze in der Skyline von Frankfurt geschaffen, es ist ein bemerkenswertes ökologisch orientiertes Bauwerk. Im ersten Obergeschoss liegt ein der Öffentlichkeit zugängliches weiträumiges Restaurant und die Lobby. Der Grundriss des Turmes ist ein Dreieck an dessen Ecken die Verkehrs- und Installationskerne angeordnet sind, in dessen Mitte sich ein über 160 m hohes Atrium erhebt. Neun Turmgärten, jeweils 200 m² groß, sind die grünen Lungen des Hauses; sie können von den Mitarbeitern als Kommunikations- und Pausenbereich genutzt werden. Ein bei Bürohochhäusern ungewöhnliche Rahmenkonstruktion überspannt stützenfrei die über 34 m breiten Gärten. Die zweischalige Klimafassade erlaubt Energieeinsparung und natürliche Kühlung – bis heute wohl einzigartig im Hochhausbau. Die Fenster der Innenschale lassen sich öffnen, so dass natürliche Frischluftzufuhr bis ins 50. Obergeschoss gewährleistet ist. Die Turmgärten schrauben sich spiralförmig auf der Ost- Süd- und Westseite in die Höhe. Jeder Himmelsrichtung liegt dabei ein botanisches Thema zugrunde; im Osten: asiatische Vegetation, Süden: mediterrane Vegetation, im Westen: nordamerikanische Vegetation. Jeder Mitarbeiter kann an etwa zwei Drittel der Tage im Jahr die Lüftung selbst steuern durch individuelles Öffnen oder Schließen der Fenster. Statt üblicher Klimatechnik wurde ein Kühldecken-System mit Wasserlauf zur Kühlung der Räume entwickelt. Geheizt werden die Räume mit konventionellen Heizkörpern. Durch ökologisch wirksame Maßnahmen in der Gebäudetechnik wird eine Energieeinsparung von 30 % gegenüber herkömmlichen Bürotürmen erreicht.

Die alte Reichsstadt Frankfurt, Krönungs- und Messestadt, war, wie Merian es in seiner Vogelschau so schön dargestellt hat, ein in Jahrhunderten gewachsenes Gefüge. Manches kostbare davon ist bis heute erhalten geblieben. Durch moderne Architektur hat die Stadt ein neues Gesicht erhalten in dem aber die alten Konturen noch erkennbar sind, als Ausdruck ihrer Wandlungsfähigkeit und Kontinuität. ∎

Das Gebäude der Commerzbank, der höchste Büroturm Europas.
The building of the Commerzbank, the highest office tower of Europe.

Gallus-Green, in Niederrad and at the airport. The City-House of 1975 located at the "Square of the Republic", with its 143 m transgressed significantly the hundred-metre mark for the first time. The demand for office space also led to greater pressure on the city council, to issue permits for larger building ground spaces and ever growing construction heights. The Euro-Tower, now the headquarters of the European Central Bank, 148 m, with access from the West-side to the old part of the city and at the Gallus-Green, has become a signal of a new development in the historic quarter, which has also led to the permission of construct-ing further in height than the steeple of the Cathedral (94 m). This is when the grouping of skyscrapers started on

Die Deutsche Bibliothek, 1997.
The German Library, 1997.

both sides of the Taunus-/Gallus-Green, which provides a good space for resting with its broad park and the colonnades. Presently, these greens are almost completely surrounded by skyscrapers. An impressive great architectural space that can be experienced parting from "Alte Oper" (the old opera) as well as from the south. The twin towers of the Deutsche Bank, 155 m height, 1984, have within this urban concept of construction an ex-cellent space-creating effect. The mirrored, in-clined towards each other highly towering glass forms on a prismatic foot, decisively give the city image of Frankfurt its characteristic.

The visitors to Frankfurt's exhibitions are already able to see from far the exhibition tower with its 256 m in height, by the architects Murphy and Jahn, in its telescope form and with the pyramid as its utmost final peak and perceive it like a sym-bol of the fair. The same is valid for the Torhaus towering on the Westside of the exhibition centre with 117 m height by O. M. Ungers, which mas-terly bridged the difficult situation within a trian-gular of tracks and a gate opening.

One office tower, which was supposed to exceed all other in Europe, whose construction failed however because of the veto of one neighbour, was the so-called Campanile, planned south of the main train station with 265 m height. An invest-ment of billions failed because of the neighbour-hood-protecting building regulations and the

stubbornness of one per-son! Also this can be found in Frankfurt.

Meanwhile, at the Kaiser-platz was built the highest office tower of Europe, the Commerzbank Centre, with 259 m plus antenna 300 m in height. A gigantic, but at the same time gay appearing work of construction for 2.400 workplaces and exemplary for the new generation of skyscrapers.

Sir Norman Foster has not only created an im-portant accent of town construction with the Com-merzbank and the peak of the skyline of Frank-furt, it is a remarkable work that is ecologically oriented. On the first floor there is a spacious restaurant open to the public and a lobby. The ground plan of the tower is a triangle that has cor-ners that provide the transport and installation fa-cilities and in the middle of which an atrium over 160 m arises. Nine tower gardens, each 200 m² in size, are the green lungs of the house; they can be used by the employees as communication and rest areas. A framework construction unusual for sky-scrapers spans over the 34 m wide gardens with-out pillars. The two-shell air-conditioned façade allows the saving of energy and natural cooling – until today probably unique in the construction of skyscrapers. The windows of the inner shell can be opened so that natural fresh air is ensured up

to the 50th floor. The tower gardens wind them-selves upwards in spiral-shape on the east, south and west side. Each direction has thus one botan-ic theme as a basis; in the east: Asian vegetation, south: Mediterranean vegetation, in the west: North American vegetation. Each employee can control for around two thirds of the day the air-conditioning himself by individually opening or closing the window. Instead of the usual air-con-ditioning technology a system of roof cooling was developed with water supply for cooling the rooms. The rooms are heated with conventional heating. Through ecologically effective measures of building-technologies savings in energy of 30 % are achieved compared to common office towers.

The old imperial City of Frankfurt, city of corona-tions and exhibitions was, as Merian portrayed it so fittingly in his bird's eye view, a conglomerate grown together in centuries. Some of its valuable treasures have remained preserved until today. Through modern architecture the city has ob-tained a new face in which the old outlines can still be recognised, enhancing the expression of its versatility and continuity. ■

Weiler Tief- und Rohrleitungsbau GmbH

Geschäftsführer/Manager:
Dipl.-Ing. Axel Zobel

Gründungsjahr/Year of Foundation:
1962

Mitarbeiter/Employees:
ca./approx. 120

Umsatz/Turnover:
ca./approx. 30 Mio. DM

Geschäftstätigkeit/Business Activity:
- Rohrleitungsbau
- Kabelverlegung
- Tiefbau
- Straßenbau
- Containerdienst
- Winterdienst
- Notdienst an Versorgungs- und
  Entsorgungsleitungen
- Transportleistung von Baugeräten
- Baumanagement von der Planung
  bis zur Ausführung
- Pipeline fitting
- Draw-in systems
- Building constructions and civil engineering
- Road construction
- Container service
- Street and pavement service
- Winter service
- Care of greens
- Emergency service of supply and waste
  disposal lines
- Transport service of construction equipment
- Construction management from planning
  up to execution

Anschrift/Address:
Im Kalk 3–5
D-60437 Frankfurt/Harheim
Telefon   +49 (6101) 40 40 2
Telefax   +49 (6101) 40 41 18

Weiler – eine gute Adresse in Frankfurt

Weiler – a good Address in Frankfurt

Der Saugbagger.

The hydraulic dredger.

Besser sein – immer besser werden", so lautet die Philosophie, die sich das Bauunternehmen Weiler in Frankfurt/Harheim auf die Fahnen geschrieben hat.

In den letzten Jahren waren durch die Zusammenschlüsse bei den Energieversorgern und durch neue Anbieter in der Telekommunikation besondere Herausforderungen zu bewältigen. Durch das ausgezeichnet ausgebildete Fachpersonal, die perfekte Organisation und Koordination konnte diese Wegstrecke mit großem Erfolg gemeistert werden, so dass der Name Weiler Bauunternehmen im Ballungsraum Rhein/Main wohl nicht mehr wegzudenken ist.

Seit fast 40 Jahren ist das Unternehmen Weiler zuverlässiger Partner für alle Aufgabenstellungen rund um den Bau. Mit über 120 Mitarbeitern werden Projekte in jeder Größenordnung, in hoher Qualität, termingerecht ausgeführt.

Um allen Anforderungen gerecht zu werden, steht bei Weiler neben der hohen Innovationsbereitschaft auch die permanente Fort- und Weiterbildung der Mitarbeiter an oberster Stelle. So ist das Unternehmen Weiler im Besitz des DVGW-Zertifikates G1 u. W1 und seit langer Zeit Mitglied im Güteschutz Kanalbau. Darüber hinaus ist die Firma Weiler anerkannter Fachbetrieb nach WHG § 19.

Gute Gründe, um mit Weiler Kontakt aufzunehmen. Wir freuen uns auf Ihren Anruf! ∎

To be better – always becoming better", this is the philosophy which the construction company Weiler in Frankfurt/Harheim has taken up as its cause.

During the last years, special challenges had to be overcome because of the mergers of energy suppliers and new providers that emerged in telecommunications. Through the excellently qualified expert personnel, a perfect organisation and co-ordination this temporary phase could be surpassed with great success, so that the name Weiler Construction Company can hardly loose its presence in conurbation zones.

Since almost 40 years, the Weiler Company has be a reliable partner for all tasks arising around construction. With over 140 employees, projects of any size are carried out in high quality and according to agreed datelines.

In order to comply with this high requirement, Weiler gives priority, apart from preparedness to innovation, also to a permanent further and continuous education of employees. Thus the Weiler Company will be certified according to ISO 9002 and has been since long a member of the grade protection for canalisation. Furthermore, the company Weiler is a recognised expert enterprise for pipeline fittings and a certified company according to WHG § 19.

Good reasons for establishing contacts with Weiler. We are glad to receive your call! ∎

132

Ganzheitliche Konzepte für den Wohnungsbau

Integral Concepts for Housing Construction

Modernisierte Wohnanlage.
Modernised Appartment Buildings.

INDUSTRIA
Bau- und Vermietungsgesellschaft mbH

Geschäftsführer/Manager:
Reiner Geiß
Dietmar Pendzialek

Aufsichtsratsvorsitzender/
Chairman of the Supervisory Board:
Jürgen Eckert

Mitarbeiter/Employees:
derzeit 21/presently 21

Anschrift/Address:
Postfach 100862
D-63008 Offenbach am Main
Telefon   +49 (69) 83 83 98-0
Telefax   +49 (69) 83 77 99
E-Mail   info@industria-gmbh.de
Internet   www.industria-gmbh.de

INDUSTRIA was founded on 21st January 1954 as a social housing enterprise of the state of Hesse, the "Gemeinnütziger Wohnungsbau hessischer Unternehmen GmbH" and is since 1995 a corporation of the Degussa AG. Until the middle of the seventies, the company strategy entailed mainly to construct social housing subsidised with public or fiscal funds for employees of Degussa AG. In view of the changed market structures however, INDUSTRIA evolved in the nineties from a purely rental association into an innovative properties association, and even more so since 1997, as the new share holder is the Degussa Bank GmbH.

Main fields of business activities of INDUSTRIA are:
• Letting and administration of self-owned appartment holdings
• Renovation and sale of self-owned and thirdparty appartment holdings
• Administration of renovated freehold appartment buildings as well as maintenance services for external holdings
• Newly-built property and sale of inexpensive typified condominiums.
In co-operation with the share holder Degussa Bank INDUSTRIA offers to parties interested the purchase of flats or houses the tailor-made financial provision at favourable conditions. The aim is to present integral concepts of solution to the client in order to enable especially for young families the acquisition of property. ■

Die INDUSTRIA wurde am 21. Januar 1954 als „Gemeinnütziger Wohnungsbau Hessischer Unternehmen GmbH" gegründet und ist seit 1995 Konzerngesellschaft der Degussa AG.
Bis Mitte der 70er Jahre war die Unternehmensstrategie, überwiegend öffentlich geförderte oder steuerbegünstigte Mietwohnungen für Mitarbeiter der Degussa AG zu bauen. Im Hinblick auf veränderte Marktstrukturen entwickelte sich die INDUSTRIA in den 90er Jahren von der reinen Vermietungsgesellschaft hin zu einer innovativen Immobiliengesellschaft, und dies verstärkt, seit 1997 der neue Gesellschafter Degussa Bank GmbH heißt.

Kerngeschäftsfelder der INDUSTRIA sind:
• Vermietung und Verwaltung eigener Mietwohnungsbestände
• Umwandlung und Verkauf eigener und fremder Mietwohnungsbestände
• Verwaltung der umgewandelten Eigentumswohnanlagen sowie Verwaltungsdienstleistung für externe Bestände
• Neubau und Verkauf von preiswerten typisierten Reihenhäusern.
Gemeinsam mit dem Gesellschafter Degussa Bank bietet die INDUSTRIA für Kaufinteressenten von Wohnungen oder Häusern maßgeschneiderte Finanzierungsangebote zu günstigen Konditionen. Ziel ist es, dem Kunden ganzheitliche Lösungskonzepte aufzuzeigen, um insbesondere auch jungen Familien den Immobilienkauf zu ermöglichen. ■

Reihenhäuser sind vor allem bei jungen Familien gefragt.
Condominiums are especially favoured by young families.

econos:
financial services consultancy of choice

Die econos consulting Gruppe, ein Tochterunternehmen der Deutschen Bank, ist im Management-, IT- und Organisationsbereich tätig und bietet ein breites Spektrum an Beratungsdienstleistungen, besonders in der Strategie-Implementierung und im Change-Management.

Den Kern der econos-Vision bildet die Überzeugung, dass der wichtigste Beitrag eines Beraters für den Kunden darin liegt, ihn zu befähigen, die sich durch den fortwährenden Wandel bietenden Möglichkeiten nutzen zu können. „Wenn man auf die sich verändernden Umweltbedingungen keinen Einfluss hat, sollte man sicher gehen, dass alle sich aus dem Wandel bietenden Vorteile genutzt werden", erläutert Ralf Müller, econos Geschäftsführer.

Ausgehend von der Erkenntnis, dass die besten Mitarbeiter die ständige Herausforderung suchen, wurde einer Gruppe engagierter Berater aus dem Inhouse-Consulting der Deutschen Bank die Möglichkeit gegeben, ihre Leistungen auch externen Kunden anzubieten.

econos wurde von drei Partnern und einem Kernteam von 30 Beratern im Frühjahr 2000 gegründet und hat sich bereits als ausgewählter Partner für große Unternehmen in und außerhalb der Finanzbranche etabliert. Bis zum Ende 2000 ist die Zahl der Arbeitnehmer auf 70 gestiegen und die Einkünfte auf über 9 Millionen Euro. Damit wurden alle Erwartungen übertroffen. Durch ausgeprägte Fachkenntnisse und jahrelange Erfahrungen begleiten die econos-Berater eine breite Palette von Projekten auf drei Kontinenten. Büros in Frankfurt und London bestehen bereits.

„Der Bedarf an Re-engineering, Systemintegration und -migration in der Finanzbranche ist ungebrochen. Hierbei können unsere Kunden auf unsere Expertise zählen", sagt Jan Kirchoff. econos

bietet in vielen finanzdienstleistungsspezifischen Bereichen ihre Beratung an. Dazu gehören: Trade Advisory-Services, Operations Control und Risikomanagement. Patrick Wilson fasst den Wettbewerbsvorteil von econos zusammen: „Mit unserem umfassenden Verständnis des Zahlungsverkehrsgeschäftes, der Markttrends, der erforderlichen Systemveränderungen und aufsichtsrechtlichen Erfordernisse, sind wir mit econos ideal positioniert, um unsere Kunden beim Erhalt und Ausbau ihrer Wettbewerbsfähigkeit zu unterstützen.

„Mit der Veränderung der traditionellen Wertschöpfungsketten unter dem Einfluss des technologischen Wandels und der Verbreitung der neuen Medien sehen sich viele Unternehmen neuen Herausforderungen ausgesetzt. Beim Aufbau eines integrierten B2B-Marktplatzes verlaufen die Grenzen zwischen der industriellen, der logistischen und der finanziellen Dimension des Geschäftes", erklärt Ralf Müller. Um diesen neuen Trends zu begegnen, bietet econos seine Leistungen entsprechend auch Unternehmen außerhalb der Finanzindustrie an.

Während der verschiedenen Phasen der Unternehmensgründung bietet das Unternehmen seinen Kunden fachmännische Unterstützung (Start-ups, neue Produkte und Dienstleistungen, neue Vertriebswege und Märkte) von der Entwicklung der Geschäftsidee über die Machbarkeitsstudie, bis zur Erstellung des Geschäftsplanes und dem operativen Start des Unternehmens an. „Der integrierte Beratungsansatz – mit einer eigens hierfür entwickelten Methode – geht sogar noch weiter als bis zur Gründung des Unternehmens: „Bei einer Expansion können wir über unser umfangreiches Netzwerk Hilfe bei der Partnersuche geben, so zum Beispiel für das Outsourcing bestimmter Leistungen", sagt Ralf Müller. Starkes Wachstum und Restrukturierungsprogramme ge-

hen einher mit der Erfordernis nach effizient gemanagten Geschäftsprozessen, einem maßgeschneiderten ERP-System, erfolgreichem Customer-Relationship-Management und einem ganzheitlichen Human-Resources Ansatz. Diese Felder sind ein zentraler Bestandteil des Service-Portfolios von econos.

Als ein junges und schnell wachsendes Unternehmen ist es econos gelungen, eine einzigartige Arbeitsumgebung und -kultur zu schaffen. Die econos Berater haben einen breit gefächerten beruflichen Hintergrund und kommen aus den verschiedensten Ländern. „Unsere Mitarbeiter schätzen, dass econos die flexible Arbeitsatmosphäre eines Start-ups mit der globalen Dimension und dem Erfahrungsschatz eines Großunternehmens kombiniert", sagt Ralf Müller. „Durch dieses Potenzial unserer Mitarbeiter sind wir im Beratungsmarkt bestens positioniert." ∎

Die econos Geschäftsführung: Patrick Wilson, Jan Kirchhoff, Ralf Müller (v. links).

The econos executive board: Patrick Wilson, Jan Kirchhoff, Ralf Müller (f. left).

The econos consulting Group is the Deutsche Bank spin-off consultancy for management, IT and organization. econos offers a wide spectrum of consulting services focused on three main areas: strategy implementation, change management, and performance improvement.

At the core of the econos vision lies the recognition that the most valuable contribution a consultancy can make to its clients is to enable them to harness the forces of change at work in the financial sector today to realize their full potential. "If you can't act on the underlying causes of change, you should make sure that all opportunities associated with that change are fully exploited" explains Ralf Müller, managing partner at econos.

Realizing that continuous challenge is a major driver to retain and attract the best people, a dedicated group of Deutsche Bank consultants were set free to proactively offer their services to external clients. Founded in the spring of 2000 as a subsidiary of Deutsche Bank AG by three partners and a core team of 30 consultants, econos has already established itself as a partner of choice for major corporate players both in and outside of the financial industry. By year-end 2000, the number of employees had risen to 70 and revenues had topped the 9 million Euro mark, far exceeding original expectations. Using skills, experience and knowledge gained over many years of in-house activity, econos' consultants manage a wide range of projects internally and externally across three continents. Offices in Frankfurt and London have already been established.

"There is a continuous need in the financial services industry for re-engineering, integration and migration which we can serve with our wide-ranging expertise" says Jan Kirchoff, one of the managing partners. econos offers consulting services over a broad spectrum of banking-related fields, including trade advisory services, continuous link settlement (CLS), operations control, global payments and global risk management/regulatory risk reporting. Patrick Wilson, managing director, summarizes econos' competitive advantage in the area of banking advisory services: "with its comprehensive understanding of the payments business, the market trends and the

regulatory/system changes required, econos consulting is ideally placed to assist its clients to ensure that they remain competitive. In addition, having Deutsche Bank as a founding member of econos allows us to offer the expertise and skills that some institutions may lack in the fields of trade, payments and operations, covering the entire process from front to middle to back office."

As traditional value chains are being reconsidered and reengineered under the influence of technological change, the development of new media and the advent of new products/services, many companies are faced with daunting competition challenges. "When setting up an integrated B2B e-marketplace, the industrial, financial and logistical dimension all converge and the challenge is then to come up with the most appropriate solution in terms of end-user satisfaction, strategic fit and profitability," explains Ralf Müller.

To respond to these new trends, econos also offers its services to non-financial institutions. In many projects, econos provides expert assistance to its clients throughout the various phases of the creation of new ventures (startup companies, new products and services, new distribution channels, new market), from the development of the business concept to the conducting of feasibility analyses, the drafting of business plans and the operational setup of the company. "In accordance with our integrated approach to consulting, the assistance we provide to our clients does not end once a venture has been launched," says Ralf Müller. "In a business expansion project for instance, econos can draw on its extensive network to assist in the finding of a partner, be it for outsourcing or for potential alliances." In addition, growing and restructuring companies typically require efficient business process management, customized ERP systems, a successful customer relationship management (CRM) system and a comprehensive human resources approach. Each of these fields is a cornerstone of econos' integrated consulting approach.

A young and rapidly growing company, econos has been successful in creating a unique working style. Consultants typically come from a variety of professional (IT, consulting, operations, HR) and national backgrounds. "Employees are especially appreciative that the company has been able to combine the flexibility and atmosphere of a start-up with the global dimension and depth of expertise usually associated with larger, longer established institutions," explains Ralf Müller. "Because econos employees feel a tremendous sense of empowerment, we are well positioned to tackle the increasingly demanding consulting market." ■

Geschäftsführung/Executive Board:
Jan Kirchhoff, Ralf Müller, Patrick Wilson

Verwaltungsrat/Supervisory Board:
Dr. Hans Kraus (Chair), Bernd Sperber, Andreas Ritter

Gründung/Foundation:
econos consulting GmbH
Gegründet am 1. März, 2000
Tochtergesellschaft der
Deutschen Bank AG
econos consulting Ltd.
Gegründet am 1. Mai 2000
100%ige Tochtergesellschaft der
econos consulting GmbH

econos consulting GmbH
founded March 1, 2000
subsidiary of Deutsche Bank AG
econos consulting Ltd
founded May 1, 2000
100% subsidiary of econos consulting GmbH

Mitarbeiter/Employees:
70 (Stand 31.12.2000/at year end 2000)

Geschäftstätigkeit/Business Activity:
- eSystem integration
- Strategic implementation management
- launch centre: organizational and technical setup of new ventures
- Business Process Management
- ERP integration
- Trade advisory services
- CLS advisory and implementation
- Operations control
- Global payments consultancy
- Global risk management

Anschrift/Address:

Zentrale/Head Office
Breitlacherstraße 94
D-60489 Frankfurt am Main
Telefon   +49 (69) 7 68 06-9
Telefax   +49 (69) 7 68 06-650

Büro London/London Office
3rd Floor
145 Leadenhall Street
GB-London EC3V 4QT
Telefon   +44 (20) 76 56 34 00
Telefax   +44 (20) 76 56 34 01

E-Mail   info@econos-consulting.com
Internet   www.econos-consulting.com

135

Frankfurt am Main – Stadt der Verbindungen und Begegnungen

Frankfurt on the Main – A City of Connections and Encounters

Frankfurt am Main ist als internationaler Verkehrsknotenpunkt seit Jahrhunderten eine Stadt der Begegnung von Menschen aus allen Himmelsrichtungen und verschiedensten Kulturen. Hier war eine Furt, also ein Flussübergang. Nachdem die Franken das Rhein-Main-Gebiet erobert hatten – vor ihnen lebten hier Kelten, Römer und Alemannen – war es der Franken Furt, wo man Fuhrwerke durch den Main zog, bis die 1222 erstmals bezeugte Alte Brücke gebaut wurde. Der Flussübergang der Nord-Süd-Verbindung kreuzte sich hier mit alten Handelswegen, die sich nach Norden, Osten, Westen und Süden in verschiedene Richtung verzweigten. An diesem zentral erreichbaren Ort errichtete der Frankenkönig und spätere Kaiser Karl der Große eine Königspfalz, in die er im Jahr 794 die geistlichen und weltlichen Amtsträger zu einer Reichsversammlung zusammenrief. Er wurden Fragen des Glaubens, der Administration und eine einheitliche Währung für das Frankenreich geregelt, das damals Westeuropa und Oberitalien umfasste.

Nach der Teilung des Fränkischen Reiches wurde Frankfurt, während der Herrschaft der Karolinger, Hauptstadt des östlichen Reichsteils, aus dem Deutschland hervorging. Später wurden hier immer wieder Reichstage und bedeutende politische Zusammenkünfte abgehalten. In der Zeit der Staufer begann der Aufschwung der Stadt. Seit 1147 wählte man hier mehrfach die deutschen Könige, so 1152 Friedrich Barbarossa, bis 1356 Kaiser Karl IV in der Goldenen Bulle Frankfurt am Main zum ständigen Wahlort bestimmte. Gewählt wurde im Kaiserdom, wo seit 1562 auch die Krönungen stattfanden. Gefeiert wurde im Kaisersaal des Römers. Frankfurt am Main wurde damit ein Ort zentraler politischer Ereignisse, bei denen Menschen aus ganz Europa zusammenkamen.

Die Stadt unterstand unmittelbar nur dem Kaiser. Mit der Zeit gelang es ihr, ihre Selbstverwaltung auszubauen, die politischen Spitzenämter zu übernehmen, bis schließlich 1312 der Rat den Bürgermeister wählen durfte. Seit 1372 war Frankfurt freie Reichsstadt.

Die günstige Verkehrsanbindung am Schnittpunkt der Fernhandelswege und über den Main an den Rhein sowie die politische Konstellation unter dem Schutz der Kaiser ließen einen bedeutenden Handelsplatz entstehen, von dem seit dem

Dr. Albrecht Magen

Der Autor wurde 1929 in Breslau geboren. Nach Verfolgung der Familie durch die Nationalsozialisten und Vertreibung aus Schlesien Schulabschluss und Beginn des Studiums der Rechtswissenschaft in Thüringen. Dort 1946 Eintritt in die CDU. Wegen oppositioneller Betätigung gegen das kommunistische Regime 1948 Flucht nach Frankfurt/Main. Nach Ablegung beider Staatsprüfungen, Promotion und Austauschstudium in USA in der Wirtschaft tätig. Von 1971 bis 1991 Vorstandsmitglied und Arbeitsdirektor eines Industrieunternehmens. Daneben im Verbandswesen und in der Kommunalpolitik aktiv. 1989 Stadtverordneter, ab 1993 ehrenamtlicher Stadtrat in Frankfurt. Seit März 2000 Dezernent für Integration, zuständig für das Amt für multikulturelle Angelegenheiten und die Ausländervertretung.

The author was born 1929 in Breslau. After the persecution of his family by the National socialists and the expulsion from Schlesia, termination of his school education and begin of law studies in Thuringia. There he joined the Christian Democratic Union in 1946. Because of opposition activities against the communist regime, flight to Frankfurt/Main in 1948. After passing both state examinations successfully, doctorate and exchange studies in the USA, active in the field of economy. From 1971 till 1991 Member of the Board and Operational Director of an industrial enterprise. Besides this, active in the system of associations and in communal politics. 1989 town councillor, from 1993 on honorary town councillor in Frankfurt. Since March 200 Head of Department of Integration, in charge of the office for multicultural matters and the aliens' representation.

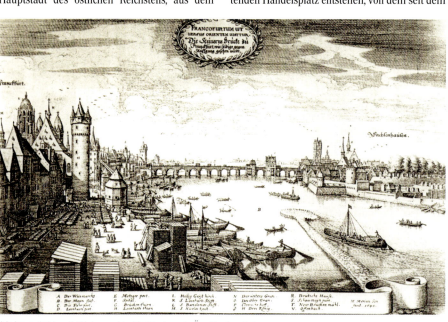

Mainansicht mit Weinmarkt, M. Merian d. Ä., Kupferstich, 1646, Historisches Museum, Frankfurt a. M.

View of the Main and Wine Market, M. Merian the Elder, etching, 1646, Historic Museum, Frankfurt on the Main.

„Warhafter und Eigentlicher Schauplatz Der Weit berühmten Franckfurter Meß" (Der Römerberg zur Messe). Johann Albrecht Jormann, Frankfurt a. M., Buchdruck mit Titel-Kupferstich (1696), Historisches Museum, Frankfurt a. M.

"Truthful and Real Location of the Widely Famous Franckfurter Mass" (The Römerberg at Fair-Time). Johann Albrecht Jormann, Frankfurt on the Main, Letterpress with Title-etching (1696), Historic Museum, Frankfurt on the Main.

Being an international node for transport, Frankfurt on the Main has been since centuries a city of encounters of people from all parts of the world and from the most varied cultures. Here, there was a ford that is a river crossing. After the Franks had conquered the Rhein-Main area – before these the Celts, Romans and Alemans lived here – it used to be the Franken Ford, where carriages were pulled through the Main until the Old Bridge was built, which is testified in 1222 for the first time. The river crossing for the North-South connection met here with old trade routes that branched out to north, east, west and south into different directions. At this centrally accessible the King of the Franks and later Emperor Carl the Great built a royal palace into which he called in the year 794 the clerical and secular office bearers to an imperial German assembly. Questions of faith, administration and a unified monetary system were stipulated for the Franconian Empire, which extended in those days over Western Europe and Upper Italy.

After the Franconian Empire was divided, Frankfurt became the capital of the Eastern part of the empire, during the rule of the Carolingians, which gave birth to Germany. Later, on many occasions German imperial senate assemblies and important political gatherings were held here. In the Stauffer period the upsurge of the city began. Since 1147, frequently the German kings were elected here like Friedrich Barbarossa in 1152, until, in 1356, Emperor Karl IV determined Frankfurt on the Main to be the permanent election place in "The Golden Bull". The election took place in the Imperial Cathedral, were also the coronations were held since 1562. Celebrations were held in the imperial hall of the Römer. This made Frankfurt on the Main a place of central political events, at which people from all over Europe came together.

The city stood under the direct orders of the Emperor alone. By the time it succeeded extending its self-administration, to take on top political posi-

tions until in 1312 the council was allowed to elect its own mayor. Since 1372 Frankfurt has been a free imperial city.

The favourable transport connections at the centre of remote sales routes and across the Main to the Rhine as well as the political constellation under the protection of the Emperors gave way to the establishment of an important trade centre that has been reported about since the 12th century. In the year 1240, Emperor Friedrich II took, always in August, travelling merchants on their way to the Frankfurt Fair under his protection. Meanwhile, the road crossing the St.-Gotthard-Pass was fortified as a sales route. Apart from the classic connection over the Brenner, on which trade blossoming since the crusade with oriental goods (Chinese silk, spices and much more) was effected from Venice first to Augsburg and Nuremberg, a shorter transport connection from Genoa and Upper Italy over the Swiss Alps to Basle the Rhine and the roads of the Rhine valley was created. This

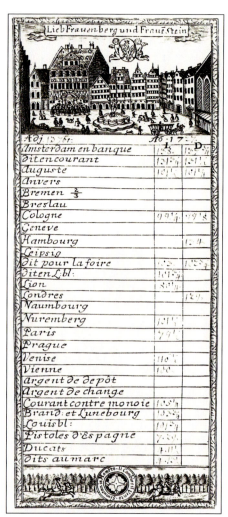

 zeigt oben die Beschriftung „Lieb Frauenberg und Frauestein".

Foto des ältesten erhaltenen Wechselkurszettels von 1727 aus Frankreich, Historisches Museum, Frankfurt a. M.

Photograph of the oldest preserved rate of exchange receipt of 1727 from France, Historic Museum, Frankfurt on the Main.

12. Jahrhundert berichtet wird. Im Jahr 1240 stellte Kaiser Friedrich II die jeweils im August zur Frankfurter Messe reisenden Kaufleute unter seinen Schutz. Zur gleichen Zeit wurde die Straße über den Sankt-Gotthard-Pass als Handelsweg ausgebaut. Neben der klassischen Verbindung über den Brenner, auf der der seit den Kreuzzügen aufblühende Handel mit Orientwaren (chinesische Seide, Gewürze und anderes mehr) von Venedig zunächst nach Augsburg und Nürnberg betrieben wurde, trat damit eine kürzere Verkehrsverbindung von Genua und Oberitalien über die Schweizer Alpen nach Basel zum Rhein und den Straßen des Rheintals. So konnten die kostbaren Waren schneller und einfacher nach Frankfurt gebracht werden, zum Teil mit dem Schiff von Mainz auf dem Main nach Frankfurt.

Im Gegenverkehr von Nord nach Süd wurden aus dem zunächst weniger entwickelten Nordeuropa vor allem Rohstoffe gehandelt, so Wolle aus England, Flandern und den nord-östlichen Gebieten des Kontinents. Die bedeutendsten Umschlagplätze waren zunächst die Messen in Städten der Champagne, die aber 1320 zusammenbrachen, teils als Folge des Hundertjährigen Krieges zwischen England und Frankreich, teils weil der Wollexport im Interesse der eigenen Produktion unterbunden wurde. Frankfurt rückte in die Position der Champagne-Messen ein.

So wurde die Stadt zum Transithandelsplatz für Waren aus allen Richtungen, für die Erzeugnisse aus dem Orient, die über Venedig, Pisa und Genua kamen, für Früchte und Gewürze aus dem Mittelmeerraum, für Wolle und Pelze aus dem Norden, für Heringe aus dem Ostseeraum, Vieh und Pferde aus Osteuropa, Farbstoffe und Metallwaren aus Thüringen und Sachsen. Schmuck, Gold und Edelmetalle wurden in der Halle des Rathauses zum Römer gehandelt. Der Handel mit Tuchen zog auch Tuchfabrikationen in Frankfurt nach sich. Die Messe wuchs so stark, dass Kaiser Ludwig im Jahr 1333 eine zusätzliche Frühjahrsmesse genehmigte und Zollfreiheit für den Messeverkehr im Reich verkündete. Noch mehr als die politischen Versammlungen führten die Messen regelmäßig Tausende von Menschen aus allen Herren Länder in die Stadt. So beschrieb Humanist Ulrich von Hutten 1510 die Messe: „Weither suchen die Völker sie auf und wandern die Menschen, denn für die Waren der Welt ist sie der wimmelnde Markt."

Zum kaufmännischen Handel gesellten sich aber noch weitere Tätigkeiten. Ein ganz neues Produkt kam hinzu, das schnell vom intellektuellen künstlerischen Einzelstück zur gewerblichen Ware wurde: das Buch. 1440 hatte Gutenberg den Buchdruck erfunden, 1454 seine Werkstatt von Mainz nach Frankfurt verlegt. Die Verbreitung von Büchern nahm einen solchen Aufschwung, das bereits 1480 die Buchmesse eröffnet wurde. Die Buchgasse erinnert heute noch an ihren historischen Platz. Buchdrucker und Verlage ließen sich hier nieder, und die Stadt blieb bis ins 18. Jahrhundert der führende Handelsplatz für Bücher, der Grundlage für umwälzende geistige Entwicklungen.

Alle diese verschiedenen Geschäfte erforderten auch differenzierte Systeme der Finanzierung. Eine Vielzahl von Münzen ganz unterschiedlicher Herkunft und Wertigkeit waren im Umlauf. Bargeld mitzuführen, war umständlich und bei den unsicheren Verhältnissen gefährlich. So musste der bargeldlose Zahlungsverkehr, das heißt das Wechselgeschäft, eingeführt werden. Schließlich konnten viele Geschäfte nur auf Kredit abgewickelt und zum Teil mussten sie durch Wechsel-

kredite finanziert werden. Das sich international verbreitende Geld- und Kreditgeschäft fand auch in Frankfurt im Gefolge der Messen einen Standort. Die Frankfurter Messen waren Fälligkeitstage für die begebenen Wechsel. Die Geldverleiher gingen später dazu über, auch den wachsenden Bedarf von Fürsten und Städten durch Anleihen zu finanzieren, deren Übertragbarkeit ermöglicht werden musste. So wurde 1585 die Börse als Ort geregelter Finanztransaktionen gegründet.

Im Vergleich zu seiner wirtschaftlichen Bedeutung war Frankfurt eine verhältnismäßig kleine Stadt. Im 15.und 16. Jahrhundert hatte es 10.000 bis 20.000 Einwohner, also einen Bruchteil der Menschen, die zu den großen Veranstaltungen in die Stadt kamen. Zugewanderte Bevölkerungsgruppen hatten als „Beisassen" hier ihren Wohnsitz und nahmen mit eingeschränkten Befugnissen am wirtschaftlichen Geschehen teil.

Zu nennen sind zunächst die Juden, die im Mittelalter gegen Zahlung einer Abgabe unter besonderem kaiserlichen Schutz standen und anfangs frei in der Stadt lebten, bis ihnen der Rat nach Erwerb des Schutzverhältnisses vom Kaiser die Judengasse als Ghetto zuwies. Auf der einen Seite waren ihnen die von den Zünften kontrollierten Handwerksberufe in der christlichen Stadt versperrt, auf der anderen unterlagen sie nicht dem Verbot, Zinsen für den Geldverleih zu erheben, das die Kirche 1179 für ihre Gläubigen verhängt hatte. So wurden sie vielfach Geldverleiher, deren Bedeutung, durch das für eine wachsende Wirtschaft unverzichtbare Darlehensgeschäft ständig zunahm. Der in Zeiten individueller oder allgemeiner Bedrängnis wachsenden Schwierigkeiten zwischen Schuldnern und Gläubigern führten wie an vielen Orten zu Antisemitismus und Vertreibungen. Aber mit der Zeit wurden die Juden immer wieder zugelassen (in Frankfurt ständig seit dem Anfang des 17. Jahrhunderts) und als Einwohner mit besonderem Status akzeptiert, bis sich im 19. Jahrhundert die Emanzipation durchsetzte.

Weitere Menschen fremder Herkunft und anderen Glaubens kamen als Verfolgte in die seit 1535 streng lutherische Stadt. Dies waren die aus Frankreich und vor allem aus den spanischen Niederlanden vertriebenen Calvinisten. Eine beachtliche Gruppe stammte aus der mehrfach umkämpften und blockierten Stadt Antwerpen, die auch besondere handwerkliche und vorindustrielle Fertigkeiten z. B. in der Baumwoll- und Seidenweberei mitbrachte. Diese Menschen waren gleichzeitig eine Bereicherung für die Stadt. 1595 stellten diese 4.000 religiösen Flüchtlinge etwa 15–20 % der Bevölkerung. Auch wenn sie wegen ihres fremden Glaubens nicht alle Rechte

Am Mainufer.

was a way to bring the valuable merchandise faster and easier to Frankfurt, partly also by ship on the Main from Mainz to Frankfurt.

In the traffic in the opposite direction from North to South raw materials were traded from the still lesser developed Northern Europe, like wool from England, Flanders and the Northeastern areas of the continent. The most important trade centres were first the fairs in the cities of the Champagne, that collapsed however in 1320, partly as a result of the hundred-year-war between England and France, partly because of the export of wool was prohibited in the interest of its own production. Frankfurt moved up to the position of the Champagne-fairs.

Thus, the city became a transitory trading place for goods coming from all directions, for products from the Orient that came via Venice, Pisa and Genoa, for fruits and spices from the Mediterranean area, for wool and furs from the north, for herrings from the Baltic Sea area, cattle and horses from Eastern Europe, artificial colouring and metal wares from Thuringia and Saxony. Jewellery, gold and precious metals were traded in the hall of the town hall adjoining the Römer. The trading with cloth brought also the cloth manufacturing industry to Frankfurt. The fair grew so much that Emperor Ludwig gave permission for an additional spring fair in the year 1333 and announced tax free trade for the fair traffic in the Empire. But more than the political assemblies, the fairs brought regularly thousands of people from all parts of the world into the city. Thus described the humanist Ulrich von Hutten 1510 the fair: "From far folks seek it and people travel, 'cause for the goods of the world it is the swarming market."

But to the commercial trade were added further activities. A completely new product emerged that rapidly transformed from an intellectual artistic individual piece to a commercial commodity: the book. 1440 Gutenberg had invented the letterpress, 1454 his workshop was transferred from Mainz to Frankfurt. The dispersion of books took such an upsurge that as early as 1480 the book fair was started. The book alley even today reminds us of its historic place. Printers and

At the Mainufer.

editorials settled down here, and the city remained up into the 18th century the leading trading place for books, the basis for transforming intellectual developments.

All these different business activities also made differential systems of finance necessary. A number of coins of completely varied origin and value were in circulation. To carry ready cash was awkward and dangerous given the insecure conditions. Thus, the cashless money transactions, that is the exchange transactions, were introduced. Finally, many business transactions could only be carried out by taking loans and had to be financed sometimes by credit on bills. The internationally spreading monetary and credit businesses also found in Frankfurt a good location, as a result of the fair. The dates of the Frankfurt Fairs were due dates for the issued bills. The moneylenders afterwards also resorted to finance the growing demand of counts and townships through loans that had to be transferable. Thus, in 1585 the stock exchange was founded as a place for regulating financial transactions.

Compared to its economic importance, Frankfurt was a relatively small city. In the 15th and 16th century it had 10.000 to 20.000 inhabitants, that is a fraction of the people that came to Frankfurt for the great events.

Immigrated groups of the population had here as citizens without full civic rights so-called "Beisassen" their domicile and participated with limited authorizations in economic activities.

First of all must be mentioned the Jews that in the middle Ages stood against payment of a tax under special imperial protection and in the beginning

lived freely in the city, until the council assign to them - after having acquired the protection status from the Emperor – the Jewish Alley as a ghetto. On the one hand, the crafts and skilled trade professions controlled by the guilds were barred to them in the Christian city, on the other hand, they did not fall under the law that prohibited the taking of interest for lending money stipulated by the Church in 1179 for their faithful. Thus they frequently became moneylenders, whose importance grew continuously through the loan business indispensable for a growing economy. The difficulties growing in times of individual or general pressures between debtors and creditors led in many places to anti-Semitism and expulsions. But by and by the Jews were always admitted again (in Frankfurt permanently since the begin-

Anno 17	Ady 27:87 In Francoforte.	
Venetia	-	117
Vienna	-	100
Norimbergo	-	101
Augusta	-	101
Lipsia	-	04
Dito infiera	-	01
Parigii	-	7
Lione	-	
Bremen	-	104
Praga	-	
Breslau	-	100
Naumburg	-	
Hamburgo	-	13
Anversa	-	133
Amsterdam in Banco	-	141
Dito Cor.	-	134
Collonia	-	100
Londen	-	133
Argentina	-	
Deposito	-	10
Moneta Dieambio	-	103
Corr. gegen Müntz	-	10
Brandb. Lüneb. u. Sächs. ꝛc.	-	0
Fürstliche Zweydrittel.	-	103
Edict gegen Müntz	-	108
Pistoletten	-	7:30
Louis Dor	-	7:31
Ducaten almarco	-	4:12
Ducaten alpeso	-	4:10

Alte Kursliste eines Frankfurter Geldwechslers von 1721 in italienischer Sprache, Historisches Museum, Frankfurt a. M.

Old list of exchange rates of a Frankfurt moneychanger of 1721 in Italian language, Historic Museum, Frankfurt on the Main.

erhielten, leisteten sie doch wirtschaftlich ihren bleibenden Beitrag. Sie trugen maßgeblich zur Gründung der Frankfurter Börse und zur Entwicklung des überörtlichen Finanzgeschäfts bei.

Im 17. und 18. Jahrhundert gab es dann weiterhin einen Zuzug einiger italienischer Kaufmannsfamilien, die zunächst als Südfruchthändler in die Stadt kamen, ab Mitte des 18. Jahrhunderts auch im Handel- und Bankgewerbe ebenfalls eine führende Rolle spielten.

Dass Frankfurt nach dem Dreißigjährigen Krieg, also ab der Mitte des 17. Jahrhunderts einen kontinuierlichen Aufschwung erlebte, obwohl in Leipzig eine konkurrierende Messe entstand, verdankt die Stadt auch den wirtschaftlichen Aktivitäten der verschiedenen Zuwanderergruppen, denen allmählich auch Freiheiten und Rechte eingeräumt wurden. Natürlich trugen entscheidend auch die Bürger der Stadt das Wachstum wie die Bankiersfamilie Metzler und Bethmann. Die Gemeinsamkeit, die sich im Laufe der Jahrhunderte entwickelte, würden wir heute „Integration" nennen.

Einen erheblichen Umbruch brachte das 19. Jahrhundert. Während nach den napoleonischen Kriegen in Frankfurt zunächst viel von der herkömmlichen Zunftverfassung wiederhergestellt worden war, begann in Europa die Entwicklung der industriellen Gesellschaft. Die Frankfurter Bankiers betrieben mit gutem Erfolg ihre Finanzgeschäfte, aber der neuen Entwicklung schloss sich die Stadt nur zögernd an. Die Beratungen des Paulskirchenparlaments, zu dem 1848/49 Menschen aus vielen Regionen strömten, wurden mit viel Anteilnahme begleitet. Der Versuch, ein geeintes und demokratisch verfasstes Deutschland zu schaffen, scheiterte jedoch.

Eine tiefgreifende Veränderung ergab sich für Frankfurt durch die unter Bismarck erkämpfte kleindeutsche Einigung unter preußischer Führung. Die Stadt wurde zur preußischen Provinzstadt. Berlin wurde nicht nur die politische Hauptstadt, sondern auch die Finanzzentrale des Reiches. Frankfurt und die umliegenden, später eingemeindeten Vororte konnten aber dank der 1867 eingeführten liberalen Gewerbeordnung eine rasante industrielle Entwicklung nehmen, die auch dem Frankfurter Bürgertum zugute kam. Menschen aus anderen Teilen Deutschlands zogen in die schnell wachsenden Großstadt und die später eingemeindeten Vororte. Der hier angesammelte Reichtum ermöglichte nicht nur wirtschaftliches Wachstum, sondern auch hervorragende Einrichtungen wie die prächtige Oper und eine von Bürgern gestiftete zunächst städtische Universität. Nazizeit und Krieg brachten einen für die Stadt

verheerenden Einbruch. Die jüdische Bevölkerung, etwa 30.000 Menschen, zum Teil hervorragende Persönlichkeiten der Stadt, wurde bis auf wenige Überlebende ermordet oder vertrieben. Die Stadt wurde bei den Bombenangriffen im März 1944 erheblich beschädigt. Vor allem der schöne historische Stadtkern sank in Schutt und Asche. Ein großer Teil der Bevölkerung war evakuiert und konnte erst nach Jahren zurückkehren.

Es kamen aber auch neue Bevölkerungsgruppen, Vertriebene und Flüchtlinge aus Ost- und Mitteldeutschland, sowie die „Displaced Persons", vornehmlich Juden aus Osteuropa, die hier eine neue, heute wieder 7.000 Mitglieder umfassende jüdische Gemeinde begründeten.

In die ruinierte Stadt waren im März 1945 als Sieger amerikanische Truppen eingezogen, die sich zunächst streng von der deutschen Bevölkerung absonderten. Doch die politische Entwicklung führte dazu, dass aus Feinden innerhalb weniger Jahre Freunde, während die Vereinigten Staaten und Deutschland Alliierte wurden. Über Jahrzehnte waren in der Stadt 30.000 amerikanische Soldaten mit ihren Familien stationiert. Sie lebten mit der deutschen Bevölkerung in guter Nachbarschaft zusammen. Institutionen wie das Amerika-Haus, die amerikanische Handelskammer in Deutschland und die Steuben-Schurz-Gesellschaft arbeiteten an der Verfestigung der deutsch-amerikanischen Beziehung. AFN, der Sender der amerikanischen Streitkräfte war ein Favorit der Jugend und trug dazu bei, dass der Jazz und die aus ihm entwickelten Musikarten in Frankfurt eine europäische Heimat fanden. Das Leben in der Stadt hat viel vom American way of life übernommen.

In den Nachkriegsjahren nahm die Stadt dann in Anknüpfung an ihre alten Traditionen einen erstaunlichen wirtschaftlichen Aufschwung. Messe und Buchmesse wurden wiederbegründet und nehmen heute einen führenden Platz in der Welt ein. Nachdem hier 1948 die Währungsreform verkündet wurde und Ludwig Erhard die Aufhebung der Bewirtschaftung durchsetzte, trat die D-Mark ihren Siegeszug an, und Frankfurt, als Bankenplatz institutionalisiert, konnte eine führende Rolle im europäischen Finanzwesen einnehmen, heute auch als Sitz der Europäischen Zentralbank. Die Stadt beherbergt zur Zeit 370 Kreditinstitute und Bankrepresentanzen, davon 230 ausländische, die annähernd 60.000 Menschen beschäftigen. Zahlreiche Versicherungen, Finanzdienstleister und für diese tätige Berufsgruppen sichern zusammen mit den Banken mehr Arbeitsplätze als die herkömmliche Industrie, die aber auch noch ihre Bedeutung hat. Das erstaunliche Wachstum ging ein-

Verleihung des Friedenspreises des Deutschen Buchhandels 1997 an den türkischen Schriftsteller Yasar Kemal in der Frankfurter Paulskirche am 19. Oktober 1997. Oberbürgermeisterin Petra Roth beglückwünscht gemeinsam mit dem Vorsteher des Börsenvereins des Deutschen Buchhandels, Dr. h. c. Gerhard Kurtze, den Preisträger.

her mit dem Zuzug von Führungskräften, Spezialisten und Arbeitnehmern zunächst aus Berlin und den Wirtschaftszentren Mitteldeutschlands, später aus Europa und der ganzen Welt.

Alle diese Aktivitäten waren und sind nur möglich, weil Frankfurt in den hochentwickelten Formen unserer Zeit seine Bedeutung als Verkehrsknotenpunkt behalten hat, aus dem es sich einmal entwickelte.

Jährlich kommen mehr als 20 Millionen Besucher in die Stadt, schätzungsweise 70 % von ihnen aus geschäftlichem oder anderem beruflichen Anlass, 30 % als Touristen. 300.000 Kraftfahrzeuge passieren täglich das Frankfurter Kreuz. Über den Flughafen reisen jährlich 46 Millionen Passagiere. Den Frankfurter Hauptbahnhof passieren jährlich 90 Millionen Menschen. Durch den Bau des Fernbahnhofs am Flughafen und am Frankfurter Kreuz entsteht ein integrierter Knotenpunkt ganz besonderer Art. Zu alledem kommen noch die modernen Medien. Das Glasfasernetz in 600 km Rohrleitungen sorgt für optimale Kommunikation in der Stadt. 80 % der deutschen Internetverbindungen laufen über Frankfurt, und im Großraum Frankfurt sind mehr als 1.000 IT-Unternehmen angesiedelt.

Endowment of the Peace Prize of the German Book Trade in 1997 to the Turkish Writer Yasar Kemal in the St. Paul's Cathedral of Frankfurt on 19th October 1997. Chief Mayor Mrs. Petra Roth bestows her felicitations on the prize bearer together with the Principal of the Exchange of the German Book Trade Association, Dr. h.c. Gerhard Kurtze.

ning of the 17th century) and accepted as inhabitants with special status, until in the 19th century their emancipation prevailed.

Further people of alien origin and other faith came as persecuted persons into the since 1535 strictly Lutheran city. These were the Calvinists expulsed from France and above all from Spanish Netherlands. A strong group came from the often disputed and blockaded City of Antwerp, that also could boast of special craftsmanship and pre-industrial skills for example in cotton and silk weaving. These people were enriching the city at the same time. In 1595, these 4.000 religious refugees represented around 15-20 % of the population. Although they did not receive all rights because of their alien faith, they contributed to the economy in an everlasting way. They bore an important part in the foundation of the Frankfurt Stock Exchange and in the development of non-local finance business.

Then, in the 17th and 18th centuries there was further immigration of some Italian merchant families that first came as merchants of citrus and tropical fruits into the city, but from the middle of the 18th century on also played a leading role in trade and bank business. The fact that Frankfurt expe-

rienced after the thirty-year-war, that is from the middle of the 17th century on a steady upswing, although there emerged a competing fair in Leipzig, the city owed also to the economic activities of the various groups of immigrants to whom were conceded slowly certain freedoms and rights. Of course, also the citizens of the city bore parts of the growth of the city, like the bankers family Metzler and Bethmann. The nature of community that developed during the course of these centuries we would call today "integration".

A considerably radical change brought the 19th century. While after the Napoleonic Wars first there was much reconstructed of the common guild laws, in Europe the development of industrial societies was beginning. Frankfurt's bankers were succeeding very well at doing their finance businesses, however, the city only hesitatingly joined new developments. The consultations of the parliament of St. Paul's Cathedral, to which in 1848/49 people from many regions poured in, were accompanied with great concern. The intent to create a unified and democratically constituted Germany failed however.

A far-reaching change for Frankfurt was brought about by the small-German unification under Prussian leadership. The German became a Prussian provincial town. Berlin not only became the political capital, but as well the financial centre of the Empire. Nevertheless, thanks to the liberal Commercial Regulations introduced in 1867, Frankfurt and the adjoining suburban town, that were later incorporated into the city, were able to take a tremendous industrial development which was also beneficial for the upper middle class and bourgeoisie of Frankfurt. People from other parts of Germany relocated into the rapidly growing large city and into the later incorporated suburban towns. The wealth accumulated here did not only enable economic growth, but also the building of such excellent and magnificent institutions like the opera and, at that moment, state university endowed by citizens.

During the Nazi era and the war the city experienced a catastrophic collapse. The Jewish population, about 30.000 inhabitants, partly outstanding personalities of the city, was killed or exiled apart from a few survivors. The city was considerably damaged during the bomb raids in March 1944. Above all, the beautiful historic city centre was completely destroyed. A great part of the population was evacuated and was only able to return after many years.

But also new ethnic groups came here, exiles and refugees from East and the Middle of Germany as

well as the "displaced persons", mainly Jews from Eastern Europe that established here a new Jewish community that has today again 7.000 members.

The victorious American troops had entered the ruined city in March 1945 and they practised a strong segregation from the German population at first. But the political development lead to the situation that within a few years enemies became friends, while the United States and Germany become allies. Over the decades about 30.000 American soldiers were stationed in the city with their families. They lived with the German population in good neighbourhood. Institutions like the America House, the American Chamber of Commerce in Germany and the Steuben-Schurz-Association worked for the fortification of German-American relations. AFN, the radio station of the American forces was a favourite with the youth and contributed to the fact that jazz and the musical styles developed from it found a European home. Life in the city has taken on a lot from the American way of life.

In the years after the war, following its old traditions the city then took an astonishing economic upsurge. The fair and the book fair were re-established again and today take a leading place in the world. After here in 1948 the monetary reform was announced and Ludwig Erhard achieved the lifting of the controls, the D-Mark started its triumphal march and Frankfurt, by now being institutionalised as a banking centre, was able to play a leading role in the European finance system, today even as headquarters of the European Central Bank. At present, the city is domicile to 370 credit institutions and bank branches, of these 230 are foreign, that employ almost 60.000 people. Numerous insurance companies, other financial services and groups of professions active for them secure together with the banks more workplaces than the common industry that nevertheless still remain important. The astonishing growth went together with the move of manager, specialists and employees at first from Berlin and other economic centres of Middle Germany, later on from Europe and the whole world.

All these activities were and are only possible, because Frankfurt has been able to maintain in the highly developed forms of our time its importance as transport node from which it had once departed from.

Every year, more than 20 million visitors come to the city, an estimated 70 % for business reasons or other professional interest, 30 % as tourists. 300.000 motor vehicles daily cross the Frankfurt

Diese vorbildliche Anbindung mit allen Mitteln des Verkehrs und der Kommunikation dienen aber nicht nur der Wirtschaft. Die Stadt ist mit ihrer Universität, den Hochschulen und wissenschaftlichen Einrichtungen, drei Max-Planck-Instituten, ihren Museen und den Kunststätten zugleich ein geistiges Zentrum, in dem sich Menschen aus der ganzen Welt begegnen.

In seiner Bevölkerungsstruktur ist Frankfurt am Main international geworden wie nur wenige Metropolen der Welt. 1960 lebten unter 670.000 Einwohnern 25.000 Ausländer. 1970 waren es 79.000, 1980 war ihre Zahl auf 135.000 gewachsen, 1990 auf 150.000. Jetzt, im Jahre 2000 sind unter den 650.000 Einwohnern 180.000 Ausländer gemeldet. Das sind 28 % der Bevölkerung. Sie stammen aus etwa 180 Nationen mit schätzungsweise 200 Muttersprachen.

Die hohe Zahl dieser ausländischen Mitbürger erklärt sich zum Teil aus der Rolle der Stadt als europäische Finanzmetropole und internationaler Wirtschaftsstandort. In dieser Situation ist es ganz selbstverständlich, dass hervorragende Spezialisten aus der ganzen Welt in wissenschaftlichen Instituten, Forschungseinrichtungen, bei Banken und in verschiedenen Dienstleistungen arbeiten. Sie bilden eine international orientierte business community. Die Stadt ist nach besten Kräften bemüht, ihnen den Aufenthalt hier angenehm zu gestalten, und damit Frankfurt auch menschlich attraktiv für das internationale Wirtschaftsgeschehen zu machen.

Der größte Teil der Nichtdeutschen stammt aber von jenen Menschen ab, die vor Jahrzehnten vornehmlich in unsere Industrieunternehmen geholt worden sind. Hauptsächlich sind es Türken, Italiener, Griechen, Spanier, Portugiesen, Marokkaner und Bürger der früheren jugoslawischen Staaten. Sie kamen als Gastarbeiter, die nach einigen Jahren heimkehren sollten und wollten, aber viele von ihnen sind hier heimisch geworden. Die meisten ihrer Kinder und Kindeskinder bleiben in Deutschland, auch wenn sie an ihren kulturellen Traditionen oder, wie zum Beispiel die schätzungsweise 78.000 Muslime, an ihren überlieferten Religionen festhalten. Mit 12 % der Bevölkerung bilden sie die drittgrößte Religionsgruppe.

Für die Stadt und die verschiedenen öffentlichen Institutionen ergibt sich dadurch eine große Aufgabe für eine behutsame Integrationspolitik, die einerseits das friedliche Zusammenleben im Rahmen der deutschen Verfassungs- und Gesellschaftsordnung sichert, andererseits die Eigenarten der verschiedenen Bevölkerungsgruppen in

Toleranz respektiert. Eine besondere Aufgabe stellt sich dabei mit Blick auf die jugendlichen Ausländer, die in bestimmten Jahrgängen fast die Hälfte der Frankfurter Jugend ausmachen. Diese müssen in der Schul- und Berufsausbildung so gefördert werden, dass sie unter den Bedingungen der Wettbewerbswirtschaft hier leben und arbeiten können.

Die Stadt Frankfurt widmet sich dieser Aufgabe mit erheblichem Aufwand. Sozial- und Sprachprogramme begleiten die ausländischen Mitbürger. Neben den jeweils fachlich zuständigen Stellen widmet sich im Magistrat der Stadt ein besonders eingerichtetes Dezernat Integration mit dem Amt für multikulturelle Angelegenheiten der Unterstützung ausländischer Gruppen und ihren Aktivitäten wie auch der Konfliktvermittlung an sozialen Brennpunkten. Hier sind noch große Aufgaben zu lösen, bei denen es auf viel Verständnis aller beteiligten Gruppen ankommt. Bisher sind größere gewaltsame Auseinandersetzungen zwischen verschiedenen nationalen Gruppen vermieden worden. In den Schulen, am Arbeitsplatz wie überhaupt in der Stadt herrscht Frieden. Sicher kommt es auch zu Konflikten, aber die Zahl der Delikte in Frankfurt am Main ist rückläufig, die Aufklärungsquote steigt und die Kriminalität ist geringer als in anderen multiethnischen Großstädten der Welt.

Die technische und wirtschaftliche Veränderung schreitet zügig voran, zwangsläufig auch die menschliche in unserer Stadt. Fast 30 % der Ehen werden zwischen Deutschen und Ausländern oder Ausländerinnen geschlossen. Unter der hier heranwachsenden Jugend liegt der Anteil der Ausländer und der Deutschen fremder Herkunft bei 40 bis 50 %. Alle demografischen Prognosen rechnen für die nächsten Jahrzehnte mit einem deutlichen Anwachsen der nichtdeutschen Einwohnerschaft.

Der weiter steigende internationale Verkehr wird immer Menschen aus allen Teilen der Welt nach Frankfurt bringen. In ihrer Verflochtenheit und menschlichen Vielfalt ist die Stadt zur „Hafenstadt" geworden.

Frankfurt am Main kann und wird die Herausforderung des Zusammenlebens und -wachsens bewältigen, indem es in Anknüpfung an seine historische Entwicklung eine weltoffene und humane Stadt bleibt. Das ist neben den vielen Wegen der Kommunikation die menschliche Grundlage auch für einen interessanten und erfolgreichen Wirtschaftsstandort. ■

Quellen: Holtfrerich: „Finanzplatz Frankfurt", C. H. Beck, 1999
Meinert: „Frankfurter Geschichte", Waldemar Kramer, 5.Aufl., 1977

Bildmontage multiethnischer Bürger vor der Kulisse der Bank-Hochhäuser, als Illustration der modernen internationalen Stadt.

Collage of multi-ethnic citizens in front of the background of bank skyscrapers, as illustration of a modern international city.

Motorway Cross. Via the airport, 46 million passengers travel yearly. Yearly, 90 million people pass through Frankfurt's main train station. Because of the newly built long-distance train station an integrated transport node of a special kind has been constructed. Added to all these are the modern media. The glass fibre network within 600 km of cable work ensures an optimal communication in the city. 80 % of German internet connections run via Frankfurt, and in the greater Frankfurt area more than 1.000 IT companies have settled down.

These exemplary connections with all means of transport and communication do not only serve the economy. With its university, the polytechnic colleges and economic institutions, three Max-Planck-Institutes, its museums and the spaces for art an intellectual centre at the same time, in which people from all over the world meet.

In its population structure, Frankfurt on the Main has become an international metropolis like only very few in the world. In 1960, amongst 670.000 inhabitants 25.000 were foreigners. 1970 there were 79.000, 1980 their number had risen to 135.000, 1990 to 150.000. Now, in the year 2000 amongst the 650.000 inhabitants, 180.000 are registered aliens. These are 28 % of the population. They originate from around 180 nations and have an estimated 200 mother tongues.

The high number of these alien co-citizens results partly from the role of the city as European finance metropolis and international business location. In these situations it is very natural that excellent specialists from all over the world work in scientific institutes, research institutions, with banks and in various service sectors. They form an internationally oriented business community. The city endeavours its utmost to make their stay here as pleasant as possible and thus, to make Frankfurt also humanely attractive for the international commerce.

The largest part of non-Germans however, originates from those people that were brought above all into our industrial enterprises decades ago. Mainly, they are Turks, Italians, Greeks, Spaniards, Portuguese, Moroccans and citizens of the former Yugoslavian states. The came here as foreign workers that were supposed to return to their home countries after a few years, but many of them settled down here. Most of the children and grandchildren will stay in Germany, even though they keep their cultural traditions or their handed down religion, like for example an estimated 78.000 Muslims do. With 12 % of the population theirs is the third largest religious group.

For the city and its varied public institutions this means, that a great responsibility for delicate politics of integration arises, which on the one hand secures a peaceful co-existence within the frame of the German constitutional and social order, and on the other hand respects the characteristics of the various groups of population in tolerance. A special task emerges in this respect in view of the young foreigners that in certain age groups make up half of the youth in Frankfurt. These have to be supported in their school education and vocational training in such way that they can live and work here under the conditions of economic competition.

The City of Frankfurt is dedicated to this task with enormous engagement. Social and language programmes accompany the foreign co-citizens. Apart from the corresponding expert departments responsible, in the municipal city council there is a specially established integration department called the "Amt für multikulturelle Angelegenheiten" (Dept. for Multi-Cultural Matters) for the support of foreign groups and their activities as well as for the mediation in conflict situation at socially hot spots. There are still great problems to be resolved which need a lot of understanding of all the groups involved. Until now, violent confrontations between the various national groups have been avoided. In schools, workplaces as in the city on the whole, there is peace. Surely there are conflicts, but the number of crimes in Frankfurt on the Main is going down, the quota of resolved cases is rising and the crime rate is lower than in other multi-ethnic large cities of the world.

The technical and economic change is rapidly moving on. Almost 30 % of all marriages are registered between Germans and male or female foreigners. The share of foreigners amongst the youth growing up here and the Germans of foreign origin is at 40 to 50 %. All demographic forecasts predict for the coming decades a marked rise of the non-German population.

The further increasing international transport will always continue to bring people from all over the world to Frankfurt. With its interconnections and human diversity the city has become a "harbour".

Frankfurt on the Main can and shall master the challenge of co-existence by remaining an open and human city and linking up with its historic development. This is, apart from the many ways of communication, the human basis also for an interesting and successful business location. ■

Sources: Holtfrerich: "Finanzplatz Frankfurt", C. H. Beck, 1999
Meinert: "Frankfurter Geschichte", Waldemar Kramer, 5th Edition, 1977

Personal – der zentrale Schlüssel für Entwicklung

Personnel – the main Key for Development

Centrum für internationale Migration und Entwicklung (CIM)
Eine Arbeitsgemeinschaft der Deutschen Gesellschaft für Technische Zusammenarbeit (GTZ) GmbH und der Zentralstelle für Arbeitsvermittlung (ZAV) der Bundesanstalt für Arbeit (BA)
A joint operation of the Deutsche Gesellschaft für Technische Zusammenarbeit (GTZ) GmbH and the Central Placement Office (ZAV) of the Federal Employment Institute (BA)

Gründungsjahr/Year of Foundation:
1980

Geschäftstätigkeit/Business Activity:
CIM vermittelt im Rahmen der Entwicklungszusammenarbeit Personal in Entwicklungs- und Reformländer. Zurzeit arbeiten über 700 CIM-Fachkräfte in mehr als 80 Ländern.
CIM finds within the framework of development co-operation personnel for developing and reforming countries. At present, more than 700 CIM-experts work in more than 80 countries.

Besuchen Sie unseren Stellenmarkt im Internet unter www.cimonline.de

Visit our job market in the Internet under www.cimonline.de

Anschrift/Address:
Barckhausstr. 16
60325 Frankfurt am Main
Telefon   +49 (69) 71 91 21-0
Telefax   +49 (69) 71 91 21-19
E-Mail   cim@gtz.de
Internet   www.cimonline.de

Der Stellenmarkt im Internet.
The job market in the Internet.

CIM-Homepage.
CIM-homepage.

CIM ist ein Personalvermittler mit entwicklungspolitischem Auftrag. Es vermittelt im Rahmen der Entwicklungszusammenarbeit der Bundesregierung und in Kooperation mit der Privatwirtschaft qualifizierte Fachkräfte nach Afrika, Asien, Lateinamerika und nach Mittel- und Osteuropa.

Mit seinem Programm „Integrierte Fachkräfte" hilft CIM Arbeitgebern in diesen Ländern dabei, auf dem europäischen Arbeitsmarkt hoch qualifizierte Fachkräfte anzuwerben. Denn oft fehlen für wichtige Arbeitsplätze berufserfahrene Fachleute. „Integriert" sind diese Fachkräfte deshalb, weil sie wie einheimische Arbeitnehmer zu den ortsüblichen Bedingungen eingestellt werden – mit denselben Rechten und Pflichten. Weil Arbeitgeber in Entwicklungs- und Reformländern den deutschen Fachkräften gewöhnlich keine höheren Vergütungen als einheimischen Mitarbeitern bezahlen können, bietet CIM Zuschüsse zum lokalen Gehalt und zur deutschen Sozialversicherung.

CIM stellt hohe Anforderungen an die Qualifikation Integrierter Fachkräfte. Fachkompetenz, langjährige Berufserfahrung und gute Fremdsprachenkenntnisse werden vorausgesetzt. Die Fachkräfte müssen zudem besonders mobil und flexibel sein, soziale und interkulturelle Fähigkeiten mitbringen und idealerweise schon einmal im Ausland gearbeitet haben. Mehr als 80 % der ausgewählten Kandidaten haben eine akademische Ausbildung. An CIM können sich auch Fachkräfte aus Entwicklungsländern wenden, die in Deutschland aus- oder fortgebildet wurden, hier bereits Berufserfahrung gesammelt haben und in ein Entwicklungsland zurückkehren möchten. Sie werden von CIM im Rahmen des Programms Rückkehr und Reintegration gefördert. ■

CIM is an agency for personnel with a political development mission. It finds, within the framework of development co-operation with the Federal Government and in co-operation with the private sector of economy, qualified specialists for Africa, Asia, Latin America and Middle and Eastern Europe. With its programme "Integrated Experts" CIM supports employers in these countries in recruiting highly qualified specialists on the European labour market. Frequently, for important workplaces professionally experienced specialists cannot be found. These specialists are "Integrated" because they are employed like local employees on the customary local terms – with the same rights and duties. Because employers in developing and reforming countries usually can not pay the German specialists higher remunerations as their local workers, CIM offers supplements to the local salaries and to the German social insurance.

CIM sets high standards on the qualifications of integrated experts. A specialised competence, long-year's professional experience and profound knowledge of foreign languages are pre-conditions. The specialists must furthermore be mobile and flexible, possess social and inter-cultural capacities and ideally have worked abroad before. More than 80 % of selected candidates have an academic education. Also specialists from developing countries that have received their education or further education in Germany and have gained some professional experience here may direct their applications to CIM, if they wish to return into a developing country. They are especially promoted by CIM within the framework of their return and reintegration programme. ■

Vermittelt werden Fachkräfte für Entwicklungsländer.
Specialists for developing countries are placed.

Rechtliche Lösungen für Neue Medien

Legal Solutions for the New Media

Im traditionellen Umfeld widmet sich die Sozietät aktuellsten Themen.
In a traditional environment the law firm is dedicated to the most current topics.

Wilkinson Barker Knauer, LLP, hat 1993 das Frankfurter Büro im Hinblick auf die Öffnung des Deutschen Telekommunikationsmarktes errichtet. Die Sozietät hat vor diesem Zeitpunkt über das Büro in Washington, DC, bereits das damalige Postministerium in Regulierungs- und Liberalisierungsfragen beraten. Das Mandantenfeld im Deutschland reicht von Telekommunikationsunternehmen jeder Art (Stadtnetzbetreiber, Verbindungsnetzbetreiber, (Mobilfunk-) Service Provider, Mehrwertdiensteanbieter) bis hin zu Unternehmen aus dem Bereich Internet und Neue Medien.

Wilkinson Barker Knauer, LLP, hat sich auf die Fragen der Telekommunikationsregulierung spezialisiert. Hierzu gehören Lizenzfragen ebenso wie die Zusammenschaltung der Netzbetreiber und die Entgeltregulierung. In den letzten Jahren wurde die Tätigkeit der Sozietät auf die Betreuung von Mandanten bei der Finanzierung ihres Geschäftsbetriebs erweitert. Dies umfasst das gesamte Spektrum der Finanzierungsfragen von der Start-Up Phase bis zum Börsengang sowie die Begleitung bei Finanztransaktionen (Private Placement, Merger & Aquisition). Bei dem Bereich des Internets und der Neuen Medien ist Wilkinson Barker Knauer, LLP, auch wettbewerbsrechtlichen Fragen und zum Schutz gewerblicher Rechtsgüter (Domain-Namen, Warenzeichen) tätig.

Mitarbeiter von Wilkinson Barker Knauer, LLP, sind selbst oder für Mandanten in einer Reihe von Interessenvereinigungen tätig. ∎

Wilkinson Barker Knauer, LLP, has established in 1993 its Frankfurt office in view of the opening of the German telecommunication market. The law firm has from this moment on consulted via the Washington DC office even the former Post Ministry in matters of regulation and liberalisation. The fields of clients in Germany extends from telecommunication companies of any kind (city network providers, connection network providers, mobile radio network service providers, added-value service providers) up to enterprises from the fields of Internet and the New Media.

Wilkinson Barker Knauer, LLP, has specialised itself to assist in regulatory affairs in telecommunication. This includes both licensing issues as well as the switching together of connections of network providers and the regulation of payments. In the last years, the activities of the association have been expanded to assist clients in the financing of their business operations. This includes the complete spectrum of financing matters beginning at the start-up phase up to the introduction at the stock exchange as well as accompanying finance transactions (private placements, mergers & acquisitions). In the field of Internet and the New Media, Wilkinson Barker Knauer, LLP, is also active in issues of legislation on competition and in the protection of commercial objects of legal merit (names of domains, trade marks).

Employees of Wilkinson Barker Knauer, LLP are active themselves or in representation of clients in a number of interest groups. ∎

WILKINSON ⟩ BARKER ⟩ KNAUER ⟩ LLP

Wilkinson Barker Knauer, LLP

Rechtsanwälte/Lawyers:
Richard J. Leitermann, Dipl. Kfm. (Partner)
Dr. jur. Joachim Ramm, M.C.L. (Univ. of III./Partner)
Robert H. Leitermann, Dipl. Kfm. (Of Council)
Dr. Florian Wäßle (Associate)
Wiebke Gorny (Associate)

Gründungsjahr/Year of Foundation:
1993

Mitarbeiter/Employees:
12

Geschäftstätigkeit/Business Activity:
• Telekommunikationsregulierung
• Corporate Finance
• Merger & Aquisition
• Vertragswesen
• Gewerblicher Rechtsschutz / Urheberrecht
• Wettbewerbsrecht
• Regulation in telecommunication
• Corporate Finance
• Mergers & Acquisition
• arrangements
• Industrial property law/Intellectual property
• Law of competition

Anschrift/Address:
Am Opernplatz 2
D-60313 Frankfurt am Main
Telefon   +49 (69) 208 76
Telefax   +49 (69) 297 84 53
Internet   www.wbklaw.com

Neue Medien werfen viele neue rechtliche Fragen auf.
New Media pose many new legal questions.

Messe: weltweit operierend, mit starker regionaler Verankerung

The Fair: Operating Worldwide, strongly rooted in the Region

Unermüdlich schlägt er den Takt der arbeitenden Stadt. Der „Hammering Man" am Fuße des Messeturms versinnbildlicht, was sich hinter den modernen Fassaden der Frankfurter Architektur verbirgt: die gebündelten Aktivitäten einer starken Wirtschaftsregion. Ein pulsierendes Netzwerk, das die Kapital- und Handelsströme in Bewegung hält.

Messeplatz Frankfurt

Eine Quelle dieses Zuflusses liegt unmittelbar in der Nähe des „Hammering Man": die Frankfurter Messe (Gesellschafter: Stadt Frankfurt 60 Prozent und Hessen 40 Prozent). In gesteigerter Kaufkraft und zusätzlichen Umsätzen lassen sich die Synergiewirkungen von Stadt und Messe in Zahlen fassen: Über 2 Millionen Besucher und über 36.000 Aussteller nahmen im vergangenen Jahr an den Frankfurter Veranstaltungen teil. Mit einem in der Unternehmensgeschichte einmaligen Rekordumsatz von 539 Millionen Mark (Vergleichsjahr 1997: 470 Millionen Mark) konnte im

Jahr 1999 erstmals die Schallmauer von 500 Millionen Mark durchbrochen werden.

Die Messe entwickelt dabei eine Sogwirkung, von der die unterschiedlichsten Branchen profitieren: der Messestandbau, die Hotellerie und Gastronomie und das Frankfurter Taxigewerbe. Aber auch die Kommunikationsbranche und der Einzelhandel werden zusätzlich belebt. Die Messe Frankfurt ist tief in der Region verwurzelt, und die Verwurzelung in Region und Stadt lässt sich in konkrete Zahlen fassen: Frankfurter Messen bringen über drei Milliarden Mark in das Rhein-Main-Gebiet und sichern rund 30.000 Arbeitsplätze.

Besonderes Qualitätsmerkmal der Frankfurter Messen ist ihr im internationalen Vergleich markant hoher Anteil ausländischer Aussteller. Bei den internationalen Fachmessen kommen über 56 Prozent der ausstellenden Unternehmen aus dem Ausland. Aus fast 180 Nationen reisen die Besucher an.

Eingang City der Messe Frankfurt am Main.

City Entrance to the Frankfurt Fair.

Michael von Zitzewitz

Der Autor wurde 1945 in Aalen geboren und studierte in Hamburg und München Volkswirtschaftslehre. Ab 1976 war er bei der Lehndorff Vermögensverwaltung GmbH tätig, ab 1981 als stellvertretender Geschäftsführer. Von 1983 bis 1992 war er Stellvertretender Direktor der Deutsche Bank AG, Frankfurt, mit den Zuständigkeiten: Vertrieb aller Kapitalanlageprodukte mit Immobilien, Geschäftsführer und Vorstandsvorsitzender (Präsident) verschiedener Immobiliengesellschaften im Inland und in den USA und Japan. Anschließend wurde er Geschäftsführer der Commerz Grundbesitz Investmentgesellschaft mbH, Wiesbaden, (CGI) der Kapitalanlangegesellschaft der Commerzbank und der DBV/Winterthur. Seit dem 1. Januar 1999 ist er Vorsitzender der Geschäftsführung der Messe Frankfurt GmbH.

The author was born in 1945 in Aalen and studied political economy in Hamburg and Munich. From 1976 on, he worked with the Lehndorff Vermögensverwaltung GmbH, from 1981 on as Vice General Manager. From 1983 till 1992 he was Vice President of the Deutsche Bank AG, Frankfurt, with the following responsibilities: sale of all capital investment products with properties, General Manager and President of various property companies in Germany and the USA and Japan. Afterwards he became Managing Director of the Commerz Grundbesitz Investmentgesellschaft mbH, Wiesbaden (CGI), the joint capital investment corporation of the Commerzbank and the DBV/Winterthur. Since the 1st January 1999 he is Chairman of the Board of the Messe Frankfurt GmbH.

Torhaus-Service Center.

Torhaus Service Centre.

Untiringly he beats to the rhythm of the working city. The "Hammering Man" at the foot of the fair tower symbolizes all that is hidden behind the modern façade of the Frankfurt architecture: the bundled activities of a strong economic region. A pulsating network that keeps the capital and commercial flow in motion.

Exhibition Centre Frankfurt

One source of this stream lies directly in the vicinity of the "Hammering Man": the Frankfurt Fair (Associates: City of Frankfurt 60 percent and the State of Hesse 40 percent). In an increased purchase power and additional sales the effects of the synergy of the city with the fair can be measured in numbers: more than 2 million visitors and more than 36.000 exhibitors participated last year in the events in Frankfurt. With unique record sales, unequalled in the history of the company, of 539 million Marks (year of comparison 1997: 470 million Marks), for the first time the magic figure of 500 million Marks has been surpassed.

Furthermore, the fair develops a certain suction effect, which is beneficial to most varied branches: construction of exhibition stands, the hotel and catering businesses and the taxi trade of Frankfurt. But also the communication branch and the retail sector are stimulated additionally.

The Frankfurt fair is deeply rooted in the region and these roots into the city and the region can be expressed in concrete numbers: The fairs of Frankfurt bring more than three billion Marks into the Rhein-Main area and secure around 30.000 workplaces.

One significant characteristic of the quality of the Frankfurt fairs is their markedly high share of foreign exhibitors, when internationally compared. For the international specialist trade fairs more than 56 percent of exhibiting companies come from abroad. Visitors come from almost 180 nations.

The Frankfurt Fair is a worldwide operating company with a clear home location: Frankfurt on the Main. Here lie the roots of its trade fair business, which is flourishing since 1240 already in this lo-cation. Meanwhile the Frankfurt Fair is the second largest exhibition centre worldwide. Its main focus form the guiding fairs of the consumer branches (Ambiente, Premiere, Tendence), textiles (Heimtextil, Interstoff, Techtextil), motor vehicles & technique (Automechanika, ISH, IFFA, Texcare, Light + Building), communications & leisure time (Musikmesse, Infobase, Cavis). Additionally there are worldwide renowned guest events, like the International Automobile-Exhibition (IAA), the Frankfurt Book Fair and the ACHEMA of the chemical sector.

Location and land development

Imbedded into the city structure of Frankfurt, with the great advantages of fast accessibility and direct connection to the infrastructure of the region, the Frankfurt Fair disposes of presently more than around 290.000 square metres of areas in halls and around 76.000 square metres of open air exhibition ground. Thus, it attains a worldwide-recognised location advantage.

With the recently started Southern extension of the fair grounds the Frankfurt Fair uses a one-in-a-million-years' chance to continue the successful business development and to provide the necessary areas. On the area of the former goods tracks, which are about to be available, the Frankfurt Fair is going to be extended by around 16 hectares.

This means an extension of its area of around 40 percent. As early as 2001, for the IAA-private car

Congress Center Messe Frankfurt.

Congress Centre of the Frankfurt Fair.

Blick über das Frankfurter Messegelände.

View across the Frankfurt fair grounds.

Die Messe Frankfurt ist ein weltweit operierendes Unternehmen mit einem klaren Heimatstandort: Frankfurt am Main. Hier liegen die Wurzeln des Messegeschäfts, das an diesen Standort bereits seit 1240 floriert. Mittlerweile ist die Messe Frankfurt der zweitgrößte Messeplatz weltweit. Schwerpunkte bilden die Leitmessen in den Branchen Konsum (Ambiente, Premiere, Tendence),Textil (Heimtextil, Interstoff, Techtextil), Auto & Technik (Automechanika, ISH, IFFA, Texcare, Light + Building), Kommunikation & Freizeit (Musikmesse, Infobase, Cavis). Hinzu kommen weltweit renommierte Gastveranstaltungen wie die Internationale Automobil-Ausstellung (IAA), die Frankfurter Buchmesse und die ACHEMA im Chemiesektor.

Standort und Geländeentwicklung

Eingebettet in die Stadtstruktur Frankfurts mit den großen Vorteilen der schnellen Erreichbarkeit und der unmittelbaren Anbindung an die Infrastruktur der Region, verfügt die Messe Frankfurt derzeit über rund 290.000 Quadratmeter Hallenfläche und rund 76.000 Quadratmeter Freigelände. Die verschaffen ihr einen weltweit anerkannten Standortvorteil.

Mit der bereits begonnenen Süderweiterung des Messegeländes nutzt die Messe Frankfurt eine Jahrhundertchance, die erfolgreiche Geschäftsentwicklung fortzusetzen und die erforderlichen Flächen anzubieten. Auf dem freiwerdenden Gü-

tergleisgelände wird sich die Messe Frankfurt um rund 16 Hektar erweitern. Dies bedeutet eine flächenmäßige Ausdehnung um rund 40 Prozent.

Bereits zur IAA-Pkw im Jahre 2001 wird eine neue Messehalle, die Halle 3, mit einer Kapazität von rund 40.000 Quadratmetern Ausstellungsfläche fertiggestellt sein. Das Gebäude wurde von dem bekannten britischen Architekten Nicholas Grimshaw entworfen und wird durch die Hochtief AG und die Bilfinger + Berger Bau AG errichtet. Zusätzlich entstehen weitere 40.000 Quadratmeter Freifläche. Die Gesamtinvestitionen dieses ersten Erweiterungsabschnitts, bei dem die Messe Frankfurt selbst als Bauherr fungiert, belaufen sich auf rund 250 Millionen Mark.

Durch zwei weitere Baumaßnahmen – das Messe-Parkhaus auf dem Rebstockgelände und der Neubau des Forums – wird die Qualität des Geländes und dessen Logistik zusätzlich verbessert. Das Messe-Parkhaus ist seit Dezember 2000 betriebsbereit und steht ab Januar 2001 zur Heimtextil erstmals zur Verfügung. Es bietet unseren Besuchern dann 5.400 Stellplätze. Die Bauarbeiten für das Forum wurden in diesem Frühjahr 2000 begonnen und ab Sommer 2001 wird die Messe Frankfurt, in der Kombination Festhalle, Congress Center und Forum, ihren Kunden ein ganz neues Gastronomie-, Konferenz- und Ausstellungsangebot machen. In einem ansprechenden Ambiente können dann rund 2.000 Personen exklusiv bewirtet werden.

Nach Beendigung dieser ersten Ausbaustufe wird das Frankfurter Messegelände über 335.000 Quadratmeter Hallenfläche und rund 121.000 Quadratmeter Freigelände verfügen.

Auslandsaktivitäten der Messe Frankfurt

Im Zuge der Internationalisierungs-Strategie hat die Messe Frankfurt als erste deutsche Messegesellschaft schon in den achtziger Jahren ein globales Veranstaltungsnetz aufgebaut. Die erste Auslandsveranstaltung, die Interstoff Asia, fand 1987 in Hongkong statt. Im Jahr 1999 wurden insgesamt 31 Auslandsmessen, mit 5.294 Ausstellern und 764.079 Besuchern, durchgeführt. Die Messe Frankfurt verfügt heute neben 64 Repräsentanzen für über 100 Länder über sieben eigenständige Tochtergesellschaften in Japan, den USA, Hongkong, Singapur, Brasilien, Indien und Italien. Weltweit arbeiten mehr als 100 Mitarbeiter für die Messe Frankfurt.

Mit der erfolgreichen Internationalisierung hat die Messe Frankfurt ihre weltweite Kompetenz im Messegeschäft dokumentiert und zugleich den Standort Frankfurt als Ausgangspunkt der Brands erheblich gestärkt. Die Sogkraft des Standortes für Aussteller und Besucher, die bereits Kunden im Ausland sind, nach Frankfurt zu kommen, ist groß.

Diese Strategie, die Weltmärkte mit unseren Kernkompetenzthemen zu besetzen, wird die Messe Frankfurt in aller Intensität weiterführen. Auf diesen ersten Schritt folgt jetzt der zweite, die Scout-Strategie. Die Messe Frankfurt bietet ein hochkarätiges Marketinginstrument an, hinter der eine weltweit anerkannte Kompetenz und Marktführerschaft steht. Dieses Potenzial wollen wir weltweit nutzen. Dazu wird die Messe Frankfurt ihre Tochtergesellschaften nutzen, denn diese repräsentieren die hohe Kompetenz der Messe Frankfurt für Konzeption und Durchführung von Messen und verfügen zusätzlich über die notwendigen Marktkenntnisse vor Ort. In den Auslandmärkten sollen neue Messethemen geortet und aufgespürt werden. Neue Themen im Ausland, die vielleicht zunächst nur örtliche Relevanz haben, können sich langfristig zu weltweiten Kernkompetenzen der Messe Frankfurt entwickeln und die Brands von morgen sein. Gleichzeitig eröffnen wir für unsere bestehenden Kunden den Zutritt auf neue Märkte. Am Standort Frankfurt entwickeln wir über ein eigenes Innovationsmanagement neue zukunftsweisende Messethemen. Dies verstehen wir unter Globalisierung des Messegeschäftes, das auf diesem Wege den Entwicklungen auf den Weltmärkten folgt. ∎

event, a new fair hall, the hall 3, with a capacity of around 40.000 square metres of exhibition grounds is going to be erected. The building was designed by the well-known British architect Nicholas Grimshaw and is being constructed by Hochtief AG and the Bilfinger + Berger Bau AG. The total investment for this first segment of expansion, at which the Frankfurt Fair itself acts as building sponsor, amount to around 250 million Mark.

Through two further construction projects – the Fair Car Park on the Rebstock grounds and the newly built forum – the quality of the grounds and its logistics are improved additionally.

The Fair Car Park was ready for operation in December 2000, and since January 2001 it has been opened for the Heimtextil for the first time. It provides 5.400 places to our visitors. Construction work for the forum where started in 2000 in spring and from summer 2001 on, the Frankfurt Fair shall present a completely renewed offer to its clients in terms of restaurant, conference and exhibition provision. In an appealing atmosphere around 2.000 persons can then exclusively be catered for.

After finishing the first section of this extension, the Frankfurt fair grounds will dispose of more than 335.000 square metres of areas in halls and around 121.000 square metres of open-air fair grounds.

Activities abroad of the Frankfurt Fair

Within its strategy of internationalisation, the Frankfurt Fair established already in the eighties as first German Fair association, a global network for events. The first event abroad, the Interstoff Asia, took place in Hongkong in 1987. In the year 1999 a total of 31 foreign fairs, with 5.294 exhibitors and 764.079 visitors were carried out. The Frankfurt Fair today disposes – apart from 64 representative offices for more than 100 countries – of seven self-sufficient dependencies in Japan, the USA, Hong Kong, Singapore, Brazil, India and Italy. Worldwide, more than 100 employees work for the Frankfurt Fair.

With a concept of successful internationalisation, the Frankfurt Fair has documented its competence in the trade fair business and has also strengthened considerably Frankfurt as a location for a starting point of brands, at the same time. The pull of the location is great for exhibitors and visitors, which are already clients abroad, to come to Frankfurt.

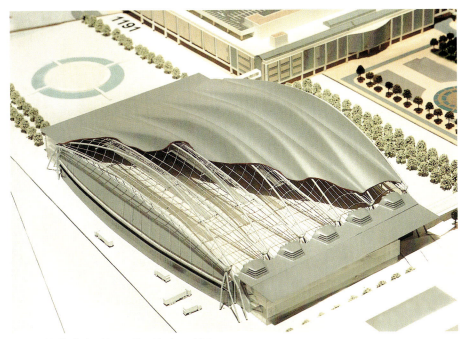

Modell Halle 3 der Messe Frankfurt am Main.

Model of Hall 3 of the Frankfurt Fair.

This strategy, to saturate world markets with our core competences, is going to be continued by the Frankfurt Fair in all its intensity. The next, second step will follow now, which is the scout strategy. The Frankfurt Fair offers a high-calibre marketing instrument, which is backed by a worldwide-recognised competence and market leadership. This potential we want to use worldwide. For this purpose the Frankfurt Fair will make use of its dependencies, because these represent the high competence of the Frankfurt Fair for conception and implementation of fairs and they dispose in addition of the necessary knowledge of local mar-

kets. Within the foreign markets, new themes for fairs are to be located and tracked down. New themes abroad that may at first only have local relevance, but may develop in the long run to be worldwide core competences of the Frankfurt Fair and become the brands of tomorrow. At the same time, we open up access for our existing clients to new markets. In the location of Frankfurt we develop through an in-house innovation management new future-oriented themes for fairs. This is what we understand by globalisation of the trade fair business, which thus follows the developments on the world markets. ■

Halle 5.1.

Hall 5.1.

Das japanische Tor an Halle 9.

The Japanese Gate at Hall 9.

149

Messe Frankfurt GmbH

Geschäftsführer/Manager:
Michael von Zitzewitz, Vorsitzender
Dr. Michael Peters
Gerhard Gladitsch

Gründungsjahr/Year of Foundation:
Die erste urkundliche Erwähnung der Messe
Frankfurt stammt aus dem Jahre 1160.
1907 wurde die Messe- und Ausstellungs-
gesellschaft gegründet. Seit 1982 existiert das
Unternehmen in seiner heutigen Form, der Mes-
se Frankfurt GmbH.
The first documented mentioning of the frankfurt
Fair dates from the year 1160. In 1907, the Fair
and Exhibition Corporation was founded.
Since 1982, the company exists in its present
form, the Messe Frankfurt GmbH.

Mitarbeiter/Employees:
Messe Frankfurt GmbH: 550
Messe Frankfurt Konzern: 801

Umsatz/Turnover:
1999: 539 Mio. DM
2000: 600 Mio. DM

Geschäftstätigkeit/Business Activity:
Organisation und Durchführung von
internationalen Fachmessen im In- und Ausland
Organisation and execution of international
specialist fairs domestically and abroad.

Anschrift/Address:
Ludwig-Erhard-Anlage 1
D-60327 Frankfurt am Main
Telefon   +49 (69) 75 75-0
Telefax   +49 (69) 75 75-64 33
E-Mail   info@messefrankfurt.com
Internet   www.messefrankfurt.com

*Weithin sichtbar – das Torhaus
der Messe Frankfurt.*

*Visible from far
– the Torhaus of the Frankfurt Fair.*

Pulsierendes Zentrum –
die Messe Frankfurt

The Frankfurt Fair – A Pulsating Centre

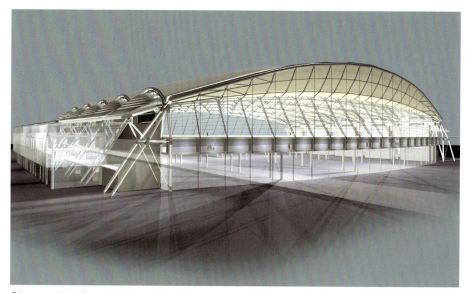

Die neue Halle 3 – ein Beispiel für richtungsweisende Messearchitektur.
The new Hall 3 – an example of trend creating exhibition architecture.

Die Messe Frankfurt ist einer der bedeutend-sten Messeplätze der Welt. Mit 37 Messen und Veranstaltungen, auf denen Aussteller und Besucher aus der ganzen Welt ins Gespräch und ins Geschäft kamen, präsentierte sie im Jahr 2000 ein höchst internationales Ausstellungsangebot. Zusätzlich werden jährlich noch rund 280 Kongresse, Tagungen und Events in der Festhalle und im Congress Center erfolgreich durchgeführt.

In Frankfurt finden die weltgrößten Fachmessen der Branchen Konsumgüter, Auto+Technik, Textil und Kommunikation+Freizeit statt. Jahr für Jahr stellen auf dem Gelände bis zu 42.000 Aussteller ihre Neuheiten vor und treffen auf ein Forum von bis zu 2 Mio Besuchern, die sich über zukunftsweisende Entwicklungen und innovative Produkte informieren.

Während auf 42 Auslandsmessen, u. a. in Rußland, China, Südostasien, den USA und Südamerika, neue Märkte eröffnet werden, sorgen eine permanente Modernisierung und Vergrößerung des Geländes in Frankfurt (die neue Halle 3 hat eine Kapazität von rund 38 000 m²) und das neue Forum für ein ganz neues Gastronomie-, Konferenz- und Ausstellungsangebot. Auch die Region um Frankfurt profitiert durch zusätzliche Einkommen in hohem Maße von den Messen – im Jahr 2000 betrug die Umwegrentabilität rund 4,1 Milliarden DM mit einem daraus resultierenden Fiskaleffekt für Stadt und Land von ca. 458 Mio. DM.   ■

The Frankfurt Fair is one of the most important exhibition centres of the world. With 37 exhibitions and events, in which exhibitors and visitors from the whole world can initiate talks and businesses, the fair presented in the year 2000 a highly international offer of exhibitions. In addition, annual number of around 280 congresses, seminars and events are carried out in the Festhalle and in the Congress Center.

In Frankfurt, the world's largest specialist fairs take place of such branches as consumer goods, Car+Technic, Textiles and Communication+ Leisuretime. Year after year up to 42.000 exhibitors present their innovations and meet a forum of upto 2 million visitors that want to be informed about future-oriented developments and innovative products.

While on 42 exhibitions abroad, including in Russia, China, South-East Asia, the USA and South America, new markets are opened, a permanent modernisation and extension of the fair grounds in Frankfurt (the new hall 33 has a capacity of around 38.000 sqm) and the new Forum ensure a completely new restaurant, conference and exhibition provision. Also the region around Frankfurt benefits through additional income to a great extent from the fairs – in the year 2000 the detour-profitability amounted to around 4,1 billion DM with a herefrom resulting fiscal effect for the city and state of Hesse of approx. 458 million DM.   ■

Die Nummer 1 der neuen Anbieter im Festnetz

The Number 1 of the new Providers in Land Networks

Mannesmann Arcor AG & Co

Gesellschafter/Corporate member:
Mannesmann Arcor AG & Co. sind:
Vodafone Group Plc (rd. 74%)
Deutsche Bahn AG (rd. 18%)
Deutsche Bank AG (rd. 8%)

Gründungsjahr/Year of Foundation:
1997

Mitarbeiter/Employees:
Mannesmann Arcor beschäftigt rd. 6.600
Mitarbeiter (Stand 30.09.2000), die in der
Zentrale und in den neuen Regionen tätig sind.
Mannesmann Arcor employs around 6.600
people (status 30.09.2000), who work in the
headquarters and in the new regions

Umsatz (1999)/Turnover (1999):
rd. 1,02 Mrd. EUR (1,99 Mrd. DM)

Geschäftstätigkeit/Business Activity:
Telekommunikations-Anbieter
Telecommunications Provider

Arcor Standorte/Arcor Locations:
Sitz der Zentrale ist Eschborn bei Frankfurt.
Um Präsenz im gesamten Bundesgebiet zu zeigen,
ist Arcor in neun Städten mit Regionalleitungen
vertreten: Berlin, Dresden, Essen, Frankfurt am
Main, Hamburg, Hannover, Köln, München und
Stuttgart. Von hier aus kümmern sich die Arcor
Mitarbeiter um die Belange der Kunden.
Zahlreiche Stützpunkte garantieren ein flächen-
deckendes Service- und Vertriebsnetz im
gesamten Bundesgebiet.
Seat of the Headquarters is Eschborn near
Frankfurt. In order to demonstrate presence across
the whole state, Arcor is present in nine cities
with regional managements: Berlin, Dresden,
Essen, Frankfurt on the Main, Hamburg, Hanover,
Cologne, Munich and Stuttgart. From these places
the Arcor employees take care of the concerns of
the customers. Numerous supporting points
guarantee a complete surface cover of service and
sales networks within the whole state.

Anschrift/Address:
Kölner Straße 5
D-65760 Eschborn
Telefon   +49 (69) 21 69-0
Telefax   +49 (69) 21 69-44 44
E-Mail   arcor@arcor.net
Internet   www.arcor.net

Mannesmann Arcor ist in Deutschland die Nummer 1 der neuen Anbieter für Tele-kommunikation im Festnetz. Mit seinem eigenen bundesweit flächendeckenden Sprach- und Daten-netz von über 50.000 km Länge bietet Arcor seinen Kunden das volle Spektrum an Sprach-, Daten- und Mehrwertdiensten sowie Internet-, Multimediaservices und E-Business-Lösungen.
1999 startete das Unternehmen mit einem kom-fortablen und günstigen ISDN-Anschluss inklu-sive Ortsgesprächen und kostenlosem Internet-zugang. Ende 2000 waren bereits 75 Ortsnetze an das Arcor-Netz angeschlossen.
In großen deutschen Städten schaltet Arcor für das Internet und die Datenübertragung den Turbo ein und schließt Kunden mit breitbandigen DSL-Zugängen über die vorhandene Telefonlei-tung an. Der DSL-Anschluss (mit 128 kBit/s oder 768 kBit/s) ist die Basis für eine Vielzahl von Services, von denen Privat- und Geschäftskunden gleichermaßen profitieren. Der Clou: Alle DSL-Dienste gibt es zum monatlichen Festpreis, der Flatrate. ∎

Mannesmann Arcor is in Germany the num-ber 1 of the new providers of telecommuni-cations within the land network. With its own extensive national voice and data network of more than 50.000 km length Arcor offers it's customers the full spectrum of voice, data and added-value services as well as Internet and mul-ti media services and e-business solutions. In 1999, the company started with a comfortable and inexpensive ISDN-connection including city calls and high speed Internet. By the end of 2000, already 75 local networks were connected to the Arcor-network.

In large German cities Arcor uses for the Internet and data transfer the turbo and connects the cus-tomer with broadband DSL-accesses via the ex-isting telephone lines. The DSL-connection (with 128 kBit/s or 768 kBit/s) is the basis for a multi-tude of services from which private and business clients profit in the same way. The point is: all DSL-services are provided at a monthly fixed price, the flat rate. ∎

Seit 10 Jahren internationale Rechtsberatung in Frankfurt

International Law Consultancy Since 10 years in Frankfurt

Frankfurt ist eine der zentralen Adressen für internationale Kanzleien in Deutschland geworden. Shearman & Sterling, die 1873 in New York gegründete Sozietät mit Praxis in amerikanischem, deutschem, englischem und französischem Recht, hat dies schon vor zehn Jahren erkannt und nach Düsseldorf sein zweites Büro in der Mainmetropole eröffnet und inzwischen mit großem Erfolg ausgebaut. Hierzu schreibt das JUVE-Handbuch 2000/2001 über Wirtschaftskanzleien: „Shearman & Sterling verzeichnet einen Erfolg nach dem anderen, besonders in der Bank- und Finanzrechtspraxis. Das Frankfurter Büro hat durch das Hinzukommen wichtiger Partner von Schilling, Zutt & Anschütz im nahegelegenen Mannheim eine Kerngruppe von Experten im Gesellschaftsrecht hinzugewonnen. (…) In Frankfurt arbeiten bereits einige angesehene M&A Anwälte. Auch die Praxisgruppe Steuerrecht hat einen guten Ruf."

Die deutschen Büros sind schwerpunktmäßig in den Bereichen Gesellschaftsrecht, Kapitalmarktrecht, M&A, Projektfinanzierung, strukturierte Finanzierung, nationales und internationales Kartellrecht sowie im internationalen Steuerrecht tätig. Die Praxisgruppen werden durch spezialisierte Fachbereiche wie Arbeitsrecht, Umweltrecht, Immaterialgüterrecht etc. ergänzt.

Shearman & Sterling hat in den letzten Jahren aus Frankfurt heraus bei zahlreichen großen nationalen und internationalen Aktienemissionen deutsche, schweizerische und österreichische Gesellschaften beraten. „Global offering" und „dual listing" aus einer Hand von Unternehmen am Neuen Markt und an der Nasdaq bzw. der New York Stock Exchange zählen zu den besonderen Stärken von Shearman & Sterling.

Bereits seit einiger Zeit gilt S&S als einer der Marktführer bei Börsengängen. Dr. Stephan Hutter und seine Partner Georg Mühlmann und Michael Leppert wurden beide nachdrücklich empfohlen. Konkurrenten und Mandanten gleichermaßen zeigen sich von der runden Praxis beeindruckt.

Beispielhaft einige Mandate: in Deutschland Emittenten wie Bayer, Dresdner Bank, Continental, Medigene, Pixelpark, SGL Carbon, GPC und Konsortialführer bei Kapitalmarkttransaktionen für Aventis, IFCO Systems, Celanese, Kamps, Adlink, Jobs & Adverts, Carrier One; in der Schweiz Konsortialführer bei der Privatisierung des Flughafens Zürich und bei Kapitalmarkttransaktionen für Gesellschaften wie Tamedia, Blue Window, Actelion, Day Interactive und Private Equity Holding; und in Österreich Konsortialführer bei den Privatisierungen von Austria Tabak und TelekomAustria und bei Kapitalmarkttransaktionen für Gesellschaften wie Austrian Airlines, Libro, AT&S und Pankl Racing Systems.

Zu den weltweiten Transaktionen gehörten u. a.: der Zusammenschluss Morgan Stanley/Dean Witter Discover, Verhandlungen zu NAFTA mit der mexikanischen Regierung, die Privatisierung von China Telecom, die Akquisition von Paramount Communications durch Viacom und der Zusammenschluß von DaimlerChrysler.

International betrachtet ist Shearman & Sterling eine global operierende Sozietät, in der die Vision eines weltumspannenden Serviceangebotes für Mandanten Realität geworden ist; so arbeiten beispielsweise in Frankfurt deutsche und amerikanische Anwälte in ihren jeweiligen Jurisdiktionen, um nationalen wie internationalen Mandanten aus Bank-, Versicherungs- und Industriebereichen den bestmöglichen Service zu bieten. ∎

Im Frankfurter Westend Carree hat S&S ihren Sitz ab April 2001 mit Büros für bis zu 100 Anwälte.

Within the Westend quarter of Frankfurt S&S has its headquarters from April 2001 on with offices for up to 100 lawyers.

Shut Down
Restart
Merge

GO

Frankfurt has become one of the central addresses for international law firms in Germany. Shearman & Sterling, the society founded in 1873 in New York with experience in American, German, English and French law, had recognised this as early as ten years ago and opened after Düsseldorf, its second office in the metropolis on the Main and has expanded meanwhile with great success. In this respect, the JUVE-Handbook 2000/2001 on business law firms writes: "Shearman & Sterling have scored one success after the other, especially in the practice of banking and financial law. The Frankfurt office has won through the association with important partners of Schilling, Zutt & Anschütz of nearby Mannheim, a core group of experts in the field of corporate law. (…) Already, some renowned M&A lawyers are working in Frankfurt. Also the group of practitioners in fiscal law enjoys a good reputation."

The German offices are mainly active in the fields of corporate law, law of capital markets, M&A, project financing, structured financing, national and international cartels law as well as in international fiscal law. The groups of practitioners are complemented by specialised expert fields such as law of employment, environment law, industrial property law.

Shearman & Sterling has been consulting from its Frankfurt base German, Swiss and Austrian corporations during a number of large national and international launches of share issues. "Global offering and "dual listing" from one provider of enterprises of the New Economy and at the Nasdaq or the New York stock exchange are among the particular strengths of Shearman & Sterling.

Already for some time now S&S is regarded as one of the market leaders for introductions into the stock exchange. Dr. Stephan Hutter and his partner Georg Mühlmann and Michael Leppert have both been strongly recommended. The comprehensive law firm impresses competitors and clients alike. Here are some examples of client agreements: in Germany, issuing corporations like Bayer, Dresdner Bank, Continental, Medigene, Pixelpark, SGL Carbon, GPC and lead manager at capital market transactions for Aventis, IFCO Systems, Celanese, Kamps, Adlink, Jobs & Adverts, Carrier One; in Switzerland lead manager at the privatisation of the Airport Zurich and at capital market transactions for corporations like Tamedia, Blue window, Actelion, Day Interactive and Private Equity Holding; and in Austria lead manager at privatisations of Austria Tabak and Telecom Austria and at capital market transactions for corporations like Austrian Airlines, Libro, AT&S and Pankl Racing Systems. Among the worldwide transactions are included: the merger of Morgan Stanley/Dean Witter Discover, negotiations regarding NAFTA with the Mexican government, the privatisation of China Telecom, the acquisitions of Paramount Communications by Viacom and the merger of DaimlerChrysler.

Viewed internationally, Shearman & Sterling is a globally operating professional association, which has made reality the vision of a worldwide service provision for clients; thus for example, in Frankfurt German and American lawyers are engaged in their corresponding jurisdictions in order to provide the best possible service to national as well as international clients from the fields of banking, insurance and industry. ∎

Dr. Stephan Hutter,
Office Managing Partner Frankfurt.

Dr. Stephan Hutter,
Office Managing Partner Frankfurt.

SHEARMAN & STERLING

M&A/M&A:
Dr. Klaus Anschütz, Mannheim
Dr. Hans Diekmann, Düsseldorf
Dr. Roger Kiem, LL.M., Frankfurt
Dr. Anton Klösters, Düsseldorf
Dr. Alfred Kossmann, Düsseldorf
Rolf Koerfer, Düsseldorf
Dr. Thomas König, Frankfurt
Dr. Thomas Liebscher, Mannheim
Dr. Jochem Reichert, Mannheim
Dr. Harald Selzner, Düsseldorf
Dr. Heino W. G. Rück, Mannheim
Georg F. Thoma, Düsseldorf
Rainer Wilke, Düsseldorf
Dr. Martin Winter, Mannheim

Private Clients/Private Clients:
Dr. Stephan Scherer, Mannheim

Arbeitsrecht/Employment law:
Dr. Georg Jaeger, Mannheim

International Arbitration/International Arbitration:
Richard Kreindler, Frankfurt

Intellectual Property/Intellectual Property:
Dr. Jost Kotthoff

Kartellrecht/Cartels Law:
Hans-Joachim Hellmann, LL.M., Mannheim
Dr. Hans Jürgen Meyer-Lindemann, Düsseldorf

Corporate Finance/Corporate Finance:
Dr. Stephan Hutter, Frankfurt
Michael A. Leppert, Frankfurt
Johann Georg Mühlmann, Frankfurt

Internationales Steuerrecht/International Tax Law:
Dr. Hanno Berger, Frankfurt
Reinhard F. Stockum, Frankfurt
Wolfgang Tischbirek, Frankfurt

Anzahl der RA/Number of lawyers:
über/more than 900

Anzahl der Partner/Number of Partners:
196

Anzahl Associates/Number of associates:
über/more than 700

Mitarbeiter/Employees:
über/more than 2.000

Niederlassungen/Branches:
Abu Dhabi, Peking, Hongkong, London,
Menlo Park, New York, Paris, San Francisco,
Singapur, Tokio, Toronto, Washington D.C.

Anschrift/Address:
Mainzer Landstraße 16
D-60325 Frankfurt am Main
Telefon   +49 (69) 9711-1000
Telefax   +49 (69) 9711-1100
E-Mail   germany@shearman.com
Internet   www.shearman.com

Kaiserpfalz und Wolkenkratzer

Imperial Palace and Skyscrapers

Kaiserpfalz und Wolkenkratzer heißt der Titel einer bemerkenswerten Fernsehserie, die vom Hessischen Fernsehen ausgestrahlt wird und auf beträchtliches öffentliches Interesse gestoßen ist. Sie bietet ein Kompendium kunstgeschichtlicher Denkmäler in Hessen von der Romanik bis zur Gegenwart, und eigentlich wartet sie auf Verlängerung zurück über die Phase der römischen Kultivierung bis in die Anfänge vorgeschichtlicher Besiedlung.

Mit dem Titel „Kaiserpfalz und Wolkenkratzer" könnte auch ein Blick über Kunst und Kultur der Rhein-Main-Region überschrieben sein, der an den hessischen Grenzen nicht endet, sondern das südliche Rheinland-Pfalz mit Mainz und das nördliche Bayern mit Aschaffenburg einbezieht. Von Ferne längst als wirtschaftlich prosperierende, einheitliche Region um das Zentrum Frankfurt angesehen, beginnt im Innern das Bekenntnis zur Region und die Identifizierung mit ihr zu wachsen. Die Rhein-Main-Region folgt damit einer Gesetzmäßigkeit, die sich im Europa der Regionen zunehmend herauskristallisiert. Definitionen aus dem historisch-traditionellen Kern heraus, deutlich gezeichnete Profile erweisen sich als zukunftsträchtige Basis für Offenheit und Selbstbewusstsein im globalen Handeln.

Partizipation

Wirtschaftliche Erfolge sind ohne kulturelle Fermente undenkbar. Aus künstlerischen Entwürfen übertragen sich Phantasie und Kreativität; sie zirkeln neue Blickwinkel und Wahrnehmungsweisen ab, sie lassen veränderte Wirklichkeit erkennen und provozieren damit die Entwicklung geeigneter Instrumentarien ihrer Gestaltung. Überlebte Konventionen bleiben dabei verbraucht zurück, historisiert in einem Depot aus Vergangenem, aus dem zukünftig gleichwohl geschöpft werden kann.

Immerfort aktuell bietet Kultur Jedem und Tag für Tag jene Ingredienzien, deren der Einzelne zur Komposition seines Tagesablaufs bedarf. Jeder

Prof. Dr. Herbert Beck

Der 1941 in Hanau am Main geborene Autor studierte von 1961–1967 Kunstgeschichte, Archäologie und Germanistik in München und Frankfurt am Main. 1969 übernahm er die Leitung des Liebieghauses Museum Alter Plastik in Frankfurt am Main. Seit Oktober 1994 ist er Direktor sowohl des Städelschen Kunstinstituts und der Städtischen Galerie als auch des Liebieghauses Museum Alter Plastik.

The author, born 1941 in Hanau on the Main, studied art history from 1961 – 1967, archaeology and German studies in Munich and Frankfurt on the Main. In 1969, he took over the Management of the Museum of Old Plastics of the Liebig House in Frankfurt on the Main. Since October 1994 he is director of the Städel Art Institute as well as of the Municipal Galleries and the Museum of Old Plastics of the Liebig House.

wählt und bestimmt aus Vielfalt und Qualität das Niveau seines eigenen Lebensstils. Arbeit und Freizeitgestaltung verschmelzen aus diesen Elementen zur unauflösbaren Verbindung wiedererkennbarer Individualität.

Bei aller Vielfalt und Qualität der über die Region hin verbreiteten künstlerischen und kulturellen Substanz bedarf es der andauernden Förderung neu zu schaffender Werke der Literatur, der Musik, der Bildenden Kunst und ihrer experimentellen Verzahnung. Daraus öffnen sich Spielräume des Hörens, Sehens und Denkens, mithin erweiterte Ansätze auch der interpretativen Umgestaltung der geschichtlichen Werke. Gedankenreichtum und Phantasie lassen

„Goethe in der römischen Campagna" von Tischbein.
"Goethe in the Roman Campagna" by Tischbein.

154

Senckenberg-Museum, Frankfurt am Main.

Senckenberg-Museum, Frankfurt on the Main.

Imperial Palace and Skyscrapers is the title of a remarkable television series being shown on the regional television of Hesse and has caused considerably public interest. It offers a compendium of art historical monuments in Hesse starting from Romanesque times till the present, and it is waiting really for prolongation back to the phase of the Roman cultivation to the beginnings of pre-historical settlements.

The title "Imperial Palace and Skyscrapers" could also have been given to an overview across art and culture of the Rhein-Main region, which does not end at the borders of Hesse, but includes the Southern Rhineland-Palatinate with Mainz and Northern Bavaria with Aschaffenburg. Having long been accepted as an economically prospering region around the nucleus of Frankfurt, now in the interior the commitment to the region and the identification with it is beginning to grow. The Rhein-Main region is thus following a natural law that is becoming more and more evident in a Europe of regions. Definitions emerging from a historical-traditional core and clearly marked profiles are proving to be a future oriented basis for openness and self-confidence in global activities.

Participation

Economic successes are unthinkable without cultural ferments. From artistic sketches fantasy and creativity are transferred; they encircle new points of view and forms of perception, make visible a changed reality and thus provoke the development of suitable instruments for their forming. Outlived conventions are left behind worn out, historicized in a depot of the bygone, from which can in future however be drawn creative spirit.

Always up-to-date, culture offers to everyone and everyday such ingredients that the individual needs for the composition of his daily routine. Everyone selects and determines from the diversity and quality the level of his own lifestyle. Work and the structure of leisure time melt from these elements into an insoluble interrelation of recognizable individuality.

With all the diversity and quality of the artistic and cultural substance dispersed across the region, there is a need for continuous encouragement of newly created works of literature, music, fine arts and it's experimental linkage. From these, spaces of hearing, seeing and thinking evolve and conse-

quently extended approaches also of an interpretative reshaping of the historical works. Richness in thought and fantasy let the works of art grow across generations, comparable to the long-lasting constructions of cathedrals in the middle Ages, but without ever reaching the completion. The chance of the epoch for each newly created work of art lies in this contextual possibility of growth. It resembles a power nucleus resting in itself, whose potency is activated by individual participation of the ones interested in art. These themselves become shareholders with an increased, productive capital.

Access

Probably no one disposes presently of a complete pool of information of all cultural possibilities in the Rhein-Main region. If one only looks at the treasure of knowledge of the Johann Wolfgang Goethe-University, which has just acquired a new campus by moving into the Poelzig-building and thus an opening bracket towards the public. This uncertainty is a result of the exploding development of local cultural life during the last twenty

„Mädchenbildnis" von Sandro Botticelli.
"Picture of a girl" by Sandro Botticelli.

Kunstwerke über Generationen hin wachsen, vergleichbar dem im Mittelalter langwährenden Kathedralenbau, ohne aber je zu einem Abschluss zu kommen. Die epochale Chance jedes neu geschaffenen Kunstwerks liegt in dieser inhaltlichen Wachstumsmöglichkeit. Sie gleicht einem in sich ruhenden Kraftkern, dessen Potenz erst aktiviert wird durch individuelle Teilhabe der an Kunst Interessierten. Diese selbst werden dabei zu Mitbesitzern mit erhöhtem, produktiven Kapital.

Zugriff

Derzeit verfügt wohl niemand über einen lückenlosen Informationspool aller kulturellen Angebote der Rhein-Main-Region. Richtet man nur den Blick auf den Wissensschatz der Johann Wolfgang Goethe-Universität, die sich mit dem Umzug in den Poelzig-Bau gerade einen neuen Campus, eine Klammer zur Öffentlichkeit hin schafft. Diese Unübersichtlichkeit ist eine Folge der explosionsartigen Entfaltung lokalen kulturellen Lebens während der letzten zwanzig Jahre: in Festivals, in Ausstellungen von Museen oder Kunstgalerien, der großen Theater, Opern- und Konzerthäuser, der privaten Theater, der Freien Szene und Experimentierbühnen, in Lesungen und Vortragsveranstaltungen, Open-Air-Konzerten, der leichten Muse ebenso wie der Kirchenmusik, des Varieté und der Orchester, der Musikpflege in Chören und Vereinen und darüber hinaus durch das unerschöpfliche Potenzial, das aus der Identität zugewanderter Bürger mit ihren heimischen Kulturen sprudelt.

Die Möglichkeit gezielter Auswahl sowohl im Hinblick auf eigene kreative Aktivität als auch der stringenten Gestaltung des individuellen kulturellen Tagesprogramms ist aber Grundbedingung eines funktionierenden Kulturlebens. Überdies kann die umfassende Informationsmöglichkeit der Kooperation der Kulturschaffenden selbst dienen und damit eine qualitative Verbesserung des Angebots bewirken.

Die Entwicklung einer praktikablen Infrastruktur von der Information über ein regionales Ticketing-System bis hin zur Optimierung der Verkehrsangebote ist eines der derzeit drängendsten Desiderate. Mit seiner Behebung werden für die Verantwortlichen erhebliche Mühen in Planung, Umsetzung und Finanzierung verbunden sein. Doch ein gutes Ergebnis stellt Erfolge in Aussicht nicht nur hinsichtlich vereinfachter und dadurch vervielfachter Nutzung des kulturellen Angebots, nicht nur im Hinblick auf das Ziel wachsender regionaler Identität. Sondern nicht zuletzt dank der damit unweigerlich verbundenen Vergleichsmöglichkeit zwischen den verschiedensten kulturellen Leistungen werden Defizite zu den europaweit konkurrierenden Regionen erkennbar werden und möglicherweise zum qualitativen Niveausprung herausfordern.

Zentrum Frankfurt

Die Hochhaus-Silhouette gibt dem Bild der Stadt ihren in Deutschland und Europa unverwechselbaren Charakter. Sein Ursprung war begleitet von heftigen Konflikten. So widersprüchlich und heftig die Diskussion einst, so bemerkenswert die Akzeptanz heute bis hin zu verbreitetem Stolz auf die kennzeichnende Singularität. Nicht zähe Diskussion um Bauhöhe und Standort, sondern verkürzte Planungsphasen scheinen vielen angelegen, um den Modernisierungsprozess der Stadt auch nach außen hin deutlich zu markieren.
Ein Wendepunkt zwischen Ablehnung und Anerkennung lässt sich mit dem Wolkenkratzer-Festival vor drei Jahren verbinden. Dieses lud die Öffentlichkeit ein, über ein Wochenende Besitz zu nehmen von Höhepunkten, die rare Weitblicke ermöglichen. Stand- und Blickpunkte, aussichtsreich erneuerte Bilder fordern seit jeher den wechselvollen Zugriff auf Wirklichkeit heraus und tragen wesentlich dazu bei, den jeweiligen Begriff von Realität zu definieren. Das Nahe gegenüber dem Fernen zu bestimmen, das Notwendige gegenüber dem Nützlichen und schließlich Überflüssigen, das Utopische in Relation zum Leidvollen über Sinneseindrücke zu erfahren, entspricht konstanten, menschlichen Anliegen.

Für diesen Zweck freilich nicht errichtet, ist den Wolkenkratzern der Stadt gleichwohl dieser Sekundärnutzen zugewachsen. Im Prozess kultureller Aneignung gewinnen die Symbole finanzieller und wirtschaftlicher Kraft an Bedeutungsebenen hinzu. Dessen bewusst, fördern die Unternehmen zunehmend die früher mehr oder weniger ausschließlich von der öffentlichen Hand finanzierten Kulturinstitute und tragen damit wesentlich zu kulturellen Bindungen bei. Public private Partnership bezeichnet die Ergänzung und Fortentwicklung bürgerlichen Mäzenatentums in der modernen Bürgergesellschaft.

Ihre Gestaltung zunehmend selbst zu bestimmen und gelungene Ergebnisse persönlich zu repräsentieren, ist mithin eine Forderung der Stunde. Über Entwicklungspotenziale verfügt Frankfurt in Fülle. Auflagenstarke Tageszeitungen, international führende Verlage, Literaten und Vermittlungsinstanzen schaffen während des Festes der Buchmesse und aus Anlass von Preisverleihungen städtische Öffentlichkeit. Dasselbe gilt für große Konzerte, die nach Kulmination in musikalischen Frankfurt-Festen rufen; nicht weniger für die breite Museumslandschaft, der leicht Glanzlichter durch temporäre Ausstellungsereignisse aufzusetzen wären. Und das Theaterleben Frankfurts mitsamt den nahgelegenen Städten der umgebenden Region gar, verfügt über institutionalisierte Voraussetzungen, die durchaus nicht im Schatten der renommierten europäischen Kulturmetropolen stehen müssen.

Beispiel Städel

Die kulturelle Leistungskraft von Stadt und Region läßt sich durch Aufzählen ihrer Denkmäler und Institutionen allenfalls erahnen. Zur Verdeutlichung ihrer Ziele und Möglichkeiten bedarf es der konkreten Exemplifizierung. Niemals Residenzstadt, verfügt Frankfurt nicht über alte, höfische Sammlungen. Die Pflege von Kunst und Wissenschaft nahmen hier die Bürger selbst in die Hand. In den fürstlichen Kunstkammern angesammelte Objekte der Natur und der Kunst verbildlichten den Kosmos. Ihre Trennung in Naturmuseen einerseits und Kunstmuseen andererseits erfolgte mit fortschreitender Differenzierung der Wissenschaften im späten 18. Jahrhundert.

In Frankfurt entsprachen dem die bürgerlichen Stiftungen der Senckenbergischen Naturforschenden Gesellschaft und des Städelschen Kunstinstituts im ersten Viertel des 19. Jahrhun-

years: in forms of festivals, exhibitions of museums or art galleries, the great theatres, the opera and concert houses, the private theatres, the fringe and experimental stages, in readings and lecturing events, open-air concerts, of light entertainment as well as church music, of variety and orchestras, the cultivation of music in choirs and clubs and furthermore, through the unceasing potential that effervescently emerges from the identity of immigrated citizens with the cultures of their homelands.

The possibility of a targeted selection with view to ones own creative activity as well as to the stringent structure of an individual daily cultural programme however, is the basic condition for a functioning cultural life. Furthermore, a comprehensive possibility for information can serve the co-operation of creative people in culture themselves and thus result in a qualitative improvement of offers.

The development of a practical infrastructure reaching from information and a regional ticketing system to optimising the possibilities of transport is one of the present most urgent suggestions for acquisition. To solve this, the responsible authorities will have to exert considerable effort in planning, realisation and financing. However, a good result will provide successes not only concerning simplified and thus a multiplied use of the cultural offers, also with a view to the goal of a growing regional identity. But ultimately thanks to the herewith undoubtedly connected possibili-

„Blendung Samsons" von Rembrandt.

"The dazzling of Samson" by Rembrandt.

ties of comparison between the varied cultural services, the deficits against the European wide competing regions will become visible and possibly challenge to dare a qualitative jump into another level.

Frankfurt
the Focus

The skyline silhouette gives the cityscape it's in Germany and Europe unmistakable character. Its origin was accompanied by tremendous conflicts. As contradictory and intense the discussion was once, as remarkable its acceptance is today up to a widespread pride about the characteristic singularity. Not tough discussions about construction height and location, but shorter planning phases seem to be the concern of many, in order to mark clearly the process of modernisation of the city also externally.

A turning point between rejection and recognition can be related to the skyscraper festival three years ago. This invited the public to take possession for one weekend of peaks that enable rare and far sights. Standpoints and viewpoints, promising renewed images challenge since the varied access to reality and contribute considerably to define the corresponding concept of reality. To determine the near against the distant, the necessary against the beneficial and finally the superfluous, to experience the utopical in relation to

the painful over an impression of the senses, this corresponds with constant human concern.

Certainly not built for this purpose, the skyscrapers of the city have nevertheless acquired this secondary usefulness. In the process of cultural appropriation the symbols of financial and economic power are gaining in levels of importance. Conscious of the latter, the enterprises promote increasingly the cultural institutes formerly more or less exclusively finance by public authorities and thus contribute essentially to cultural relations. Public private partnership describes the complementation and further development of middle class patronage in a modern society of citizens.

To determine its shape increasingly by itself and to represent successful results personally is consequently the demand of the present. There is enough potential for development in Frankfurt. Daily newspapers, strong in circulation, internationally leading publishers, literati and authorised agencies create during the feast of the book fair and on the occasion of prize awards a public awareness for the city. The same is valid of great concerts that call for a culmination in musical Frankfurt-celebrations; not least of the broad andscape of museums, to which could easily be added starlights because of temporary exhibition events. And the theatre life of Frankfurt, with its nearby cities of the surrounding region even, disposes of the institutionalised preconditions,

„Vornehme Dame mit Hündchen" von Pontormo.

"Elegant Lady with small dog" by Pontormo.

Blick über die Frankfurter Skyline.

View across the Frankfurt skyline.

Gemälden des 14. Jahrhunderts bis zur Gegenwart internationalen Ranges, die in Deutschland nach Berlin, Dresden und München in ihrer Bedeutung an vierter Stelle genannt wird. Sie wird umgeben von Einheiten eigenständiger Dynamik und Anziehungskraft: von der Graphischen Sammlung, die ihrerseits zu den wichtigsten in Deutschland zählt, mit einer Ausstellungshalle für wechselnde Präsentationen aus dem reichen, etwa 100.000 Papierarbeiten umfassenden Bestand; Von dem Ausstellungshaus für frequentierte, temporäre Sonderausstellungen, die zur Positionierung Frankfurts als Kulturstadt beitragen; von einer großen Buchhandlung, die den Sektor der Kunstbuchproduktion umfassend bereitstellt; von einem Café-Restaurant, das über den üblichen Museumsservice hinaus zu abendlicher Geselligkeit einlädt; schließlich von einem Veranstaltungsbereich für Feiern, für Feste, für Events.

Damit ist in Frankfurt zum Konzerthaus Alte Oper, zu Oper/Schauspiel/TAT/Ballett und Mousonturm ein weiterer Magnet entstanden, um gesellschaftliches Leben zu bündeln. Solcher Orte bedarf es insbesondere zu Zeiten extremer Individualisierung. Fortschreitende Emanzipation eröffnet dem Einzelnen heute Freiräume, wie sie vergleichbar in der neueren Geschichte nur die Epoche der Aufklärung ermöglicht hat. Seitdem stellt sich aber auch drängend die Frage nach dem Verhältnis von Individuum und Gemeinschaft. Zu einer Antwort beizutragen, sieht das Städel sich, gerade als bürgerliche Stiftung, aufgerufen.

Lust zu wecken auf Bilder, ohne der Last des geschichtlichen Bildungskanons unterworfen zu sein, ist ein Ziel. Ebenso das Vertrauen auf die eigene ästhetische Kompetenz in Relation zu umfänglich verfügbaren, wissenschaftlich-methodischen Bildexegesen. In der Welt des Expertentums ist der eigenen Sinneswahrnehmung eine neue Domäne erschlossen. Das Schlüsselwort des neuen Städel heißt Ästhetisierung. Sie setzt Sinne und Verstand zueinander in genussvolle Spannung, an der die Öffentlichkeit uneingeschränkt partizipieren kann. Von seiner Natur her ist das Museum ein Ort öffentlicher Kommunikation. Hier mündet individuelle Entfaltung, angereichert mit künstlerischer Substanz, in Lebensstile hohen Niveaus. Diese Dynamik begründet die gesellschaftlich konstitutive Kraft der Institution Museum. Grundlagen dafür hat auch das Städel nun geschaffen, um gemeinsam mit der vielfältigen Kulturszene in Frankfurt und der Region ein zukunftsorientiertes Modell sozialer, politischer und ökonomischer Funktionsfähigkeit fortzuentwickeln und weithin zu veranschaulichen. ■

derts. Später ergänzt wurden diese durch kommunale Museumsgründungen und schließlich abgerundet durch das kürzlich eröffnete „Museum regionaler Kunst – Haus Giersch", einer wiederum privaten Stiftung im Geist traditionellen Mäzenatentums.

Flaggschiff der Kunstmuseen Frankfurts und der Region ist das Städel, die „älteste und bedeutendste Museumsstiftung in Deutschland".

Das Städel erfuhr in den letzten Jahren eine durchgreifende konzeptionelle und bauliche Erneuerung, die überwiegend durch Zuwendungen von privater Seite finanziert werden konnte. Ziel war die Konstruktion eines urbanen Ortes, der breite Öffentlichkeit über die Ausbildung unterschiedlicher Leistungskomponenten generiert.

Im Zentrum des Städel steht die ästhetisch möglichst perfekt präsentierte Sammlung von

which by no means have to stand in the shadow of the renowned European cultural cosmopolitan cities.

The example of the Städel

The cultural power of performance of the city and region can merely be guessed by counting its monuments and institutions. In order to clarify its aims and possibilities, a concrete example is needed. Having never been a residential city, Frankfurt does not dispose of old collections of courts. The citizens themselves dealt here with the cultivation of art and science. Objects of nature and art collected in art chambers of the courts gave form to the cosmos. Their division in natural museums on the one hand and art museums on the other proceeded with the growing differentiation of the sciences in the late 18th Century.

In Frankfurt, these corresponded to the citizen foundations of the Senckenbergische Naturforschende Gesellschaft (a natural research society) and of the Städel Art Institute in the first quarter of the 19th Century. Later on, these were extended by communal foundations of museums and finally complemented by the recently opened "Museum of regional Art – The House Giersch", again a private foundation in the spirit of traditional patronage.

Showcase of the art museums of Frankfurt and its region is the Städel, the eldest and most important museum foundation in Germany". The Städel experienced in the last years a thorough conceptual and structural renovation, which was possible to be financed mainly through private contributions. Aim was the construction of an urban place that would generate a broad publicity about the formation of the most varied service components.

In the focus of the Städel is the aesthetically as perfect as possible presented collection of paintings of the 14th century up to the present of international rank, which is mentioned in Germany after Berlin, Dresden und Munich in fourth place in its importance. It is surrounded by units of independent dynamism and attraction: By the graphic collection, which in itself is amongst the most important in Germany, including an exhibition hall for changing presentations from the rich funds, comprising of around 100.000 works on paper. By a large bookstore, which comprehensively offers the section of production of art books. By a café restaurant that beyond the usual service of museums invites to an evening's sociability; and finally by a section for arrangement of celebrations, feasts and events.

Thus, in Frankfurt has emerged a further magnet adding to the concert house AlteOper, to the opera/Theatre/TAT/Ballet and Mousonturm places, where sociable life can be gathered. Such places are necessary especially in times of extreme individualisation. A progressing emancipation opens spaces of freedom to the individual today, as have only been made possible comparably in the recent history by the time of the renaissance. Since then, however, also the question is arising urgently as to the relation of the individual and society. The Städel considers itself to be called to contributing an answer, especially being a citizen's foundation.

One aim is, to create a desire for paintings, without being subjected to the burden of the historical education-canon. Also a confidence in one's own aesthetic competence in relation to expositions of paintings, disposable in volumes and various scientific methods. Within the world of expertise, the own perception of the senses has acquired a new domain. The key word of the new Städel is Aesthetication. It sets the senses and the intellect into a lustful thrill to each other, in which the public may participate unlimited. By nature, the museum is a place of public communication. Here flows together individual unfolding, enriched with artistic substance into highly evolved lifestyles. This dynamism is founded in the socially constituting force of the museum as an institution.

The basis for this has now also been created by the Städel in order to continue to develop and make visible from afar together with the diverse cultural scenery in Frankfurt and its region a future-oriented model of social, political and economic functionality. ∎

„Madonna" von Barbara Da Modena.

"Madonna" by Barbara Da Modena.

Provadis: Wegbereiter für Unternehmerischen Erfolg

Provadis: Precursor for Entrepreneurial Success

Mit über 300 Bildungsangeboten ist Provadis
einer der größten Anbieter im Rhein-Main-Gebiet.

*With more than 300 educational opportunities Provadis
is one of the largest providers in the Rhein-Main region.*

Labortechnik finden alle am beruflichen Erfolg Interessierten das passende Programm. Für die Bereiche Betriebswirtschaft, Informatik, Chemie und Biologie sind weiterführende Qualifzierungsmaßnahmen im Angebot, die mit einem akademischen Grad abgeschlossen werden können.

Das Konzept von Provadis endet nicht bei der innovativen Weiterbildung. Provadis qualifiziert junge Menschen in über 20 Berufen. Mit professionellem Know-how, an modernsten Geräten, mit hochkarätigen Ausbildern und den neuesten Methoden garantiert Provadis eine hohe Qualität bei der Erstqualifizierung. Ob in Ausbildungsberufen im Bereich Produktion und Technik, zu denen beispielsweise Chemikant/in, Pharmakant/in oder Prozessleitelektroniker/in zählen, oder in kaufmännischen Berufen wie Industriekaufmann/frau und Fremdsprachenkorrespondenten/innen, in den IT-Berufen Fachinformatiker/in, Informatikkaufmann/frau oder aber auch in labortechnischen Berufen – Provadis öffnet jungen Menschen mit zukunftsorientierten Ausbildungsberufen alle Türen und Tore zu der modernen Arbeitswelt.   ∎

D ie Provadis Partner für Bildung und Beratung GmbH ist eines der größten Unternehmen für Bildung und Beratung im Rhein-Main Gebiet. Die Dienstleistungspalette des Frankfurter Unternehmens reicht von der Managementberatung bis zur Erstqualifikation – ein breiter Brückenschlag, der gerade die „Einzigartigkeit" des Unternehmens auszeichnet.

Die Management-Consultants von Provadis unterstützen ihre internationale Kunden bereits bei der Strategieentwicklung, optimieren – basierend auf den für den Geschäftserfolg erforderlichen Erfolgsfaktoren – die Geschäftsprozesse und richten die Organisationsstrukturen neu aus. Mit Pragmatismus wird die Implementierung durch Know-how-Transfer auf Schlüsselpersonen (der Berater geht – das Wissen bleibt im Kundenunternehmen) umgesetzt. Als Servicegarantie für den Kunden gilt: Beratungsprojekte werden erst bei erfolgreicher Umsetzung der Konzepte in die

Praxis als abgeschlossen angesehen. Die Stärke im Managen von Veränderungsprozessen resultiert aus der langjährigen Erfahrung im Managementtraining und -coaching in den Schwerpunktthemen Zusammenarbeit und Führung. Provadis verfügt über umfangreiche Erfahrungen bei der Neuausrichtung von Unternehmen in der Prozessindustrie, Gesundheitswesen, Banken und öffentlichen Einrichtungen.

Auf Wunsch und nach Bedarf begleitet Provadis Menschen in Unternehmen über die gesamte berufliche Laufbahn. Das umfangreiche Portfolio an Weiterbildungsmaßnahmen ermöglicht die praxisgerechte, flexible und kreative Entwicklung der Mitarbeiter analog der immer schnelleren Veränderungen in den Anforderungen der Arbeitswelt. Bei den 300 verschiedenen Angeboten aus den Bereichen Management und Führung, Management Skills, Kommunikation, Betriebswirtschaft, Marketing, Sprachen, PC-Kurse, Produktions- und

---

Bildungs- und Beratungsleistungen

- Erstqualifizierung (Ausbildung)
  In über 20 Berufen aus Produktion, Technik, Labor, Betriebswirtschaft und Informatik
- Weiterführende Qualifizierung mit anerkanntem Abschluss – Meister-, Techniker- und Fachhochschulkurse für Chemie, Biologie, Betriebswirtschaft und Informatik
- Weiterbildung
  General Management, Führung und Verhalten, Kommunikation, Sprach-, PC-, SAP-Kurse sowie individuelle, an betriebliche Rahmenbedingungen angepasste Seminare aus Labor, Produktion und Technik sowie Betriebswirtschaft und Arbeitstechniken
- Unternehmensberatung und -entwicklung, Strategieentwicklung und Umsetzung, Neuausrichtung von Organisationen und Geschäftsprozessen, Markt- und Wirtschaftlichkeitsanalysen, Kundenzufriedenheitsanalysen, Interkulturelles Management, Management von Veränderungsprozessen sowie integrale Personalentwicklung

Trainings- und Schulungszentrum Provadis Akademie.
Training and Instruction Centre of the Provadis Academy.

Partner für Bildung & Beratung

Provadis
Partner für Bildung und Beratung GmbH

Geschäftsführer/Manager:
Dr. Udo Lemke

Gründungsjahr/Year of Foundation:
Ausgegliedert aus Hoechst-Konzern seit 1997

Mitarbeiter/Employees:
ca./approx. 150

Umsatz/Turnover:
ca./approx. 30 Mio Euro

Beratungs- und Umsetzungsprojekte im
nationalen und internationalen Umfeld/
Consulting and implementation projects
within the national and international field:
ca./approx. 50

Teilnehmer in Trainings,
Seminaren und Coachings/
Participants in trainings,
seminars and coaching:
ca./approx. 9.000

Gesamtzahl der Auszubildenden/
Total number of trainees:
ca. 1.200 mit mehr als 60 Partnerunternehmen
approx. 1.200 with more than 60 partner companies

Anschrift/Address:
Industriepark Höchst
D-65926 Frankfurt am Main
Telefon   +49 (69) 305-8 18 24
Telefax   +49 (69) 305-8 48 48
E-Mail   info.provadis@provadis.de
Internet www.provadis.de

The Provadis Partner für Bildung und Beratung GmbH (Provadis Partner for Education and Consulting) is one of the largest companies for education and consulting in the Rhein-Main area. The range of services provided by the Frankfurt enterprise extends from management consulting to the first qualification – thus bridging a wide gap, which expressly distinguishes the "unique characteristic" of the enterprise.

The management consultants of Provadis support the international clientele as early as at the strategy development stage, they optimise – based on the success factors necessary for business success – business processes and adjust organisational structures. With a pragmatic approach the implementation is carried out through transfer of know-how to key persons (the consultant goes – the know-how stays in the client-company). The valid service guarantee for the client is: consulting projects are viewed as completed only on successful realisation of the concepts in practice. The strength in the management of modification processes results from a long-year's experience in management training and coaching with main focus on the subjects of co-operation and leadership. Provadis disposes of extensive experience in restructuring of companies in the processing industry, health care, banking and public institutions.

If desired and according to requirement, Provadis accompanies people in companies over the complete period of their career.
The extensive portfolio in further education measures enables a practice-oriented, flexible and creative development of employees in line with the ever faster changing requirements of the working world. In the 300 different offers from the fields of management and leadership, management skills,

communication, business economics, marketing, languages, PC-courses, production and laboratory techniques, everyone interested in professional success can find the suitable programme. For the fields of business economics, information technology, chemistry and biology secondary qualification measures are provided, which can be completed with an academic graduation.

The concept of Provadis does not end with an innovative further education. Provadis qualifies young people in more than 20 professions. With professional know-how, at the most modern equipment, with high-calibre trainers and the latest methods Provadis guarantees a high standard of quality at first qualification stage. Whether in training professions of the fields of production and technical science, which include for example the professions of chemist, pharmacist or process control electronics, or in commercial professions like industrial merchant and bi-lingual correspondent, in the IT-professions IT- specialist and IT-merchant as well as in professions of laboratory technicians – Provadis opens doors for young people with future-oriented training professions to the modern working world. ■

Services of education and consulting

- First qualification (training/apprenticeship)
  In more than 20 professions of production, technical science, laboratory, business economics and information technology
- Secondary qualification with recognised certification master craftsmanship, technician and polytechnic courses for chemistry, biology, business economics and information technology
- Further Education
  General management, leadership and behaviour, communication, language-, PC-, SAP courses as well as individual seminars from laboratory, production, and technical science as well as business economics and working techniques, adjusted to corresponding internal framework conditions of the companies
- Company consulting and development, strategy development and implementation, restructuring of organisations and business processes, market and profitability analyses, customer satisfaction analyses, intercultural management, management of modification processes as well as integral personnel development

Frankfurt am Main – die Hauptstadt des Tourismus in Deutschland

Frankfurt on the Main – Capital of Tourism in Germany

Frankfurt am Main ist ein Banken- und Finanzplatz von europäischer Bedeutung – dass Frankfurt jedoch auch ein Zentrum des deutschen Tourismus ist, wissen in der Regel nur Insider.

Die Entwicklung der Stadt Frankfurt am Main wurde in der Vergangenheit maßgeblich geprägt durch:

- die Erteilung des Messeprivilegs
- den Bau des Flughafens
- den Sitz der Deutschen Bundesbank.

Die Zukunft wird ferner bestimmt werden von der Europäischen Zentralbank, denn sie ist die optimale Voraussetzung zur Positionierung der Stadt Frankfurt am Main als Wirtschafts- und Finanzplatz in Europa. Frankfurt ist die Hauptstadt des Tourismus in Deutschland, denn bis auf ganz wenige Ausnahmen befinden sich alle ausländischen Fremdenverkehrsämter in unserer Stadt. Die wichtigsten touristischen Veranstalter haben

ihren Sitz in Frankfurt oder in der Region Frankfurt Rhein-Main. Bedingt durch den Flughafen sind mehr als 140 Fluggesellschaften hier registriert und ansässig.

Diese eingangs genannten Ereignisse stehen in unmittelbarer Wechselwirkung zueinander und haben sich in den Jahren gegenseitig befruchtet.

Der Ausgangspunkt der Entwicklung der Stadt Frankfurt am Main zu einem bedeutenden europäischen Zentrum war sicherlich die Erteilung des Messeprivilegs, welches der Stadt vor dem Hintergrund ihrer geografischen Lage erstmals im Jahre 1240 erteilt wurde.

Die steigende Zahl der Messen, die zunehmende Bedeutung der Messen und die Ausweitung der Angebote haben über Jahrhunderte die Entwicklung der Stadt positiv gefördert. Die jährlichen Konsumgütermessen setzen ästhetische Maßstäbe und sind gleichzeitig Barometer für

Günter Hampel

Der Autor war ab 1971 Persönlicher Referent bei Prof. Hilmar Hoffmann, Kulturdezernent der Stadt Frankfurt am Main, anschließend Büroleiter bei Prof. Hoffmann und schließlich Leiter des Dezernatsbüros. 1984 wurde er Geschäftsführender Direktor von Oper, Schauspiel und Ballett der Stadt Frankfurt am Main, 1989 Leiter des Verkehrsamtes der Stadt Frankfurt am Main. Seit 1995 ist Günter Hampel Geschäftsführer der Tourismus + Congress GmbH Frankfurt am Main.

The Author was from 1971 on Personal Advisor of Prof. Hilmar Hoffmann, Head of the Department of Culture of the City of Frankfurt on the Main, afterwards Chief of the Office with Prof. Hoffmann and finally Head of the Department. 1984 he became Managing Director of the Opera, Theatre and Ballet of the City of Frankfurt on the Main, 1989 Head of the Department of Transport of the City of Frankfurt on the Main. Since 1995 Günter Hampel is Director of the Tourismus + Congress GmbH Frankfurt am Main.

die wirtschaftliche Entwicklung in den nächsten 12 Monaten.

Die Beurteilung Frankfurts als Tourismusstandort muss sich lösen von der herkömmlichen Betrachtungsweise, in der Tourismus zwangsläufig mit der privat motivierten Reise – dem „traditionellen Urlaubsereignis" – gleichgesetzt wird. Grundlage für die Bewertung des Begriffes Tourismus und der Bedeutung des Wirtschaftsfaktors Tourismus für einen Standort leitet sich aus der Definition

Am Römer.

At the Römer (town hall).

162

Alte Oper.

The Alte Oper.

F rankfurt on the Main is a banking and finance place of European importance – the fact that Frankfurt is also a centre of German tourism is generally only known by insiders.

The development of the City of Frankfurt on the Main has been characterised in the past mainly by:

- the granting of fair privileges
- the construction of the airport
- the seat of the Federal Bank of Germany.

The future will be determined further by the European Central Bank, for she is the optimal precondition for the positioning of the City of Frankfurt on the Main as an economic and financial place in Europe. Frankfurt is the capital of tourism in Germany, because – apart from some few exceptions – all foreign tourism offices are seated in our city. The most important tour organisers have their headquarters in Frankfurt or the Rhein-Main region around Frankfurt. Due to the airport, more than 140 airlines are registered and seated here.

The events mentioned in the first instance are in direct reciprocal effect to each other and have been mutually stimulating during the years.

The starting point for the development of the City of Frankfurt on the Main to become an important European centre has surely been the granting of fair privileges, which were conceded to the city be-

cause of its geographic location in the year 1240 for the first time.
The increasing number of fairs, the rising importance of the fairs and the expansion in exhibitors have promoted over the centuries the development of the city positively. The yearly consumer goods fairs set aesthetic standards and are measuring sticks for the economic development of the following 12 months at the same time.
The evaluation of Frankfurt as a location of tourism must be detached from the common method of observation, which sees tourism as being unavoidably equal to privately motivated travel – "the traditional holiday event". Basis for an evaluation of the term tourism and the importance of the economic factor tourism for a business location can be derived from the definition of the WTO. She says that the term tourism includes business as well as leisure travel – the only determining criterion being a movement outside the normal working and living environment. This is of such importance because for this kind of travel also in future the term tourism will be taken as a basis.

Tourism in the modern sense does not only influence the hotel and restaurant business but also, to a

considerable extend, the retail trade, transport sector and other service providers like cultural event presenters etc.
Frankfurt's inner city is characterised by its quality as international business and commercial location. The yearly turnover from tourism amounts to 2,5 billion DM and can be segmented according to a survey of Prof. Dr. Gugg as follows:

- to hotels	25 %
- to restaurants	38 %
- to the retail trade	24 %
- to transport and other	13 %.

More than 30.000 workplaces alone are directly dependent on tourism. The City of Frankfurt for example, receives taxes for turnover related to tourism of 38 Million DM.

The reasons for a journey to Frankfurt on the Main are manifold. 70 % are professional reasons. These may include the visit of a fair, a meeting with a bank, a seminar, a congress or other reasons. Nevertheless, the remaining share of 30 % should not be underestimated, because over 1,3 Million lodgings are for private reasons.

The value of a location for tourism can be observed in differing parameters; I would like to mention two: an important one is the relation of overnight stays to the size of the city, that is to its inhabitants – in this comparison Frankfurt on the Main is in 2nd place nationally after Heidelberg and stands out considerably before its competitors Berlin and Munich. The same thing can be said about the relation between hotel beds to inhabitants: also in this case, the concentration is very high compared to the low number of inhabitants.

In reality, 2.214.600 persons visited Frankfurt on the Main in the year 1999, which also stayed overnight; they remained for 3.831.678 nights,

Palmengarten.

The Palmgarten.

Gut besuchte Straßencafés – mehr als 20 Millionen Tagesgäste kommen jährlich nach Frankfurt am Main.

Well-visited street cafés – more than 20 million daily guests visit Frankfurt yearly.

der WTO ab. Sie sagt, dass unter dem Begriff Tourismus sowohl Geschäfts- wie Freizeitreisen subsumiert werden – allein ausschlaggebend für das Kriterium Tourismus ist die Bewegung außerhalb des normalen Arbeits- und Wohnumfeldes. Dies ist deshalb wichtig, weil für diese Art von Reisen auch zukünftig der Begriff Tourismus zu Grunde gelegt wird.

Tourismus im modernen Sinne beeinflusst nicht nur das Beherbergungsgewerbe, die Gastronomie, sondern in erheblichem Maße auch den Einzelhandel, das Transportwesen und sonstige Dienstleister wie Kultureinrichtungen usw. Frankfurts Innenstadt ist geprägt vom internationalen Geschäfts- und Wirtschaftsstandort. Die vom Tourismus abzuleitenden Umsätze sind jährlich mit mehr als 2,5 Mrd. DM zu beziffern und teilen sich nach einer Studie von Prof. Dr. Gugg wie folgt auf:

- auf die Beherbergung   25 %
- auf die Gastronomie   38 %
- auf den Einzelhandel   24 %
- auf Transport und Sonstiges 13 %.

Allein mehr als 30.000 Arbeitsplätze sind unmittelbar vom Tourismus abhängig. Die Stadt Frankfurt beispielsweise erhält aus dem vom Fremdenverkehr getätigten Umsätzen 38 Mio. DM Steuereinnahmen.

Die Anlässe für eine Reise nach Frankfurt am Main sind vielfältig. 70 % sind berufliche Anlässe. Dies können der Besuch einer Messe, ein Meeting bei einer Bank, eine Tagung, ein Kongress oder

sonstige Anlässe sein. Gleichwohl ist der mit 30 % verbliebene Anteil nicht zu unterschätzen, denn es sind immerhin über 1,3 Mio. Übernachtungen, die private Anlässe haben.

Die Wertigkeit des Tourismusstandortes kann man an unterschiedlichen Parametern ableiten; zwei will ich nennen: ein wesentlicher ist die Relation Übernachtungen auf die Größe der Stadt, also auf die Einwohner bezogen – in diesem Vergleich steht Frankfurt am Main an 2. Stelle bundesweit nach Heidelberg und hebt sich weit vor seinen Konkurrenten Berlin, München ab. Gleiches kann man für die Relation Hotelbetten/Einwohner vornehmen: Auch hier ist die Konzentration für die geringe Zahl der Einwohner sehr hoch. Real waren im Jahr 1999 2.214.600 Personen in Frankfurt am Main, die auch übernachteten; sie blieben 3.831.678 Nächte, was einer Steigerung zum Jahresergebnis 1998 von 7,83 % bedeutet. Genauso wichtig für den Wirtschaftsfaktor Tourismus und damit für den Standort ist die so genannte Zahl der Tagesgäste, die ohne die täglichen Einpendler aus dem Umland ermittelt wird. Diese Zahl ist schwer zu erfassen, sie liegt aber in Frankfurt am Main mit Sicherheit bei mehr als 20 Millionen Besuchern.

Der Hotelstandort Frankfurt steht bundesweit im Vergleich der Umsätze ganz oben. Immobilien für Hotelneubauten sind deshalb nicht lange am Markt. Die Liste der Interessenten für neue Investitionen in Frankfurt am Main ist groß.

Ein Vergleich zu den unmittelbaren Konkurrenten in Deutschland ist sinnvoll. Aus dem Profil der Ziel-

gruppen sind hierbei lediglich Berlin und München vergleichbar. Frankfurt am Main hat knapp 52 % seiner Gäste aus nichtdeutschsprachigen Märkten. Der Anteil der Stadt München liegt bei 43,7 %, der Anteil der Stadt Berlin bei 25,26 %. Die übrigen Städte sind weit von diesen Prozentsätzen entfernt.

Frankfurt am Main rangiert im Bereiche der Gäste aus USA bundesweit auf Platz Nr. 2 hinter München, vor Berlin. Gleiches gilt für den japanischen Markt: Hier ist Frankfurt am Main Nr. 2 hinter München, vor Berlin. Wenn man jedoch die Addition der Gesamtübernachtungen aus dem asiatischen Raum zu Grunde legt, rangiert Frankfurt am Main mit 471.571 Nächten vor München (406.231) und Berlin (197.676). Die übrigen Großstädte, beispielsweise sei Hamburg genannt, sind in diesem Segment für Frankfurt am Main keine Konkurrenz, denn Hamburg liegt fast am Ende mit 105.017 Übernachtungen.

Die Bedeutung Frankfurts für den Tourismusstandort Region Rhein-Main leitet sich aus der Schaffung der Synergien mit den Städten Mainz, Wiesbaden, dem Umlandverband ab. Deshalb wird seit Jahren eine touristische Vermarktung gemeinsam mit dem Rheingau, den Vorzügen des Odenwaldes, des Taunus – um nur einige zu nennen – vorgenommen.

Der Tourismusstandort Frankfurt am Main in der Zukunft ist der Tourismusstandort Frankfurt Rhein-Main. Nur in der Bündelung der Strategien, der Angebote und der Vernetzung der Vertriebswege wird die Region im Wettbewerb der Regionen Bestand haben und sich weiter international positionieren und positiv entwickeln können.

Wichtige, zukunftsweisende Entscheidungen sind in der Vergangenheit getroffen worden. Eine der wichtigsten ist der Germany Travel Mart 2000/2005/2010, der gemeinsam von den Städten Frankfurt am Main, Mainz, Wiesbaden, dem Umlandverband und der Region durchgeführt wird.

Ein Indiz für die gute Kooperation der Region ist auch im Hotelreservierungssystem der Tourismus + Congress GmbH Frankfurt am Main „Frankfurt Regio-Soft" zu sehen, in dem 240 Hotels aus über 65 Gemeinden zusammenarbeiten.

Der Wirtschaftsfaktor Tourismus mit 30.000 Arbeitsplätzen und 2,5 Mrd. Umsatz wird an Bedeutung gewinnen, je größer die Vermarktungseinheit wird, wobei die Zukunft nicht in der politischen Begrenzung auf das Stadtgebiet, sondern in der großräumigen, Stadt- und Landesgrenzen überschreitenden Vermarktung liegt. ■

which signifies an increase against the yearly result of 1998 of 7,83%.

Just as important for the economic factor of tourism and therefore for the business location, the so-called number of day visitors that is arrived at without the daily commuters from the suburbs. This number can only be found with great difficulty, it lies in Frankfurt on the Main with certainty however at more than 20 million visitors.

Frankfurt as a business location for hotels is nationally on top of the list when comparing turnovers. This is why properties for new constructions of hotels are not for sale on the market for very long. The list of interested investors for new hotels in Frankfurt on the Main is very long.

A comparison to the direct competitors in Germany is useful. From the profile of target groups, only Berlin and Munich can be used for this comparison. Frankfurt on the Main draws 52% of its guests from non-German speaking markets. This share lies for the City of Munich at 43,7%, the share for the City of Berlin is at 25,26%. The remaining cities are far away from these percentage rates.

Frankfurt on the Main ranges in the field of guests coming from the USA nationally on place no. 2 behind Munich and before Berlin. The same is valid for the Japanese market: here Frankfurt on the Main is no. 2 behind Munich and before Berlin. However, if one takes as basis the total overnight stays of the Asian region, Frankfurt on the Main ranges with 471.571 nights before Munich (406.231) and Berlin (197.676). The remaining large cities, Hamburg for example, are in this section no competition for Frankfurt on the Main since Hamburg lies almost at the end of the scale with 105.017 overnight stays.

The importance of Frankfurt for the Rhein-Main region as a business location for tourism derives from the creation of synergies with the Cities of Mainz and Wiesbaden and the Association of Surrounding Communities. For this reason, since many years a concerted tourism marketing is being practised together with the Rheingau, the benefits of the Odenwald and the Taunus regions – just to name a few.

Frankfurt on the Main, the tourism business location, will be in future the Frankfurt Rhein-Main business location. Only by combining strategies, offers and the networking of marketing avenues, the region can prevail in the competition against other regions and position itself further internationally and develop positively.

Important and future-oriented decisions have been made in the past. One of the most important being the Germany Travel Mart 2000/2005/2010, which has been carried out together by the cities of Frankfurt on the Main, Mainz, Wiesbaden, the Association of Surrounding Communities and the Region.

One proof for the good co-operation in the region can be seen also in the system of hotel reservations of the Tourismus + Congress GmbH, Frankfurt on the Main, called "Frankfurt Regio-Soft" in which 240 hotels from over 65 communities work together.

Tourism as a factor of the economy, with its 30.000 workplaces and 2,5 billion turnover, will even increase in importance the larger the marketing union grows, whereby the future lies not in the political limitation of its city area, but in a greater, more expansive marketing crossing over city limits and regional limits. ■

Die Frankfurter Skyline am Abend.

The skyline of Frankfurt in the evening.

Amadeus AG
Stresemannallee 30
D-60596 Frankfurt am Main
Telefon   +49 (69) 9 68 76-314
Telefax   +49 (69) 9 68 74-399
Internet   www.AmadeusAG.de   S. 82

Accenture GmbH
Otto-Vogler-Straße 15
D-65843 Sulzbach
Telefon   +49 (6196) 57-60
Telefax   +49 (6196) 57-50
Internet   www.accenture.com   S. 26

awell Dienstleistungs GmbH
Rudolf-Diesel-Straße 20
D-65760 Eschborn
Telefon   +49 (6173) 32 12 66
Telefax   +49 (6173) 64 08 57   S. 83

Centrum für internationale Migration & Entwicklung
Barckhausstraße 16
D-60325 Frankfurt am Main
Telefon   +49 (69) 71 91 21-0
Telefax   +49 (69) 71 91 21-19
Internet   www.cimonline.de   S. 144

CommerceBay GmbH
Hamburger Allee 2–10
D-60486 Frankfurt am Main
Telefon   +49 (69) 7 92 04-0
Telefax   +49 (69) 70 04 86
Internet   www.commercebay.de   S. 76

Deininger Unternehmensberatung GmbH
Hamburger Alle 2–10
D-60486 Frankfurt am Main
Telefon   +49 (69) 79 20 40
Telefax   +49 (69) 70 04 86
Internet   www.deininger.de   S. 77

Deutsche Bank AG
Taunusanlage 12
D-60325 Frankfurt am Main
Telefon   +49 (69) 910-00
Internet   www.deutsche-bank.de   S. 36

Deutsche Telekom AG
Kundenniederlassung Deutsche Telekom AG
Emil-von-Behring-Str. 8–14
D-60439 Frankfurt am Main
Telefon   +49 (69) 909-30
Telefax   +49 (69) 909-3 32 99
Internet   www.telekom.de   S. 58

3i Deutschland Gesellschaft für Industriebeteiligungen mbH
Bockenheimer Landstraße 55
D-60325 Frankfurt am Main
Telefon   +49 (69) 71 00 00-0
Telefax   +49 (69) 71 00 00-59
Internet   www.3i.com   S. 24

DG Diskontbank GmbH
Friedrich-Ebert-Anlage 2–14
D-60325 Frankfurt am Main
Telefon   +49 (69) 74 47-31 00
Telefax   +49 (69) 74 47-32 00
Internet   www.dg-discontbank.de   S. 44

econos consulting Group
Breitlacherstraße 94
D-60489 Frankfurt am Main
Telefon   +49 (69) 7 68 06-9
Telefax   +49 (69) 7 68 06-650
Internet   www.econos-consulting.com   S. 134

Ernst & Young
Deutsche Allgemeine Treuhand AG
Eschersheimer Landstraße 14
D-60322 Frankfurt am Main
Telefon   +49 (69) 152 08-01
Telefax   +49 (69) 152 08-280
Internet   www.ernst-young.de   S. 46

ESA –
Elektronik Stark- und Schwachstromanlagen GmbH
Berner Straße 35
D-60437 Frankfurt am Main
Telefon   +49 (69) 3 90 01-0
Telefax   +49 (69) 3 90 01-433
Internet   www.esa-thyssenkrupp.de   S. 111

Flughafen Frankfurt/Main AG (FAG)
D-60547 Frankfurt am Main
Telefon   +49 (69) 690-0
Telefax   +49 (69) 690-7 76 90
Internet   www.flughafen-frankfurt.com   S. 53

GESAT mbH
Gesellschaft für Software,
Automatisierung und Technik mbH
Hanauer Landstr. 121a
D-60316 Frankfurt am Main
Telefon   +49 (69) 96 21 80-10
Telefax   +49 (69) 96 21 80-99
Internet   www.gesat.com   S. 121

Haden Drysys GmbH
Berner Straße 76
D-60437 Frankfurt am Main
Telefon   +49 (69) 50 91 94-0
Telefax   +49 (69) 50 91 94-99   S. 110

Hotel Kempinski Gravenbruch
An der Bundesstraße 459
D-63263 Neu-Isenburg
Telefon   +49 (6102) 505-0
Telefax   +49 (6102) 505-900
Internet   www.kempinski-frankfurt.com   S. 52

hpi GmbH
Industriepark-Höchst
D-65926 Frankfurt am Main
Telefon   +49 (69) 305-165 08
Telefax   +49 (69) 35 95 01
Internet   www.hpigmbh.de   S. 109

Hessischer Rundfunk
Anstalt des öffentlichen Rechts
Bertramstraße 8
D-60222 Frankfurt am Main
Telefon   +49 (69) 15 51
Telefax   +49 (69) 155 29 00
Internet   www.hr-skyline.de   S. 119

Ice Field Dry Ice Engineering GmbH
Industriepark-Höchst C343 & C346
D-65926 Frankfurt am Main
Telefon   +49 (69) 308 52-403
Telefax   +49 (69) 308 52-404
Internet   www.icefield.de   S. 108

INDUSTRIA
Bau- und Vermietungsgesellschaft mbH
Postfach 100862
D-63008 Offenbach
Telefon   +49 (69) 83 83 98-0
Telefax   +49 (69) 83 77 99
Internet   www.industria-gmbh.de   S. 133

Interxion Telecom GmbH
Hanauer Landstraße 312
D-60314 Frankfurt am Main
Telefon   +49 (69) 401 47-0
Telefax   +49 (69) 401 47-199
Internet   www.interxion.com   S. 69

INVESTNET Deutschland
Trading-Software & Service GmbH
Hochstraße 49
D-60313 Frankfurt am Main
Telefon   +49 (69) 92 10 17-0
Telefax   +49 (69) 92 10 17-80
Internet   www.investnetwork.com   S. 68

KoSa GmbH & Co. KG
Lyoner Straße 38a
D-60528 Frankfurt/Main
Telefon   +49 (69) 305-3555
Telefax   +49 (69) 305-81921
Internet   www.kosa.com   S. 120

Mannesmann Arcor AG & Co
Kölner Straße 5
D-65760 Eschborn
Telefon   +49 (69) 21 69-0
Telefax   +49 (69) 21 69-44 44
Internet   www.arcor.net   S. 151

Messe Frankfurt GmbH
Ludwig-Erhard-Anlage 1
D-60327 Frankfurt am Main
Telefon   +49 (69) 75 75-0
Telefax   +49 (69) 75 75-64 33
Internet   www.messefrankfurt.com   S. 150

MKI GmbH
Taunusstraße 52–60
D-60329 Frankfurt am Main
Telefon   +49 (69) 242 942-0
Telefax   +49 (69) 242 942-99
Internet   www.mki.net   S. 102

von Oertzen GmbH & Co. KG
Mainzer Landstraße 250-252
D-60326 Frankfurt am Main
Telefon   +49 (69) 7 59 04-0
Telefax   +49 (69) 7 59 04-249
Internet   www.von-oertzen.de   S. 118

Pricewaterhouse Coopers
Unternehmensberatung GmbH
Lurgiallee 5
D-60439 Frankfurt am Main
Telefon   +49 (69) 59 76-80
Telefax   +49 (69) 59 76-81 09
Internet   www.pwcglobal.com/de
           www.ebusinessisbusiness.com   S. 16

Priority Telecom Germany GmbH
Nibelungenplatz 3
D-60318 Frankfurt am Main
Telefon   +49 (69) 95 90 95-0
Telefax   +49 (69) 95 90 95-11
Internet   www.prioritytelecom.com/de   S. 60

Provadis – Partner für Bildung
und Beratung GmbH
Industriepark-Höchst
D-65926 Frankfurt am Main
Telefon   +49 (69) 305-8 18 24
Telefax   +49 (69) 305-8 48 48
Internet   www.provadis.de   S. 160

Shearman & Sterling
Mainzer Landstraße 16
D-60325 Frankfurt am Main
Telefon   +49 (69) 9711-1000
Telefax   +49 (69) 9711-1100
Internet   www.shearman.com   S. 152

Siemens Axiva GmbH & Co. KG
Industriepark-Höchst
D-65926 Frankfurt am Main
Telefon   +49 (69) 305-305 69
Telefax   +49 (69) 305-305 68
Internet   www.axiva.com   S. 92

Verlagsgruppe
Frankfurter Allgemeine Zeitung GmbH
Hellerhofstraße 2–4
D-60327 Frankfurt am Main
Telefon   +49 (69) 75 91-0
Internet   www.FAZ.com/de/net   S. 74

Weiler Tief- und Rohrleitungsbau GmbH
Im Kalk 3–5
D-60437 Frankfurt/Harheim
Telefon   +49 (6101) 40 40 2
Telefax   +49 (6101) 40 41 18   S. 132

Wilkinson Barker Knauer, LLP
Am Opernplatz 2
D-60313 Frankfurt am Main
Telefon   +49 (69) 208 76
Telefax   +49 (69) 297 84 53
Internet   www.wbklaw.com   S. 145

Zürich Gruppe
Solmsstraße 27–37,
D-60486 Frankfurt am Main
Telefon   +49 (69) 71 15-0
Telefax   +49 (69) 71 15-33 58
Internet   www.zuerich.de   S. 90

Wirtschaftsstandort Frankfurt am Main
Business Location Frankfurt on the Main

Verlag/Publishing House
EUROPÄISCHER WIRTSCHAFTS VERLAG GmbH
Ein Unternehmen der MEDIEN GRUPPE KIRK HOLDING AG
Groß-Gerauer Weg 1 in D-64295 Darmstadt
Telefon   (06151) 17 70-0
Telefax   (06151) 17 70-10
LeoPro   (06151) 17 70-48
E-mail   ewv@medien-gruppe.com

Internet/Internet
Homepage www.medien-gruppe.com
www.standort-deutschland.com

Herausgeber/Publisher
Christian Kirk ©
in Zusammenarbeit mit der Stadt Frankfurt am Main

Realisation/Production
MEDIA TEAM Gesellschaft für Kommunikation mbH
Dieses Projekt wurde realisiert unter Mitarbeit der Wirtschaftsförderung Frankfurt GmbH und der Autoren Dieter Posch, Petra Roth, Dr. Frank Niethammer, Dr. Hartmut Schwesinger, Friedrich von Metzler, Albrecht Glaser, Dr. Wilhelm Bender, Gerd Simon, Heinz Huth, Hans-Wolfgang Pfeifer, Hans-Peter Griesheimer, Jürgen Heyne, Prof. Dr. Rudolf Steinberg, Dr. Hans Günter Gassen, Volker Sparmann, Jörg Lunkenheimer, Prof. Rudolf von Staden, Dr. Albrecht Magen, Michael von Zitzewitz, Prof. Dr. Herbert Beck, Günter Hampel sowie in der Organisation Judith Nießner, Ute Rühl, Christopher Zulauf und Christiana Weber (Schlussredaktion)

Chefredaktion/Editor-in-Chief
Heinz-Dieter Krage

Produktionsleitung/Production Manager
Mirko Emde

Grafik & Satz/Graphics & Typesetting
Kerstin Rutscher, Martin Müller, Eva-Maria Prinz

Bildnachweis/Picture Credits
Autoren der Artikel, portraitierte Unternehmen, Ingo Bach – Messe Frankfurt, Jochen Beyer, Uwe Dettmar, Ursula Edelmann, Wolfgang Eilmes, Helmut Fricke, Historisches Museum Frankfurt am Main, Lothar G. Humla, IHK Frankfurt, Martin Joppen, Markus Kirchgessner – Messe Frankfurt, Mirko Krizanovic, Kurt Lauber, Fotostudio Michels, Nickl & Partner, Presseamt der Stadt Frankfurt, Matthias Schüssler, Torsten Silz, Helmut Stettin – Messe Frankfurt, Marco Stirn, Tourismus + Congress GmbH, Verkehrsverbund Rhein-Main, VG Bild-Kunst, Welzel – Messe Frankfurt, Horst Zielske – Messe Frankfurt.

EBV, Computer to Plate/EBV, Computer to Plate
digitaltype GmbH, Darmstadt

Druck/Printers
Eduard Roether GmbH, Darmstadt

Papier/Paper
Rhein-Main-Papier GmbH & Co.KG, Bochum, Senden, Darmstadt. Papiersorte: Volley®Silk matt, 135 gr/m^2

Umsetzung für Internet/Internet Implementation
InMediasRes GmbH, Darmstadt

ISBN/ISBN
3-932845-39-0, Ausgabe 2001/2002